LEARN ASTROLOGY

A Guide for Absolute Beginners

Leoni Hodgson

All rights reserved

Copyright © Leoni Hodgson
February 2020

No part of this publication may be reproduced, stored in a retrieval system, or transmitted in any form or by any means, electronic, mechanical, photocopying, recording or otherwise, without the prior written permission of the author.

ISBN: 978-0-6483012-3-3

About the Author

Leoni Hodgson works professionally as a practitioner and teacher in several specialist areas in the esoteric arts. Astrology (DMNZAS - Diploma Member of the NZ Astrological Society 1982, and the PMAFA - Professional Member of the American Federation of Astrologers 1983), Esoteric Psychology (MA in Esoteric Psychology and Ph.D. in Esoteric Philosophy), Raja Yoga and Esoteric Healing (INEH Certificate).

About this Book

Beginners to astrology will find it easy to follow this well laid-out tutorial. An overview of the science is given in the first few pages. Then greater depth is added in the following chapters - the Signs, Planets, Houses and Aspects are all explained in detail, individually, and as they work together to form a natal chart. Exercises are given with worksheets, to help interpret planets, in signs, in houses, in aspect to each other. Love and Relationships, Career, Health, Children and Death are all explained in detail, with example charts so that students themselves can study these vital areas of life and work with them. A chapter on calculating a natal chart manually (Placidus style), is given, for those who wish to go to this depth. Birth charts for Helen Reddy and Princess Diana are used as examples. A chapter on looking forwards into the future or the past covers Secondary Progressions, Solar-arc Directions, Transits, Eclipses and Solar Return charts. This book contains everything needed to learn how to read an astrology chart proficiently and to investigate important life areas. The way the book is written trains the student to read a chart from the psychological angle. But what truly sets this extraordinary tutorial apart from others, is that it also trains the student to read the spiritual potential in the chart - the soul's purpose in the life.

Other Books Written by the Author

Journey of the Soul.
A Handbook for Esoteric Psychology and Astrology.
Originally published 2000.

Medical Astrology.
Discover the Psychology of Disease using Triangles.
Published February 2018.

Astrology of Spirit, Soul and Body.
A Handbook for Esoteric Astrology.
Published November 2018.

Acknowledgements

This book is dedicated to the world service work of the Tibetan Master Djwhal Khul.

Loving thanks to my dear husband Jim who supports me in every way in all my endeavours. Many thanks to my dear friend Jeanni Monks, who assisted in the production of the book.

CONTENTS

Astrology, Introductory Overview 1

Chapter 2. The Planets 27

Chapter 3. The Houses 47

Chapter 4. Planets in Signs and Houses 59

Chapter 5. Planets in Aspect 109

Chapter 6. Exercises to Interpret a Natal Chart 137

Chapter 7. Love, Career, Health, Children & Death 151

Chapter 8. Manual Calculations - Natal and Progressions. 167

Chapter 9. Looking to the Future 183

    1. Secondary Progressions 184

    2. Primary or Solar-Arc Directions 186

    3. Transits 186

    4. Eclipses 188

    6. Solar Return Charts 190

Appendix *192*

Glossary *195*

Index *200*

ASTROLOGY, INTRODUCTORY OVERVIEW

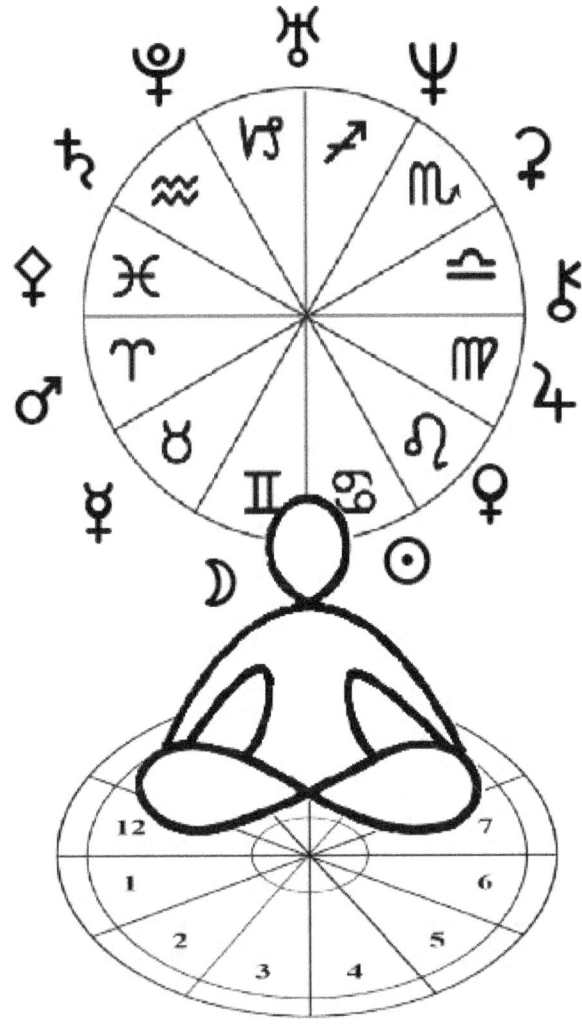

Introductory Overview

Astrology has actually nothing to do with the stars but is the 5000-year-old psychology of antiquity and the Middle Ages. [1]

This book has been written for students who are new to astrology.
If this is you, then welcome to a science that will literally change your life.

Astrology is a science of energies. Scientists study energy and devise many ways to control and use it for human consumption. Astrologers are also scientists. The astrology energies have been studied for thousands of years by sages and yogis, who observed the impact of these forces upon consciousness, on nature and life. This knowledge and its application to the personal life constitutes the foundation of modern astrology.

Astrology can therefore be defined as:

> Astrology is a science that relates the universal to the particular, that draws a parallel between the forces of constellations, stars and planets to life on earth. The natal (birth) astrology chart relates these conditioning and governing energies to ourselves, incorporates us into the fabric of the universe and lays out in graphic form, the potential realisation of "self."

"Know thyself," is the ancient Greek aphorism.

This has been echoed down the ages by wise men including Socrates, Plato and Aristotle. The statement implies that, if we are to live more meaningful and fulfilling lives, we should first understand clearly our principles, our motives and the bedrock of the nature from which our goals and aspirations arise; then to act in accordance with these in the outer life - intelligently and knowledgeably. Astrology is the science that enables us to do that.

> The personal natal astrology chart is composed of the constellations and planets combinations at the time we are born. This chart arrangement represents our psychological energies and how we are predisposed to use them - the strengths, weaknesses and adjustments that need to be made to bring about an increased awareness of self.

As we increase self-awareness, our capacity to lead a rich and fulfilling life increases. This is because we are clearer about who we are, what we want and how to go after and get what we want. Whether the goal is material or spiritual (aspiring to something higher and finer), self-understanding increases our capacity to achieve life success. Astrology assists us in this process. Our job is to make internal adjustments to bring us into harmony with universal flow, which will then support us in whichever direction we decide to go.

Astrology is also a science of cycles. It enables us to map the various energy and life-cycles that we go through. This knowledge - the best time to start and end things, is invaluable for life success.

To this end, in this book, the basic essentials of astrology have been presented and in a way that will help students begin to read charts quickly. A further section "Looking to the Future," will teach students how to read life-trends and cycles and how to use them wisely. Chart calculation has also been included for those who would like to explore further in that direction.

However, this book is very different to most other astrology text-books.

This is because an evolutionary or self-development aspect has been incorporated into the descriptions for each sign and planet. The entire philosophy upon which this book is based is that we are incarnating souls on a journey to enlightenment (Spiritual awareness). This means our birth chart is karmic - what we have inherited from our past lives. A synonym of soul (the higher spiritual aspect of our nature) is "consciousness." As we acquire knowledge and apply it in our everyday lives, we become wiser, more discerning and consequently our consciousness and our understandings about ourselves, of others and of the world expands. Our soul-awareness increases. This expansion of consciousness is the plan or purpose of the soul for us in this life. This book is based upon this notion.

<u>Upon this note</u> reader, welcome to the study of the greatest science known to mankind.

[1] Carl G. Jung, Letters, vol. 1, 1973

In this introductory section, a brief overview of the components of astrology are introduced. This will help students to grasp the broad scope of the science before delving into any details.

1. Overview of the Twelve Signs.

Technically, the zodiac signs are 30-degree segments of the *ecliptic* (the apparent path of the Sun around the Earth). The zodiac of signs is known as the "Tropical Zodiac".

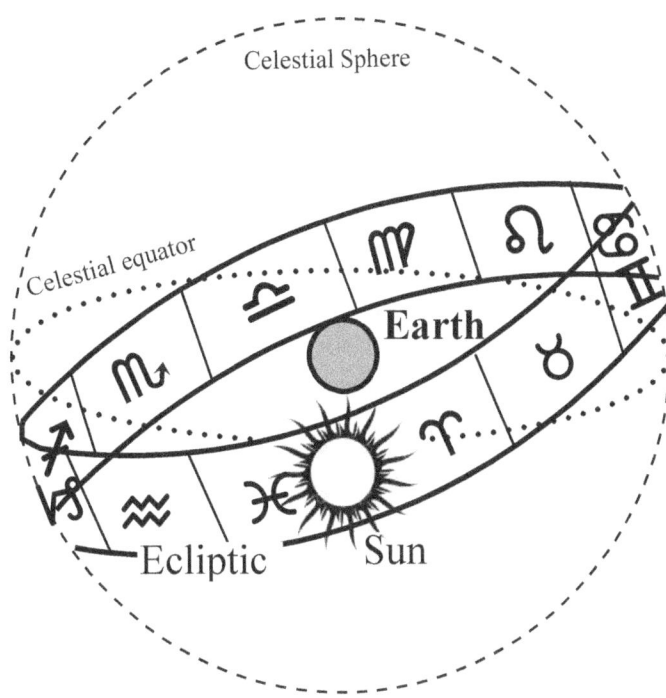

- The signs no longer line up with the constellations of the same name due to the earth's wobble. The *celestial sphere* is an imaginary orb around the solar system, with Earth at its centre. This is the basis of "earth based" or Tropical Astrology that we use today. Symbolically, everything rotates around the ego, which the Earth represents.

- Although, physically it is illusory, it is a very valid science, because "energy follows thought". The world we live in has been created by our collective thoughts and actions and astrology represents this reality. Esoterically, the energies of the constellations do flow through the signs of the same name.

- In the diagram you can see that the ecliptic or zodiac looks like a circular movie screen. A small picture of the Sun is shown moving around the strip.

- Astrology maps the movement of the Sun and planets across the zodiac, as viewed from Earth.

The zodiac signs and ruling planets are the agents used by the constellations for distribution of their energies to man and to all forms of life on earth. Here is a chart listing the signs, dates and attributes.

Signs - Elements - Modes - Symbols

	Signs		*Element*	*Modes*	*Symbols*
♈	Aries	Mar 21 - Apr 21	Fire	Cardinal	Ram
♉	Taurus	Apr 22 - May 20	Earth	Fixed	Bull
♊	Gemini	May 21 - Jun 21	Air	Mutable	Twins
♋	Cancer	Jun 22 - Jul 22	Water	Cardinal	Crab
♌	Leo	Jul 23 - Aug 23	Fire	Fixed	Lion
♍	Virgo	Aug 24 - Sep 22	Earth	Mutable	Virgin
♎	Libra	Sep 23 - Oct 22	Air	Cardinal	Scales
♏	Scorpio	Oct 23 - Nov 21	Water	Fixed	Scorpion
♐	Sagittarius	Nov 22 - Dec 20	Fire	Mutable	Centaur
♑	Capricorn	Dec 21 - Jan 19	Earth	Cardinal	Goat
♒	Aquarius	Jan 20 - Feb 18	Air	Fixed	Water-bearer
♓	Pisces	Feb 19 - Mar 20	Water	Mutable	Fishes

2. Overview of the Planets and Asteroids.

Each sign is ruled by one or two planets. The signs distribute their energies via their ruling planets. The planets receive the energies pouring from their sign, add their own particular force, then distribute this modified force to man and to the world.

The inner, personal planets

The personal planets represent different parts of our immediate psychology, hence "personal". These are the Sun, Moon, Mercury, Venus and Mars.

- The Sun represents the personality or ego.
- The Moon represents the emotions.
- Mercury represents the mind.
- Venus represents the affections, sometimes wisdom.
- Mars represents the passionate emotions and desire.

The outer, growth planets

The rest of the planets from Jupiter to Pluto, they represent evolutionary forces that continually make an impact upon our personal consciousness, forcing us to grow psychologically and spiritually. These impacts can be mapped via astrology. They occur as the outer planets orbit around the sun and make connections to the personal planets in the natal chart.

- Jupiter represents expansion and growth.
- Saturn represents karma, discipline, limitations, adversity and opportunities to make changes as a consequence.
- Uranus represents sudden changes; it awakens us to the new.
- Neptune represents forces of refinement, devotion and idealism.
- Pluto represents the forces of destruction, death and transformation.

The Asteroids

There are many asteroids and not everyone uses them. Only five are widely used. Chiron is the most popular. Its impact is more enduring. It moves outside of Saturn and its orbit around the Sun takes approximately 50 years. With the exception of Chiron, the other four - Vesta, Juno, Ceres and Pallas; these are related to female goddesses of the Greek and Roman pantheon.

- Vesta, Goddess of Hearth and Home, represents dedication to a cause.
- Juno, chief goddess and wife of Jupiter, represents our attitudes to marriage and to the spouse.
- Ceres, Goddess of Agriculture, represents the influences of nurturing upon the human soul.
- Pallas Athena, Goddess of Wisdom and Truth, represents mental creativity and intelligence.
- Chiron was the "wisest and justest of all the centaurs." He represents childhood wounds and wisdom through experience.

The planets and asteroids are all explained in greater detail later.

Signs		Ruling Planets	
♈	Aries	♂	Mars
♉	Taurus	♀	Venus
♊	Gemini	☿	Mercury
♋	Cancer	☽	Moon
♌	Leo	☉	Sun
♍	Virgo	☿	Mercury
♎	Libra	♀	Venus
♏	Scorpio	♂♇	Mars, Pluto
♐	Sagittarius	♃	Jupiter
♑	Capricorn	♄	Saturn
♒	Aquarius	♅	Saturn, Uranus
♓	Pisces	♃♆	Jupiter, Neptune

Personal planets

☉	Sun
☽	Moon
☿	Mercury
♀	Venus
♂	Mars

Growth planets

♃	Jupiter
♄	Saturn
♅	Uranus
♆	Neptune
♇	Pluto

Asteroids

⚶	Vesta
⚵	Juno
⚳	Ceres
⚴	Pallas Athene
⚷	Chiron

3. The Houses.

The chart is divided by 12 houses or regions, to represent all life departments on earth.

The houses are of equal or unequal size depending upon the house system used. Two of the most popular systems are Placidus (unequal house size) and Equal House (equal size houses).

When a planet is located in a house, the affairs of that house are activated. A more complete description of the houses is given in a later chapter. Here are the basic meanings of the twelve houses.

House 1	The self
House 2	Money, values
House 3	Communication, neighbours
House 4	Home and family
House 5	Lovers, pleasure, hobbies
House 6	Work, health
House 7	Marriage, Partners
House 8	Sex, death, transformation
House 9	Beliefs, morals, religion, the world
House 10	Status, fame
House 11	Friends, groups
House 12	Privacy, self-undoing

4. The Aspects.

Aspects are specific geometric angles between planets. In the accompanying horoscope, these are shown by the lines in the middle of the chart and by the grid underneath it.

Planets orbit around the Sun at different speeds. The faster planets approach slower planets, form aspects with them and then separate. When an aspect is in effect, energy flows between the two planets. Aspects in the natal chart show character, how different parts of the personality work together.

The Major Aspects

    ☌ Conjunction (unites)

    □ Square (blocks)

    △ Trine (flows with)

    ☍ Opposition (fights)

Almost major aspects

    ✶ Sextile (constructive growth)

    ∠ Semi-square (interference)

    ⚻ Inconjunct/ quincunx (out of balance)

Minor aspects (two of several)

    ⚼ Sesquiquadrate (conflict, disruption)

    Q Quintile (latent talent)

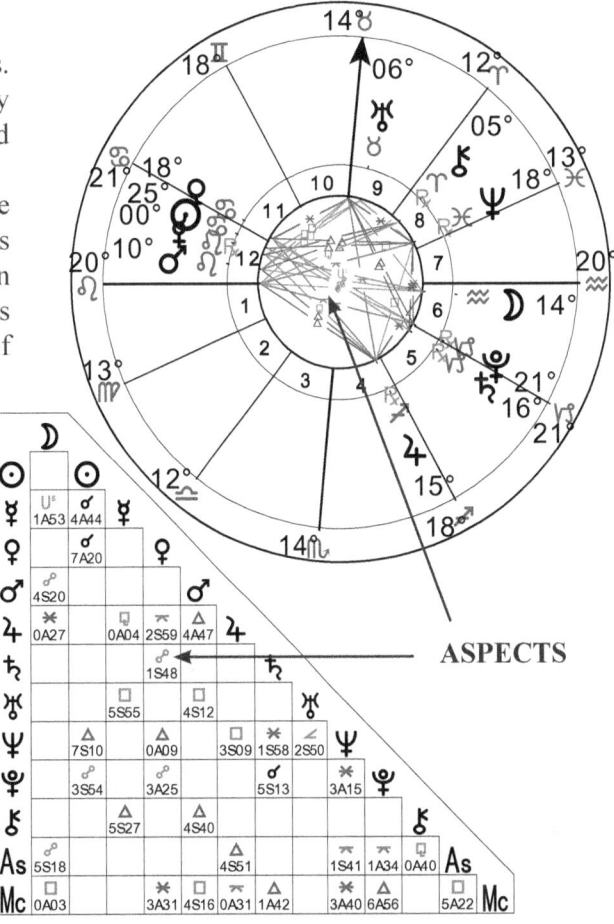

5. Keywords Summary Page.

Personal planets as they represent our psychology.

☉	Sun	The personality. The ego, identity, personality, the lower-self, the father, authority.
☽	Moon	The emotions. Instincts, habits, nurturing/ mothering qualities, women; negative beliefs.
☿	Mercury	The mind. Communication, travel, speech, thought, young people; tricking, lying.
♀	Venus	The affections, love. Relationships, young women, mistresses; promiscuity.
♂	Mars	Desire, passionate emotions. Courage, competitiveness, young men; anger, hate, combat.

Transforming planets as they affect our psychology.

♃	Jupiter	The urge to grow, to understand, generosity. Expands, enhances; exaggerates, boasts.
♄	Saturn	Ambitions, sense of duty, responsibilities. Disciplines; limits, checks.
♅	Uranus	Urge to be free, independence. Awakens to the new, changes; rebels.
♆	Neptune	Urge for spiritual union, idealism. Refines, dissolves; deludes.
♇	Pluto	Urge to control, to survive. Transforms, destroys; obsesses.

Asteroids and qualities they give.

⚶	Vesta	Dedication, devotion, duty, mission, purification.
⚵	Juno	Marriage, married life; betrayal, infidelity, jealousy.
⚳	Ceres	Mothering, nurturing, nourishing, self-esteem.
⚴	Pallas	Executive ability, mental-creativity, problem solving.
⚷	Chiron	Wisdom, healing, healer; childhood wounds.

Signs as they influence our psychology.

♈	Aries	Hot and assertive. Aspires, creates, explores, leads; burns, erupts.
♉	Taurus	Practical, grounded, earthy, stable. Endures, possesses; stubbornness.
♊	Gemini	Intelligence, communication, duality. Adapts, socialises, thinks.
♋	Cancer	Emotions, moods, sensitivity. Defends, nurtures, protects.
♌	Leo	Dignity, grand, royal; arrogance. Leads, radiates, rules; bullies, roars.
♍	Virgo	Practicality, discrimination, intelligence. Analyses; criticises, nit-picks.
♎	Libra	Intelligence, diplomacy, fairness; indecision. Balances, flirts; procrastinates.
♏	Scorpio	Emotional intensity and privacy; vengefulness. Fights, reacts, retaliates.
♐	Sagittarius	Aspirational beliefs; excess. Aims, expands, pursues, searches, visions; boasts.
♑	Capricorn	Practical and ambitious; meanness, stinginess. Assesses, calculates, disciplines.
♒	Aquarius	Intelligence, friendship, humanitarianism, science. Knows, thinks, separates; aloof.
♓	Pisces	Emotions, idealism, artistic; naivety. Believes, feels, flows, sympathises, trusts, serves.

Houses.

1. The self: appearance, image we project, personal interests, physical body. Asc: image, life approach.
2. Money: personal possessions, resources, values.
3. Communications: early education, environment, neighbours, short distance travel, siblings, writings.
4. Home: family, mother, one's "roots".
5. Hobbies, recreation: children, personal creativity, lovers, pleasures, romance.
6. Work, health: acute health conditions, co-workers, service, skills.
7. Marriage, other people: open enemies, partnerships, relationships.
8. Death, emotional traumas, inheritances, losses, occult groups, other's money, sex, transformation.
9. Collective mind: beliefs, higher learning, morals, foreign lands and foreigners, religion.
10. Father, career, status: authority, government, public recognition. MC: high goals.
11. Friends, groups, organisations: politics, revolution, social reforms.
12. Self-undoing, subconscious, the hidden: confinement, privacy: large institutions.

6. To Learn Natal Astrology.

- Students should work with their own chart to start with. Comparing what we know about ourselves with the chart, helps to build up confidence.
- Learn the symbols and keywords for the Signs and Planets.
- Use the "Keywords Summary Page" frequently while you learn.
- Read and absorb the chapters on Signs - Planets - Aspects - Houses
- Do the Interpretation Exercises.
- Practise interpreting natal charts until interpretation begins to flow. It is like driving a car. First you learn what each part of the car involved in driving is called. Then you put them together to get things moving. Then you practice until you can do this smoothly and can drive the car. Astrology is similar - learn the symbols, put them together and learn to read what they mean fluently.
- The key to success in astrology is to practise reading charts on an ongoing basis. The website astro.com has thousands of charts.

7. The ethics of astrology work.

A private natal chart reading contracted between a client and the astrologer should be subject to all rules of confidentiality that credited counselling agencies and health professionals are bound by. In such a case, under no circumstances should the client's identity or personal details be revealed publicly, unless permission has been granted. However, just as health professionals gather and use health details of their patients (anonymously), when doing research and to improve the science; so, should astrologers. We all read charts of celebrities that are posted online - for instance, permission has never been granted by the British Royal Family to have or read their charts. But we all read them and learn from them. We also set up charts for famous people once birth details are known and read them. But when a client consults an astrologer under the expectation that any intimate details revealed will be kept private - that must be respected.

8. In Summary.

Energies are simply the forces of Space or Deity at work in the universe. They flow
- through the signs
- to the planets
- into man via his etheric chakras (energy vortices)
– into the houses, which is into physical life.

There are many branches of astrology. Those who use it as a psychological or spiritual tool know that it is an interpretive key that gives immediate insight into a person's psyche and the best way to advise people who are having difficulties.

Those who persevere in their efforts to read a natal chart and master the Science of Astrology, they are developing skills that can greatly benefit people who are going through difficulties in their life.

As has been emphasised before, the key to success in astrology is to reading charts on an ongoing basis.

> *Obviously astrology has much to offer psychology, but what the latter can offer its elder sister is less evident. So far as I judge, it would seem to me advantageous for astrology to take the existence of psychology into account, above all the psychology of the personality and of the unconscious.* – Carl G. Jung

CHAPTER 1.
THE SIGNS

A. THE SIGN COMPONENTS

In this section, the zodiac signs are explained. They are twelve evolutionary experiences or classes composed of four elements, a mode or rate of vibration, a symbol (usually an animal), and are related to the seasons.

1. The Elements of each sign.

Each sign is related to an element of life - fire, earth, air and water.

Fire keywords:
Enthusiastic
Fiery
Initiative
Inspirational
Zeal
Aggression

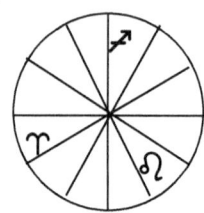

Fire: Aries – Leo - Sagittarius

In the average person born in Aries, Leo or Sagittarius, the fire element relates them to the passions and desires of the Emotional or Astral Plane (emotional and astral are synonymous terms). At the higher level, fire relates people to spiritual aspiration. Fire gives heat, enthusiasm, assertiveness and brilliance. Fiery people are courageous, inspiring and creative. Negatively expressed: fire is projected aggressively, selfishly, rashly. Lack of fire: such people have difficulty inspiring others, may lack enthusiasm for life or desire for adventure and exploration.

Air keywords:
Airy
Networking
Thinking
Social
Communicative
Superficial

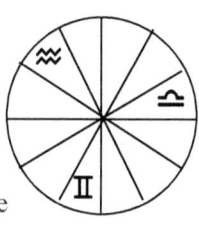

Air: Gemini – Libra - Aquarius

Air is related to the Mental Plane. This means that the masses born in Gemini, Libra or Aquarius are having their minds stimulated and are being taught to think and to analyse. When the mind is awake and the Spiritual Path is being approached, the intuition develops, a faculty related to the air element. Although the goal is for air people to work with their minds, the average person is still greatly influenced by the emotions. But generally, air people are light, gay, like socialising and talking. Negatively expressed: they can be superficial, deceitful, ungrounded, airy-fairy. Lack of air: difficulty with communicating in a social setting.

Water keywords:
Emotional
Feeling
Flowing
Sensitive
Watery
Wet

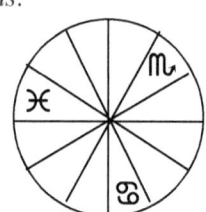

Water: Cancer – Scorpio - Pisces

The water element is related to the Emotional Plane which means that people born in water signs are having their emotions stimulated, developed and purified. Unless there are repressive factors in the chart, water-people have a strong feeling nature. They are emotionally expressive, intuitive, highly sensitive and seek to understand life through how they feel. Negatively expressed: they are over-emotional, naive, delusory. Lack of water: such people lack sensitivity, empathy and have difficulty with emotional expression.

Earth keywords:
Caution
Down-to-earth
Earthy
Grounded
Practical
Plodding

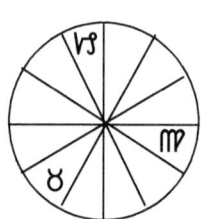

Earth: Taurus – Virgo - Capricorn

The earth element is related to the Physical Plane, which means people born in Taurus, Virgo and Capricorn are being taught to be practical, down-to-earth and non-emotional in the way they approach life matters. Earth people take things slowly, but when something is grasped, it is not released or forgotten easily. Negatively expressed they are slow to think and move and can be very rigid and stubborn. Lack of earth: such people have difficulty staying grounded because they live either in the world of the emotions or of the mind.

2. The Modes or Rates of Vibration of each sign.

Matter has three rates of vibration: Cardinal (rajas, fast, mobile); Fixed (tamas, slow, inert); and Mutable (sattva, flexibility, rhythm). Each sign that has a planet in it will influence that planet (the function the planet is related to), with its vibration. Some people have one dominant mode, which means that vibration (fast, slow or flexible), will greatly influence their expression. Others are a mixture of vibrations and expressions.

Cardinal: Aries, Cancer, Libra, Capricorn.

The cardinal mode brings activity, it moves in a very direct, outgoing, potent manner. In the "hare and tortoise" fable, the hare represents the cardinal mode. The hare was faster, but made mistakes and had to go back and fix these, arriving at the finish line with the tortoise. This mode gives leadership abilities, rapid expression and an independent manner. Negatively expressed, there is inattention to detail and domineering, impatient and ruthless traits.

Cardinal keywords:
Assertive
Direct
Fast
Independent
Leadership
Restlessness

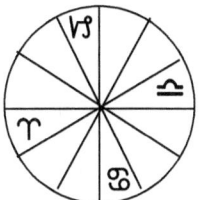

Fixed: Taurus, Leo, Scorpio, Aquarius.

The fixed mode gives stability. In the race with the hare, the tortoise moved slowly in a straight line, ensuring everything was properly done as it progressed. The tortoise represents fixed mode. This mode gives steadiness, stability, staying-strength, power to endure, loyalty, patience and consistency. Negatives are rigidity and stubbornness. The fixed signs are thought to be the most powerful signs of the zodiac because of the condensed nature of their force and staying power.

Fixed keywords:
Determination
Endurance
Resistant to change
Stable
Stubborn

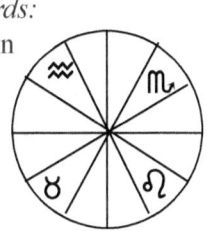

Mutable: Gemini, Virgo, Sagittarius, Pisces.

The mutable mode brings flexibility, adaptability, lightness and change. Mutable people have softer, more pliable natures, are the easy-going people of the zodiac and consequently, people enjoy their company. They like to keep moving and are curious about life and people. Their negatives are being superficial, ungrounded, being unconvincing and non-committal.

Mutable keywords:
Adaptable
Changeable
Flexible
Following
Friendly
Weak

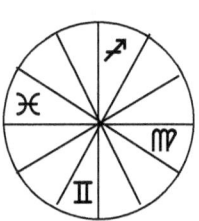

3. Sign Decanates.

Each astrology sign has 30 degrees and three sections or decanates (decans) of 10 degrees each. Two of these decans are influenced by the other two signs of the same element.

Each sign rules its own first decan. The next subsequent sign of the same element governs the second decan. The third sign of the same element governs the third decan. Let us look at the three fire signs to clarify how this works.

The 3 decans of Aries are ruled by: 1) Aries. 2) Leo. 3) Sagittarius.
The 3 decans of Leo are ruled by: 1) Leo. 2) Sagittarius. 3) Aries.
The 3 decans of Sagittarius are ruled by: 1) Sagittarius. 2) Aries. 3) Leo.

The ruling planets also rule the decans; therefore:

The 3 decans of Aries are ruled by: 1) Mars. 2) The Sun. 3) Jupiter.
The 3 decans of Leo are ruled by: 1) Sun. 2) Jupiter. 3) Mars.
The 3 decans of Sagittarius are ruled by: 1) Jupiter. 2) Mars. 3) The Sun.

From this we can see that it makes a difference which decan of a sign that a house cusp or planet falls in. For instance, if the Sun was in the first decan of Sagittarius the person would be more typically Sagittarian than if born in the 2nd decan (coloured by Aries and Mars), or 'the 3rd decan (coloured by Leo and the Sun). The same rule is applied to the signs of the other elements.

4. Sign symbols: represent the nature of each the signs.

Each sign has a symbol, which is usually an animal. But not always. There are non-animal symbols for the air signs and for Virgo. The symbol of each sign represents certain characteristics that colour the expression of people born with planets or ascendant in the sign. If a person's consciousness is still ruled by selfishness, the lower traits of the symbol will demonstrate. Higher, more altruistic people will demonstrate higher characteristics of the symbol.

Aries: The Ram. The Ram gives its people an accentuated head, which is often proportionally larger than the rest of the body and a grizzled, irritated look. It also gives a muscular, compact body, with no excess body fat and medium height. The characteristics it gives are leadership qualities, territorial attitudes, passion, urgency, strong desires and a powerful will to be and do. Negatively, the Ram is aggressive. When it cannot get its way, it puts its head down and races forward to crash obstacles out of its way.

Taurus: The Bull. In appearance, the Bull gives its people a solid and well-formed body. Men are muscular and women can be voluptuous. They are slow moving, tend to plod-along when they walk. In character, the Bull imparts strength of will, tenacity and a stable and steady nature. Normally calm and steady, it is happy to graze alone. But if anyone challenges it, invades its space or tries to take its possessions, it will charge to destroy the interloper.

Gemini: The Twins. With a human symbol, Geminis are supposed to be more "human" in appearance and character than their relatives in animal signs. This generally means they are more mental in their life approach and less inclined to succumb to their emotions or "animal" passions. In appearance, the twins are usually slim and youthful looking. In character, they are dual-natured and can happily travel two different paths in life at the same time. Negatively, this can mean duplicity and lies. But overall, the symbol of the Twins represents human communication and socialising.

Cancer: The Crab. In appearance, the Crab gives strong forearms and hands to its people - the better to provide for the family and for self-protection. There is a chest emphasis and women may have ample breasts, which this sign rules. When walking, these people often sidle from side to side, as the crab does. In character, they are highly protective and defensive - which the crab's shell represents. Retreating into their own private world when hurt, they stay there, hidden away in their shell until their moods lift and they feel it is safe to emerge.

Leo: The Lion. Physically, the Lion gives a thick, flowing mane of hair - a mark of maturity, virility and fertility that helps to attract a mate. It also gives a regal gait and prideful set of head. In character, the Lion gives innate leadership talent, immense courage and willingness to face up to danger to protect the family. It gives a noble manner, dignity in its dealings, generosity and large-heartedness. But once betrayed, the Lion will not easily trust again or forgive. It likes to roar to get attention.

Virgo: The Virgin. Having a human symbol, Virgos are supposed to be more "human" in their life approach, more mental and less influenced by the animal appetites. Virgos certainly are this. In appearance, they have youthful appearances, with fine features and well formed, slim bodies. To character, the Virgin gives modesty, shyness, innocence, purity. However, the shrewish old-maid (a negative symbol), gives nagging, criticalness and querulous nit-picking.

Libra: The Scales. The Scales are used to balance and in appearance this suggests a well-proportioned body, which many natives of this sign have. The scales are the only non-organic representative in the zodiac family and is a symbol of justice and fairness. More advanced members of Libra are endowed with these characteristics. However, not everyone is at that level and in most cases, there is a lack of balance and procrastination.

Scorpio: The Scorpion. Its people move speedily and fleetly, like the scorpion that darts quickly and agilely to inject venom into its prey. Often their arms are longer proportionally - the scorpion grabs its prey before killing it. Characteristics are watchfulness, being vigilant for danger and being aggressive and vengeful with enemies. The Scorpio person is a battle machine - the sign gives warriorship to its people - the practices, occupation, or status of a warrior. There are two higher symbols, the Eagle and the Phoenix. The Eagle represents the soaring intellect of an evolved native of this sign; and the Phoenix, its transformative power.

Sagittarius: The Centaur. It has a horse body and the torso of a man. In mythology, centaurs were very lustful and aggressive creatures and these characteristics are given to their people. Unchecked, Sagittarian's indulge their appetites, are gamblers and womanisers. They are also bold and adventurous, global travellers who love to cover long distances rapidly. In appearance, this family group are given the loose-limbed, rangy and strong-legged attributes of the Centaur or horse - another symbol. There are two higher symbols for Sagittarius. The Archer and the Arrow. The Archer represents the human soul who is no longer half-animal, but controls his appetites (being seated on the horse); and the Arrow represents the soaring spiritual nature of the advanced Sagittarian.

Capricorn: The Goat. In appearance, the Goat is a careful but fleet-footed creature, who clip-clops his way across rocky terrain and who is able to climb mountains. These attributes are imparted to its people, who use them to further their ambitions and to scale the heights of government, corporate and political power. They are group-oriented and like to join organisations with like-minded people. In appearance, Goat people have a dour and serious look. They have thin and darkish hair, a compact and sinewy body, bony knees and large feet.

Aquarius: The Water-Bearer. With a human symbol, Aquarian's are more mental in their life approach and are cooler and less disturbed by their emotions or passions than other signs. They are also oriented to helping others, enjoy friendly citizenship and like to pour out their wisdom and knowledge to benefit the world. They will also instigate a revolution if that is the only way to make worthwhile changes. Selfish Aquarian's use their knowledge and power to benefit themselves. In appearance, they are a good-looking people, tall, well-shaped, have a high and well-defined forehead and an intelligent look.

Pisces: The two Fishes. The natural habitat of the fishes is the ocean. In appearance, they have a svelte look and seem to glide forward as they move, like their animal counterparts. They have dreamy, very beautiful, soulful eyes and fine hair that drifts about as if being moved by unseen currents. Their natural habitat is the world of feelings and they like to ride emotional waves and currents. But they are less likely to be trapped by their feelings when compared with the other water signs Cancer and Scorpio. This is because they are always ready for the next experience and new sensations.

5. The Sign Glyphs.

A glyph is a hieroglyphic character or symbol. Mostly, the Sign Glyphs are interpreted mundanely. But they represent the characteristics of the sign on three levels - physical, soul and spiritual. Deeper meanings can be found in all the glyphs.

Aries. Physically, the glyph depicts the face and horns of the Ram - the animal representative of this sign. Very often in Aries people, you can see arched eyebrows and a strong straight nose (before it gets broken), that warns all who approach to beware. The glyph also represents the fountain of youth, the verve of new beginnings and the welling up of spontaneous self-confidence - traits of this sign's energy. At a higher level, Aries' glyph represents the spontaneous outpouring of spiritual energy.

Taurus. Physically, the glyph represents the Bull's head and horns. Looking deeper, the horns over the circle of spirit, suggests the desire nature is more dominant than the spiritual side - the circle is always a symbol for oneness, for God. The brightest star in Taurus and also one of the brightest stars in the night sky, is the first magnitude, red giant Aldebaran. It is also known as Buddha's Star, the Star of Illumination, God's Eye, and the Eye of the Bull. Consequently, throughout the ages Aldebaran has been spiritually recognized as a channel of divine power and this is represented by the orb in the glyph - spiritual light shining through consciousness.

Gemini. This is the sign of the celestial Twins, Pollux and Castor. Pollux is the brightest star in Gemini and represents the spiritual aspect in man that is waxing in power. Castor represents the personal, mortal side of man that wanes in intensity when the Spiritual Path is pursued. The two pillars of the glyph also represents the duality of nature - matter and spirit, which is imparted to those born in the sign of the twins. Between the pillars a doorway can be seen. When Gemini's balance their nature and turn their curiosity to an inner search for understanding, this door opens and leads to a higher, more integrated level of consciousness.

Cancer. Physically, the glyph represents the two claws of the Crab, pointing to the grasping and very protective nature of the sign energies. It can also represent the two female breasts that nourish babies - an area of life that Cancer rules. The spiritual goal in Cancer is to balance the emotions and to bring them under the control of the soul-illumined mind. At this higher spiritual level, the upper and lower arms of the glyph represent this balance: the lower arm can be seen to represent the quiescent personality, which is now in balance and harmony with the dominant soul, represented by the higher arm.

Leo. This glyph represents the lion's mane or tail and suggests the sense of pride and puffed-out chest that this sign engenders in some. It also suggests a head-dress, such as a mitre worn by bishops and senior abbots, crowns and other head symbols that kings and important people wear. At a higher level, this suggests an open crown chakra, which occurs in the spiritually advanced. Staying with this theme, the brightest star in Leo and the 22nd brightest star in the sky, is Regulus, also called the "Royal Star." It is said to bring good fortune to those who receive its blessing.

Virgo. The arm in the glyph folds over, representing the virginity and celibacy of this sign. At a higher level, the three legs also represent our triple form (mind, emotions, physical), that imprison the soul that is bound to the material world. The Christ Spirit is birthed into consciousness in Virgo, and the bulge suggests a purified nature pregnant with spirit. The brightest star in Virgo is Spica, a first magnitude blue giant. It is also known as "Alpha Virginis" - the first Virgin.

Libra. Latin: "Balance". The Scales represent the weighing attributes of this sign, and its task is to balance us on all levels of our nature - physical, emotional, mental. Its higher goal is to balance the opposites of spirit and matter - to bring our material nature into harmony with our spiritual source. When this balance is found, entry to another, higher level in consciousness is possible - through the arch. The brightest star in Libra is Zubeneschamali. It is the only star to appear green to the naked eye. This is interesting because esotericists believe the green (3rd) ray flows through Libra.

Scorpio. The upturned arrow indicates potent male sexuality. Scorpio is the sign that rules the sex organs and sex - especially male sexuality, so the glyph is very descriptive. The upturned-arrow also suggests the sword of Mars, a ruler of this sign - Scorpio is the warrior sign. The three legs represent the mind, emotions and physical natures that are now at war with the soul, which trying to control them. At a higher level again, the arrow represents the soul breaking free from the binding shackles of the material world. The brightest star in Scorpio is Antares, one of the Royal Stars of Persia called "The Watcher of the West." Antares: Greek, means "rival to-Ares" - "opponent to-Mars", because it has a reddish hue similar to that of Mars.

Sagittarius. This symbol depicts the arrow of the Centaur, aiming to higher realms. In Greek mythology, centaurs were followers of Dionysus, the God of Wine. Consequently, they were considered savage, rowdy and boisterous and were governed by their lower desires. The "uncivilised" Sagittarius is such a type. In the more advanced type, the arrow is now being fired by a human, the Archer, who gallops across the plains - symbolising the modern-day world-traveller who explores the world to increase his or her understanding. The latest version is the Arrow itself, representing the intuition and a soaring aspiration for something higher and finer in life. This is the mark of a spiritually advanced person who is on a search for enlightenment.

Capricorn. In this mysterious symbol, we can see the Mountain Goat or Sea-Goat, which has the head of a goat with the tail of a fish. Another symbol is the Makara, a crocodile-like, mythical sea creature in Hinduism. The Makara is a vehicle of the river goddess Ganga and the sea god Varuna; it guards gateways and thresholds to throne rooms and temples. The energy of this formidable sign ignites an incentive to improve oneself. The upwards pointing arm of the glyph represents the urge to climb a mountain. The younger, inexperienced soul climbs the mountain of materialism; the more advanced soul climbs the mountain of spirituality. In this sense, the glyph can be considered a symbol for spiritual initiation, since this is the goal in this sign.

Aquarius. Although it is an air sign, the energies of Aquarius are related to the flow of healing waters. Its name begins with "aqua" and in Latin, it means "cup bearer" or "water bearer." The symbol depicts water. At the lower level, these are the emotions. The sharp corners in the symbol can represent disruptive energies or mental rigidity that some in this sign display. The upper wave can be seen to represent a balanced intelligence that has harmonised the emotional life - the bottom wave. Ultimately, this is a symbol of open-ended spiritual energy pouring forth to help the needy and impoverished.

Pisces. The two arcs represent the two Fishes. In Pisces, the Fishes represent the masses of humanity. The downwards swimming fish represents the blinded soul who is descending into glamour, chaos and illusion. The upwards-turned fish represents the soul that is seeking release from matters hold and is swimming towards the light of wisdom. When the soul gains control of the lower nature, the binding cord is cut. The soul absorbs the personality and enlightenment occurs.

Mode:
cardinal - fast

Element: fire

Animal: Ram

Ruler:
Mars

Hercules Labour in Aries: Capture of the man-eating mares.

The mares were killing everyone. Hercules and his friend Abderis, captured them. But Hercules was so proud of his deed he instructed Abderis to herd the mares while he went off to brag. But Abderis was weak, the horses killed him and escaped. Grieving, Hercules completed the task alone.

Moral: think before acting and complete tasks.

B. THE SIGNS

1. Aries (March 21 - April 22).

Keynotes: Creation - Being - Activity - Synthesis - Strife

Fast and direct fire, hot, fiery, aggressive - "I Am first and Best!" The symbol is the Ram, which symbolises the aggressive nature of these people. The fiery energies of Aries produces people who are fast in action, easily aroused, youthful, naive, courageous with high energy. They are good at initiating activity, but poor at follow through because of a short attention span. Natural leaders and directors of men; they are exciting to follow because of the speed they work and risks they take. They are fighters, highly assertive and are always striving to master every situation they are involved with. The immature Aries rushes in to do battle at every opportunity and is a troublemaker. The more mature, thinking Aries plots a careful strategy and rarely loses, for he is a master in the art of skilful battle.

In relationships they are ardent and when courting need to be the hunter. But they are territorial and jealous. As a fire sign they are easily aroused but are also easily bored and can move on quickly. But they will stay with the person who can contain and feed their fire.

The Spiritual Goal: Aries represents an opportunity to illumine the mind, then use it to control the wild Arian personality and to direct the will intelligently in initiatives that benefit humanity.

Aries rules: the first house and is related to number 1. People: soldiers, young men, warriors. Generally: masculinity, rams. Season: spring. Colour: red. Stones: bloodstone, diamond. Metal: iron.

Anatomy and Health. Aries rules the head, the head, eyes and brain. Typical Aries characteristics give medium height, a strong brow, eyebrows, nose and jaw. Physique is compact and sturdy. Health problems occur with the above anatomy - headaches, stroke, fevers, eye and brain problems etc.

Vocations. Aries are suited to any career which allows them to express their initiative, ideas, physical dexterity and drive. They are natural managers and supervisors, suited to selling, marketing, travelling, the military and any career involved with machinery, utensils, metals, weaponry, sports, competition, hairdressing and surgery.

Planets in Aries

- The Sun: is exalted. In advanced man, it represents spirit that has come to full expression because of the evolutionary process. In undeveloped man it represents egoism.
- Venus: in detriment. In the advanced person, the light of the lower sensuous nature fades as the light of the soul grows. In average man, lower desire dominates.
- Saturn in Aries: this is a karmic position, indicating that individuals need to be responsible with their use of power.

Keywords. Positive: action-oriented, active, adventurous, ardent, assertive, bold, brave, commanding, competitive, confident, courageous, dareviltry, daring, dynamic, energetic, enterprising, enthusiastic, fast-moving, fiery, forceful, hot, independent, initiating, leading, quick-acting, out-going, passionate, pioneering, straight-forwards, urgent. *Negative:* aggressive, arrogant, babyish, childish, combative, disingenuous, fool-hardy, hotheaded, headstrong, impatient, impulsive, inflammatory, irresponsible, leaps before looking, naive, quick-tempered, rash, reckless, selfish, strife, tactless, undisciplined, unthinking, war-like.

2. Taurus (April 23 - May 21).

Keynotes: Desire - Illumination - Will - Directed Purpose

Mode:
fixed - slow

Element:
earth

Animal:
bull

Ruler:
Venus

Fixed – earth, practical, down-to-earth, enduring - "I Desire," "I Have." The Bull symbolises the powerful desires and appetites of this sign. The energies of this sign give the most down to earth of the zodiac people - steady, stable, reliable, predictable, very determined, with ordered habits, likes and dislikes. Once they have experienced or learnt something, they never forget. When Taurus energy is expressing negatively it produces stubbornness, laziness and greed. Taurus people are normally easy to get along with, but when aroused can be very destructive.

They make the most loyal partners, friends and associates. When Taureans commit, they usually stay bonded – as long as their earthy needs are being met. Ruled by Venus, they are romantic, sensual and have a strong sex drive. They need tangible demonstrations of love.

The Spiritual Goal: Taurus gives us the opportunity to control the lower appetites. This is achieved by transmuting desire into aspiration, impressing higher spiritual will on the lower will and bringing Spiritual Light into the mind and life.

Taurus rules: the second house and is related to number 2. People: artisans, artists, beautiful Venus-like men and women, decorators. Generally: banks, bulls, earth, finance, luxury, land, money. Season: mid-spring. Colour: green. Stones: emerald. Metal: copper.

Anatomy and Health. There are two types - the earthy who have thick and shoulders and are chunky in body. Venus types have beautiful faces and bodies. Taurus rules the throat, neck and thyroid and this typically is where problems occur. Taurus' partner-sign is Scorpio, which rules the reproductive area.

Vocations. They are suited for jobs that call for reliability, practical application and commitment. Taureans do well with finance, working the land, real estate, handling food or luxury items. Venus' influence gives artistic talent and many Taureans have beautiful voices.

Planets in Taurus
- Moon: exalted. Form or material life controls the nature.
- Uranus: it falls in this earth sign. This accentuates the wide divide between the lower appetites of the personality and the lighted soul, which is so marked in Taureans. Uranus awakens an inner response to the light, leading ultimately to full spiritual illumination.
- Mars: in detriment. This adds to the warlike nature of Taurus but also gives the incentive to struggle towards light and understanding.

Keywords. Positive: compact, concrete, consistent, constant, dependable, desire, determined, devoted, direct, dogged, down-to-earth, earthy, enduring, faithful, firm, forbearing, grasps, hands-on, insistent, loyal, owns, patient, persevering, persistent, physical, practical, pragmatic, prosperous, realistic, reliable, resolute, resolved, sensual, solid, steadfast, steely, stable, stoical, strong-willed, tangible, tenacious, tolerant, trustworthy, uncompromising. *Negative:* conflicted, desirous, destructive, greedy, hard, headstrong, hedonistic, on the horns of the bull, indolent, inflexible, jealous, lazy, over-love of luxury, materialistic, mulish, obstinate, placid, possessive, rigid, rushes blindly, self-indulgent, stiff, stubborn, over-sensual, self-indulgent, slothful, slow, stubborn, unbending, uncontrolled appetites, unimaginative, unmovable, wilful.

Hercules Labour in Taurus: Capture of the Cretan Bull.

Hercules sought and eventually captured the bull in the maze of Minos on the island of Crete. He rode the bull back to a holy place on the mainland, using a gleaming star on the bull's forehead to light the way.

Moral: ride the bull of lust and do not be ridden by it.

Mode: mutable - adaptable.

Element: air.

Animal: human twins.

Ruler: Mercury.

Labour in Gemini: Finding the Golden Apples.

Hercules meandered about as he searched. He did not recognise his higher self who came several times to give advice. He wrestled with desire and for aeons was under the spell of Busiris, arch-deceiver. Eventually freed he saved Prometheus and Atlas, then found the apples.

Moral: stay focused on the task.

3. Gemini (May 22 - June 20).

Keynotes: Fluidity - Recognition of Duality - Soul Control

Changeable - air, communicative, social - "I Think." The symbol for this sign, the Twins, represents the dual, oscillating and restless nature of these people. They have fewer animal traits than the other signs, which means they are less likely to be ruled by their passions. Gemini energies produces people that are airy, adaptable, social and communicative. They have logical minds capable of processing facts and data with accuracy and speed. They are good conversationalists on a wide variety of subjects, talented in many ways and clever with their hands. Their restless inquisitiveness takes them through many experiences from which they have the opportunity to develop discrimination. Negatives of this sign are shallowness, superficial behaviour, restlessness, being easily bored, gossiping, telling lies and being deceitful.

They are entertaining lovers, but their restlessness, inquisitiveness and the dual nature of this sign means they can have more than one relationship on the go at the same time. Their emotional attachments can be as changeable as their minds and they need a lot of freedom.

The Spiritual Goal: Gemini provides us with the opportunity to control the unstable nature of the personality by illuminating the mind and bringing it under soul control. This means developing discrimination, discernment and refining life values so that intelligent love is developed and expressed.

Gemini rules: the third house and is related to number 3. People: accountants, acquaintances, adolescents, children (older), communicators, educators, handymen, in-betweeners, interpreters, journalists, linguists, messengers, neighbours, public speakers, reporters, sales-people, traders, travellers, twins, youths, young people; liars and thieves. Generally: commerce, communication trade, short-distance travel. Season: late spring. Colour: yellow. Stones: agate, opals. Metal: Mercury.

Anatomy and Health. Typical Gemini characteristics give height, a slender build and clear, sparkling and intelligent eyes. Gemini rules the shoulders, arms, hands, lungs and breathing passages. They are susceptible to asthma, lung disorders, nervous strain and diseases, speech defects, emphysema and bronchitis.

Vocations. Any of the communication or information industries suit them such as office work, administration, book keeping, education, academia, teaching, writing, lecturing, reporting on the world situation through social or political commentary, selling, marketing and travel.

Planets in Gemini

- In its own sign, Mercury is in its dignity. But no other planet falls or is exalted. The developmental goal is to find inner balance and to avoid all extremes of behaviour.

Keywords. Positive: academic, adaptable, adjustable, articulate, bookish, brainy, bright, casual, changeable, chatty, clever, communicative, dual, educated, eloquent, erudite, flexible, fluent, fluid, inquisitive, intellectual, intelligent, inventive, knowledgeable, learned, lively, mental, neighbourly, networking, rational, sagacious, smart, sociable, speak, talkative, variable, versatile, youthful, wise, witty. *Negative*: airy-fairy, anxious, cunning, deceitful, gossipy, highly-strung, inconsistent, nervous, nervy, neurotic, restless, shallow, superficial, tricky, two-faced, ungrounded, unstable.

4. Cancer (Jun 21 - Jul 22).

Keynotes: Instinct - Intellect - Intuition

Mode: cardinal - fast.

Element: water.

Animal: crab.

Ruler: Moon.

Fast moving water-emotions, nurturing, sensitive, defensive - "I Feel." The energies of Cancer produces people who are the most emotional in the zodiac family. Their symbol is the Crab, representing a defensive, retiring and aggressive nature. They are tenaciousness and highly intelligent when it comes to protecting their family or fulfilling their emotional and security needs. This sign symbolises motherhood, family, nurturing and Cancerian's need the comfort and security of a home. Positively expressed, Cancer brings inner serenity and peace and the ability to nurture others wisely and sensitively. Expressed negatively, there are exaggerated emotions, fluctuating moods, a tendency to be clingy and crabby.

Cancerian's are tactile, sensuous and sensitive lovers. They need someone to fuss over. Insecurity causes them to cling to partners and ask for constant demonstrations of love and affection. If they give their hearts, they find it very difficult to leave or to let go of a relationship.

The Spiritual Goal: Cancer provides us with the opportunity to develop the intellect and purify the emotional body so they are no longer a playground for negative thoughts and emotions. When the mind is freed from illusion it becomes a prism for the light and love of the soul.

Cancer rules: the fourth house and is related to number 4. People: babies, domestics, infants, families, females, mature women, mediums, mothers, nurses, pregnant women and women generally, wives, the public and masses. Crabs, domesticity, the home, milk, mother's milk, the sea-shore, white or colourless liquids. Season: early summer. Colour: white. Stones: moonstone, pearls. Metal: silver.

Anatomy and Health. Typical Cancerian characteristics give shortness in height, pale skin, moon faces, high cheekbones, moist, dreamy and unsure eyes. Top heavy, they put on weight easily through water retention. Cancer rules the breasts, stomach and pale fluids in the body. Health problems centre around these areas.

Vocations. Industries that involve nurturing, healing, domesticity, hospitality, service, working with the public generally, those that involve female issues - reproductive health, mothering and child-raising. Organising and administrative positions in any area of service (an extension of their superior home-making skills); via higher ruler Neptune, careers that have to do with the sea and with spirituality.

Planets in Cancer
- The Moon: it is dignified in Cancer.
- Venus: in this sign emotionalism interferes with clear and rational thought.
- Mars: it falls and is a source of emotional conflict.
- Jupiter and Neptune: exalted. Jupiter gives the ability to build homes, families, prosperity. Neptune gives psychic sensitivity, both at higher and lower levels.
- Saturn: in detriment. This is karmic. It indicates a person who has built emotional walls for self-protection to the extent that the feelings are repressed and it is difficult to relate intimately with others. These walls must be brought down.

Keywords. Positive: caring, cautious, domestic, contemplative, emotional, emotionally-expressive, empathetic, feeling, gentle, imaginative, inclusive, intuitive, maternal, mothering, nurturing, protective, retiring, sensitive, shrewd, sympathetic, tenacious, watery, womanly. *Negative*: backwards-looking, clingy, concealing, crabby, defensive, emotionalism, hiding, hyper-sensitive, insecure, moody, over-protective, over-sensitive, smothering, wet.

Hercules Labour in Cancer: Capture of the Doe.

Artemis (instincts) daughter of the Moon, and Diana (the intellect) daughter of the Sun, both laid claim to the doe and they tried to foil Hercules in his efforts to capture it. But capture it he did and he took it to the holy shrine of the Sun God.

Moral: overcome the lower nature and strive for wisdom (the doe).

5. Leo (July 23 - August 22).

Keynotes: Self Consciousness - the Will to Know - the Will to Rule

Mode:
fixed - slow.

Element:
fire.

Animal:
lion.

Ruler:
the Sun.

Hercules Labour in Leo: Slaying the Nemean Lion

Hercules was sent to kill the lion. It attacked but Hercules was too strong. The lion hid in a cave that had two entrances. Hercules blocked off one entrance and entering through the other, choked the lion to death with his bare hands.

Morals: energy should not be given to the rampant lion of the ego.

Concentrated – fire, proud, dignified, regal, intelligent - "I Rule!" Leo produces people who need to be central, stand in their own power, express their own truth, apply their own will. The symbols - the Lion and the Sun, greatly typify their nature. They love holding centre court and need an adoring public. They are natural leaders, have a warm charisma which makes them very attractive and are naturally generous and warm-hearted. When Leo energy is expressed negatively it produces arrogance, vanity, laziness, susceptibility to flattery and hypersensitivity to criticism.

Romantic, ardent and truly passionate, Leo's need a partner who can return this fire with equal measure. Possessive and territorial, they are unforgiving if a partner is unfaithful. Some Leo's like to gather a harem.

The Spiritual Goal: Leo provides us with the opportunity to integrate the personality so that a self-conscious, self-empowered personality emerges. Then, to bring it under soul control so that creative power flows through it for the good of the whole. The 1st initiation, control of the physical appetites, is related to Leo.

Leo rules: the fifth house and is related to number 5. People: authority figures, children via the fifth house, dignitaries, fathers, heads of state, husbands, kings, leaders and mature men generally, presidents, princes, princesses, queens, rulers, sovereigns and teenagers. Season: mid-summer. Generally: lions. Colour: gold, orange. Stones: jasper, topaz. Metal: gold.

Anatomy and Health. Leo rules the heart and spine. Natives of this regal sign are handsome with thick beautiful manes of hair, strong, well-proportioned heads, facial features and bodies. With a dignified bearing, they emit a solar glow. Leo rules the heart, spine, the cardiovascular system and the immune system. They are susceptible to heart conditions.

Vocations. Any area of leadership: manager, leader, statesman, supervisor, self-employment. Standing at the heart of an organisation or working with hearts, such as a heart surgeon. They make fine sports people, work well with children and in all creative areas - art, theatre, acting, performance and dance.

Planets in Leo

The Sun is dignified in its own sign. However, no planet falls or is exalted. The advanced Leo is free from outside control, is king and ruler of the life. The power of Saturn and Uranus weaken in Leo, except in the case of the initiate who responds to the esoteric influence of Uranus.

- Uranus: in detriment. The power of the mind symbolised by Uranus is reduced. In spiritually advanced people, the soul has illumined the mind.
- Saturn: in detriment. Difficult karma awaits those who misuse power.

Keywords. Positive: authoritative, benevolent, beneficent, big-hearted, bold, bountiful, brave, broad-minded, ceremonious, courageous, courtly, creative, determined, dignified, direct, dominant, enthusiastic, expansive, expressive, faithful, fearless, gallant, generous, grand, heart-felt, heroic, hospitable, expressive, kind, kingly, lordly, loving, loyal, magnanimous, majestic, noble, open-hearted, optimistic, princely, proud, radiant, regal, resolute, royal, self-aware, self-confident, self-conscious, self-control, stately, straight-forward, strong willed, warm-hearted, warm, warmth. *Negative:* arrogant, boastful, conceited, controlling, dogmatic, dominating, egocentric, egoistic, extravagant, head-strong, hedonistic, lazy, melodramatic, narcissistic, pompous, prideful, self-centred, self-important, vain.

6. Virgo (August 23 - September 22).

Keynotes: "Christ in you, the hope of glory"

Changeable – earth, dutiful, discriminating, fastidious - "I Analyse." The symbol is the modest Virgin - quiet, shy and unassuming, chaste and fastidious. Virgo produces people who are found in all manner of administration work, who quietly keep the wheels of organisations ticking over. They are loyal and devoted servers who can be relied upon in any crisis. Practical, ultra-reliable, discriminating; they have shrewd minds suited to analytical, detailed and precision work. There is a natural interest in diet, health and hygiene. Negatively expressed, Virgo energy produces a super-critical, driven, fussy, over-meticulous perfectionist. Or conversely, someone who realising the high standards cannot be reached, gives up trying and is a slob.

Virgos love with their minds and they want their relationships and partners to be perfect. If this is not moderated, their tendency to criticise can ruin unions. They tend to be faithful and loyal, but have a curiosity which may sometimes cause them to go outside their primary relationship. Unless Mars is strong, they can be too cerebral and lack passion. Any faults aside, their willingness to please makes them agreeable partners.

The Spiritual Goal: Virgo provides us with the opportunity to develop discrimination and use it to bring about the purification of the physical, astral and mind bodies. This will reveal the inner light - the Christ consciousness, love and wisdom. The goal then is to serve.

Virgo rules: the sixth house and is related to number 6. People: celibates, healers, servants, virgins and workers. Generally: agriculture, wheat. Season: late summer, Colour: beige, summer colours. Stones: sapphire. Metal: Mercury.

Anatomy and Health. Typically, Virgo gives height. Its people are wiry, neat and well made - with tidy small features, hands and feet. They are either very well-groomed, or sloppy in dress. Virgo rules the intestines and colon.

Vocations. Virgos are suited to the health, healing and nutrition industries, to education, customer service, clerical and any work that requires great attention to detail. They make excellent accountants, analysts, research scientists, librarians, administrators, communicators, servers and servants.

Planets in Virgo

- Mercury: dignified. This strengthens the mind. Mercury reaches its full power in this sign because Virgo is intelligence and the hidden Christ is wisdom or pure reason.
- Venus: falls. When materialism dominates the nature, then ignorance rules wisdom (Venus), which then disappears and vanishes into the darkness.
- Neptune: in detriment. Sensitivity is not evident during the early stages of the Path when the personality nature, particularly lower mind, is being developed.
- Jupiter: in detriment. Inclusive love is hidden in the depths of ignorance.

Keywords. Positive: accurate, analytical, astute, chaste, conscientious, demure, diagnostic, diligent, discerning, discriminating, dutiful, economical, exact, exacting, fastidious, helpful, innocent, intelligent, logical, maidenly, meticulous, modest, organised, practical, precise, pure, as pure as the driven snow, rational, reliable, reserved, selective, serene, shy, sinless, specific, vestal, virgin, watchful, work-skills. *Negative*: anxious, critical, fussy, inhibited, judgemental, narrow-focused, narrow-minded, nervy, neurotic, nit-picking, over-critical, passive-aggressive, perfectionist, petty, picky, tunnel-vision, worrying.

Mode: mutable - adaptable.

Element: earth.

Animal: human virgin.

Ruler: Mercury.

Hercules Labour in Virgo - the Girdle of Hippolyte

Venus gave the girdle to Hippolyte the Amazon Queen. She was instructed to give it to Hercules but wanted to keep it. Hercules seized the girdle and killed her. But later repented and saved a maiden in distress.

Moral: making mistakes is normal on the Path. Atone and keep going forwards.

Mode: cardinal - fast.

Element: air.

Animal: the scales.

Ruler: Venus.

Hercules Labour in Libra: Capture of the Boar

While searching for the boar in the mountains, Hercules met Pholos, a centaur. They drank wine belonging to the centaurs, causing a fight and centaurs were killed. Hercules found the boar, and drove it down the mountain by its hind legs. This was amusing to onlookers.

Moral: lower desire must be conquered.

7. Libra (September 23 - October 22).

Keynotes: Balance - Equilibrium - Justice

Fast – air, striving for balance and harmony, "I Weigh." Libra produces people who are airy, charming and graceful. With good minds, they mix well socially and are interesting and witty conversationalists. Diplomatic and cooperative, they have a strong sense of justice and make good mediators and peacemakers. Negative use of Libran energy produces procrastinators, people who sit on the fence and who cannot make a decision, people who avoid conflict because they lack courage.

This is the sign of relationships. Libran's need a partner. They prefer handsome looks and will be disappointed if the real person does not match the exterior. While in love, they are romantic, ardent and very attentive. But if the partner fails to measure up, they can lose interest. However, they don't like to end things and will manipulate the partner into making the break.

The Spiritual Goal: Libra provides us with the opportunity to develop balance, moderation, right equilibrium between all opposites and to express goodwill on earth so that harmony prevails.

Libra rules: the seventh house and is related to number 7. People: advocates, ambassadors, artists, attorneys, barristers, counsellors, decorators, designers, lawyers, partners, spouses. Generally: the arts, the law and all legal matters, marriage, scales and one-on-one unions intimate and professional. Season: early autumn. Colour: pastel green. Stones: quartz, marble. Metal: copper.

Anatomy and Health. Typical Libran characteristics give medium height with perfect proportions, perfect features, flawless skin, unmatchable charm. Libra rules the kidney area, the urinary tract, the middle spinal area and pancreas endocrine glands.

Vocations. Libran's are suited to careers in the legal and justice services and those that involve mediation and counselling such as psychology, the diplomatic service, conflict resolution and relationship counselling. They have artistic talent and a flair with colour, so are suited to the arts, beauty, fashion, decorating industries, or where personal presentation, charm and good looks count.

Planets in Libra

- Saturn: it is exalted. At the point of balance, people have an opportunity to use the intellect wisely, to make the right choice, or face further negative karma.
- Mars: in detriment. In this sign of interlude, the power of desire is lessened. This enables the mind to be developed.
- The Sun: it falls. Neither personality nor soul dominate in the pure Libran. With balance achieved, esoterically they tune each other out. Unless there are other factors in the chart (in the psychology), this manifests as a life that is relatively conflict free.

Keywords. Positive: accommodating, advocates, ambassadorial, artistic, balanced, beautiful, blends, charming, cooperative, coordinates, counsel, decorative, decorous, delicate, design, diplomatic, discerning, discreet, easy-going, fair, harmonising, judicious, just, kind, likable, matches, moderate, peaceful, polite, prudent, refined, relating, romantic, sociable, subtle, tactful, thoughtful, understanding, unions, urbane, valuing. *Negative:* ambivalence, changeable, dependent, dithering, equivocating, falters, flirtatious, hesitant, indecisive, pleasure-seeking, procrastinating, puts off the inevitable, shallow, superficial, teetering, torn, unbalanced, undecided, unreliable, vacillating, wavering.

8. Scorpio (October 23 - November 22).

Keynotes: Struggle - Strength - Test - Trial - Triumph

Mode: fixed - slow.

Element: water.

Animal: scorpion.

Rulers: Mars and Pluto.

Concentrated and intense water-emotions, passionate, powerful, dangerous - "I Fight." Scorpio produces people who are deep, emotional and passionate. With very strong wills and long memories, they are intense about anything they are involved with. Warriors of the zodiac, they fight to win and usually go straight for the jugular (that is, to win at first strike). The symbol is the Scorpion, representing the highly reactive, aggressive and at times dangerous nature of these people. When the lower influence of the Scorpion is strong and people are driven by their desires, they can do bad things - use their force to hurt others. When the Eagle is stronger, fearless, courageous leaders and protectors of the weak are produced - also healers who give their strength willingly to those in need. Being a water sign, Scorpio's are gifted with intuition and Pluto, God of the Underworld, gifts them with deep insight.

They are possessive, territorial, passionate, jealous, loyal and devoted and would fight to protect loved ones. They can also be controlling and manipulative.

The Spiritual Goal: Scorpio provides us with the opportunity to resist and to triumph over the illusions, rampant desires and deceits of the lower emotional life. This marks the 2nd spiritual initiation, control over the astral-desire nature.

Scorpio rules: the eighth house and is related to number 8. People: assassins, executioners, sexual predators, soldiers, tax-men and warriors. Generally: criminal elements, death, eagles, garbage, inheritances, latrines, the military, phoenix, scorpions, sex, taxes, toilets, the underworld, waste, weapons. Season: the middle of autumn. Colours: red, black. Stones: topaz. Metal: iron, plutonium.

Anatomy and Health. Typical Scorpio characteristics of the eagle-type are piercing magnetic eyes, a strong, proud face with high-cheekbones and a hooked nose. The Scorpion type is shorter, thickset, physical and dark. Scorpio rules the sexual and reproductive areas, which is where problems often occur.

Vocations. Scorpio is a healing sign and rules vocations connected with the healing of emotions such as - psychology, transformational inner healing, the healing of emotional trauma, of sexual problems and all problems caused by unresolved emotional wounds. It governs esoteric studies and participation in occult work and rituals. Scorpio people are also suited to industries involved with blood, sexuality, death and birth; sanitation, the underworld, the military, weaponry, subterfuge, machinery, surgery, water, oil, the stock-market, investments, unions and politics.

Planets in Scorpio

- Uranus is exalted. It develops the scientific mind and enables the spiritually advanced in Scorpio to live the occult life and leave the mystic way behind.
- Venus is in detriment. In average man, sex dominates. In the advanced person, soul-love and wisdom are on the ascendancy.
- The Moon falls. In the final victory in Scorpio, the instinctual life (the Moon), is entirely vanquished and defeated and desire killed out.

Keywords. Positive: assertive, brave, courageous, deep, determined, emotional-depth, faithful, focused, forceful, impassioned, insightful, intense, intuitive, magnetic, mysterious, passionate, penetrating, perceptive, possessive, powerful, probing, psychological, regenerating, reserved, resourceful, sexual, transforming, victorious, warrior-like, watchfulness, will-power. *Negative:* brooding, brutal, compulsive, cruel, dangerous, desirous, destructive, fixed, forceful, jealous, obsessive, resentful, sadistic, secretive, tyrannical, unforgiving, vindictive, wilful.

Hercules Labour in Scorpio: Destroying the Lernaen Hydra.

The hydra had nine angry heads that breathed flames. Hercules attacked it, but two heads grew back for every one he severed. Hercules was being defeated. But then he had the inspiration to raise the hydra aloft and when its connection with the mud was broken, it died.

Moral: hold the mind up in the light.

9. Sagittarius (November 23 - December 21).

Keynotes: Aspiration - Orientation - Direction

Mode: mutable - adaptable.

Element: fire.

Symbol: the centaur.

Ruler: Jupiter.

Hercules Labour in Sagittarius: Killing the Stymphalian Birds.

Man-eating birds attacked and killed people. They lived and hid in the marshes. To bring them into the open, Hercules clashed cymbals together. When the birds rose in panic at the noise, Hercules mounted his winged horse and killed them with his arrows.

Moral: weed out negative thoughts and words.

Changeable – fire, focused, one-pointed, Idealistic - "I Vision." The energies of Sagittarius produces travellers and searchers - at three levels. There are three symbols for this sign - the Centaur represents those ruled by their lower desires; the Archer represents those oriented to a higher way of life, the Arrow represents the intuitive initiate. Sagittarians are enthusiastic world travellers and/ or travel mentally through abstract study. They are devotional, idealistic, intellectual people who are highly motivated when in pursuit of their goals. When its energy is negatively expressed it produces individuals who have difficulty keeping their energies focused and who can be undisciplined with food, drink, gambling, sex and moral issues.

Sagittarian's are warm while they love, but they move on easily. Passion is often focused on areas outside of the personal. The ideal partner is a kindred soul who is independent, likes to travel and intellectualize.

The Spiritual Goal: Sagittarius provides us with the opportunity to develop harmlessness in thought and speech, to aspire towards a higher aspirational life and to redirect the energies to new and more idealistic goals.

Sagittarius rules: the ninth house, is related to number 9 and the preparation required for spiritual initiation. People: archers, church people, foreigners, journeymen, philosophers, promoters, propagandists, Secretaries of State and world travellers. Generally: arrows, centaurs, churches, embassies, horses, morals, philosophies, religions, universities and the world. Season: late autumn. Colour: turquoise, purple. Stones: amethyst, turquoise. Metal: tin.

Anatomy and Health. The sign gives height and breadth, strong hips and thighs, a toothy, 'horsey' look and a tendency to gallop quickly from goal to goal. Sagittarius rules the liver, hips and thighs. Common problems are gout, sciatica, obesity, jaundice and liver disease.

Vocations. Sagittarius people are suited to careers that are connected to the raising of the consciousness or soul of man - for example, philosophy, higher education, religion, academia, publishing and library work. They are suited to travel vocations and those involving foreign countries such as import-exporting, foreign correspondence or ambassadorial work. Promotional work also suits them such as selling, marketing and gambling. Sagittarius is also a very athletic sign (it governs locomotion), and rules in particular, athletics, archery and javelin throwing.

Planets in Sagittarius

- No planet is exalted in Sagittarius and no planet falls. Sagittarius is esoterically regarded as a sign of balance and of no extremes; there is no great fall and no exaltation. This indicates that Sagittarian's must walk an even way between the pairs of opposites, a central, balanced path. This enables them to travel fast upon the Spiritual Path.
- Mercury: in detriment. In time, wisdom supersedes the logical mind.

Keywords. Positive: adventurous, aspiring, big-hearted, convivial, direct, enthusiastic, expansive, exploring, focused, freedom-loving, generous, good-humoured, honest, independent, jovial, large-hearted, magnanimous, one-pointed, optimistic, outspoken, philanthropic, philosophical, promotes, straightforward, travels far, venturesome, visionary, wise. *Negative:* blunt, boastful, bragging, dogmatic, exaggerating, extravagant, gossipy, gambles, insensitive, irresponsible, over-confident, predatory, restless, self-righteous, squanders, tactless, wasteful, zealous.

10. Capricorn (December 22 - January 21).

Keynotes: Effort - Struggle - Strain - Initiation

Direct – earth, cautious, shrewd, ambitious, practical - "I Work." The energies of this sign produces people who are down-to-earth and very ambitious. The Goat - hardy and aggressive is their symbol. They get to the top of their mountain, into a position of power, through sheer hard work and determination. They are cautious, disciplined, reliable and always get the job done. Conservative, they obey rules and regulations and when in power can be authoritarian, expecting others to observe all formalities and traditions as well. Higher types express tolerance, wisdom and understanding. Expressed negatively, Capricorn people can be cold, lack joyfulness, be ruthless, calculating, rigid, miserly and cruel. Capricorn people look old when young and seem to look more youthful as they age.

They are not sentimental people and will assess the benefits a partner can bring. But they are loyal and supportive and will work hard to make a relationship work. Psychologically, they need partners who are emotionally demonstrative, who can draw them out of their reserve.

The Spiritual Goal: Capricorn provides us with the opportunity to overcome greedy ambition - represented by the Goat, and to kneel in humility before the Divine and offer the life in service.

Capricorn rules: the tenth house, is related to number 10 and to spiritual initiation. People: authority figures, executives, judges, policemen. Generally: aging, crocodiles, goats, law enforcement, mountains; old age. Season: early winter. Colours: black, brown. Stones: amber, onyx. Metal: lead.

Anatomy and Health. Typical Capricorn characteristics give medium height, a sinewy body, an angular head with a goat-like look, a gaunt face, worried features and small, dark, shrewd eyes. Capricorn rules the skeleton, spine, knees and skin. Typical problems are trouble with joints, deafness and dental problems.

Vocations. Capricorn is a leadership sign and its people are suited to managerial or executive positions that give power and authority, especially in government, corporations, large institutions, conservative organisations and politics. Also, industries connected with the land such as real-estate, mining and minerals; and those related to death and time.

Planets in Capricorn
- Mars is exalted. The God of War and producer of conflict triumphs in the life of the undeveloped and average person, who fights to satisfy his ambitions. For the more evolved person, this material sign provides the battleground between the lure of the old established, covetous, habits and new, higher impulses.
- Moon: it is in detriment. In the evolved person, form-life no longer controls.
- Saturn: is dignified. It is potent in Capricorn. For the more evolved person, this gives a powerful mind and intellect and liberates the soul from form control. Otherwise, it strengthens greed.

Keywords. Positive: abstemious, ambitious, careful, cautious, conservative, conventional, deliberate, disciplined, dry, economical, enterprising, frugal, hard-working, ordered, patient, practical, pragmatic, provident, prudent, reserved, resourceful, responsible, sensible, shy, spartan, tenacious, traditional, wise. *Negative:* avarice, avid, calculating, canny, close-fisted, cold, crystallizing, cunning, fatalistic, grudging, limited, materialistic, mean, miserly, Machiavellian, niggardly, parsimonious, pessimistic, power-hungry, rigid, stubborn, status-seeking.

Mode: fixed - slow.

Element: earth.

Symbol: the goat.

Ruler: Saturn.

Hercules Labour in Capricorn: Slaying Cerberus, Guardian of Hades.

Hercules travelled down into Hades, the underworld, to rescue Prometheus who was guarded by Cerberus. The dog had three heads. Hercules defeated it by choking it to death. He freed Prometheus who then gave man the gift of fire.

Moral: ruthlessly greedy people will have to face the consequences of their actions.

Mode: cardinal - fast

Element: air

Symbol: Water-Bearer.

Ruler: Uranus

Hercules Labour in Aquarius: Cleansing the Augean Stables

For thirty years, the great cattle stables of King Augeas had not been cleaned. The air was putrid and pestilence was sweeping the land. Hercules broke down a wall surrounding the stables and diverted two rivers through them, cleansing them within a day.

Moral: the healing waters of God will wash away sins.

11. Aquarius (January 22 - February 19).

Keynotes: Group Consciousness - World Service

Concentrated – air, they intellectualize, are group conscious - "I Know." Aquarius energies produces people who are detached, mental and universal - in outlook and opinion. They are preoccupied with social and political issues and how society can be changed for the better - their symbol is the Water-Bearer. Group and friendship oriented, they seek the company of people they can share their ideas and visions with. Revolutionaries at heart, they can be eccentric and unorthodox. Aquarian energy expressed negatively produces narrow and prejudiced views.

This is not a romantic or passionate sign. Aquarian's are intellectuals who need partners who are also friends, and who will support their efforts to improve society. They are often accepting of alternative types of relationships.

The Spiritual Goal: Aquarius provides us with the opportunity to develop the scientific mind, to become more inclusive and group conscious and to develop the heart and intuition of a World Server. Then use these qualities in humanitarian interests to promote right human relations across the globe.

Aquarius rules: the eleventh house and is related to number 11. People: architects, eccentrics, humanitarians, information technology experts, reformers, revolutionaries, scientists, water-bearers and world-servers. Generally: air-planes, computers, groups, new technology, organisations, science, water, water-pots. Season: middle of winter. Colour: electric blue. Stones: amethyst. Metal: uranium.

Anatomy and Health. Typical Aquarian characteristics are height and a light complexion. They have an air of thoughtfulness about them, an intelligent brow and can talk. Aquarius rules the calves, ankles and electric signalling in the nervous system. They can suffer circulation problems and leg cramps.

Vocations. Aquarius people are suited to careers that improve civilisation generally, that salvage, reform and uplift - such as the United Nations, welfare work and the promotion of right-human-relations and brotherliness. They are also suited to careers that cater for the expression of new ideas, originality, the modern and new, which offer variety, change and alternative options such as the esoteric sciences that includes astrology. This sign is related to science, so other suitable careers are those that deal with new technology, computers and scientific research.

Planets in Aquarius

No planet is exalted and no planet falls. This is because the advanced Aquarian (who has worked through all the signs in previous lives), has reached a point of balance and is no longer held by the pairs of opposites. He has surmounted all the tests of human life and stands free, distributing life, symbolised by the two wavy lines of the Aquarius symbol.

- The Sun (the physical Sun) is in detriment. The personality (Sun) has its power lessened in this group-conscious sign. The 3rd spiritual initiation occurs when the light of the personality is "put out" by the light of the soul (the Sun).

Keywords. Positive: affable, civilized, cordial, detached, dispassionate, eccentric, free and free-spirited, friendly, group-awareness, group-conscious, honest, humane, independent, individualistic, intellectual, intelligent, inventive, liberal, loyal, maverick, mental-originality, original, reforming, right-detachment, unconventional, universal. *Negative*: aberrant, abnormal, aloof, chaotic, contrary, cool, detached, deviant, dogmatic, erratic, intractable, nervousness, nervy, opinionated, rebelliousness, rigidity, unfeeling, unpredictable, wild.

12. Pisces (February 20 - March 20).

Keynotes: Bondage - Detachment - Death

Mode: mutable - adaptable

Element: water

Symbol: fishes.

Rulers: Jupiter, Neptune

Compassionate, Sacrificing, Inclusive - "I Serve." Pisces produces people who are watery, emotional, fluid and compassionate. Like their symbol the two Fishes, they ride the currents of life and can change direction from moment to moment - the whole world is their ocean. Servers of humanity, it is easy for them to "walk in the shoes of others" and as a result are compassionate, accepting and tolerant people. Piscean energy expressed negatively produces fantasy-dreamers, people who are ungrounded, naive and unrealistic. Too trusting and gullible, they often find themselves in victim-type situations. With hyper-sensitive emotions, they may try to escape from the hardship of life through drugs, alcohol, fantasy or religious cults.

Pisceans need continuous emotional demonstrations and they will swim in search of someone else if the current partner is not delivering in this area. They often fantasise about the ideal partner and project this image on to those they meet. Such unrealistic expectations usually lead to disappointments.

The Spiritual Goal: Pisces provides the opportunity to detach from the nonessentials in life and serve humanity with compassion, tolerance and understanding.

Pisces rules: the twelfth house and is related to number 12. People: alcoholics, artists, drug addicts, mediums, missionaries, poets, priests, psychics and servers. Generally: boats, fish, the ocean. Season: late winter. Colour: sea-green. Stones: coral, jade. Metal: tin.

Anatomy and Health. There are two Pisces types - the dolphin (sleek and compact) and the whale (large and ponderous). Both have moist and gentle eyes, pale skin, some have pouting lips and the feet may be like flippers. Pisces rules the feet and lymph glands and its people are susceptible to gout, viruses, mucus discharges, addictions, psychosomatic illnesses, oedema and lymph troubles.

Vocations. Pisces people are suited to the serving, sacrificial, healing, nurturing, caring and volunteer industries. They are often found working with people afflicted with serious physical or mental health issues, who have addictions, are incarcerated or are dying. They are also drawn to religion, to spiritual and mystical careers. Often talented artists and musicians, they excel in storytelling, theatre, music, acting, film and fantasy.

Planets in Pisces

- Venus is exalted. In the advanced person, all personal selfishness has been dissolved away leaving the ability to love unconditionally. In average man, naivety in love matters.
- Mercury falls. In ordinary man, the power of mind weakens when the emotions dominate consciousness. Later, in the spiritually advanced person, the power of the mind ends - it is no longer required. The intuition takes its place.

Keywords. Positive: artistic, caring, charitable, compassionate, dissolves, dreamy, emotional, empathetic, feeling, fluid, gentle, forgiving, healing, humane, idealistic, imaginative, introspective, intuitive, kind and kind-hearted, merciful, musical, mystical, perceptive, poetic, receptive, sacrificing, selfless, sensitive, serving, spiritual, sympathetic, tender, visionary, understanding, watery, *Negative:* addictive, no boundaries, confused, debilitating, delusional, disingenuous, escapist, fantasising, impractical, impressionable, indolent, naive, over-sensitive, secretive, unclear, vague, victim-consciousness, weak-willed.

Hercules Labour in Pisces: Capture of the Red Cattle.

On Erytheia, the monster Geryon was holding cattle unlawfully. Hercules killed him and his two-headed dog, but spared the shepherd Orthrus. He sailed with the cattle and Orthrus back to the mainland and offered them to Athena, Goddess of Wisdom.

Moral: eventually, all souls return to God.

CHAPTER 2.
THE PLANETS

A. ABOUT THE PLANETS.

Planets can be read on three levels. As part of the psyche - for example, Mars rules the passions. As a body part - Mars rules the reproductive organs. As an outer experience, a thing or person - Mars rules conflict, war, military weapons and aggressive young men. In this chapter, the components that make up a planet's nature are explained.

1. Planets have personalities and rule Signs.

Each planet has its own quality. It also carries the energy of the sign it rules. In classical astrology certain planets were considered unfortunate, malefic - Mars, Saturn, Uranus, Neptune and Pluto. Venus and Jupiter were considered fortunate, benefic. In Psychological Astrology, the malefics represent "shadows" within our psyche. In Esoteric Astrology, they represent spiritual forces which urge us to transform and grow.

In society, the planets represent people.

    Sun: autocrats, dictators, kings, leaders, presidents, prime ministers, rulers.
    Moon: mothers, wives, women generally and those who are mature or pregnant.
    Mercury: interpreters, messengers, scribes, travellers.
    Venus: lovers, mistresses, young attractive women.
    Mars: fighters, hoodlums, soldiers, young men, youths.
    Jupiter: church people, gamblers, philosophers, teachers, long-distance travellers, university professors.
    Saturn: authority figures, elders, grandparents, law enforcers, old people, professionals, wise people.
    Uranus: anarchists, eccentrics, revolutionaries, scientists, social reformers.
    Neptune: con-men, priests, shamans, spiritual healer, visionaries.
    Pluto: assassins, criminals, healers, executioners, rubbish or sewerage disposers, spies.

2. Planets Retrograde (℞).

The Sun and Moon are never retrograde. The symbol for retrograde is a capital R with a stroke across the lower part. Retrograde occurs when a planet appears to be moving backwards as a faster planet passes it. It is interpreted as being karmic. Because of the misuse of a function in a previous life, the individual is being re-educated in the right use of the principles symbolised by the planet. It is important mainly for Mercury, Venus, Mars - the personal planets that represent the mind, affections and passionate emotions. Mercury retrograde indicates lessons to do with communicating correctly; Venus retrograde, lessons with love and relationships; Mars retrograde, lessons to do with desire and sexual expression. The outer, slow-moving, transformative planets are retrograde often. In their case, the retrograde phase simply prolongs the learning experience.

3. Planet dispositors.

"Disposit" is an astrology term that can be defined as one planet having power over another. A planet disposits any planet which is in the sign it rules. This dispositing planet modifies the disposited planet. For example, if Mars the God of War is disposited in Libra, then Venus' energy will tone down or modify its aggression. The unruly traits will be socialised to a certain extent.

4. Mutual Reception.

Two planets that are located in each other's signs, are said to be in mutual reception. This brings a harmonising effect between the two planets. For example, Mars in Libra and Venus in Aries, are in mutual reception. So are the Moon in Capricorn and Saturn in Cancer. Ordinarily, these planets would be hostile to each other so mutual reception is fortunate. In the personality it shows a reconciliation between the two factors involved, increased harmony between two previously warring aspects.

5. Planet glyphs.

Planet glyphs (☉, ☽, ☿, etc), are usually broken down into three common elements: A circle denoting spirit or mind, a crescent denoting the soul or the emotions, and a cross denoting the physical body.

6. Planet strengths by sign.

Dignity. This occurs when a planet is located in the sign it rules, such as Saturn in Capricorn. The planet's positive qualities are strengthened.

Exalted. This occurs when a planet is in the sign which enhances its power. Once again, the particular qualities the planet represents are strengthened and enhanced. Exaltation is a planet's most positive expression.

Detriment. This occurs when a planet is located in a sign opposite its own - such as Saturn in Cancer, the sign opposite Capricorn. The positive traits represented by the planet are weakened and the negatives are strengthened. This will manifest through the personality as a negative trait and dysfunctional behaviour, until corrected.

Falls. This occurs when a planet is located in the sign opposite to that in which it is exalted. The negative behavioural pattern is more acute and it takes greater effort to correct it.

Planet Strengths by Sign

Signs	Dignified *strengthened*	Exalted *strengthened*	In Detriment *energy distorted*	Falls *energy distorted*
Sun	Leo	Aries	Aquarius	Libra
Moon	Cancer	Taurus	Capricorn	Scorpio
Mercury	Gemini-Virgo	Aquarius	Sagittarius-Pisces	Leo
Venus	Taurus-Libra	Pisces	Scorpio-Aries	Virgo
Mars	Aries-Scorpio	Capricorn	Libra-Taurus	Cancer
Jupiter	Sagittarius-Pisces	Cancer	Gemini-Virgo	Capricorn
Saturn	Capricorn	Libra	Cancer-Leo	Aries
Uranus	Aquarius	Scorpio	Leo	Taurus
Neptune	Pisces	Cancer	Virgo	Capricorn
Pluto	Scorpio	Aries	Taurus	Libra

7. Planet Strengths from other factors.

An unaspected planet. There are no major aspects to other planets. This is very important if the planet affected is one of the personal planets - the Sun, Moon, Mercury, Venus and Mars. It symbolises an undeveloped and alienated part of the psyche which needs to be integrated back into the personality. The dispositor planet holds the key to integration.

> For example: unaspected Mercury in Libra. This represents communication difficulties, perhaps an inability to speak out about relationship issues. Because Venus disposits Mercury, it holds the key to healing these difficulties. If for instance, it was in Capricorn in the tenth house - these difficulties could be helped through developments associated with the career, such as good public speaking skills.

Most elevated planet. This is the planet closest to the MC of the chart. What the planet symbolises - and the sign it is in, will have an important influence on the life for good or ill.

Afflicted planets. A planet is afflicted if it is in a sign where it falls or is in detriment, if it is unaspected or retrograde. A planet is also afflicted if it has multiple hard aspects to other planets. This distorts/ cripples/ impairs the planet's expression.

8. Planets, void of course.

Applies to a planet that has completed all aspects to other planets before leaving the sign it is in. In this period, before the new sign is entered, the planet lacks creative force and no new tasks should be started.

9. Planet Patterns.

There are six recognised Planetary Patterns (each one representing a recognised personality type), and a seventh non-conformist pattern – the Splay.

Bowl. The planets are in six consecutive signs or houses. Individuals with this pattern are self-contained and have high ideals or goals which they strive to realise. Personal sacrifice is a quality often demonstrated. The lead planet (i.e. the first planet after going through the empty part of the chart in an anticlockwise direction) provides the driving force; the end planet symbolises the goal.
EG. Uranus as the lead and the Moon as the end planet. This individual is innovative and open to the new and unorthodox (Uranus), especially when seeking emotional satisfaction or goals in which there is an emotional (Moon) investment.

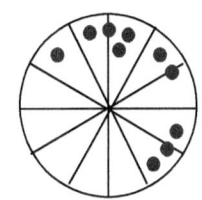

Bucket. A single planet opposes all planets on the opposite side. The energy generated by the large group of planets will try to find release through the single planet. It is crucial therefore that the function symbolised by this planet is working well, or congested energy, anger and frustration will result. If Mars is the handle, the energies are gathered up and delivered enthusiastically and with "punch". Saturn will give a measured, cautious delivery. The handle can have a maximum of 2 planets.

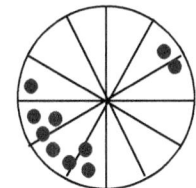

Bundle. The planets are contained within a trine, four signs or four houses. This cocktail of forces gives a very intense personality type. Bundle people are single-minded, self-mobilised trail blazers and self-sufficient. They can build something from nothing. They can also be inhibited, obsessive, selfish and very self-centred. They tend to put all their eggs into one basket and this can be catastrophic for them if things go wrong and everything comes crashing down. They have to start building from new.

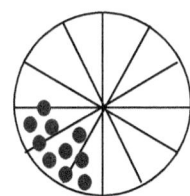

Locomotive. Planets fill two thirds of the chart. These personality types have a driving urge to action. They are often involved with solving the community's problems. They are idealists and will work hard to achieve their aspirations. They start movements then leave them to their followers to manage, going out after new challenges. There is much in common with the Bowl type, but the Locomotive is more adventurous. Apply the lead/ end planet principle.

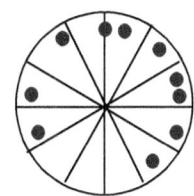

Seesaw. In this pattern type, the planets oppose each other across the chart. These personality types thrive on conflict and excitement. Their natural inclination is to swing to extremes and back and forth - this is the root of their problem. They need to practise moderation in all things, look for the middle-way, try to centre themselves in the midst of emotional upheavals.

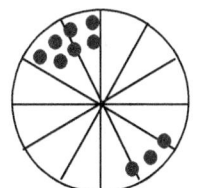

Splash. Not more than one planetary conjunction or 4 houses empty. This personality type can be more impersonal than the others - they tend to take a broad view of life. They are very versatile and can do several things at once. This could lead to a "jack of all trades, master of none" approach to life. If discipline is applied, they can coordinate their energies into a specialised direction.

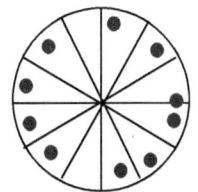

Splay. There are three irregular groups in the pattern - but any other non-conforming planet arrangement fits into this category. These are the nonconformists of the zodiac who do not fit neatly into any of life's pigeon holes. They are very intense, independent and will not allow others to tie them into predictable patterns. They have the ability to direct their energies constructively into several specialised directions.

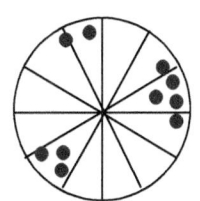

10. The "Gifts" the Gods give to the Planets named after them.

Sun. The symbol for the Sun is the eye of Ra, of Father-God. The Sun gives power and status, confident masculine assertiveness and leadership. It also gives an ability to light up a room just by making an appearance. A bright, glowing complexion and thick, bright-coloured hair that surrounds the head like a nimbus, are its physical attributes.

Moon. The Moon is a symbol of Mother-Matter. She gives a silvery sheen (physically or emotionally) - pale, milky skin and contrasting dark hair. In character, the Moon bestows mature femininity, shyness and modesty.

Mercury. The Messenger of the Gods, is fleet-footed, slim and youthful looking. He passes these characteristics on to those in his signs along with long, loose limbs, height and an Adam's Apple. His people are cerebral, are the messengers of the zodiac, presenting their ideas through all manner of communications.

Venus. The Goddess of Beauty gives good looks to her people - charm, beautiful skin, full and curving lips, dimples, long eyelashes and curvaceous or well-formed bodies. Physically they are often the most beautiful-looking members of the zodiac. Venus also gives many blessings that benefit relationships. The sex-drive is more compelling in Taurus (the sign of desire), than it is in cerebral Libra.

Mars. The God of War gives a warlike nature to its people. Higher types are assertive, courageous, brave and fight for causes they believe in. Younger souls are aggressive bullies. Mars gives the body of a warrior, compact, fit, strong, active, lean and muscular.

Jupiter. He was the king of the gods, of the sky and thunder. Renowned for his good humour and largesse, he was also a boozer and womaniser. He gives these traits and a love of intoxicating drinks, rich food and excesses. He was also considered wise, and brotherly love and wisdom are the higher qualities he confers.

Saturn. In appearance, Saturn is usually depicted as dour looking, thin, troubled, dark; and when he is pictured with a scythe as the Reaper of Souls, he looks dangerous. These traits he gives to his people, along with a long pointy chin and a large, dipping nose.

Uranus. Ouranos is a Sky-God. His force is electrical and Uranian people look like they have had a shock, with wild, sparkling eyes and kinky, curling hair. They are individualists who walk to the beat of their own drum - rebels who want to change the world.

Neptune. The King of the Oceans gives devotion, idealism, a spiritual orientation and a very sensitive and empathetic nature. In appearance, Neptunian types are svelte, other-worldly looking, who glide when they move and carry a magical aura about them.

Pluto. God of the Underworld. The picture is Anubis, the Egyptian God of the Dead. Pluto adds darkness and a swarthy appearance. Sometimes his people have a body part that is disproportionate or misshapen. It also gives a formidable will and power to transform psychologically.

B. THE PERSONAL PLANETS AND ASCENDANT

The personal planets represent our psychology and are fully explained in this section. The personality is represented by the Sun, the mind by Mercury, love and affection by Venus, and emotions by the Moon and Mars. Although it is not a planet, the ascendant is included.

1. The Ascendant.
How we approach life and how people see us - the image we project.

The ascendant is one of the four angles in the chart and is also the cusp of the first house. The other angles are the descendant, which is also the seventh house cusp; the nadir, the bottom of the chart and the cusp of the fourth house in Placidus; and the MC (medium coeli), the zenith or top of the chart and the cusp of the tenth house in Placidus. The sign on the ascendant represents our approach to life, how we view the world and how others see us. This approach will either hinder growth and progression or support it. The planet that rules the sign on the ascendant, is called the "chart ruler". It will influence the life in some vital way. It represents where we will focus our ascendant-sign forces to discover more about our self and about the world.

The Spiritual Goal. At a higher level, the ascendant represents the soul's purpose in the incarnation. This consists of the positive development of the ascendant sign qualities and their expression. This will balance out the egotistical traits of the personality - represented by the Sun sign. In Esoteric Astrology, the esoteric ruler of the ascendant sign is the higher ruler of the chart. Its nature, sign and house extend the message of the soul. It tells us what we have to do and where to further our soul development. This means we should examine both the traditional and esoteric rulers of the ascendant if we are interested in spiritual growth.

Astrology Signs and Planet Rulers

Signs	*Exoteric ruler - governs the personality*	*Esoteric ruler: represents soul influence*
Aries	Mars	Mercury
Taurus	Venus	Vulcan
Gemini	Mercury	Venus
Cancer	Moon	Neptune
Leo	Sun	Sun v. Neptune
Virgo	Mercury	Moon v. Vulcan
Libra	Venus	Uranus
Scorpio	Mars, Pluto	Mars
Sagittarius	Jupiter	Earth
Capricorn	Saturn	Saturn
Aquarius	Uranus, Saturn	Jupiter
Pisces	Jupiter, Neptune	Pluto

V = veiling, or being a channel for the forces of the second planet, which occurs when we are on the Spiritual Path and are applying purification disciplines.

Aspects to the Ascendant. Planets located near the angles are very influential, especially those on the ascendant and in the first house. If a planet is actually conjunct the ascendant it greatly influences how we approach life and how people experience us. But all planets in the first house are important in how we identify as "the self" (usually the prerogative of the Sun), because this is the house of "self".

Anatomy. the ascendant sign (and the ascendant planet ruler), colour physical appearance. The first house that is associated with the ascendant, governs the head and brain. It is the birth-point.

Keywords. Appearance, approach to life, beginnings, brain and head, early environment, image, mannerisms, perception of life, physical body, physical traits, projection into life.

The Sun's symbol represents God (the dot) in the universe (the circle).

The **Sun rules** Leo and is **dignified** when placed in its own sign.

The Sun is **exalted** in Aries.

The Sun is in **detriment** in Aquarius.

The Sun **falls** in Libra.

"The soul is light symbolically, for it is like the rays of the sun, which pour out into the darkness". Bailey, Esoteric Astrology page 132.

2. The Sun.

The nature and power of the conscious self, the personality.

The Spiritual Goal. This is to develop, integrate and express the powers of the personality positively and potently.

Overview. In our psychology, the Sun symbolises the ego, the individuality, the "I Am I" centre of the personality - how the inner essence, power and authority of the lower self is expressed. If the Sun is well-placed it gives a strong will, a strong and positive character, determination to achieve the goal, vitality and a strong constitution.

The Sun takes its colouring from the sign it is in. The Sun Sign traits are the characteristics that form the heart of the personality. The Sun is the heart of the chart as far as the personality goes - and in the average person, the other planets are satellites of the Sun.

The Sun at birth, symbolises the level of personality integration or maturity that has been achieved so far. Its sign and situation in the chart show the opportunities that have been given in this incarnation to take this further. The positive qualities of the Sun sign must be developed and the negative traits balanced out. This will help to integrate the various facets of the personality into a unified whole, which we then demonstrate as confidence of character and mature and wise action.

This important evolutionary step is symbolised by the Sun's sign - Leo. In the 12 signs, Leo represents the development and integration of the personality. When this integration occurs, the soul begins the long battle (over lifetimes), to bring the personality under its influence and control. This is achieved by purifying the negative traits of the Sun sign and strengthening the positive qualities.

The Sun rules: the sign Leo, the fifth house. People: authority figures, dignitaries, fathers, husbands, kings, leaders, men generally and mature men. Generally: daytime, power, light and sunlight. Day of the week: Sunday. Colours: gold, orange-yellow and orange-red. Stones: topaz, diamonds. Metal: gold.

Vocations. All leadership careers, such as managers, authority figures, presidents, statesmen, rulers, dignitaries, magistrates, organisers and bankers. Also, careers that show off the personality, such as acting.

Aspects to the Sun. Easy aspects give confidence and a strong sense of self. The Sun in the 1st or 10th houses, or conjunct the MC or ascendant strengthens its power. Hard aspects give a strong but abrasive personality. Unaspected, retrograde or in fall or detriment; this can result in a weak, unintegrated personality.

Anatomy. The Sun rules the heart, cardiovascular system, spine, vitality, the constitution, the immune system. The stronger the Sun is in the chart by sign, house or aspect, the stronger is vitality and the immune system.

Keywords. Positive: authoritative, brilliant, confident, dignified, the ego, father, generous, identity, individualistic, heat, leadership, life-force, light, masculine, mature, noble, paternal, the personality, powerful, prideful, the self and self-expression, solar, strong and strong-willed, vital, vitality, warm, wisdom. *Negative*: arrogance, conceited, despotic, egotistical, haughty, ostentatious, self-important, tyrannical, weak-willed.

Verbs. Positive: alight, blazes, bully, embraces, flames, heats, illumines, inflames, leads, lights, loves, radiates, warms, shines, throws light on, vitalises. Negative: burns, devitalises, scalds, scorches, sears.

3. The Moon.

How we express the emotions and our unconscious reactions.

The Spiritual Goal. The Moon represents an opportunity to break old, limiting, unconscious, emotional patterns; to clear out baggage from the past.

Overview. In our psychology, the Moon represents the emotions and the subconscious mind and its contents - our automatic, unconscious beliefs, habits, responses and instincts. The esoteric term for these responses is "the prison of the soul-pattern" - the modern, psychological term is "negative core-belief". These automatic responses are reactions to painful, past-life emotional experiences. They consist of reactions like outrage and anger and any self-protective actions we instinctively take. But all these reactions are related to the unresolved emotional incident and they will continue until inner healing occurs. The Moon sign and its position in the chart shows the nature of the pattern, where it is triggered and where we will have conflict until healing takes place. When this has been achieved, when the astral nature is clear and balanced, the positives of the Moon Sign demonstrate and in turn create harmony in the environment.

The **Moon rules** Cancer and is **dignified** when placed in its own sign.

The Moon is **exalted** in Taurus.

The Moon is in **detriment** in Capricorn.

The Moon **falls** in Scorpio.

The Moon rules: Cancer and the fourth house. People: babies, domestics, infants, families, females, mature women, mediums, mothers, nurses, the public, the masses and wives. Generally: domesticity, the home, moonlight, pregnancy, night-time, the nurturing and protective instincts. Day of the week: Monday. Colours: violet, silver, white. Stones: moonstones, opals. Metal: silver.

Aspects to the Moon. Easy aspects give easy emotional expression. This does not necessarily mean that the emotions are mature and poised. Most people are in the process of bringing this about. Hard aspects indicate difficulty expressing the emotions - with Jupiter, Uranus and Mars, "over-the-top" or volatile emotions. With Saturn and Pluto, repressed emotions. Lunar-Pluto aspects eventually lead to explosive, emotional eruptions. Moon unaspected: emotional isolation, great difficult in relating emotionally, in getting on with other people in a domestic setting.

Vocations. Generally, careers that are related to the traditional roles of women - domestic, caring, healing, nurturing and serving. For example, catering, cooking, domestics, dress-making, hospitality, nursing, teaching, minding children and public-service industries. Today, with gender definition dissolution, more men are entering traditional "female" trades.

Anatomy. The breasts, digestion, female functions, stomach.

Orbit. the Moon's orbit around the Sun takes approximately 27 days.

Keywords. Positive: emotional, fecundity, feelings, feminine, fertile, fruitful, habits, imaginative, instincts, intuitive, maternal, moist, moody, the national mood, parenting, people, protective, psychic, the public, receptive, sensitive, tribal, women. *Negatives:* anxious, changeable, damp, emotion, fretful, inconstant, infertile, inner-conflict, moody, psychic, restless, smother-love, unstable.

Verbs. Positive: cherishes, defends, digests, dreams, emotes, feels, hesitant, imagines, intuits, nurtures, protects, reacts, receives, responds. *Negative:* agonises, chills, struggles, sulks, vacillates.

The Moon's Nodes

The Moon's Nodes are not planets. They are the two points at which, the orbit of the Moon crosses the ecliptic. The north-node is related to the positive Moon and also to Uranus - indicating how we can progress forwards positively into the future. The south-node is similar to the negative Moon and to Saturn, representing baggage from the past that hinders positive progression.

Keywords - North: moving forwards into the future, positive goals, progressive, soul direction, spiritual growth, the "new". *South:* backtracking, going backwards, the past, tied to the past, retrogressive, the "old."

Mercury's symbol represents Mercury's winged hat and the caduceus.

Mercury rules Gemini

and Virgo,

and is **dignified** when placed in one of its own signs.

Mercury is **exalted** in Aquarius.

Mercury is in **detriment** in Sagittarius

and Pisces.

Mercury **falls** in Leo.

"Mercury, the star of the intuition." Bailey, Cosmic Fire, page 370

4. Mercury.

The way the mind works - how we think and communicate.

The Spiritual Goal. Mercury represents an opportunity to develop and illumine the mind and use it to bring the psyche into alignment with the soul, and the life generally into balance and harmony.

Overview. Mercury represents the mind and is associated with all processes of thought - the intellect, logic, all left-brain activities, the ability to perceive, relate, associate, remember and use knowledge. It governs communication in all its forms. At a higher level it represents the abstract mind, then higher still it represents buddhi, the intuition (intelligence without the concrete mind).

Mercury rules: Gemini, Virgo and the third and sixth houses. People: accountants, acquaintances, adolescents, older children, communicators, educators, handymen, interpreters, journalists, linguists, messengers, neighbours, news-media, opinion-polls, public speakers, reporters, scribes, traders, travellers, youths, young people; liars and thieves. Generally: commerce, trade, short-distance travel. Day of the week: Wednesday. Colour: yellow. Stones: agates. Metal: mercury, quicksilver.

Aspects to Mercury. Easy aspects give mental prowess and good communication skills. Hard aspects or Mercury in detriment or falling - difficulties in communication because of things like narrow-mindedness, mental aggression, dismissing what others have to say without acknowledgement, being too judgmental, or fear of speaking out. Unaspected: The mind lacks proportion and balance and this results in difficulties with communication.

Vocations. All careers connected with communication, education, sharing ideas, travel and commerce - book binders, book sellers, conflict resolvers, counsellors, diplomatic services, educators, holiday organisers, interpreters, journalists, linguists, mediators, merchandisers, office-workers, orators, publishers, reporters, salespeople, satirists, teachers, trades people, translators, travel guides and writers,

Anatomy. The shoulders, arms, hands, lungs, organs of speech and nervous system.

Orbit. Mercury's orbit around the Sun takes 88 days.

Keywords. Positive: clever, cognizant, communicative, dexterous, discriminative, eloquent, fleet-footed, illuminating, intelligent, intuitive, literary, mental, messenger, networking, opinions, quick-witted, reason, understanding, versatile, witty, writing. *Negative:* changeable, deceitful, dishonest, flighty, forgetful, gossipy, indecisive, nervy, nervous, restless, shallow, superficial, worrying.

Verbs. Positive: analyses, articulates, chatters, cognises, communicates, comprehends, contacts, converses, discriminates, expresses, forgets, gestures, illumines, intuits, mediates, messages, nervous, networks, reasons, speaks, speeds, talks, texts, thinks, travels, understand, worry, writes. *Negative:* cheats, gossips, lies, steals, thieves, tricks, worries.

> *Mercury illumines the mind and mediates between the soul and the personality, being the Messenger of the Gods. This mediatorship, in the first instance, produces an inevitable opposition between the pairs of opposites and a long drawn out conflict. This conflict finally works out into victory and the dispelling of illusion through the illumination of the lower mind.* [1]

---

[1] Bailey, Alice, A. Esoteric Astrology, page 100

5. Venus.

How we express affection, give and receive personal love.

Venus' symbol represents a hand mirror or necklace; also female genitalia.

The Spiritual Goal. At the higher level, Venus represents the soul and the beautification of consciousness - of the lower self; and refinement of values. It provides the soul with an opportunity to develop the ability to love intelligently.

Overview. In our psychology, Venus represents our ability to give and receive love and affection and how we generally relate with others. The positive qualities of the sign Venus is in, represent the positive ways we love - that sign, and planets that make hard aspects to Venus, their negatives traits indicate how we sabotage relationships. If we are having difficulties and want to improve relationships, these are the areas that need transforming.

Refining everything it touches; Venus develops sound values based on goodness and justice - it represents all things good and beautiful. Its location in the chart shows where we can beautify the nature, establish right-human-relations and express love-wisdom. We achieve this by reasoning our way through issues intelligently and by learning to relate with others and to perceive the world with kindness and love.

Venus rules Taurus

and Libra

and is **dignified** when placed in one of its own signs.

Venus rules: Taurus, Libra and houses 2 and 7. People: celebrities, girls, maidens, artists, decorators, fashion culture, feminists and femininity, high society, lawyers, lovers, marriage, mistresses, models, musicians, socializers and young attractive women. Generally: the arts, beauty, fashion, make-up, money. Day of the week: Friday. Colour: pastel colours. Stones: beryl, jade, lapis lazuli. Metal: brass, copper.

Aspects to Venus. Easy aspects give finesse in relationships, charm and ease in social settings. Hard aspects or Venus unaspected, in detriment or falling; it brings relationship difficulties. The ability to give affection, to be at ease in an intimate relationship is impaired and needs to be healed - the chart pattern will indicate what is wrong and how this should be done.

Venus is **exalted** in Pisces.

Venus is in **detriment** in Scorpio

and Aries.

Vocations. Careers in finance, law or handling money - for instance banking, money lender, all services and industries concerned with the law, with legal matters and legislation - barristers and lawyers. Vocations concerning mediation and the arts - counselling, diplomacy, human resources and industrial mediation; beautification, decorating, designing, fashion, luxury goods, modelling, social events organiser.

Anatomy. Rules the throat, thyroid, kidneys and the pancreas endocrine glands.

Orbit. Venus' orbit around the Sun takes 224 days

Keywords. Positive: affectionate, appreciative, artistic, attractive, beautiful, beauty, charming, coalition, cohesive, cosmetics, cute, intelligent-love, flirtatious, harmonising, intelligent, kind, loving, love-wisdom, lucid, luxury, marriage, money, ornamentation, personal love, pleasant, pretty, relationships, romance, sensual, sentimental, sex, socially-aware, sugar, values, wealth. *Negative*: artifice, desirous, dissolute, fickle, greedy, inconstant, lazy, materialistic, narcissistic, promiscuous, selfish, self-absorbed, slothful, sluttish, vain, vulgar, ugly, weak.

Venus **falls** in Virgo.

"Venus ..the beauty of nature", Bailey, Esoteric Astrology page 683.

Verbs. Positive: adds value to, adorns, appreciates, attracts, balances, beautifies, charms, desires, enhances, flirts, harmonises, loves, marries, relates, romances, socialises, sweetens and values. *Negative*: befouls, blemishes, debases, dishonours, prostitutes, seduces, stains, tarnishes and weakens.

Mars' symbol represents Mars' shield and spear. It also represents male genitalia.

Mars rules Aries,

and co-rules Scorpio,

and is **dignified** when placed in one of its own signs.

Mars is **exalted** in Capricorn.

Mars is in **detriment** in Taurus

and Libra.

Mars **falls** in Cancer.

"Mars, the God of War," Bailey, Esoteric Astrology page 96.

6. Mars.

How we express our passions and desires.

The Spiritual Goal. Mars represents an opportunity to transmute desire into spiritual aspiration.

Overview. In our psychology, Mars represents our desires, sex, passion and bolder and coarser emotions such as aggression, anger, courage, bravery, combativeness and self-assertion. It also represents how we fight for what we want and our ability to hold on to what we get. A strong Mars helps to achieve the life ambitions.

Esoterically, Mars symbolises the way in which the blind, rebellious emotional nature has to be subdued by the soul as it seeks to impose its will upon the lower nature. Although its fiery power can thwart the soul, Mars establishes relations between opposites and is a beneficent factor. Its higher manifestation is spiritual aspiration.

Mars rules: Aries, Scorpio and houses 1 and 8. People: athletes, blacksmiths, butchers, carpenters, engineers, explorers, fanatics, fighters, gun-smiths, hoodlums, iron and steel workers, machinists, males, mechanics, military, sex workers soldiers, sports people, surgeons, young men, youths and warriors. Generally: war and conflict. Day of the week: Tuesday. Colour: red. Stones: bloodstone, flint, rubies. Metal: iron.

Aspects to Mars. Easy aspects give ease in expressing physical and sexual energy, abundant energy to benefit health, and passion and aspiration to pursue our ambitions and higher things in life. Hard aspects or Mars unaspected, in detriment or falling; these forces indicate volatile emotions - anger, aggression, selfishness and violence. The passions are undisciplined, behaviour is irresponsible. Or, if Pluto or Saturn are involved - emotional repression leading eventually to fiery explosions.

Vocations. Those that are connected with the improvement of the physical body and competition, such as athletics, body-work, surgery, physical health and exercise, sports and sports coaching, body massaging, physiotherapy and chiropractic. Careers aligned with the warriorship aspect of Mars: soldier, military officer, fighter, boxer, pugilist, swords person, assassin, abattoir worker, war and weapons. Others: exploration, hairdressing, working with instruments, machinery and metals; engineering, slaughter-houses, sex-worker.

Anatomy. Rules the head via Aries, male reproduction, sex organs and adrenal glands. Illnesses such as burns, fevers, infectious diseases, skin rashes and accidents.

Orbit. Mars' orbit around the Sun takes 687 days.

Keywords. Positive: active, aspirational, assertive, brave, combative, conflict, courageous, daring, defensive, desirous, devoted, dynamic, eager, energetic, enterprising, enthusiastic, fiery, gallant, heroic, hunting, idealistic, intense, one-pointed, passionate, self-sacrificing, sex, war, worshipful, zeal. *Negative:* aggressive, angry, argumentative, audacious, avid, bullying, brutal, coarse, combative, conflicted, covetous, cowardly, craven, crude, cruel, desirous, destructive, emotional, fanatical, filthy, forceful, friction, hot-headed, impulsive, irritation, jealous, lustful, one-eyed, pursue, rapacious, reactive, reckless, sadistic, savage, selfish, temper-tantrums, volatile, violent, war-like.

Verbs. Positive: acts, adores, battles, bullies, combats, feels, fights, hunts, idealises, idolises, pursues. *Negative:* angers, annoys, attacks, boasts, coarsens, covets, debases, defiles, dirties, forces, injures, irritates, kills, lusts, murders, rapes, retaliates, sexualises, violates.

C. TRANSFORMING PLANETS

The five non-personal planets are transformative forces. They are the agents of evolution and their interactions with the personality (planets) bring both challenging and expansive experiences that force or encourage us to change, to let go of the past and move into the future.

1. Jupiter.

The Spiritual Goal. Jupiter represents the opportunity to broaden our horizons, expand our understanding and to develop soul love and wisdom.

Overview. Jupiter expands consciousness. Its placement in the chart shows where and how our perceptions can be widened and truth and wisdom can be developed. Jupiter inspires us to take long visionary journeys, to go on spiritual quests in search of greater understanding and it directs us into areas of higher learning, such as philosophy and religion. It gives the gift of freedom and sometimes prophecy. Generally, Jupiter brings expansion, success, prosperity, abundance and rewards.

Negatively, in the average person, Jupiter expands the ego and the desire nature. The appetites are exaggerated. For example, there could be a craving for fatty foods, intoxicating drinks and for sensual experiences. Risky, irresponsible behaviours can be accentuated.

Jupiter rules: Sagittarius, Pisces and houses 9 and 12. People: entrepreneurs, gurus, lawyers, magistrates, middle-age, philosophers, professors, promoters, prophets, religious figures and wise teachers. Generally: churches, higher education, prosperity, publishing, religion and religious workers, wealth, universities. Day of the week: Thursday. Colours: royal blue and purple. Stones: amethysts. Metal: tin.

Aspects to Jupiter. Easy aspects and conjunctions to personal planets or the ascendant, gives good humour and optimism and brings expansion, rewards and prosperity. Hard aspects result in excess, extravagance, wasteful and irresponsible behaviours. These are the attitudes that have to change.

Vocations. Those in higher education, healing, religion, charitable organisations and that promote brotherliness, wisdom and universality. For example - spiritual leaders, preachers, religious workers, morality crusaders, charity workers, philanthropists, teachers, philosophers and professors. Additionally, those careers connected with advertising, international finance, long distance travel, publishing, marketing and promotion.

Anatomy. Rules the arteries, growth, the hips, the liver and thighs.

Orbit. Jupiter's orbit around the Sun takes 12 years.

Keywords. Positive: abundant, benevolent, broad-minded, brotherly, charitable, confident, enthusiastic, expansive, extroverted, fellowship, fusing, generous, good-fortune, good-humoured, good-luck, good-fortune, growth, honourable, inclusive, magnetic, moral, optimistic, philanthropic, popular, prophetic, prospering, religious, successful, understanding, visionary, wealthy, wise. *Negative:* boastful, bombastic, extravagant, fat, indolent, lawless, lazy, obese, opulent, over-confident, pretentious, prodigal, showmanship, wasteful.

Verbs. Positive: benefits, broadens, exaggerates, expands, extends, fuses, gambles, gambling, honours, includes, joins, jokes, magnetises, rewards, teaches, travels, understands, visions, widens. *Negative*: boasts, gambles, exaggerates, moralises, over-estimates, rewards, wastes.

Jupiter's symbol represents Jupiter's thunderbolt.

Jupiter rules Sagittarius

and Pisces

and is **dignified** when placed in one of its own signs.

Jupiter is **exalted** in Cancer.

Jupiter is in **detriment** in Gemini

and Virgo.

Jupiter **falls** in Capricorn.

2. Saturn.

Saturn's symbol represents Saturn's sickle.

Saturn rules Capricorn and is **dignified** when placed in its own sign.

Saturn is **exalted** in Libra.

Saturn is **dignified** in Capricorn

Saturn is in **detriment** in Cancer.

Saturn **falls** in Aries.

"Saturn is the Lord of Karma, the imposer of retribution and the one who demands full payment of all debts," Bailey, Esoteric Astrology page 105.

The Spiritual Goal. Saturn represents that aspect of nature that teaches us to live within the greater law. It teaches us discipline and responsibility through karma.

Overview. Saturn is a symbol of the Lord of Karma, who administers the Law of Cause and Effect. Simply, whatever we do, brings back an equal and opposite reaction from life. If we do good things, we receive good things; if we are bad, repercussions come our way. Saturn teaches us to be more responsible and disciplined in our approach to life and decision making. Some consider it to bring misfortune and loss, and it does when our negative behaviours warrant this.

While symbolising our fears and inhibitions, Saturn also provides the opportunity to face up to them and to heal them. It achieves this by slowing down time and crystallising the particular problem until it becomes frustrating and unbearable. We can then choose to make changes for the better or stay fixed in the pattern, which is then deepened. Saturn forces us to grow up, to work hard and to shoulder our responsibilities - in which case it brings well-earned success and respect. Saturnian people are reserved and serious and wise - the result of having to deal with the challenges that earth-life brings.

Saturn rules: Capricorn and houses 10 and 11. People: authoritarians, bankers, the elderly, law and order disciplinarians, executives, government-workers, grand-parents, professionals, stock-brokers, trustees and wise people. Generally: aging and old age, institutions, the justice system, the law, mining, real estate and time. Day of the week: Saturday. Colours: black and green. Stones: obsidian. Metal: lead.

Aspects to Saturn. Easy aspects to personal planets or the ascendant give a responsible, cautious attitude and ease with authority. Hard aspects and conjunctions indicate difficulties with authority and limitations. These need to be adjusted.

Vocations. Executive and managerial positions generally. Conservative organisations and businesses such as the government, authority bodies, prisons, law and order, banking, insurance, death, taxes and stockbroking. Construction trades such as real estate and those connected with the earth - mining, pottery, farming, etc. Also, working with the elderly and careers connected with time.

Anatomy. Knees, teeth, joints, the skeleton, problems like arthritis and depression.

Orbit. Saturn's orbit around the Sun takes 29 years.

Keywords. Positive: ambitious (healthy), ascetic, astute, authoritative, bureaucratic, cautious, conservative, constructing, contracting, deliberate, diplomatic, disciplined, economical, enduring, faithful, frugal, hard-working, just, karmic, mature, opportunity through adversity, persistent, reliable, serious, self-disciplined, self-sufficient, solid, spare, stable, steady, tactful, thrifty, trustworthy, wisdom through adversity. *Negative*: adverse, ambitious (ruthless), austere, avaricious, calculating, cold, crystallised, constricted, cynical, depressive, disciplined, fearful, hard, inhibited, introverted, limited, loss, mean, materialistic, melancholy, miserly, obstructive, pessimistic, rejection, rigid, rule-bound, secretive, severe, slow, suffocates, suspicious.

Verbs. Positive: ages, assesses, builds, chills, contracts, concentrates, consolidates, constricts, constructs, contracts, corrects, deliberates, disciplines, economises, endures, limits, persists, restricts, retires, slows, solidifies stabilises, steadies, structures, teaches. *Negative*: ages, contracts, crushes, crystallises, depresses, hardens, lessens, limits, loses, obstructs, persists, punishes, reduces, restricts, shrinks, slows and suffocates.

3. Uranus.

The Spiritual Goal. Uranus represents the radical changes and opportunities that suddenly appear in life and that force us to move forwards into the future unencumbered by old emotional baggage. It is the force of change that awakens us to "the new"

Overview. Uranus' effect on consciousness has an awakening effect. It shatters crystallisation and fosters an urge to be free. It stimulates independence and urges us to rebel against all limitations, to be different, to experiment and to be original in thought and action. Its ultimate task is to drive us forwards on the Path of Evolution.

Esoterically, Uranus develops the scientific mind giving the ability to think clearly and abstractly. It is the Awakener and, in the chart, indicates the power of the soul to shatter confining structures within the personality and the Saturnian past with the lightning power of new vision. Uranus shows where we have to open things up and experiment. Where we can most rapidly cut away old patterns and revolutionise our approach to life. Where we can initiate a new order of life and conditions and be free of all limitations.

Uranus rules: Aquarius and the eleventh house. People: anarchists, astrologers, aviators, discoverers, eccentrics, friendship, guerrillas, hierophants, insurgents, inventors, magicians, nerve-specialists, occultists, pioneers, social-reformers, revolutionaries and scientists. Generally: the abstract mind, alchemy, bohemia, cosmology, electricity, new technology and science. Colour: electric blue. Stones: amethyst. Metal: uranium.

Aspects to Uranus. Easy aspects and conjunctions to personal planets or the ascendant give an innovative, independent approach to life, the ability to lead, to embrace differences and to experiment. Sometimes it gives intellectual brilliance, talent in science and creative ingenuity. Hard aspects indicate extreme nonconformist attitudes, selfish individualism and self-centredness, avoidance of commitment, unpredictability and erratic instability.

Vocations. Generally, careers that are flexible in structure, which are related to science and technology, that are pioneering, new, alternative and that improve and reform civilisation and society. The sciences generally, pioneering initiatives, psychology, the many alternative healing modalities - astrology, cosmology, aviation, computers, electrical industries, information and entertainment technology, mobile phones, the internet, invention, renewable energy, television, the esoteric and metaphysics.

Anatomy. Rules the electrical impulses in the nervous system.

Orbit. Uranus' orbit around the Sun takes 84 years.

Keywords. Positive: altruistic, bohemian, different, electric, esoteric, free-thinking, free-will, independent, individual, impersonal, innovative, intelligent, intuitive, inventive, irregular, libertarian, magical, new, nonconforming, odd, original, progressive, self-reliant, spontaneous, sudden, unconventional, unique, universal, universality, unorthodox, unstable. *Negative:* anarchy, bizarre, chaotic, disorderly, eccentric, erratic, egocentric, explosive, inconstant, individualistic, irresponsible, licentious, mayhem, mutinous, noncompliant, radical, rebellious, selfish, spasmodic, violent, volatile, wild.

Verbs. Positive: awakens, betters, changes, electrifies, evolves, experiments, improves, initiates, invents, originates, progresses, radically changes, reforms. *Negative:* rebels, repels, revolts, shocks, shatters, spasms.

Uranus' symbol is taken from its discoverer's last name - Herschel.

Uranus rules Aquarius and is **dignified** when placed in its own sign.

Uranus is **exalted** in Scorpio.

Uranus is in **detriment** in Leo.

Uranus **falls** in Taurus.

"Uranus, the planet of the hidden mystery and one of the most occult of the planets", Bailey, Esoteric Astrology page 401.

Neptune's symbol represents Neptune's trident.

Neptune rules Pisces and is **dignified** when placed in its own sign.

Neptune is **exalted** in Cancer.

Neptune is in **detriment** in Virgo.

Neptune **falls** in Capricorn.

"Neptune, Who rules the ocean, whose trident and astrological symbol signifies the Trinity in manifestation and Who is the ruler of the Piscean Age," Bailey, Esoteric Astrology page 219.

4. Neptune.

The Spiritual Goal. Neptune represents an opportunity to refine our emotions and to develop and express unconditional love.

Overview. Neptune's effect on consciousness instils a yearning for something higher and finer. It dissolves crystallisation and refines the emotions so that we are more sensitive to the soul and to higher spiritual realities and energies. It awakens an urge to transcend all limitations, to be loved unconditionally and to experience oneness with all life.

Neptune also represents "other worldliness" such as mysticism, dreams, visions, fantasies and ideals. Working negatively, it creates a desire to flee reality, to escape into an ideal world where one is safe and everything is beautiful. This is a description of our spiritual home and while this is an ultimate truth, on earth the immediate task is to overcome delusion and find the truth. It is behind the tendency in some, to wear rose-coloured glasses - a phenomenon where we distort reality so that we see what we want to see. It also shows the type of life disappointments that can trigger escapism and addictive behaviours.

Neptune rules: Pisces and the twelfth house. People: alcoholics, charlatans, con-men, dreamers, idealists, illusionists, mediums, mystics, priests, psychics, shamans, spiritual teachers (authentic or charlatans), spiritual workers and visionaries. Generally: arts (dance-film-music), dreams, drugs, intoxicants, metaphysical, the oceans, oil, pharmaceuticals, shipping, all matters spiritual. Colour: aquamarine mauve, sea-green, coral. Stones: aquamarine, lapis lazuli. Metal: platinum.

Aspects to Neptune. Easy aspects and the conjunction to personal planets or the ascendant give sensitivity, empathy, compassion, high idealism, artistic talent, a spiritual approach to life and the urge to serve. Hard aspects indicate difficulty in dealing with life's realities and a tendency to seek escape through means such as drugs, alcohol and cult groups. In some cases, easy aspects can have the same effect. Its place in the chart represents where emotional-desire needs to be transmuted into love-aspiration and where and how we should try to be kinder and more compassionate.

Vocations. Those that promote higher ideals, religion, spirituality, mysticism, psychism; that minister to the sick, suffering and addicted; that require personal sacrifice and concern, such as - nuns, monks, ministers, church helpers, nurses and spiritual healers. Vocations to do with the arts: music, dance, poetry, theatre, photography, illusion and film. Alternatively, careers connected with liquids, the ocean and oil.

Anatomy. Lymphatic system, addictions, strange diseases.

Orbit. Neptune's orbit around the Sun: takes 165 years.

Keywords. Positive: all embracing, aspiration, Christ-like, clairvoyant, compassionate, devoted, divine, empathetic, faithful, forgiving, hopeful, idealistic, inspired, spiritual, subtle. *Negative*: alcoholic, confused, covert, deceptive, defrauding, in denial, deluded, dreamy, drug-induced, escapist, fantasising, glamours, grieving, gullible, hypersensitive, impressionable, illusion, indiscriminate, manipulative, naive, strange, rose-coloured, self-deceiving, ungrounded, unrealistic, vague.

Verbs. Positive: devotes, dissolves, dreams, forgives, hopes, idealises, inspires, pretends, refines, sacrifices, sensitises, serves, spiritualises, uplifts, yearns. *Negative*: cheats, confuses, cons, deceives, defrauds, deludes, denies, fantasises, hides, misrepresents, veils.

5. Pluto.

The Spiritual Goal. Pluto represents an opportunity to eliminate limitations in our consciousness and to transform the life. It does this by totally destroying the old, so that life opens up for "the new."

Overview. As Pluto moves through each sign, it influences an entire generation. From the mass consciousness it brings up negative patterns that are due to be destroyed. For instance, as it moved through Scorpio, Sagittarius and Capricorn, the paedophilia (Scorpio) scandal in the churches (Sagittarius) and other government (Capricorn) institutions erupted, starting a great purging (Pluto).

When we step onto the Path of Spiritual Development and are strong enough to handle the challenges Pluto brings, it works at an individual level. It gives insight and the will to radically change the personality and to cut away any bad habits. Pluto's higher task is to destroy all limitations that prevent us from moving forwards spiritually. Working negatively, it indicates wilfulness and despotism. Its sign, house and aspects indicate what needs to be transformed.

It helps to understand the power Pluto wields by considering that in mythology, Pluto was God of the Underworld, with the power to take or grant life. So, it is not surprising that it was "discovered" at the time the atom was first split and the making of the atom bomb that was used to bring widespread death and destruction.

Pluto rules: Scorpio and the eighth house. People: all-powerful people, assassins, billionaires, blackmailers, capitalists, criminals, detectives, dictators, healers, magnates, manipulators, the masses, mass-murders, metaphysical healers, mobs, mob power, plutocrats, pressure groups, psychologists, researchers, spies, terrorists and tycoons. Generally: the Arrow of Death, big business, catastrophes, corporations, death and rebirth, the forces of life and death, healing, mega-power, powerful hidden forces, primeval energy, radical transformation, weapons of mass destruction, unstoppable force which destroys for good or ill, monopolies and the under-world. Colours: dark red, black. Stones: opals. Metal: plutonium and uranium.

Aspects to Pluto. Easy aspects to personal planets or the ascendant give depth, weight, intensity, substance, ease with handling power and the ability to transform the nature. Conjunctions or hard aspects indicate the potential misuse of power, egocentricity, wilfulness and stubbornness. It can also represent a fear of being annihilated and danger from greater forces.

Vocations. Positions of power and control, particularly in business, politics, the military and the criminal world - Chief Executives, plutocrats, billionaires and crime-lords. Careers in research, detection, healing and psychology. Those connected with death, destruction, elimination, refuse, sex, war and the underworld.

Anatomy. Co-rules the elimination organs and the will to survive in the adrenals.

Orbit. Pluto's orbit around the Sun takes 248 years.

Keywords. Positive: in control, deep, depth, dominant, fearless, insightful, intense, might, omnipotent, potent, powerful, an unstoppable force. *Negative:* compulsive, criminal, dangerous, dark, destructive, devastating, eruptive, forceful, lethal, manipulative, wilful.

Verbs. Positive: delves, destroys, detects, eliminates, investigates, menaces, obsesses, plumbs, probes, radically changes, rebuilds, renews, regenerates, researches, revives, transforms and transmutes. *Negative:* assassinates, blackmails, exterminates, forces, kills, massacres, menaces, murders, plunders, terrorises, threatens, tortures.

Pluto's symbol can be seen to represent the transformative power that releases the soul (the circle), from matter's hold (the cross).

Pluto rules Scorpio and is **dignified** when placed in its own sign.

Pluto is **exalted** in Aries.

Pluto is in **detriment** in Taurus.

Pluto **falls** in Libra.

"Pluto .. The arrow of God pierces the heart and death takes place.. brought about by the soul," Bailey, Esoteric Astrology page 509.

D. THE MAJOR ASTEROIDS AND CHIRON

The asteroid belt is between Mars and Jupiter and the most important asteroids are Vesta, Ceres, Pallas Athene and Juno. Vesta is closest to the Sun, then moving outwards, next is Juno, then Ceres and Pallas. Discovered at the beginning of the 19th century, astrologers made an association between these asteroids and the rise of the women's movement taking place in the West. Hence, they were given female genders and named after important female goddesses. Though secondary in importance to the planets, some astrologers say their influences are significant. They are explained more fully in this section.

Vesta was discovered by the German astronomer Heinrich Wilhelm Olbers in 1807. Its symbol was created by astrologer Eleanor Bach. It is a simplified version of other representations of Vesta's altar.

In 1804 German astronomer Karl Ludwig Harding discovered, named and created the symbol for Juno. The sceptre topped with a 7-pointed star appears to symbolise her position as Queen of the Gods.

1. Vesta.

Vesta was a Roman goddess equivalent to the Greek Hestia. She is the Virgin goddess of the hearth, home and family and is usually represented by the fire burning in her temple (⚶). Only her priestesses, the Vestal Virgins, who guarded and tended the sacred fire at the hearth, could enter. In the chart, she represents the ability to purify the nature, to guard the sacred inner fire of creativity, devotion to a mission or goal and sacrifices we have to make. Vesta also indicates the way we will contribute to the well-being of our home and family. Consequently, it is related to the traditional ruler of home and family, the Moon and is very comfortable in the fourth house.

Vesta rulerships. People: celibates, monks, nuns, sister-hoods and virgins. Generally: celibacy, chastity, fires, flames, hearth and home.

Aspects. Easy aspects to Vesta give a natural ability to retreat from mainstream life periodically for clarity and regeneration of one's passion and purpose. It also indicates sacrifices we will make willingly to further our important aims. Hard aspects can indicate we will be forced to take time out to do this, through illness or some other means. It also indicates sacrifices we will be forced to make. A Vesta transit could indicate that it is time to retreat from mainstream life for purification, contemplation and renewal of one's inner resources prior to a renewed effort towards life goals.

Orbit. Vesta's orbit around the Sun takes 3.63 years.

Keywords and phrases. Positive: chaste, committed, contemplative, dedicated, devoted, dutiful, keeper of the flame, keeping the home fires burning, the inner fire, on a mission, pious, pure, purification, going into a retreat, sacred-duty, sacred-flame, sacred sexuality, sacred space, sacrificial, serving, sexual control, spiritual commitment, virginal, virtuous. *Negative*: fanatical, isolating, promiscuous.

Verbs. Positive: Commits, contemplates, dedicates, devotes, purifies, retreats, sacrifices, serves.

2. Juno.

Juno was a Roman goddess (the closest Greek equivalent is Hera), who was married to serial-cheater, Jupiter. Consequently, she is connected with all aspects of marriage, married women or anyone in a committed or formal relationship. She was said to be jealous of her husband and angry when he gave birth to Minerva (Pallas Athena) from his own head. In the chart, Juno represents our ability to honour a marriage or formal commitment and to enhance it with loyalty and commitment. Negatively, she also represents potential problems because of jealousy and possessiveness. Juno can be read in connection with the seventh house of marriage.

Juno rulerships. People: husbands, married women, spouses, wives. Generally: committed partnerships of all types, divorce and marriage.

Aspects. Planets that make easy aspects to Juno indicate positive ways we contribute to marriage, while hard aspects indicate ways, we sabotage vital relationships through jealousy and possessiveness. Juno is most comfortable in Libra and the seventh house, since they rule marriage. Located in Aries and Scorpio, its negative traits will be triggered and these will have to be dealt with.

Orbit. Juno takes 4.36 years to orbit the Sun.

Keywords and phrases. Positive: committed union, compatible, husband, intimacy, loyalty, marriage, married life, monogamy, mutual trust, partnership, relationship, spouse, union, wife, vows. *Negative*: betrayal, divorce, fear of abandonment, infidelity, jealous, possessive, revengeful, separation, spousal abuse.

Verbs. Positive: commits, marries, trusts, relates, vows and weds. *Negative*: betrays, cheats, divorces and separates.

3. Ceres.

Ceres (Greek equivalent is Demeter) was the Roman goddess of agriculture, grain and bounteous harvests that result from wise cultivation and effort. This relates Ceres very closely to Virgo, whose symbol is sometimes seen as a maiden carrying wheat. She also represents the love a mother has for her child and nurturing, kind and benevolent qualities. In our psychology, Ceres represents the early nurturing that we received and how this affected our self-worth, our self-esteem and our ability to cope with life challenges such as separation, dependency, loss, rejection and grief. Ceres consequently, also represents how we nurture ourselves and others that we care for.

Ceres rulerships. People: field-workers, landscape designers, mothers, parents, those who nurture. Generally: agriculture, cereal, the country-side, crops, food, grain, vegetation and wheat.

Aspects. The conjunction and easy aspects indicate beneficial nurturing in childhood and as a result - healthy self-esteem and the ability to handle grief and rejection. These aspects also show how we can nurture others. Hard aspects indicate the denial of nurturing, abuse and low self-esteem. In the chart, Ceres can be read in conjunction with the Moon.

Orbit. Ceres is by far the largest of the asteroids and takes 4.607 years to orbit the Sun.

Keywords and phrases. Positive: benevolent, bountiful, cultivation, Earth Mother, encouraging, germinating, harvesting, incubating, kind, mother-love, Mother Nature, nurturing, nutrition, providing, on a rescue mission, self-esteem, self-worth, sustenance, unconditional love. *Negative*: barren, grief, grieving, loss, low esteem, rejection.

Verbs. Cultivates, fosters, harvests, nourishes, nurtures, parents, provides.

4. Pallas Athena.

Pallas Athena (Roman equivalent was Minerva) was the Greek Goddess of Wisdom, War and of skilled tradespeople. Daughter of Zeus, king of the gods, she was born from his head, fully mature and clothed in armour. From the myth we can see that she represents mental-creativity. She is wisdom in action through the logical mind. To help us learn this, Pallas takes us through periods of destruction and renewal until we learn to think more logically when solving problems and make wiser decisions.

Juno continued: The cross under the start symbolises the sacrifices demanded in marriage.

In 1801, Italian priest and astronomer Giuseppe Piazzi discovered Ceres. The symbol is a sickle, indicating Ceres' connection with agriculture. It has a relationship with the Moon, sharing maternal and nurturing qualities. Ceres' arc is like an unfinished Moon.

The symbol for Pallas, the "spear of Pallas Athena", was invented by German Hungarian astronomer, Baron Franz Xaver von Zach, in 1802.

There is a close resemblance between Pallas' symbol and that of Venus.

Esoterically, both are related to the ajna chakra of intelligent comprehension and of vision.

The symbol for the centaur Chiron, is a key with the letter K (for discoverer Charles T. Kowal). The symbol was proposed by astrologer, Al Morrison.

The key is an object symbolic of opening and closing powers, such as the power to open the door between this world and the next. In this regard, it can be seen to represent spiritual wisdom which gives access to higher realms of knowledge and existence.

Pallas Athena rulerships. People: female executives, skilled crafts-people, political strategists, tradespeople, strategists, warrior women and weavers. Generally: mental-creativity, military science, problem solving ability and wisdom.

Aspects. Easy aspects and conjunctions indicate executive ability that will lead to professional success. Hard aspects indicate over-emphasised mental approach and lack of empathy.

Orbit. Pallas' orbit around the Sun takes 4.619 years.

Keywords and phrases. Positive: brainchild, breaking glass-ceilings, crafty, creative-thought, dexterous, dispassionate, executive-ability, fertility of mind, finding solutions, game-plan, impartial, inspired-thought, intelligent, intellectual-acumen, logical, master-plan, mentally-creative, mentally-fertile, mentally-combative, problem solving skill, reasoned-argument, shrewd, single-minded, strategises, wisdom in action. *Negative*: emotionless, fixed-minded, irreverent, mentally fixates, narrow-minded, over-emphasised mentality.

Verbs. Positive: battles, comprehends, fights, ponders, strategises, thinks, understands. *Negative*: fixates.

5. Chiron.

Chiron was discovered much later than the previous asteroids - in 1977. It is a small, icy body orbiting the Sun in the outer solar system among the giant planets. Scientists now believe it is a comet - its nucleus is a mixture of icy water, gases and silicate dust. It was given the name Chiron, a centaur in Greek mythology who was a healer and teacher and who ironically, could not heal himself.

In the natal chart, Chiron is a symbol for "the inner child" or emotional development. It symbolises the emotional wounds and retardations suffered in childhood because of parental abuse or neglect - either in the current or a previous life - we can carry unhealed wounds from one life to the next. Mature Chiron represents the healing of those wounds and the wisdom and understanding gained as a result. This wisdom can then be used to help others heal their own hurts.

Chiron rulerships. People: abused children, doctors, the handicapped, healers, survivors of child abuse and "the wounded child". Generally: emotional wounds, healing, health, medicine, naturopathy, negative core beliefs, psychological wounds and service to others who suffer childhood hurts.

Aspects. Planets that form conjunctions or easy aspects indicate positive ways people supported the inner child, good emotional health and natural healing talents. Hard aspects indicate rigid beliefs and unhealed emotional wounds that are preventing healthy and mature emotional expression.

Orbit. Chiron's orbit around the Sun takes 49 years.

Keywords and phrases. Positive: doctor, healer, healing, holistic healing, holistic thinking, kind, knowledgeable, master-healer, medical knowledge, medical skills, medicine, natural healing, serving, service, teacher, wisdom through experience and wounded healer, wounds. *Negative*: abuse, afflicted, childhood wounds, crippled, emotional wounds, inability to heal, ordeals, psychological wounds and woundedness.

Verbs. Positive: heals, serves, teaches. Negative: abuses, hurts, wounds.

CHAPTER 3.
THE HOUSES

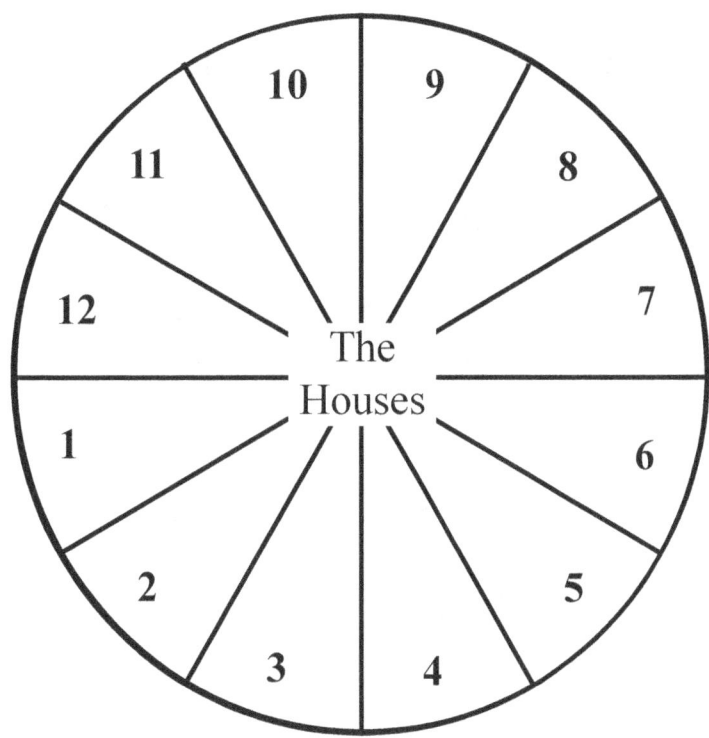

1. How the Houses and the Natal Chart are formed.

The houses are called the "mansions" of the Moon, different areas of life in this form-bound world - the Moon rules "the form." In this section the houses - how they are formed and what they mean are fully explained.

Day by day, year by year, from Earth we see the Sun and planets move through the signs. This view, of planets in signs, changes as the earth rotates on its axis once in 24-hours.

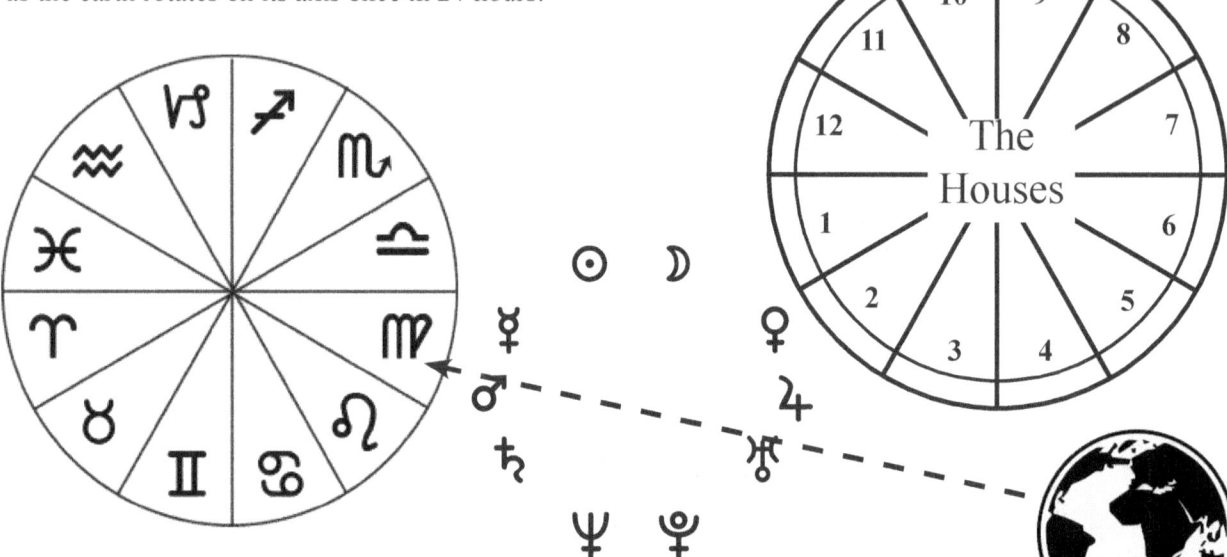

At birth, the natal chart "photo" is taken. Whichever sign is rising over the eastern horizon at that moment forms the ascendant of the chart and the beginning of the first house. In the same manner, each subsequent house cusp is related to a sign and degree.

The lower diagram tries to create the impression of looking from earth outwards. The white circle around earth, represents the houses. It becomes a zodiac chart/ the horoscope, when the planets and signs are added. It may help to imagine you are standing on earth looking out into the solar system. The immediate earth-space forms the houses. As you look through the houses out into the solar system, you see the planets and signs, which then are added to the chart.

The chart defines our relationship to the greater whole, the solar system, set at the moment of birth when the first breath is taken. The houses must not be confused with the signs. Although they are related, the houses have to do with things on earth, the signs are cosmic energies

The bottom of the chart represents midnight, the 9 o'clock point 6 am, the top of the chart noon and the 3 o'clock point 6 pm.

Although there are differences between various house systems, well-trained and intuitive astrologers can use any chart-type to give and accurate readings for their clients.

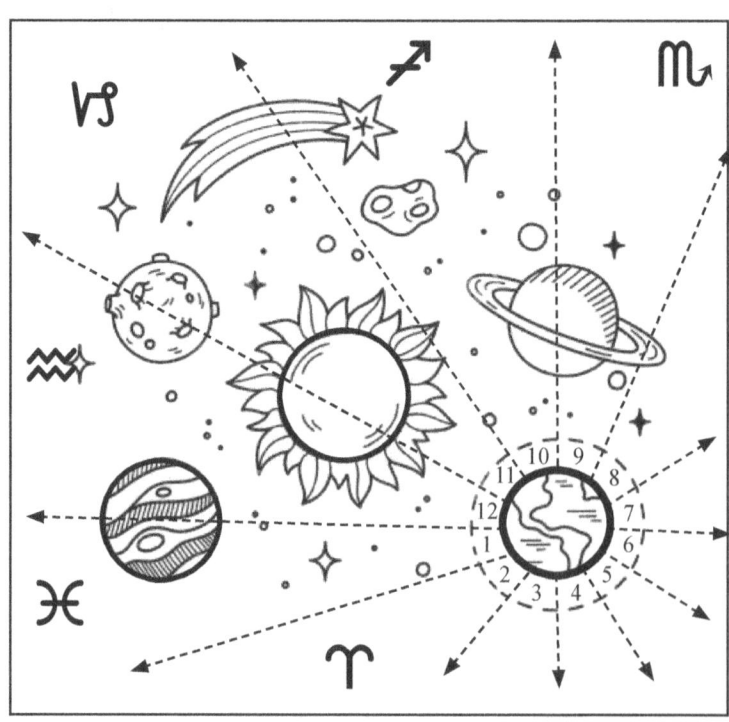

2. Components in the Astrology Chart.

The chart consists of four circles. Working with the Placidus chart-style on this page, starting from the centre and moving outwards:

a. The inner circle (1), it holds the aspect lines.
b. The narrow circle (2) has the house numbers.
c. The next large circle (3) contains the houses and planets. Each planet has written beside it, the degree and minutes of the sign it is in. The 12 dividing lines or spokes of the chart are the House Cusps (house number labels have been added for convenience). Then, depending upon the sign and degree of each house cusp, the planets all fall into one of the houses. For example:

   Mars is at 21 degrees and 17 minutes of Taurus (21♂♉17).
   Jupiter is at 23 degrees and 29 minutes of Sagittarius (23♃♐29).

d. The outer narrow circle (4), has the sign (and degree), ruling each house.

Example - CHART X

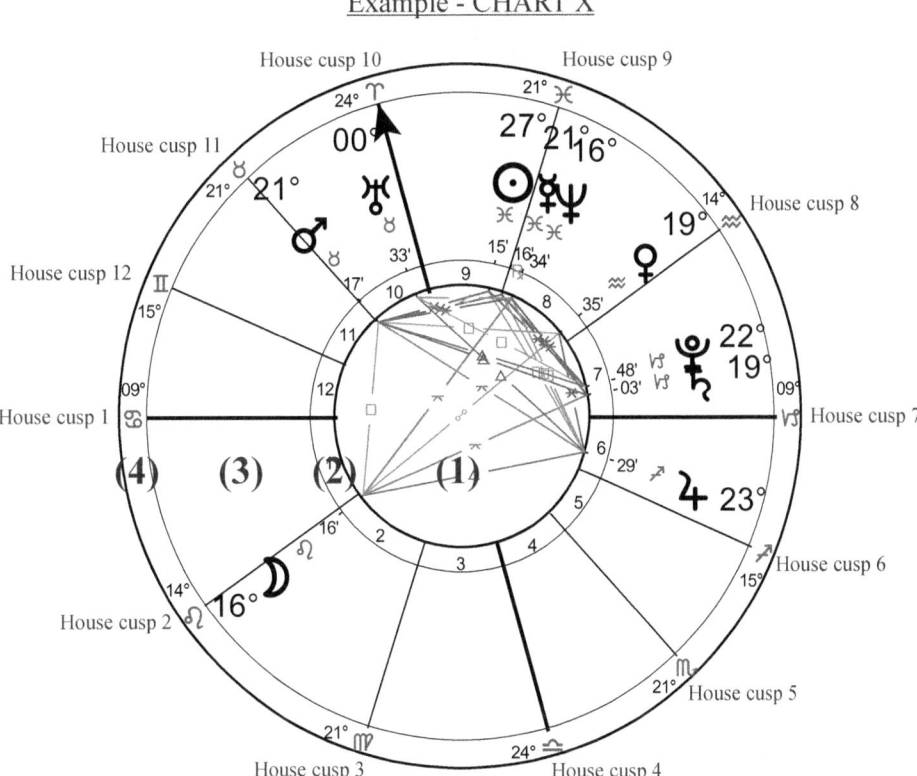

The signs ruling each house.

The 1st house cusp is at 9 o'clock - 9♋.
The 2nd house cusp is at 8 o'clock - 14♌.
The 3rd house cusp is at 7 o'clock - 21♍.
The 4th house cusp is at 6 o'clock - 24♎.
The 5th house cusp is at 8 o'clock - 21♏.
The 6th house cusp is at 8 o'clock - 15♐.
The 7th house cusp is at 8 o'clock - 9♑.
The 8th house cusp is at 8 o'clock - 14♒.
The 9th house cusp is at 8 o'clock - 21♓.
The 10th house cusp is at 8 o'clock - 24♈.
The 11th house cusp is at 8 o'clock - 21♉.
The 12th house cusp is at 8 o'clock - 15♊.

The planet positions.

The Sun is at 27♓15, in the 9th house.
The Moon is at 16♌16 in the 2nd house.
Mercury is at 21♓16 8th (only just).
Venus is at 19♒35 in the 8th house.
Mars is at 21♉17 10th (only just).
Jupiter is at 23♐29 in the 6th house.
Saturn is at 19♑03 in the 7th house.
Uranus is at 00♉33 in the 10th house.
Neptune is at 16♓34 in the 8th house.
Pluto is at 22♑48 in the 7th house.

e. On the right-hand side is a typical natal chart, without the aspect grid.
f. The chart below shows the houses on their own. Leo (20 degrees) is on the first house cusp which is always located at 9 o'clock. Virgo 13 degrees is on the second house, etc.

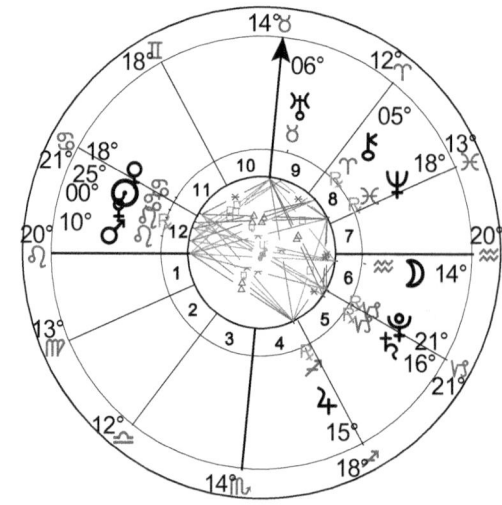

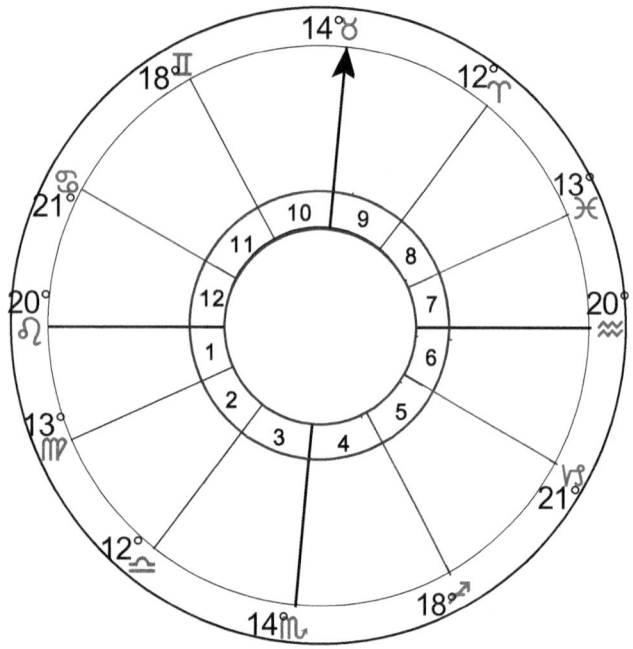

Below are the planets and the aspect lines on their own - without the houses.

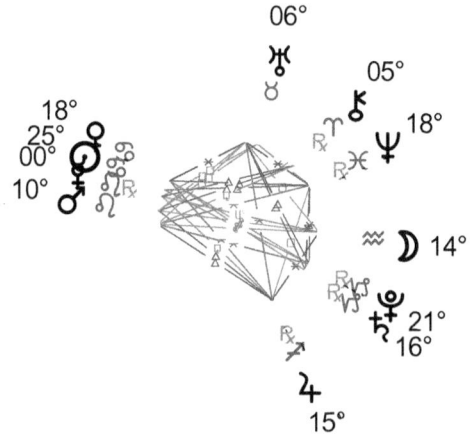

3. The Angles.

These are the four cardinal points of the ecliptic, that form the cusps of the 1st, 4th, 7th, tenth houses. These are also called the angular houses.

- The ascendant, the eastern horizon; the dawn point.
- The nadir, Imum Coeli or IC. The lowest point in the heavens and in the chart; the midnight point, the under-sky. It is the cusp of the fourth house.
- The descendant, the West horizon, the setting Sun point and cusp of the seventh house.
- The zenith, MC or Midheaven; the noon point and cusp of the tenth house.

The angles are significant because they represent our attitudes to four vital areas of life - self (East), family (nadir), marriage (West) and career (zenith).

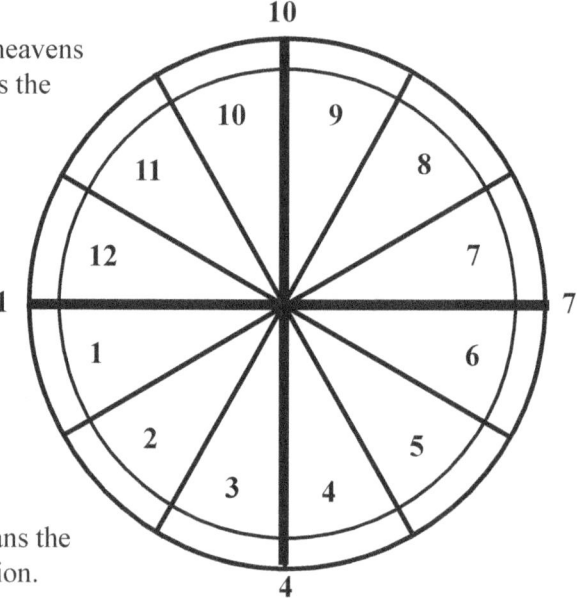

a. In Chart X on the previous page, the ascendant is in Cancer. This means the person views life through an emotional perspective.
b. The nadir or fourth house angle is in Libra, which means the balanced nature of Libra will influence family perception.
c. The descendant or seventh house angle is in Capricorn, indicating a responsible attitude to marriage.
d. The MC or tenth house angle is in Aries, indicating an urgent and dynamic approach to the career and pursuit of higher goals.

4. Angular, Succedent and Cadent Houses.

Angular houses

"Angular" is defined as being "sharp"; as houses, they are acute or vital. These are the 1st, 4th, 7th and tenth houses. They represent the physical plane cornerstones of life - self (1), home (4), partner (7) and career (10). They are dynamic, action houses which empower any planets located within them. Their energy has a potent effect in physical plane life.

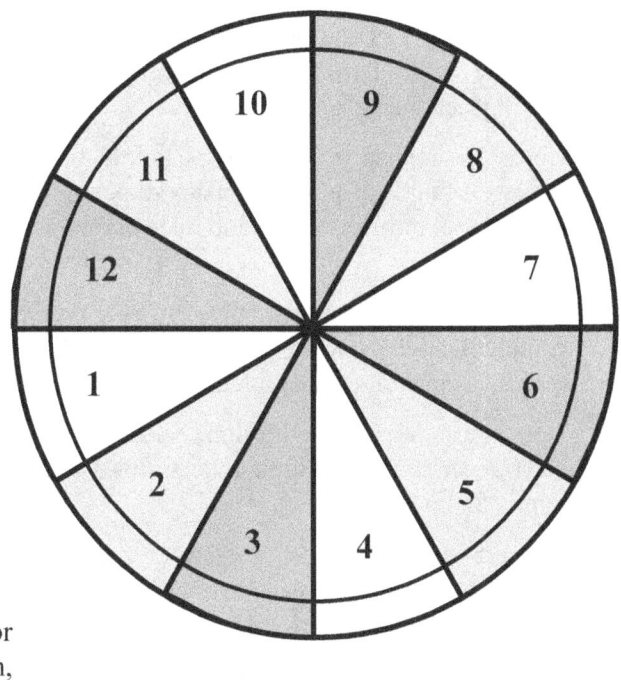

The house vibrations can also be related to the three "gunas," the three primal qualities or elements of matter according to Sankhya philosophy — rajas (action), sattva (harmony) and tamas (inertia). The angular houses carry the rajas vibration, they are action houses.

Succedent houses

"Succedent" is defined as "coming next", or "succeeding." These houses - 2nd, 5th, 8th and 11th, follow the angular houses. They are related to the Emotional Plane and determine how we feel about money (2), love (5), sex (8) and friends (11). They are "tamas" or "grounding" houses. Planets located here are also strong and are instrumental in determining whether emotional experiences in the various houses/ life areas, will be easy or difficult.

Cadent houses

The 3rd, 6th, 9th and 12th houses are the cadent houses. "Cadent" is defined as being "rhythmic" or sattvic in vibration, or harmonious - adjectives applied to mutable signs. Cadent houses are naturally ruled by the mutable signs - Gemini, Virgo, Sagittarius and Pisces. These houses are related to the Mental Plane, are more particularly concerned with the mind and with learning.

5. The Houses are related to the Seasons.

Although the odd-numbered houses are considered to be masculine and the even-numbered house feminine; collectively, the upper houses are masculine and impersonal and the bottom houses personal and feminine.

a. Spring houses 1–3, represent our early years and self-interest.

b. Summer houses 4–6, represent the things we focus on in young adulthood - home, children, work.

c. Autumn houses 7–9, represent those things important in adulthood - marriage, divorce and change; and our search for meaning in life. morals.

d. Winter Houses 10–12, represent those things important in middle and old-age - status, friends and inner reflection as life concludes.

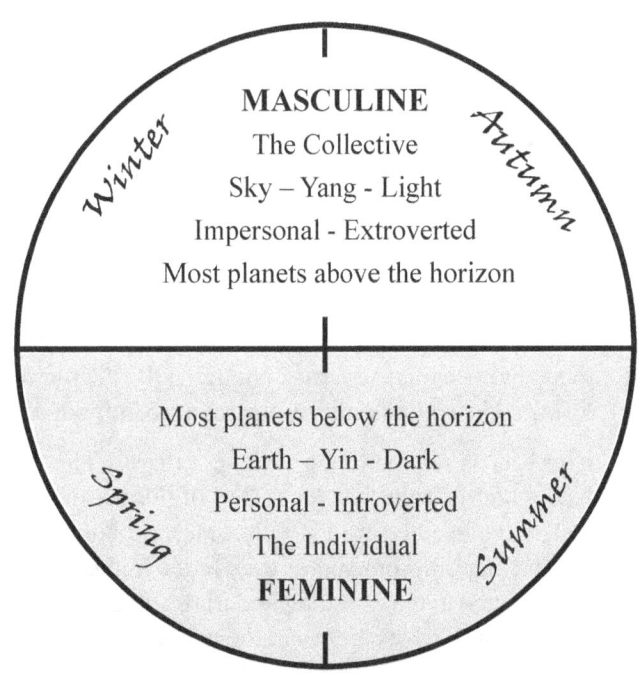

6. Each House is naturally governed by the Sign of the same number.

1. House 1 is related to the 1st sign Aries. The vibration of the number "1", emphasises the self, the "I", all personal interests and on being first and best. This captures the essence of the 1st sign Aries. The first house of self, reflects these vibrations. It represents the self, personal interests, new beginnings and birth in a physical body.

2. House 2 is related to the 2nd sign Taurus. In relation to the number "1" of spirit, "2" represents matter, "things". Taurus acquires the material possessions and things that we desire. The second house reflects the material traits of Taurus and rules our values.

3. House 3 is related to the 3rd sign Gemini, which is pre-eminently a sign of communication, travel and commerce. These attributes are also represented by the third house - it is the premier house of communication. Number "3" represents public intercourse, adding its vibration to this life area that also represents movement and interaction in the local environment.

4. House 4 is related to the 4th sign Cancer. Number "4" is the pre-eminent sign of matter and of incarnation and Cancer, the sign of birth, reflects this. Cancer and the fourth house both govern the foundation of life, family and parents.

5. House 5 is related to the 5th sign Leo. The number "5" reflects change and creativity and Leo is the creative sign. Being creative in various ways such as producing children and works of art; these are represented by both Leo and the fifth house.

6. House 6 is related to the 6th sign Virgo, which is dutiful, industrious, hard-working and rules health. These attributes are also represented by the sixth house, which governs work and work-skills, and health complications when we misuse our energies. "6" is a reckoning number, you get back what you put in.

7. House 7 is related to the 7th sign Libra. Esoterically, "7" is an ending number and the seventh house represents the ending of singularity and union with others. It is the house of marriage. Balancing life is Libra's function, especially in human relationships and both Libra and the seventh house govern important intimate unions and their balancing so that harmony prevails.

8. House 8 is related to the 8th sign Scorpio. Death and transformation into a new and higher form is represented by Scorpio and also the eighth house. It is a house of mystery and of the occult, attributes also associated with Scorpio. The number "8" governs material prosperity and the eighth house governs other people's money and taxes.

9. House 9 is related to the 9th sign Sagittarius. The number "9" is called the number of initiation - a transition into a new and higher awareness. Both Sagittarius and the ninth house represent this function, the quests and journeys required (around the world or to inner and higher realms), to expand consciousness.

10. House 10 is related to the 10th sign Capricorn. "10" is the number of perfection or culmination, prior to entering into a new cycle of progress. Perfection attracts attention, status and life rewards, which the tenth house represents. It is naturally ruled by ambitious Capricorn which craves life-power and recognition - which the 10th endows.

11. House 11 is related to the 11th sign Aquarius. Now that initiation ("9") has been taken and relative perfection ("10") has been reached, we now are ready to form close bonds with people to whom we are drawn to through shared ideals and service commitments. The eleventh house of friends and groups is related to friendly Aquarius. Numerically, the number "11" can represent a mature individual ("1"), who forms a close bond with another mature individual (the second "1"); for some higher purpose ("11").

12. House 12 is related to the 12th sign Pisces. The twelfth house of hidden things is related to mysterious Pisces and its ruler Neptune, God of the oceans. This is the house of the unconscious, of self-undoing, that is represented by Pisces' ocean, the home for those souls who are blinded by their emotions or incapacitated in some other way. In the higher sense, the number "12" - and the twelfth house, represent a completed cycle of testing and trial, and the dawning of a new cycle of opportunity. At a mystical level, the 12th and Pisces represent the unknown universe.

HOUSES

1st House and the Ascendant: individuality, expression of Self.

- The self, the head, the brain, the physical body, action in the physical body.
- The appearance, the mask worn to get approval.
- The approach to life, new beginnings, personal interests and mannerisms.
- Soul Purpose, spiritual qualities to develop.

This is the personal house. It represents our individual personal tastes and preferences, in contradiction to those of "others," who are represented by the opposite 7th. From this it can be seen that the first house is related to the planet of individuality - the Sun. The Sun is exalted - at its greatest power in Aries, which is the natural ruler of the first house. When the Sun is located here, it greatly strengthens its overall power.

Collectively, the first house, its sign, the planet ruler and the sign that it is located in - all these contribute to how we look, our appearance, our image and to things we take a personal interest in. So do any planets in the first house.

The ascendant sign is very important in our makeup, because it represents our approach to life and how we view the world. This approach will either hinder growth and forwards evolutionary progression or support it and propel us forwards. If there is a lack of integration in the personality, consciousness can identify completely with its physical form, or traits of the rising sign and any planets in the first house. Then, in defence against what it sees as a hostile world, the ego will create a mask to hide behind, a perfect image to show the world to gain acceptance and approval - the lower traits of the ascendant sign.

At a higher level, the ascendant represents the purpose of the soul that seeks to increase its light and influence in our consciousness. It can do this when we develop and express the higher, positive qualities of the ascendant sign and that of its esoteric ruler. This is the ultimate goal of the first house, to help us be authentic and transparent souls and to radiate our essential spiritual note to the world.

2nd House: The experience of Ownership.

- Possessions, personal resources.
- Personal money, personal business matters, gains and losses.
- Our values - material and spiritual.

The second house represents what we desire and value, the energies that we use to get what we want and resources that we materialise to achieve this. It generally governs money, gold and other symbols of wealth.

The way the personality values money and material possessions and goes after them, is shaped by the sign on the house cusp, its ruling planet and any planets in the house. They also indicate whether the pursuit of material fortune will be easy or hard. For instance, Jupiter in the second house trine Mars in the 10th, promises an easy flow of money from actions taken in the career.

If we are fearful about the world and are afraid that material deprivation will leave us vulnerable to be hurt and exploited, this house will represent the struggle undertaken to acquire possessions and material security. If our identity merges with our "things", if we become possessed by what we own, we will fight to protect them as if they were our very life.

The higher goal of the 2nd, is to help us transform our values from those that are purely selfish and material, to those that are inclusive and embracing of the higher and finer things in life. At this level, it represents how a source of spiritual income can be generated so that we have abundant resources to share in selfless service.

Aries, natural ruler of the 1st house.

1st House Keywords: Appearance, approach to life, birth experience, causal body of the soul, the head, the head centre, how we are seen, image, mannerisms, mask we wear, new beginnings, personal interests, physical body, purpose of the soul, the self.

Taurus, natural ruler of the 2nd house.

2nd Keywords: Attachments, personal energies, finances, gains, losses, money, personal investments, personal resources, possessions, self-worth, spending habits, spiritual values to live by, values.

♊

Gemini, the natural ruler of the 3rd house.

3rd House Keywords: Commerce, communications, daily contacts, early education, extended family, local environment, neighbours, networking, relatives, schools, siblings, short journeys, trade, writings.

Cancer, the natural ruler of the 4th house.

4th House Keywords: Family, family traditions, foundations, home, life endings, one's "roots", one's spiritual family, a parent - mother or father, Mother Earth, unhealed emotional patterns.

3rd House: The experience of Environmental Living.

- The close environment, neighbours.
- Communication and networking.
- Schools, siblings, relatives and early education.
- Short journeys, commerce, trade.
- Communication of the wisdom teachings and the antahkarana.

The third house represents all the contacts and experiences we have throughout the day that contributes to the training of the concrete mind and the development of good communication and networking skills. For instance, this house rules schools and our early formal education, which is vital for early mental development. It also rules all conversations and transactions that we have on a daily basis with neighbours, siblings, relatives and those we meet casually as we move about the local environment. The sign on the third house cusp, the house ruler and any planets in the house; these colour our attitudes to these life areas and the type of experiences we will have.

At a higher level, as the spiritual Path is approached, this house fosters - in conjunction with the ninth house; a search for higher knowledge and understanding. Self-development courses are taken and connections are made with brothers and sisters in spirit who share similar ideas. In time, as a consequent of the third house, the mind learns to be discerning, communication becomes harmless and the initial stage of the antahkarana (the bridge in consciousness that connects us with the soul), begins to be constructed. This house then, gives us the opportunity to communicate the wisdom teachings in our local environment.

To the soul, the third house represents an opportunity to develop the intellect and bring it under its control.

4th House: The experience of Home and Family.

- Family, mother, home.
- Life endings.
- Inherited roots.
- Unhealed psychological patterns.
- Mother Earth, Nature, the family of man, humanity.

The fourth house is at the bottom of the chart. It represents the foundations of life, one's family, home and a parent - most usually the mother, but this is not always the case with the modern phenomenon of single parent families. Some astrologers believe the most dominant parent (and this could be the mother), is governed by the tenth house, usually the preserve of "the father." The sign on the fourth house cusp, the house ruler and planets in the house, these colour our attitudes to this foundational part of our life and the type of experiences we will have.

The personality has its roots in the past and is shaped by experiences in early family life. If this is dysfunctional, deep psychological wounds can cripple confidence. If these remain unresolved emotionally, wherever we travel in the world or whatever we may achieve; a psychic thread binding us to the past will follow us. This will set us on search for the acceptance and emotional security we never got in early years and compel us to project our problems onto others. If we cannot break free from unhappy childhood events, our "roots" and emotional development will stay firmly anchored in the past. This does not bode well for future family harmony.

The goal of this house, is to help us develop healthy family attitudes and life roots. To the soul, it represents an opportunity to cut past-life binding links, to clean out psychological baggage and on a higher level, to serve the human family.

5th House: The experience of Creative Release.

- Children.
- Personal creativity and creative activities.
- Romance and lovers.
- Hobbies, sports and pleasure activities, recreation and re-creation.

Planets in the fifth house and the sign on the cusp, these colour our creative drives and indicates the sorts of things we take pleasure in and like to pour our creative-juice into. For instance, into hobbies, sports, risky adventures, sexual-romantic escapades and making children. This house is related to the sexual, sacral chakra, the lower creative centre. It rules children, describes our attitudes to them and our relations with them. Malefics in this house can sometimes deny children or indicate challenges or losses involving them.

The search for pleasure is a driving and dominating force in humanity and the planet ruler of the sign on the cusp and any planets in the house, these show ways the personality will seek pleasure and happiness.

The higher equivalent of sacral-centre pleasure seeking is the heart chakra and true heart-felt love. The higher goal of this house is to teach us to love unconditionally. To achieve this, we must eventually redirect our creative energies into higher, more aspirational projects. As sexual fire is moderated, the flame of higher aspiration will grow, balance will be achieved in the desire nature and consequently, heart expression will increase. At this level, the 5th represents the love and wisdom we pour out to others - especially children and younger souls.

Leo, the natural ruler of the 5th house.

5th House Keywords: Acting, adventures, amusements, children, creative activities, fun, entertainment, gambling, hobbies, pleasure, personal creativity, love affairs, recreation, risk-taking, role-playing, romance, speculation, sports.

6th House: The experience of Work, Crises and Health.

- Service, work generally, co-workers and the development of work skills.
- Health and crises.
- Small animals.
- Attitudes to food, nutrition and eating habits.

This house represents the struggles and crises we go through on a daily basis as we seek to make a living and to survive. It rules "service" generally, the daily duties and works we are responsible for, day by day. The sign on the cusp, the ruler of the house and any planets in the 6th, these colour our attitude to work and indicate some of the experiences we will have.

The sixth house is the link between the personal 1 to 6 houses and the less personal 7 to 12 houses. It symbolises the personal adjustments needed to engage with society as a whole and to make a constructive contribution. This makes this a place of reckoning for the personality. Here we have to develop skills we need to survive in life and to get along with people we work with. At this level, it represents those many life adjustments we need to make so we can integrate harmoniously with people at large (the seventh house).

If this is problematic, if we run into difficulties that cause ongoing stress, crises in the life will arise and health problems will appear. The sign on the cusp, the ruler of this sign and any planets in the house, these indicate potential illnesses that can manifest if we have trouble making the necessary adjustments. But ill health can be positive in the sense that, the soul will use it to draw attention to the problematic way we are living our lives. This gives us the opportunity to make adjustments so that healing on both physical and metaphysical levels can take place.

The first goal of this house, is to develop skills that will enable us to make a living, in work that is fulfilling and productive. The higher goal is to use our skills in selfless service.

Virgo, the natural ruler of the 6th house.

6th House Keywords: Co-workers, daily duties, diet, employees, employment, health and acute health issues, health-care, hygiene, life crises, service, skills, work, small animals.

Libra, the natural ruler of the 7th house.

7th House Keywords: Contracts, counsellors, diplomats, formal relationships, husband, lawsuits, legal matters and all those who work in the legal industries, marriage, one-on-one relationships, open enemies, other people, partnerships - intimate and professional, projection onto others, spouse, wife.

Scorpio, the natural ruler of the 8th house.

8th Keywords: Death, emotional issues, emotional trauma, inheritances, legacies, the occult, other people's money and resources, mysteries that can be uncovered, psychology, rebirth, secrets, sex, taxes, transformation, the underworld, wills.

7th House: The experience of Human Relationships.

- Others, one-on-one unions, formal partners, relationships and marriage.
- Open enemies.
- The law and legal matters.

The sign on the seventh house cusp, the ruler of the house and any planets in it, these colour our attitude to marriage, formal relationships and one-on-one partnerships. Depending upon this energy combination, we will be attracted to certain types of people and relationships and be repulsed by others. If there is a Capricorn-Saturn theme for instance, we will be more conservative in our tastes, but respond very differently and be more progressive if there is an Aquarian-Uranus emphasis.

The seventh house is a major training ground for inter-personal relationships. Those who have insecurities in this area, who are dysfunctional, who project their "stuff" onto the partner, seeing only what they expect to see - they are destined to meet people who will trigger their fears and respond in the expected negative manner. There is a cause-effect aspect at work. This is also the house of "open-enemies", and such unions often end up as open warfare, eventual divorce and a dispute over money and property - eighth house matters.

The overall spiritual goal of this house is to help us develop relationship skills so we can create harmonious unions with others and resolve conflict situations. It teaches us to be mature and loving individuals, capable of building healthy, whole and beautiful relationships. This will help attract soul mates from the same soul-group, those we are in deeper harmony with.

8th House: The experience of Transformation and Death.

- Resources of the partnership.
- Other people's money, legacies and inheritances.
- Sex.
- Intense emotional experiences and trauma that initiate efforts to change.
- Death, rebirth, transformation and major separations.
- Occult groups.

The 8th is naturally ruled by Scorpio, the sign of deep emotions and emotional battles. Consequently, this is the house of major emotional and life transformations. Psychologically, this requires the death of something old in the nature so that something new can be birthed. The sign on the cusp, the ruler of the house and any planets in the 8th, these influence how we do this and face major life challenges.

Such change can be inspired in various ways. For instance, disappointments in our sexual life, disputes over money or inherited legacies, or the traumatic death of a cherished partnership or loved one. This house is also associated with the fall-out from divorce and any disputes over shared money or property.

As major crises and disappointments arise, we are confronted with those aspects of ourselves that need to be transmuted. For some, transformation may go no further than the momentary enjoyment and loss of self, experienced with an orgasm. But others are compelled to seek permanent change and understanding. Some find this through psychological help. Others investigate the occult - the practice of spiritual disciplines. Meditation is an example. It helps to bring emotional and sexual balance as well as forge a link with the soul and higher spiritual realities.

The overall goal of this house is to help us find our inner strength when faced with loss and adversity and to transform aspects of ourselves that have become crystallised. From such achievements we gradually become balanced in the nature and more spiritually whole.

9th House: The experience of Understanding.

- Collective mind, society's beliefs, morals.
- Universities, higher study, higher schools of learning.
- Long distance travel, the world.
- Foreign lands, people, cultures.
- Formal religion, philosophy.
- Wisdom Teachings, spiritual Teachers, the Spiritual Path.

The ninth house represents the higher collective mind of humanity, the vault of knowledge and wisdom that has been produced and the teaching of this wisdom so that all can become wise and moral world-citizens. For example, universities, academic life, lecturers and professors; formal religions, religious life and priests; world philosophies and philosophers.

On a personal level, it rules those efforts we make to broaden our understanding about people and foreign cultures, the religious/ spiritual orders or topics we will be drawn to, as well as the religious beliefs and morals that we generally hold about life and the world.

The sign on the cusp, the ruler of the house and any planets in the 9th, colour our attitudes. They represent the experiences we will have in our search for wisdom, the nature of our voyage of discovery and the wise people we meet that help us to grow. For those who venture into the esoteric, Eastern teachings on the nature of "soul" and practices such as meditation and Raja Yoga will be found and applied.

The ninth house generally, gives the soul an opportunity to expand consciousness and broaden beliefs so that we will be more inclusive and tolerant towards all people's in the world, to all races and their cultures and religions. The goal is to become wise and inclusive, and to inspire others to do the same.

Sagittarius, the natural ruler of the 9th house.

11th House Keywords: Arch-deacons, ashrams, beliefs, bishops, churches, collective mind, ethics, faith, foreign lands and foreigners, God, gurus, higher learning, ideals, long journeys, ministers, morals, philosophy, preachers, religion, search for understanding, spiritual fanatics, spiritual teachers.

10th House: The experience of a Vocation, Society and Status.

- Father, authority figures, government.
- Career, professional life, ambitions.
- Status, public recognition.
- Initiation, the Master's group and work.

Located at the top of the chart, this house represents society at large and those who govern it, such as the government, leaders and the "father". It represents power, authority, status, the professional life, accolades, glories, and the contributions we make to society.

The sign on the cusp, the ruler of the house and any planets in the 10th, these colour our attitudes towards this life area, define how we can make a worthwhile contribution and what types of careers we are suited to. If those in power approve of what we have to offer then material benefit, recognition, fame and glory will follow. Disapproval on the other hand can result in public notoriety and rejection.

At the higher level, this house (and its natural sign ruler, Capricorn), govern initiation - the expansion of consciousness. There are three main initiations we pass through as we scale the mountain of spirituality - the 1st brings control over the physical appetites, the 2nd over our emotions and the 3rd brings the entire personality into alignment with the soul, our source of wisdom and love.

The 10th and its experiences prepare those who are ready to take this higher 3rd initiation - symbolically, the scaling of the mountain of spirituality and becoming a member of a Master's group. The 10th gives us the opportunity to serve a spiritual Master or Teacher in a soul-inspired vocation. To make a contribution towards world service work, thereby helping to manifest the greater good.

Capricorn, the natural ruler of the 10th house.

12th House Keywords: Ambitions, authority and authority figures, dominant parent, father, government, Masters, the Master's work, power, profession, public recognition, reputation, social standing, status, vocation. MC: high goals.

Aquarius, the natural ruler of the 11th house.

Keywords: Friends, groups and group creativity, hopes and wishes, organisations, politics, revolution, social causes, social groups, social reform.

Pisces, the natural ruler of the 12th house.

Keywords: Aloneness, asylums, behind the scenes, chronic health issues, confinement, hidden things, hidden enemies, hospitals, jails, large institutions, privacy, retreats and sanctuaries, self-sacrificing, secrets, self-undoing, subconscious, the unconscious, the universe, the unknown, unsolved mysteries.

11th House: The experience of Group-interaction.

- Friends, groups and organisations.
- Social reform, politics, revolution.
- Hopes and wishes.

We come now to the life-area that rules our social life and group-participation, and our "hopes and wishes" for a better future. The sign on the cusp, the ruler of the house and any planets in the 11th, these represent how we will seek social intercourse - the friendships we make, the groups and organisations we join because we have an affinity with the ideals they espouse and we want to put our achievements to use.

For the average person, this house represents the social customs and norms of the day that the average person participates in when interacting with others on a social level. But if our tenth house experience was difficult, if we did not achieve the status and respect we craved, then in the 11th we will express our dissatisfaction, by rebelling, by becoming a revolutionary. Our social life then will revolve around interactions with people that similarly share our dissatisfaction and activist schemes or projects to make these dissatisfactions known to the public mind.

The higher goal of the eleventh house is to help us develop group skills and to find our soul-group, a humanitarian organisation through which we can work with greater effect and power than we could on our own; to serve world need.

12th House: The experience of Isolation and Endings.

- Self-undoing, negative core beliefs.
- The unconscious, the hidden, the unknown.
- Confinement, prisons, large institutions; retreats and sanctuaries.
- Hidden enemies.
- Selfless, sacrificial service.

Generally, the twelfth house rules life endings, the manner in which we bring major cycles to a conclusion in preparation for a totally new beginning. It also rules life's rejects and casualties of life (such as criminals and the seriously ill), and places that look after them such as hospitals, hospices and prisons. It can represent people that we are unaware of because they act covertly or secretly, who affect our lives for good or ill. On a broader level, it encompasses the collective unconscious of humanity and life's unknowable mysteries.

On a personal level, this final house can represent the "too-hard" basket of life. All those unresolved emotions and uncompleted tasks we choose not to deal with at the time because they are too difficult and that we shove into the background to deal with later. It represents our very private and secret life that we want to keep hidden and away from the public gaze. The sign on the cusp, the ruler of the house and any planets in the 12th, these colour these attitudes and experiences.

More positively, it represents periods when we choose to enter into a more introspective phase of life and leave the main-stream on a self-initiated search for understanding. Even if we are forced to do so though illness, loss of employment or incarceration, this will provide an opportunity to self-analyse and identify any habits, patterns of thought, or activities that are self-sabotaging and that need to be changed or healed.

Positively, the 12th represents a place of quiet spiritual retreat for reflection and meditation, for healing and integration. Such periods help us gain clarity about what we need to do to complete major cycles successfully so that we can enter into the flow of life again without taking forwards any obstructive baggage.

CHAPTER 4. PLANETS IN SIGNS AND HOUSES

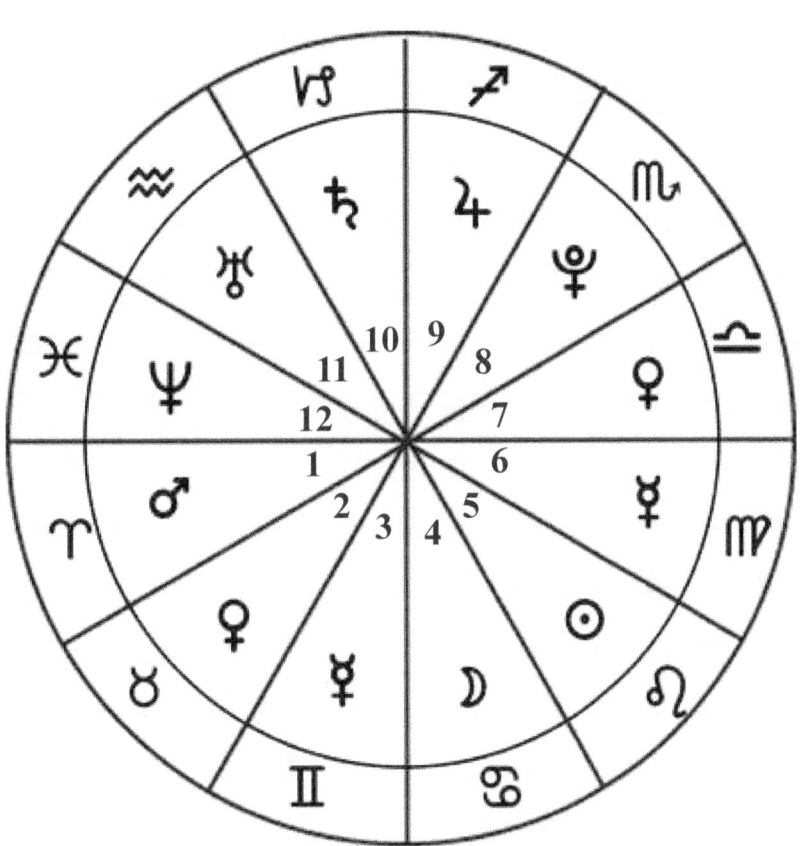

In this section, the effects of the planets, asteroids and ascendant in the signs and houses, are explored. This is the "nuts and bolts" section of the book and of astrology.

1. The Ascendant Sign.

The ascendant sign represents the way life is viewed and approached, the image and appearance. This approach is also influenced by the planet ruler of this sign, which is called the "ruler of the chart." The first part of each paragraph describes how the animal representative of the sign behaves. The second part describes the purpose of the soul, which is to develop love and wisdom through life experience. The ruler of the ascendant sign (in its sign and house), provides further information.

Aries ascendant. The Aries mask is full of fire and power. Entering life through the portals of Aries, perceptions are coloured by the aggression of the Ram. It races into life like a pugilist, to take on all comers. Mars gives it a hungry desire and an urge to fight, compete and win - the strongest and bravest taking all. The purpose of the soul is to become an intelligent, warrior leader, develop the intellect and use it to rein in the undisciplined impulses and to bring the lower life under rule and control. Those who achieve this are like tempered steel. Intelligent and confident, they stride boldly into life, leading the fight for the higher good.

Taurus ascendant. Entering life through the earthy portals of Taurus, the ego's perceptions are coloured by the raw passion of the Bull of Desire. Determined to satisfy its urges, it fixates upon its source of "food" and gallops towards its goal, fighting and struggling, determined to let nothing stand in its way. The purpose of the soul is to become a Master of Life by gaining control over the desires of the lower nature. Self-control should be applied and meditation to lift the sexual chakra forces up into the throat to feed the mental life. This brings desire under control. Those at this level can stand steady like a mountain for higher principles. They radiate light and harmony.

Gemini ascendant. Perceptions are coloured by nervous thought energy. The ego is clever, witty, and people like it for its charm. But lacking mental discipline and control, it is easily distracted, its interests and decisions alternate rapidly and it has difficulty making lasting commitments. The purpose of the soul is to observe the lower nature and use wisdom and discipline to control its restless fluctuations. This will fill the consciousness with light, will illumine the lower nature. Those at this level have become centres of radiant intelligent love, "Messengers of the Gods" with the power to speak and teach higher truths.

Cancer ascendant. The ego's perceptions are coloured by the defensive Crab and timid Moon. It scuttles into life wearing its protective "house" and hides in the shallows of the emotions. Through fear of being hurt, it puts up defensive walls to block people and love out. But amongst the crowd, life is lonely. The purpose of the soul is to purify the emotions through spiritual practises, so that soul-light permeates the nature. This will dissolve emotional negativity and fill the consciousness with the light of wisdom. Those at this level have the power to walk freely in the world of illusion as Light Bearers, people who nurture the masses in their attempts to grow spiritually.

Leo ascendant. The personality lopes forward into life like a Lion, with an arrogant intention to rule and dominate. Commanding its subjects to come and adore, it delights in its beauty, its power and glory. Feeding off the adulation it receives and roaring out its commands, it reigns supreme, acknowledging no other power. To channel the higher powers of Leo, to manifest the purpose of the soul, the ego must be decentralised and selflessness developed. This will change the whole cellular structure of the heart on both physical and metaphysical levels, so that divine love can flow through into the world. Those at this level have the power to radiate love and wisdom to the masses, to fight to uphold the highest principles and greater Law.

Virgo ascendant. The ego mask is studied perfection. Finely made with chiselled features, every movement, every word is carefully constructed to give the impression of superiority and class. It is a master in finding flaws in others, which helps to maintain the impression that it is perfect. The purpose of the soul is to purify the emotional life and refine negative ways of thinking, so that love and wisdom can flow through the purified heart and mind. As part of this, the negative traits of the Moon sign need purifying. Christ light radiates freely through the hearts of those who have achieved this, giving the power to serve humanity wisely, intelligently and with practical skill and expertise.

Libra ascendant. The ego mask is charming and pretty. But it is restless and has difficulty making decisions because it lacks inner harmony. Many relationships cause life to become a tangle of unresolved affairs. The ego tries to avoid upsetting people by being sweet - it is a "pleaser". The purpose of the soul is to balance the mind, the emotions, relationships and the entire life. Radical change is required, the awakening of consciousness to new and higher truths and interests. Those at this level have developed the ability to walk "The Noble Middle Path," have become a harmonising and peace-making influence for good in the world.

Scorpio ascendant. The ego's mask is dark. It scuttles into life as if it were a battlefield, with its weaponry honed, ready to slay all enemies. Defensive, aggressive, it fights everyone and everything as if its life depended upon it. People see this ego as being deadly and dangerous and they avoid it, as they should. The purpose of the soul is to become a spiritual warrior, which requires the elimination of self-delusion and control of the aggressive traits. Mars' house shows where the battle to achieve control and emotional balance will primarily play out. Those who achieve this have become centres of lighted intelligence with the power to fight to the death until justice prevails and truth unfolds.

Sagittarius ascendant. This mask is good-humoured and people like it. A prophet in the lower sense, it pontificates and brags. Underneath is the hungry Centaur, which gallops through life consuming - food, drink and people. Irresponsible, it laughs off life's problems and moves on to greener pastures when it exhausts its environment. The purpose of the soul is to change life direction and aim for higher goals, and when one goal is reached, to aim for another - and so on. When we are moving in the right and higher direction and as wisdom unfolds, we are given the keys of freedom to the planet. At this level, we are equipped to make a global contribution to world good - as a teacher, a prophet or as a director, guiding people to the heights.

Capricorn ascendant. The Goat is hungry for power. It wants to conquer the mountain and is manipulative, devious and controlling in its efforts. But once reaching the mountain-top of its ambitions, it has to atone for its sins. The purpose of the soul is to be ambitious for the greater good, to use one's powers, resources and influence to benefit humanitarian causes. Saturn's house indicates where karma will be met, where to shoulder responsibilities and give selflessly. Those who have achieved this will be given the opportunity to serve the greater good of humanity, to manage projects and build structures that make a difference for many.

Aquarius ascendant. Wearing its dazzling mask of mental cleverness, people are awed by the knowledge that comes out of this ego's mouth. But they cannot make a connection. Aloof and separative, it erects a wall of "superior" thought-forms, which prevents closer contact. It is a "Water-Bearer" who does not like to share. The purpose of the soul is to align the mind with the heart and then pour out love and wisdom liberally over others, to humanity, without judgment or reserve. Those who have reached this level are agents for love and wisdom, benefactors and reformers of society for the higher good.

Pisces ascendant. The ego's mask is emotional and fluid, it shifts and changes. Swimming unconsciously, it enjoys the changing currents of emotional highs and lows. Naive, it blindly trusts that all will be well and if not, it moves on easily to a new wave and to a new frolic. As the higher levels of Pisces are reached, the inner call of the soul is heard - "destroy all that stands between you and your spiritual freedom." This registers consciously, as an urge to eliminate all negative traits and attachments that bind one to non-essential material things. This is the purpose of the soul. Those who have achieved this have emerged from illusion into truth and have the power to follow in the footsteps of the Master and be a world server.

2a. The Sun in the Signs - representing personality expression.

Each sign begins with the way the personality tries to control its environment. To emphasise the point, the animal or lower traits of each sign are highlighted. This is followed by the higher goals and qualities.

Sun in Aries. The personality "Ram" is warlike, aggressive and childish. It acts before thinking and is foolish in its courage and daring. Bringing the "Ram" under intelligent control is the transformational goal. In other words, developing the intellect and using it to rein in the aggressive, lower impulses. This will enable the natural leadership qualities to flourish without the distorting effects of emotionalism and anger. The illumined Aries personality is intelligent, pioneering and courageous - it has the ability to stand alone if necessary. Those at this level have the power to destroy all shackles that bind people.

Sun in Taurus. The personality "bull" is conflicted and driven by lower desire. It is obstinate, destructive, unimaginative, lazy and greedy. "Riding the bull" is the transformational goal, to control of desire. We must develop dispassion and use the higher will to control the impulsive nature. Those with a wise and lighted Taurus personality have steadfast strength and the power to stand firm for their principles - like a mountain can withstand a storm. There is an artistic and creative side to Taurus and power to create beauty and harmony.

Sun in Gemini. The unregulated personality is symbolised by the Twins, a dual and two-faced ego. It is unstable, has a superficial thought life and is gossipy, deceitful and restless. Stabilising the over-fluid mind and curbing its restlessness is the transformational goal when the Sun is in this sign. This is achieved through daily meditation and the appreciation and expression of truth and beauty. Illumined Gemini personalities have a clear and wise intelligence. They are brilliant and powerful communicators and can inspire many with the beauty and potency of their thoughts and words.

Sun in Cancer. The personality "Crab" has moods and lives in the past, hanging on to old things and dead relationships. Stepping free from the defensive shell is the transformational goal, developing the intellect and using it to free the consciousness from emotional control. This is achieved by refusing to give in to upset moods but instead, learning how to deal with negative emotions in an intelligent and healthy manner. Those with a lighted Cancer personality protect and nourish people with kindness and compassion. They have the power to throw light onto troubled waters and to calm them.

Sun in Leo. The personality "Lion" is arrogant, vain, over-indulged and lazy. Over-dramatic and posturing, it continually draws attention to itself. Controlling the "Lion" and bringing the lower will and mind into line with the wisdom of the soul is the transformational goal. This is achieved through daily meditation and the practise of selflessness, which develops soul sensitivity. Illumined Leo personalities radiate light and wisdom. Magnetic, many will be attracted by their dignity, warmth and good-heartedness - they are benevolent leaders and teachers.

Sun in Virgo. The personality has natural intelligence and superb teaching and communication skills. But unregulated, it is insecure, hypercritical and small-minded. With a narrow focus and an irritating perfectionism, materialism rules the life. Purifying the mind of its negativity is the transformational goal. In time, this will give birth to kindness and consideration for the feelings of others. Those who have a wisdom-infused Virgo personality are distinguished by a clear and direct intelligence, dedication to selfless-service and brilliant craftsmanship. At this level, being harmless in word and deed, many will benefit from the quiet goodness and expertise they have to offer.

Sun in Libra. The unregulated personality lacks balance; it is indecisive, procrastinates, is promiscuous and dishonest. Vain and concerned with appearances, it takes advantage of others with its charm and attractiveness. "Balancing the Scales" is the transformational goal - bringing the life into balance and order. A moderate lifestyle, such as the "Noble Middle Path" as recommended by the Buddha should be followed. Spiritual discipline and the ongoing practise of honesty and integrity is required. Wisdom-infused Libra personalities are distinguished by their brilliant intellects, their judicial minds and they have the power to help many find peace and harmony.

Sun in Scorpio. The personality is symbolised by the lethal Scorpion that is dangerous, vindictive, revengeful, holds grudges and is emotionally conflicted. Self-delusion rules. Extinguishing the power and sting of the "Scorpion" and overcoming self-deception is the transformational goal. This is achieved through esoteric meditation, which teaches us to hold the mind steady in the light of intelligence and the practise of dispassion to control the emotional life. Those with a wisdom-infused Scorpio personality are intelligent and strategic warriors who use their power and strength to help the troubled and suffering.

Sun in Sagittarius. The personality centaur loves "wine, women and song". It is extravagant and boastful, a wasteful gambler who squanders life's opportunities and wounds others with thoughtless words and gossip. Curbing the appetites and developing one-pointedness and harmlessness, these are the transformational goals. Wisdom-infused Sagittarius personalities, they are distinguished by their creative and artistic talents and by the way they can inspire people to reach for their higher good. Radiating warmth, joy and confidence they lift people's spirits and many will be inspired to follow their lead.

Sun in Capricorn. The personality "Goat" is avaricious, Machiavellian, the true materialist. It is ruthless and calculating in its quest for power and control. Muting the material ambitions of the "Goat" and development of true humility are the transformational goals. But this will not happen until the hunger for the material life is exhausted. Self-discipline must be applied to bring the lower impulses under control. When the Capricorn personality is infused with wisdom, it uses its executive managerial skills and power to benefit and shape society for the greater good.

Sun in Aquarius. The unregulated personality uses its mental powers to show it is "superior". But it is also unstable, volatile, dogmatic and mentally rigid. It separates itself from people behind walls of illusory and impenetrable thoughtforms, living there in aloof solitude and weaving impractical schemes. Bringing the mind and heart into balance and reconnecting with humanity at a feeling level, is the transformational goal. This is achieved by studying the Wisdom Teachings and by following a scientific self-development plan. Those with a wisdom-infused Aquarius personality are distinguished by an acute intelligence, inclusiveness and a loving heart - qualities needed to help reform humanity for the better.

Sun in Pisces. The restless personality "fish" swims through life without clear direction and lives in a fantasy world. Hypersensitive, impressionable and naive, it sees itself as a victim. It is also cunning, controlling others through guilt, false obligation and passive aggression. Developing the intellect and using it to balance the emotions and to be less reliant on others is the transformational goal. The ruthless pruning of interests and relationships that are not core or vital is essential. When the Pisces personality is infused with wisdom, the urge to raise up humanity in some way flows through them spontaneously. This may come through the arts so that people are uplifted by wondrous creations, through healing or teaching.

2b. The Sun in the Houses.

The Sun's house is where effort should be made to develop and integrate the personality and to express its power by intelligently dominating the environment.

Sun in 1. Personality power is expressed through the image, the body, personal interests and by projecting the will spontaneously into life. The goal is to gain distinction as an individual. This means expressing power strongly and openly, facing life honestly - without a mask, being up front and becoming a leader who is a shining example of goodness and benevolence.

Sun in 2. The power of the personality is expressed through managing resources, possessions, money and business concerns. But the important goal is to be clear about the values espoused and to ensure that actions in the material world are in line with these and other important principles. This placement gives the power to attract and manage resources and possessions potently.

Sun in 3. Communications in the close environment and with relatives, is the avenue through which personality power will be expressed. The goal is to gain distinction by developing excellent communication skills and using them to convey one's truth to people, powerfully and confidently. This placement gives the power to do this and to excel at teaching and writing.

Sun in 4. The personality seeks to expresses itself through foundational relationships, with parents, in the home and with the family; generally, strengthening "roots" and traditions. The goal is to become the heart of the family, a centre of strength that family can respect and look up to. This will create a solid and healthy foundation for the family unit and will bring individual and also family distinction.

Sun in 5. Through relations with children and lovers, hobby activities and pastimes; this is where the personality will try to express its power. The goal is to gain distinction in the way creative energy is used so that pleasure and happiness is given to others - this will come back to oneself. When wisdom has been achieved, this combination gives the power to radiate love and light, especially to children and younger souls.

Sun in 6. Personality power is expressed through work and health. If there are health issues, then understanding how we may have contributed through our psychology and lifestyle will enable vital changes to be made to improve things. The higher goal is to gain distinction by developing and using skills so that we become a centre of strength that people can turn to for assistance in times of trouble. When we heal ourselves, this combination gives the power to heal others.

Sun in 7. The personality wants to express its power through important one-on-one relationships, to gain distinction in vital partnerships both personal and professional. This is achieved by being authentic, honest and assertive, but also expressing oneself in a way that meets the needs of the partner so that the relationship is improved. This combination gives the power to be a centre of strength and love that others can cling to and rely upon.

Sun in 8. Personality power will develop as inner demons and emotional hang-ups are healed, through psychological assistance or by practicing esoteric sciences such as meditation. When we can accept who we are at a deep, core level and can express this authentically, a major transformative break-through has been made - a goal of this combination. The Sun's location here, gives the power to be a guiding light in all transformative, inner healing processes.

Sun in 9. The personality wants to expand its understanding by making long journeys around the world to learn about "foreign" cultures and beliefs, or by exploring higher knowledges such as philosophy, ethics and religion. The goal is to gain distinction by becoming a centre of light, knowledge and wisdom in one or more of these areas. Then to radiate what we know so that others in turn can learn, and expand their understanding and wisdom.

Sun in 10. Life gives a lift to those with this combination, to reach and express their personality power through positions of status, power, government or rule. The goal is to gain distinction in a vocation so that people are positively impressed, to become an authority that people trust and an inspiration so that they are empowered. This combination gives the power to throw one's light over many. However, a cautionary note - this placement can bring notoriety if one runs afoul of the authorities.

Sun in 11. The personality wants to express its power amongst friends and like-minded fellows, with people who share similar ideals - socially or politically. The goal is to become a centre of love, power and authority in the group, fellowship or organisation we belong to, so that it is empowered and better able to achieve its external aims. This combination gives the power to strengthen any organisation or group we belong to.

Sun in 12. The power of the personality is temporarily dimmed with this combination. It suggests that private healing at a deep psychological or spiritual level is required, before distinction in the outer world can be made. If this is successfully undertaken, then true heart radiance and wisdom can blaze forth, healing, helping and encouraging many. This placement gives the power to heal people who are the casualties of life, the sick, infirm and mentally ill, those who have lost heart and stumble about in the dark.

3a. The Moon in the Signs - the expression of emotion.

In our psychology, the Moon represents our emotional habits and expressions. Esoterically, the Moon Sign represents the "prison of the soul pattern", the negative core beliefs that cause conflict with others and that hinder our spiritual progress. The task is to eliminate them by developing the higher sign traits.

Moon in Aries. The problem pattern is one of fast, unthinking and aggressive emotional reactions. The ego is hot-headed. It acts with blind and unthinking aggression and throws tantrums if anything or anyone blocks its way. The goal is to develop the intellect and use it to control the rash emotional impulses. Success will enable the positive strengths of Aries to be used to create dynamic and passionate connections with others.

Moon in Taurus. Uncontrolled desire, is the problem pattern. The "bull" goes after what it wants in a stubborn and destructive manner, creating chaos. Change will come when there is an intelligent study of cause and effect, how choices made under the sway of desire are a cause of trouble and steps are taken to moderate any excesses. Success brings out the positive qualities and strengths of Taurus - the power to stand strong and steadfast in the face of opposition and to build personal relationships that are light-filled, stable and beautiful.

Moon in Gemini. The problem pattern is a restless mind that trivialises, that is shallow and changeable, that lacks empathy and deceives people. Greater depth is required in all interactions and follow-through, so that ideas are manifested in some constructive and beneficial way. Success will give the power to communicate thoughts with greater clarity and empathy to the public. The response will be positive and encouraging feedback.

Moon in Cancer. Extreme defensiveness and sensitivity that leads to emotional isolation, is the problem pattern. The development goal is to develop healthy emotional expression and build a clear and lighted consciousness. This requires the development of the intelligence and balancing of the emotions. Success will give expression to the positive strengths of Cancer - power to reach out to people with love and sensitivity and ability to build light-filled and nurturing personal relationships.

Moon in Leo. The binding pattern with this combination, is that of wanting to control everyone and everything and being bullying and arrogant. The development goal is to lift the eyes from the little self to the higher spiritual Self. This will shift the focus away from the ego to the soul, the wisdom-self. The emotional nature will be purified and lightened. Success will give the ability to create personal relationships that are filled with fiery love and warmth, that are selfless and sharing.

Moon in Virgo. An emotional need to criticise people, is the problem pattern. This infects the mind, so it becomes hypercritical and demands perfection in this imperfect world. An alignment affirmation that can bring change is, "Christ in you the hope of glory." It trains the mind to see the good in people - something that Virgo's need to develop. Success will enable the positive strengths of Virgo - intelligence and kindness; to be expressed in all relationships and interactions so that people feel good about themselves.

Moon in Libra. The problem pattern (if it has not been sorted out already), is unbalanced fiery passion and shallow, frivolous living. Another way this combination works, is "playing it safe", being unwilling to create a fuss in case people are disapproving. The intelligence must be used to balance the emotions and overcome any fears that inhibit. When this is achieved, the positive qualities of Libra will shine forth through the astral nature, giving the power to create relationships that are beautiful in their power to nurture people.

Moon in Scorpio. Delusion, seeing only what one wants to see, being continually at war with everyone around, this is the problem pattern. This occurs because the emotions and desires are too powerful and distort reality. Additionally, perceived injuries are remembered and revenge attacks are continually being planned. The development goal is to lift the mind up into the light of wisdom - above the battlefield, and to look at life again - through the eyes of truth. This will develop a clear and insightful intelligence, with power to build relationships that are deep, authentic and truthful.

Moon in Sagittarius. Being driven blindly by the lower appetites is the problem. There is a too powerful desire for excess consumption (food, drink, sex), for freedom from all discipline, and an emotionally fuelled tendency to gossip and wound through speech. The development goal is to purify the desire life so that the mind can be free to focus on higher and more aspirational goals. Success will enable the positive strengths of Sagittarius to shine forth - an aspiration for that which is higher and finer; and the power to build emotional relationships that are founded on true friendship and shared ideals.

Moon in Capricorn. The problem-pattern is being ruthless, calculating and cunning to get one's way. Emotional expression is difficult in this sign of detriment for the Moon - caused by a lack of nurturing from carers in childhood. This will cause major problems in intimate relationships until healed. The development goal is to get in touch with the feelings and be more emotionally responsive to intimate partners and with the family. Success will give the power to found relationships on a bedrock of integrity and trust.

Moon in Aquarius. Separativeness, due to being too mental, individualistic and isolated from feelings and human intimacy, is the problem pattern. The goal is to learn to think with the heart, and feel with the mind and a scientific-like program should be followed to bring about this development. Success will free the positive strengths of Aquarius - the ability to make friends anywhere and at any level of society. Personal relationships will be founded on deep friendship and inclusive kindness.

Moon in Pisces. Although there is a natural ability to connect spiritually and emotionally with people and power to build relationships that are founded on openhearted trust and unconditional love; this will be sabotaged because of the problem pattern. It consists of being too emotional, having a consciousness that is too fluid and ungrounded, being subject to delusion because there is a lack of discernment and being too attached to life comforts. The intellect needs to be developed, healthy emotional boundaries constructed and the life guided more intelligently in the future. This will empower any service activities.

3b. The Moon in the Houses.

This is where lunar "bad habits" are strongest - where they cause conflict. An important task is to harmonise this area of life. This is achieved by intelligently recognizing the pattern at play, its negative effect and by striving to act in a more conscious and balanced manner. Transformed, the Moon brings harmony and balance.

Moon in 1. There is a pattern of past-life self-absorption about the appearance, the image, the body and personal interests. It is likely the emotions are on display, and life-perception is easily distorted by their instability. The goal is to face life honestly, without a mask or playing games. This requires inner work to balance and stabilise the emotions so they do not interfere when important decisions are to be made. Once the inner work has been done, this placement gives an ability to approach life with a clear awareness of self and motive, free of conditioning and denial. The public will admire this.

Moon in 2. There is a pattern of past-life materialism and greed that is driven by an emotional need for possessions and money. There could be low self-esteem, and self-valuing by what one owns - by possessions. A belief may exist that money or material things are needed to be safe and secure. The key to reversing this pattern is to find and value one's higher inner qualities, such as goodness and generosity. These are the hallmarks of souls who leave the world a better place for having lived.

Moon in 3. Communication misunderstandings and conflicts could arise with relatives and neighbours. If so, the cause is emotional over-sensitivity and holding on to negative beliefs and thoughts so that the meanings of people's words are distorted. Another manifestation of this combination, is being so busy and active with mundane things, we miss exploring our higher potential. Developing the mind through study, improving concentration and learning to speak the truth without emotion is required. This will give an ability to communicate ideas and opinions creatively to the public and to have them be very well received.

Moon in 4. This placement indicates there is heightened emotional sensitivity about family matters and bonds with parents, the family or with family traditions that may no longer be healthy. There may be codependency, a reluctance - even a psychological inability perhaps, to leave the nest and forge one's own way in life. It is important to complete unfinished family business, to grow up emotionally, and to psychologically leave home. It is important to not let binding limitations or unfair demands from the past, from family or parents prevent one from striving to reach our highest potential. When the inner work has been done, this placement gives an ability to build stable and healthy life foundations.

Moon in 5. This pattern can play out two ways. There may be the selfish pursuit of pleasure, driven by an emotional need to avoid life difficulties and responsibilities. Or, there may be unfinished past-life issues with lovers or with children that are causing conflict and these are impeding life progress. To counter-balance this, all family responsibilities should be met before time is given to pleasure activities and an effort should be made to heal enmities with children and loved ones. Positively, the healed Moon in the 5th brings nurturing relationships and creative talent.

Moon in 6. There is an emotional need to prove one's worth in daily life. This can play out as being so busy and occupied with work or attending to the normal duties and tasks of life, there is no balance or time for other activities. If so, it will lead to stress and ill health, most of which has an emotional basis. Try to balance daily duties with quiet and private recuperative time. When used positively, this placement gives an ability to develop good work skills and build a career that is attractive to the public.

Moon in 7. The pattern centres around unfinished business with significant others from a past life. It means that major relationships will be highly charged emotionally. There may be tremendous neediness so that one becomes too reliant or obsessed with the partner. Unhealed, this pattern can cause people to lose touch with the inner-self so they become a caricature of who they are and are willing to do anything to avoid being rejected. The goal is to complete unfinished business with partners and learn to move on when a relationship has died. Success gives the ability to build harmonious and loving partnerships of all types.

Moon in 8. This indicates that the desire nature needs purifying and transforming. The negative pattern consists of uncontrolled emotionalism, too powerful desires, self-torment or fear. There may be trouble with an inheritance, an ex-partner or sexual issues; or incidents as extreme as being attacked by malevolent forces. The ability to think clearly should be developed and used to balance and control the emotions.

Focus should be placed upon healing any old emotional traumas and painful memories. Becoming financially independent is another goal and together these new developments will help cut ties with an unhappy history and from the memories of people that bind us to the past.

Moon in 9. The pattern may take the form of an emotional need to be free and to travel far, to run away from the responsibilities of life. Or, a too-heavy reliance on the "rightness" of moral or religious dogma and preaching at others for their sinfulness. Some with this placement may have unfinished, past-life business with a religion or with someone from a religious setting. Whatever form the pattern may take, there is a moralizing aspect. It requires breaking ties with any religious or philosophical group that is limiting to growth and understanding. This may mean a temporary period of atheism, or finding a more inclusive and holistic philosophy to replace the old one. Achievement of this will result in the opportunity to teach cherished ideals and beliefs to an appreciative public.

Moon in 10. There is a heightened emotional need to gain respect and acceptance from authority figures, especially from the father (or mother on occasions). Or, being driven to succeed and shine in the vocation to compensate for low self-esteem. This pattern will only be healed when healthy self-confidence is developed. That will happen over time as important life goals are reached, thus proving to the insecure inner child that it is talented and worthy. This placement gives the ability to build forms or structures that lead to life success - an ability to shine one's qualities to the world.

Moon in 11. Emotional wants and needs are met through friends and groups. But if this should become a dependency to help shore up low esteem - if the associations are toxic upon the life and other important relationships; they should be cut away and new and healthier friendships should be formed. A period spent developing one's own talents and creativity, spending time with children and other people who are loved will be helpful. Inner healing will bring in time, an opportunity to work with an inclusive and healthy group and to shine within it.

Moon in 12. The ego is secretive and very private. Focus is "behind the scenes." Hiding away on one level or another is the survival strategy. Trouble comes when this urge becomes compulsive, paranoid, because of a fear that life is dangerous. Consequently, this placement offers the opportunity to bring this debilitating pattern and associated negative core beliefs into the light for healing. A deliberate effort should be made to socialise, even if only at a minimal level. Focus should be on the Sun and the house it is in.

3c. Moon's Nodes in the Signs.

The Moon's nodes are the two points at which the orbit of the Moon crosses the ecliptic. They are diametrically opposite each other. The north-node sign represents positive qualities to develop, to counterbalance past-life negatives represented by the south-node sign.

Nodes in Aries - Libra. When the Moon's north-node is in Aries, positive traits such as using the initiative, courage and assertiveness should be expressed, to counterbalance Libra south-node negatives such as indecision, procrastination and cowardliness. When the north-node is in Libra, cooperative qualities such as good manners and social skills should be expressed to counterbalance Aries south-node negatives such as selfishness, lewdness and aggression.

Nodes in Taurus - Scorpio. When the Moon's north-node is in Taurus, positive traits such as being steadfast, practical and loyal should be expressed to counterbalance Scorpio south-node negatives such as emotionalism, revengefulness, holding on to the past and nursing grievances. When the north-node is in Scorpio, the reverse is true. Emotional integrity, insightfulness and courage should be expressed to counterbalance south-node in Taurus traits such as stubbornness, materialism and greed.

Nodes in Gemini - Sagittarius. With the Moon's north-node in Gemini, good social and communication skills should be expressed to counterbalance Sagittarius south-node negatives such as boasting, irresponsibility and a lack of discipline. When however, the north-node is in Sagittarius, directness, honesty, expansiveness and wisdom should be expressed to counterbalance Gemini south-node negatives such as trickery, lying, restlessness, duality and shallowness.

Nodes in Cancer - Capricorn. When the Moon's north-node is in Cancer, healthy emotional expression is required and nurturing kindness, to counterbalance Capricorn south-node negatives such as coldness, meanness, materialism and calculating hard-heartedness. With the north-node in Capricorn, qualities such as healthy ambition, common sense and practicality should be expressed to counterbalance Cancer south-node negatives such as emotionalism, moodiness and defensiveness.

Nodes in Leo - Aquarius. With the Moon's north-node in Leo, self-assertiveness, benevolence and heart-felt expression should be expressed to counterbalance Aquarius south-node negatives such as intellectual detachment and coolness. In the reverse case, when the north-node is in Aquarius, positive traits such as humanitarianism, goodwill and brotherliness should be expressed to counterbalance Leo south-node negatives such as egoism, arrogance and selfishness.

Nodes in Virgo - Pisces. When the Moon's north-node is in Virgo, positive traits such as mindfulness and discrimination should be expressed to counterbalance Pisces south-node negatives such as being too fluid, emotional and indiscriminate. When the north-node is in Pisces, the development of positive traits such as going with the flow, compassion, trust and faith should be expressed to counterbalance Virgo south-node negatives such as being critical, narrow, miserly and materialistic.

3d. Moon's Nodes in the Houses.

North-node in 1 - south-node in 7. With the north-node in the first house, the goal is to be assertive and use one's initiative to develop a strong self-identity. This is necessary to counter-balance a past-life tendency of losing sight of oneself when married, in a formal partnership or by only serving other people's needs. It is time now for attention to be placed on personal growth and development of one's own talents and self-expression. "We cannot give to others what we do not have ourselves."

North-node in 2 - south-node in 8. With this combination we must establish our own set of values, honour and value ourselves. This may require healing emotional hurts or unhealthy sexual habits. We also must be financially independent and not rely on others to provide for us. Instead, focus on establishing life prosperity and willingly sharing with others. There is a spiritual truth that applies to this situation - "To those who give, all will be given."

North-node in 3 - south-node in 9. The goal is to develop a community-minded spirit and make new and healthy connections with people in the local environment. Learn to listen rather than preach and be open-minded to new ideas and develop good communications with siblings and neighbours. This will prevent living in an ivory tower composed of one's own rigid philosophical or religious beliefs and therefore being unapproachable.

North-node in 4 - south-node in 10. The task is to put down stable roots and ensure that the family, parents and traditional cultural values are honoured and that they take priority over the career or any search for glory. This does not mean we cannot have these. Just ensure that career drives and worldly ambitions do not become so consuming, they cause a serious breach with the important people who are foundational to the life.

North-node in 5 - south-node in 11. Development of one's creative talents and using them to bring joy to people's lives is the task - especially with children who are in our care. Avoid cutting time with them to be with friends or to pursue social interests to the detriment of this. An important goal is to spend quality time with those we love and who bring joy into our lives.

North-node in 6 - south-node in 12. With this placement, we should pour our energies into work and what we do on a daily basis. It is important to develop useful skills to make a living in a profession, industry or craft that is enjoyed. Being busy, doing something constructive, will help to give life tangible meaning and purpose. Above all else, avoid becoming a recluse and hiding away from life.

North-node in 7 - south-node in 1. Positive emphasis in the house of partnerships means we should be less self-absorbed and I-focused, and instead, develop good relationship skills and put time and energy into building positive and harmonious unions. Healthy and loving relationships should be easy to form if the effort is made - the universe is encouraging us to move in that direction.

North-node in 8 - south-node in 2. The desire nature needs to be purified and balanced and an old, debilitating psychological pattern may need to be transformed. This may mean developing a healthy and balanced sex life to overcome past life impotency, sexual promiscuity or prostitution. It may require learning to share money and resources with others to counter-balance past-life selfishness or greed. The study of psychology will aid the transformational process. So, will joining an esoteric group and practicing techniques such as mindfulness and Raja Yoga.

North-node in 9 - south-node in 3. The goal is to travel far, study widely and as a consequence, broaden one's morals, beliefs and expand consciousness and life wisdom. There is a need to rise above and leave behind, outdated ideas learned in childhood that now limit progress. Some with this placement may travel the world and have important life-changing experiences with people from foreign cultures or races.

North-node in 10 - south-node in 4. The professional life is emphasised positively. Working towards higher ambitions and aspirations should be followed, even if it requires sacrifices to be made with family duties. Such obligations have been fulfilled in a previous life so there is no reason to feel guilty as long as reaching the goal will bring benefit and rewards to the family in the long run.

North-node in 11 - south-node in 5. There is a need to develop new and finer friendships and to be involved with - and to support more fully, group or organisational interests rather than personal. It is important not to waste time on frivolous pastimes or to allow selfishness from children or lovers impede work to be done with a group of like-minded associates who want to do good in the world.

North-node in 12 - south-node in 6. Make time for quiet healing and peaceful reflections upon the greater mysteries of life, in private surroundings and in nature. Seek the serene and beautiful. This will help counter-balance a previous over-busy and duty laden life and possibly also, one that had serious health complications.

4a. Mercury in the Signs - the different ways mind expresses itself.

Mercury in Aries. Fire-mind is fast and innovative. It is an independent thinker, talks quickly and likes to think up new ideas and put them into action. Lower Aries mind is hot-headed and aggressive, it attacks without discrimination. Judgment is poor because the lower emotional impulses are stronger than mental control. When the mind is illumined, it can see the broad picture unencumbered by personal agendas and is an assertive and intelligent instrument. It gives the power to communicate messages dynamically, so that those who hear will obey and follow.

Mercury in Taurus. Earth-mind works methodically. It places importance on traditional knowledge and learns in a slow, step by step manner. But once learnt, nothing is forgotten. Lower mind is fixed and stubborn. It sticks to old ideas and dislikes learning anything new. It is wielded like a blunt club to fight and bash the opposition. The result is mental conflict and a tendency to agonise. When the mind is illumined, vision is clear and unencumbered by desire so that the light of understanding shines through. This gives the power to persevere in the search for truth until the right answer is found. This mind is an instrument of light and wisdom that conveys soul messages in a powerful, creative way.

Mercury in Gemini. Air-mind works lightly, quickly, flexibly and intelligently. It loves conversing and networking, is a fast talker and thinker, and likes collecting knowledge and data. Lower mind is restless and superficial. It likes to touch the new, the interesting and play with life, bringing it into conflict with other minds because of its duplicity. When the mind is aligned with soul-wisdom, the intuition unfolds so that it is able to receive divine ideas. This mind is wise, loving and understanding and can convey higher truths and inspirational messages. Many great spiritual teachers and orators are born with this combination.

Mercury in Cancer. Water-mind learns by osmosis - it drinks in information. It places importance on communication within the family and has a need to communicate emotional issues. Lower mind is easily disturbed. It is vague and has difficulty building clear thoughtforms. This brings it into conflict with others because the truth of any matter, or reality, can become obscured by emotionalism. When the intelligence is developed and the mind is illumined through spiritual disciplines, it is transformed into a lighted "house", an instrument that is both intelligent and intuitive - a very effective instrument through which to help the needy in the world.

Mercury in Leo. Fire-mind is bright and engaging. Grand and broad-minded, creative and intelligent - this mind is powerful when it communicates. Lower Leo mind is arrogant, controlling, over-dramatic and attention seeking. It continually tells itself and others that it has a divine right to rule. Roaring this out to the world brings it into conflict with other powerful egos. Illumination occurs when this mind is freed from the self-aggrandising ego. With intuitive light pouring through, it is a superb mental instrument to help guide and lead people. Communicating messages upon the ray of power, those who hear will obey and follow - it is the regal and dignified mind.

Mercury in Virgo. The earth-Virgo mind works precisely and exactly. This is the discriminating mind, but it can also be too critical and obsessed with a need for detail. Lower Virgo mind is focused on material acquisition and operates within a very narrow perspective. It is judgmental, querulous and makes a fuss over unimportant details. This brings it into conflict with other minds that retaliate, finding its imperfections in turn. As the mind is illumined, its boundaries broaden so that there is greater vision and wisdom. Virgo is intelligence, and the hidden Christ that is associated with this sign is the intuition or pure reason. This the higher Virgo mind demonstrates.

Mercury in Libra. The air-Libra mind is intelligent. Always seeking balance, it wants to be fair and just. A charming communicator, it is delightful to listen to. However, lower mind is unstable, over-busy, restless and swings to extremes. Lacking depth, it procrastinates, frets, dwells upon that which is frivolous, sensuous and superficial. This brings it into conflict with other duplicitous minds. As it becomes illumined and the intuition unfolds, its abstract reasoning powers are heightened. Mind then is a diplomatic, discerning, judicious and peacemaking instrument; a superb instrument for legal, counselling and diplomatic work.

Mercury in Scorpio. The water-Scorpio mind works secretively and focuses intensely. With a need to grasp hold of the truth, it delves to the core of things. It has a long memory, holds onto grudges and can sting when it speaks. Lower mind sees people and life as a battleground. It is ultra-defensive, reactive and lethal on attack with cruel thoughts and words. As the mind is illumined and the intuition unfolds, it is able to observe life from above the emotions, giving the power to see reality and the truth as it is. This is a warrior-mind that will fight injustices in the world powerfully with pen and word.

Mercury in Sagittarius. The fire-Sagittarius mind is visionary. It wants to learn, understand and grow. A born philosopher, it places importance on freedom of speech and is quick to give its opinion. Lower mind is careless with facts. It pontificates loudly, to all who listen. It harms, wounding others through too-blunt speech. This brings it into conflict with other minds that in turn, will judge. As the mind is illumined and the intuition unfolds, it becomes wise, creative and visionary; a mind that is philosophical and reasoning. With this mind we have the power to draw many to the Spiritual Path through what we say, preach and write.

Mercury in Capricorn. The Capricorn earth-mind is practical, cautious and systematic. It is very efficient in analysing problems and can quickly finding practical, workable solutions. With the wisdom of experience, it is a careful thinker and communicator and places importance on credibility and veracity. Lower mind hungers after material power. It is coercive, calculates, plots, deceives and connives to satisfy its material ambitions. This mind is illumined through altruism and the study of higher teachings and practice of spiritual disciplines. When it is illumined by the soul, it carries the power of truth in its words that can influence many.

Mercury in Aquarius. Exalted in Aquarius, this mind works intelligently and brims with original and unique thoughts. It is inventive and rebels against the old and traditional. Communicating with friends and groups is something it loves to do. But lower mind likes to demonstrate its superiority. Detached from the emotions, judgmental and dogmatic, it is not sensitive to people's feelings. It says what it thinks. This brings it into conflict with other minds that are just as judgmental in their assessments. As soul radiance proceeds and mind aligns with heart, it gives the ability to think with the heart and love with the mind. The combination of intelligence, wisdom and an awakened intuition produces one of the finest minds possible.

Mercury in Pisces. The water Pisces-mind is poetic, imaginative and intuitive - it can tune into other people's thoughts. But lower mind is vague, deluded and confused. Emotionalism affects the thought processes so there is difficulty building clear thoughtforms and distinguishing reality from fantasy. When this mind has been illumined with soul-light, it thinks and sees clearly, it dwells in the truth and in reality. This type of mind is able to communicate Christ love, wisdom and healing power to alleviate suffering.

4b. Mercury in the Houses.

Mercury's house is where we will be challenged to think clearly and intelligently about what is going on in the life. It indicates experiences that compel us to speak up and to voice our truth. If we have difficulty doing this, then a special effort should be made to overcome any fear that is causing the inhibition.

Mercury in 1. Mental focus will be on the image, on the body and on our personal interests. Because skilled oratory will be an important part of personal expression, it is vital to learn to think before speaking and to then speak in a manner that conveys thoughts clearly and as diplomatically as possible. The ascendant is related to the purpose of the soul. With Mercury in this region of the chart, becoming a communicator of truth and wisdom could be part of the soul's plan for the life.

Mercury in 2. When the mind is in the life-area of personal resources, we are required to figure out how to create a more abundant life and to create prosperity. Money may be made through communications and writings. Another goal is to study life carefully and consequently, to develop higher values to live by. Then, communicate these values and principles to the world.

Mercury in 3. With the mind located in the house of communications, we are required to learn, study and practice our communication skills so we can enhance all contacts made during the day with the words we speak and thoughts we convey. The placement indicates talent with writing and teaching and enjoyment with travelling. A career that utilises these skills will benefit the life.

Mercury in 4. The development of good communications with parents and family is important when Mercury is in the foundational area of life. If there is family dysfunction, if there are emotional wounds, then creating dialogue so that problems can be discussed and resolved, will help to create a healthier family unit. On another level, it creates an opportunity to teach, write or to run an office or commercial venture from home.

Mercury in 5. When the mind is in the life-area of personal creativity, it gives an interest in children and all pleasurable activities, such as love affairs, hobbies, speculation and sport. It is an opportunity to improve communications during our recreational periods. It also indicates talent - mental-creativity, skill with the hands in sport or art, or through communications such as in drama or film. This mind has the ability to bring much joy to children's lives.

Mercury in 6. Work and career opportunities will be enhanced by developing good communication skills. Alternatively, the hands can be used to earn a living. This combination also gives talent with healing, counselling and in administration work generally. On another level, Mercury in the house of health can indicate problems with depression, mental illness or with the nervous system. So, seeking professional help if symptoms start to appear and enunciating clearly what is going on to the practitioner, is important.

Mercury in 7. With the mind in the house of important human relationships, it shows there is much to learn about inter-personal dialogue. A requirement is the development of good, clear communications with close partners so that words are supportive and enhance unions rather than contaminate them. A career can be made in counselling, helping to heal divisions and conflict between people.

Mercury in 8. With Mercury in the mysterious eighth house, there will come a time when conflict arises in one or other of the areas of sex, death and dying, or concerning inheritances and joint resources. Major adjustments and changes to get the best out of the situation will be required, and perhaps also, emotional healing. There is an ability to use the mind as an instrument to bring about transformative change in oneself as well as in others and talent with understanding and teaching psychological and occult writings.

Mercury in 9. The goal is to expand our higher understanding through academic study, philosophy, ethics or religion. It gives an opportunity to develop the mind and become proficient in one or other of these areas. At another level, it may indicate travel to far distant places and communicating often with people from different places, races or cultures. Some with this mind like to preach and others will teach wisdom.

Mercury in 10. With the mind in the house of career and important life goals, development of effective public speaking and general communication skills should be undertaken. This is because they will be important in the career, which could also involve much travelling. On a personal level, developing good communications with authority figures and the father will be beneficial.

Mercury in 11. With Mercury is in the house of friends, groups and organisations, there is an opportunity to become an important communicator and networker in these social groups. This is also the political house and this placement provides an opportunity to excel in this area and to voice and teach humanitarian issues. On a higher level, it is an opportunity to develop harmlessness in thought and speech with friends, groups and in larger organisations.

Mercury in 12. The mind will naturally focus on private matters and may often withdraw into its own private and undisturbed world - it is inclined to be mentally secretive and withdrawn. This is fine if the life is otherwise healthy and balanced. But if there is a tendency to depression or to confuse fantasy with reality, this can be dangerous for mental health. In such cases, assistance should be sought. The placement also gives an ability to understand these sorts of troubles and to help such people. At a personal level, taking time out of the mainstream to reflect and meditate will be beneficial.

5a. Venus in the Signs - how love and affection are expressed.

We are all in the process of learning to love unconditionally and the adjustments we need to make to achieve this are embedded in the higher aspects of Venus' sign.

Venus in Aries. The affections are expressed ardently and passionately. People with this combination like to be the initiators of romance, but also to maintain their freedom and independence. A good relationship is still possible if the needs of the partner are being met. But in this sign of Venus' detriment, "love" is often expressed immaturely, aggressively and selfishly. In some, love is sex and sensuous gratification. This selfish, conditional way of loving must be reversed.

The goal is to learn to love more wisely, to appreciate the benefits of equal sharing, of cooperation and to value the higher and finer things in life. This will lead to the development of intelligent-love, which when expressed through this sign, results in relationships that are a balance of ardent fire and cooperation. The Aries soul at a leadership level, radiates the power of love to benefit all relationships.

Venus in Taurus. The affections are expressed reliably, slowly, steadily and sensually. People with this combination enjoy physical intimacy and want a solid financial base to life; consequently, there will be contentment if these are provided. So, a partner should be sought who is both sensuous and is a good provider. This is the banking sign and gives talent with handling money. At the lower level, the "bull of desire" rules "love" and relationships founded on this basis will be a battleground.

The task in Taurus, is to love more wisely and in the process, transmute lower desire into higher aspiration. This is achieved by looking for and valuing higher and finer things in oneself, in others and in life. When intelligent-love is being expressed through this sign, it results in beautiful unions that are founded upon a bedrock of loyalty and trust. The Taurus soul creates beautiful art-forms to inspire the world.

Venus in Gemini. With flirtation, fun and playful communication, people with this combination love with their minds - communications are vitally important. But they are easily bored and restless and find it easy to stray. At the lower level, love is superficial, irresponsible, non-committal and ephemeral. There is no depth of true feeling or ability to love intimately. Love remains a thought that can just fade away.

The goal is to love more wisely - with the feelings as well as with the mind. This will balance the energies of the mind and heart, so that greater depth will be given to all unions. When love is expressed intelligently in this way, relationships will be beautiful - mentally and emotionally. The Gemini soul in full bloom is profoundly wise, is a messenger who communicates wisdom to beautify the minds and hearts of all.

Venus in Cancer. These emotional people love sensitively, emotionally and defensively. They place emphasis on family relations and have an emotional need for financial and material security. At the personality level, they are needy, clingy and have many oscillating highs and lows. Fearful of being rejected and emotionally hurt, they can put up walls to protect their hearts. If this persists over time, love will be unable to get through.

The task with this combination, is to develop the intellect and let it take the lead in relationships rather than the emotions. This is because choices made when emotional are usually detrimental to the forming of healthy unions that can withstand the test of time. As the refining light of wisdom permeates the mind, greater sensitivity and appreciation of the value of others will be demonstrated and this in turn will enable beautiful love-unions to be built. The Cancer soul loves to light the way home for the masses.

Venus in Leo. These people love regally and generously. They like to be proud of the partner and are creative in showing their feelings with many grand displays of affection. Being territorial and needing to be in charge, sometimes partners are viewed as possessions - especially at the lower level where love is narcissistic and needs constant approval, appreciation and adoration. Normally loyal, some with this combination like to gather a lion's-pride of partners.

The task is to learn to love more wisely, to be a partner and friend as well as a leader in the union at some level or other. As the light of inclusive love grows, it will gradually supersede the egocentric focus, benefitting all relationships. Intelligent-love expressed through this sign results in relationships that are a balance of fiery power and sensitivity to the needs of the partner. The Leo soul uses this force to provide intelligent, wise and loving leadership to the world.

Venus in Virgo. Many in this group will want their intimate unions to be perfect and for the partner not only to be a lover, but also to be neat, punctual and to contribute financially. Normally loyal and dutiful, they themselves contribute much materially. But Venus falls in Virgo and this combination belongs to people who potentially use the critical mind to judge partners and relationships. If this impulse is not controlled, then it will kill love like a heavy frost burns and withers spring buds. The real trouble is low self-esteem. At an unconscious level, these people believe they are imperfect, even unlovable. Criticisms of others are in reality, the criticising of one's own short-comings.

The task is to learn to love more wisely, by placing greater value and appreciation on positive qualities and attributes - both one's own and those of others; and on learning to love unconditionally. This will gradually improve the quality of all relationships. The Virgo soul in full expression, is very intelligent, is kind, appreciative and thoughtful and uses these qualities to help and heal the suffering.

Venus in Libra. These flirtatious charmers have a compelling desire to be in a relationship, and want them to be harmonious and peaceful. They are very attentive to the partner and like being "in love." But at the lower level, "love" is restless and needs excitement and diversions. It becomes a sensual game, with many partners and deceit. Such relationships are unstable and many hearts will be hurt when love is treated like a game and not enough consideration is given to the feelings of others.

The task is to learn to love wisely - as a soul rather than as a personality. In Libra, this means being very considerate of the partner's needs and being just and fair in all matters concerning the union. In simple terms, loving with greater depth and feeling. Intelligent-love expressed in this way will enhance all relationships - professional and intimate. The wise and considerate Libra soul has the power to bring opposites into perfect union.

Venus in Scorpio. Sensual, intense and passionate, the sex life will be important (Scorpio rules sex). People with this combination will fight for those they love and to keep them safe. But Venus is in detriment in this sign, which means those with this combination can be possessive, jealous and threatening. They may consider the partner to be a possession and if he or she tries to escape, an enemy to be attacked. These lower traits need to be transmuted.

The task is to learn to love more wisely, and a way to do this is to meditate on all things good and beautiful. This will train the mind to dwell on higher and finer things, rather than be occupied with dark thoughts. As this is done, gradually, relationships will become more harmonious, reflecting the growing capacity to love as a soul. Intelligent-love expressed in this sign results in relationships that are based on trust and truth. The Scorpio-warrior soul, loves to go into combat on behalf of those who are weak and who suffer.

Venus in Sagittarius. People with this combination love adventurously, freely, with fun and good humour. They move easily through relationships and are attracted to fellow adventurers. At the lower level, love is like a wild untameable horse, which demands freedom and avoids responsibility and commitment. When it wants, it wants all. When it has had enough, it leaves without looking back.

The task is to love more wisely. This means balancing the freedom loving traits of Sagittarius with relationship commitments and responsibilities. If this is achieved, it will result in unions that are honest and direct and that are built upon a foundation of values and beliefs that are mutually shared - there is often a shared love of spiritual or philosophical teachings with this combination. The Sagittarius soul is very wise and learned and loves to beautify the hearts and minds of others by teaching inspirational philosophies and truths.

Venus in Capricorn. Loving cautiously and responsibly, people with this placement prefer traditional types of relationships – those that form slowly so that they are likely to be more enduring. At the lower level, ambition turns love into a commodity, as barter and a means to gain material benefit. The personality affections are controlled and there is a lack of warmth. Loneliness and rejection await those who walk this way.

The goal is to learn that love and all the benefits that a loving relationship brings, are more important than power and money, which cannot buy the former. A greater appreciation of love and of its value is required. As the mind grasps and appreciates these higher notions - since energy follows thought; gradually, beautiful and mutually fulfilling relationships will be formed. These people will flourish with a partner who can evoke their feelings. The Capricorn soul loves to shoulder heavy responsibilities so that the load of humanity is lightened and the world is beautified.

Venus in Aquarius. This group of people love intellectually and their partners also need to be good friends. They are open to having unconventional relationships and those where they are free to express their predilections. At the lower level, under the power of the lower mind - separativeness and selfish individualism blights love. Relationships are less important than the desire to experiment, to be free and independent.

The task is to learn to love wisely, which for them means thinking with the heart - to consider the feelings of others before going their individual way. This will bring about a greater appreciation of other people generally and enable more loving and inclusive relationships to form. This in turn, will lead to a greater appreciation of the whole of humanity in all its shades and colours. The Aquarius soul loves to pour out the healing waters of love upon humanity.

Venus in Pisces. The affections are expressed emotionally - those with this combination are romantics who yearn for the ideal partner, someone who will come along and sweep them off their feet. At the lower level, they can flow from partner to partner, all the time looking for a deeper spiritual connection. Childlike and avoiding responsibility, dependent upon others; they can play the victim and bind people through guilt.

The task in Pisces is similar to that in Cancer - to develop the intellect and use it to make wiser choices in relationship matters. However, Venus is exalted in Pisces and those who have this combination, find it easy to be kind and compassionate lovers. When this level of loving is accompanied with intelligence and wise action, then unconditional love flows out from them like an ocean to embrace all. The Pisces soul loves to serve humanity; to lift, to heal and save.

5b. Venus in the Houses.

Venus' house is an area of life that we can beautify with kindness and intelligent interactions. It is also a place that love and wisdom may be found.

Venus in 1. The image that people see is one of charm, grace and beauty. There may be preoccupations with the appearance - body and weight, how to attract lovers or money. The task is to transform consciousness so that it resembles the beauty of Venus. This is achieved by training the mind to look for the good and beautiful in people, to be kind and sensitive and express one's inner beauty through beautiful thoughts, words and actions. This in turn will bring back, abundant love and appreciation.

Venus in 2. Venus in the house of money can manifest as a love of luxury, possessions, money, beauty and art. At the higher level, the task is to beautify our values and attitudes to money and to bring these into right balance with our spiritual ethics. It is important also, to be clear about the principles that we want to live our lives by and to honour these and express them. Loving and appreciating life's bounties and blessings and sharing what we have with others, this will bring life abundance flowing back in return. People will love the beauty and values expressed.

Venus in 3. With the planet of love in the third house, we are being asked to follow Christ's commandment - "love thy neighbour as thyself." The task is to communicate beauty through thoughts and words - not only to those contacted in the environment, but to the wider community at large. Learning to think good thoughts and speaking only when there is something kind or positive to say, is the golden rule. We will be rewarded by attracting people into the life who will speak with love and sincerity about us in return. This placement gives the power to express beauty in writings and speech.

Venus in 4. The task is to radiate intelligent love within the family unit and home and to create family relationships that are mutually appreciative and honest. For instance, speaking with kindness and positivity and being respectful and fair. This is especially important if house rules have been broken. Taking a little extra time to explain why and how the rules contribute to family harmony, while also showing family members they are valued and appreciated - this will be rewarded by attracting love in return from the family. Venus in the 4th indicates being surrounded by beauty and joy at the end of life.

Venus in 5. This combination gives talent in the arts, the ability to craft beautiful creations and to bring joy to the lives of others - not only with artistic presentations, but with the beauty of the love we have to share. The task is to be kind and intelligently loving with children and romantic partners. As we express ourselves in this way, loving and talented people (many will be children), will be attracted into the life and give unconditional love in return.

Venus in 6. The goal is to express intelligent-love in the working life, to share wisdom and expertise with co-workers and clients and to think kind thoughts and speak wise words. Developing work skills to do this is another part of this placement - for instance, becoming a counsellor or human-resources officer. As we learn to handle everyday problems in such a manner, insecurities about being worthy will gradually heal, benefitting personal relationships and overall health. Otherwise, problems with the throat, thyroid or urinary tract could arise. True love may be found at work.

Venus in 7. The Goddess of Love is asking those with this placement, to demonstrate intelligent-love in all important partnerships. This means showing our appreciation, being honest and fair, thinking good thoughts about the partner and being always respectful. Another important goal is to end relationships kindly and leave former partners with their respect intact so they do not turn into enemies. Insecurities about being "lovable" will heal as these inner changes are made, giving the skills necessary to build beautiful, intimate unions.

Venus in 8. Transformation is required - any emotional traumas that exist should be healed, the way sexual energy is used refined, and the value placed on other people's money or rights needs adjusting. The mind must be beautified, freed from unhealthy imaginings and healthy self-love and self-appreciation should be cultivated. These changes will help bring inner peace. Venus in the 8th can foster a love of the mysterious and esoteric. It also indicates love may be found in a mysterious manner or while attending to one's self-healing.

Venus in 9. This placement encourages a search for wisdom. Firstly, by studying the Ageless Wisdom - the writings and teachings that contribute to the beautification of the collective mind and that teach universal oneness and fellowship. Secondly, by reaching out beyond one's own race, religion and culture so that a wiser understanding is gained of all the people of the world and their cultures. This combination gives the potential to become learned and to teach wisdom to others. Love may be found in a foreign place or with someone from another culture.

Venus in 10. The goal is to express intelligent love and beauty in the profession or important life work and to use one's influence to bring about greater fairness and justice in the world. If success in the world is gained, then from that position of prominence, publicly share beautiful thoughts and demonstrate kind actions. In return, love, beauty and wisdom will flow back, especially from influential people and authority figures. The love of one's life may be someone prominent in the community or who shares important life work.

Venus in 11. The task is to beautify our friendships and the groups and organisations we belong to. This is achieved by being kind and fair with our associates, becoming an inspirational and visionary force so that people by association will feel their lives enhanced and beautified. If this is done, the reward will be to attract people who will love and value us for our finer qualities, people with whom beautiful and enduring friendships can be formed. Lovers will also be friends.

Venus in 12. Love and affection are expressed quietly, behind the scenes. For instance, a love of nature, of solitude, perhaps even a very private love-affair. Adversely, there may be an attraction to psychically unhealthy people or to cults where the sex function is misused. If there is a problem with giving and receiving love, if there are negative thoughts about being unlovable; healing at a very deep level is required. In this case, a therapist, guide or teacher should be sought to help lift one's thoughts to the good and beautiful. Sometimes, Venus in the 12th points to love being found in the most unexpected places or ways.

6a. Mars in the Signs.

It represents the various ways passion and desire are expressed, how we fight for what we want.

Mars in Aries. Those with this combination express passion urgently and aggressively. They initiate activities, are spontaneous, like to take risks, are rash and accident prone. Territorial, they want to lead, to be first and best. There is bravery and courage, but it is not well directed because of jealousy, aggression and contests for control and leadership.

The evolutionary task is to fight against blind and forceful desire, to balance and control it. As this takes effect, then gradually desire is transformed into spiritual aspiration. Self-control is a momentous development in Aries and when achieved, an intelligent and assertive leader steps forth, one who fights with fiery power for the higher good.

Mars in Taurus. This group of people are stubborn if opposed and they are very territorial. The desire nature is volatile and explosive - driven by the "bull of desire" the appetites are voracious. In the rush to satisfy them, the personality swings from the heights of exhilaration to the depths of despair. But there is also tremendous bravery and courage.

In Taurus, the task is to release oneself from the hold of lower desire. As the emotions purify and desire transmutes into spiritual aspiration, gradually those with this combination emerge as warriors of light - stable and lighted vessels through which the soul can direct its power. They have the power to fight with the determined steel of higher will and persevere for as long as it takes to achieve higher goals.

Mars in Gemini. This combination links the emotional nature and mind so that the energy of the mind speeds up. There is mental acuteness and combativeness, hot and angry thoughts, volatile verbal outbursts and a lot of talk. Wants and needs are communicated assertively and defensively, sometimes aggressively. There is talent with initiating ideas and putting them into action.

The development task is to cultivate mental and emotional balance and direct Mars' force wisely so that communications remain powerful but not aggressive. As spiritual disciplines are applied and lower desire wanes, the observing consciousness will grow and glow. Working at its best, this combination gives a master orator who is powerful in debate because the mind is fast and words are used skilfully, like a rapier to foil opponents.

Mars in Cancer. Mars falls in this sign, so its negative side is often seen - angry emotions that swamp rational thought. There are moods, jealousies, grievances and resentments over past hurts. Those with this combination like to retreat into their shell, but will come out fighting to protect the home and family. They fight for those they care about.

As the emotional life refines, it lifts energy from the solar plexus up to the heart chakra so that desire transmutes into spiritual aspiration, giving the soul a clear channel through which to work. In Cancer, we fight to free ourselves from bondage to the emotions and when successful, fight to free the masses from this slavery as well.

Mars in Leo. Those with this combination are very prideful and arrogant and like to make an impact on people. The passions are expressed grandly, with flair and a lot of noise. There are explosions of anger, sulks, dramatic displays and much dismissing of people who offend from the royal presence.

The task is to displace the selfish ego from the seat of control and bring it into line with the soul (wisdom). This is achieved through character building and the application of spiritual disciplines. When successful, the soul has a clear path through which to radiate its fire. Those at this level have the power of the Sun streaming through the heart. Mars in Leo develops warrior-leaders who are inspired to fight for the greater good.

Mars in Virgo. Passion is expressed fastidiously and scrupulously. Those with this combination pursue their desires in a practical and methodical manner. They fight with "the facts", by proving themselves to be right, and can be hyper-critical if opposed. Sometimes the emotions are inhibited, resulting in passive aggression and muted spitefulness.

Positively, there is often expertise with all things manual and practical. When soul illumination purifies the emotional life and desire is transmuted into spiritual aspiration, the Christ-spirit (love and wisdom) will birth in the heart. Those at this level have the intelligence, will and talent to free humanity from ill-health, poverty and the drudgery that occurs amongst the poor and impoverished.

Mars in Libra. When Mars heats up the sacral centre, passion and excitement are demanding. But Mars is in its detriment in Libra, which means its aggressive side is somewhat muted. However, unhealed Mars in Libra indicates selfishness in relationships, conflict and arguments. There is a warlike touch to the mind so that mental barbs can be acute, if subtle. Sometimes men with this placement feel their "male-side" is not strong and feel "less manly" in comparison to testosterone types.

In the more advanced, as desire transmutes into spiritual aspiration the soul has a clear and balanced astral field through which to work. Because inner equilibrium has been achieved, it gives the power to harmonise conflicting forces in people and to generally establish peace and harmony in the environment.

Mars in Scorpio. The desires are passionate and intense, the sexual urges strong and compelling. Deep and secretive, those with this combination try to hide what they feel for protective purposes - they are warriors who do not like to show their weaknesses. They make vengeful opponents, are very territorial and fight to win. At the lower level, glamour and bias distorts reality, giving rise to churning emotions that are dark, aggressive, retaliatory and revengeful. Battles are fought, within as well as with others.

Across lives, the illumined mind gradually disperses the darkness, and desire transmutes into spiritual aspiration. The purified astral nature becomes a lighted vessel that can be used to deal intelligently with life stress. Having developed the power to fight and defeat the darkness within, now the same can be done for others.

Mars in Sagittarius. The passions are a combination of jovial humour and assertiveness. People with this combination are fiery, reactive and have an enormous appetite for sensuous and physical pleasures which they pursue with one-pointed gusto. They like travel, to explore, to seek out adventures. They can also be blunt, insensitive and attack with words. A few can be boozing, gambling, tricksters and con-men.

When desire transmutes into spiritual aspiration, these travellers re-direct their explorations towards higher and finer ideals and goals. Such people are inspirational leaders and teachers and have the power to guide men and women onto the higher way, towards their higher ideals and spiritual goals - towards the mountain top of enlightenment!

Mars in Capricorn. Passion is expressed with exacting and intelligent skill - Mars is exalted in this sign. Those with this combination pursue their ambitions in a responsible and methodical manner and have the drive to succeed. Very territorial, they can also be aggressive and controlling to get what they want and to hold onto it. Lower types will try to destroy anyone who stands between them and the success, money and power they crave. But karma awaits those who violate the Law of Love. The lower will is broken through humiliation and adversity, forcing the personality to its knees. This is a requirement for higher progression.

As wisdom shines through, ambition transmutes into an aspiration to climb the higher ethical, moral spiritual mountains. In higher Capricorn, we fight to release ourselves from the slavery of material ambition and when this is achieved, have the power and drive to serve the greater good, the Plan of God.

Mars in Aquarius. These are mental-warrior types who use the mind and forceful ideas to fight for their ideals and for what they want. Lower types, believing they are always "right", they try to defeat all opposition with facts and pointed arguments. Beliefs are aggressively defended and expressed. Thwarted, they become rebellious and unpredictable activists and anarchists.

As these emotions clear, the astral nature gradually becomes a vessel through which the soul can inspire its owner to reach out in friendship and love to the community and to all humanity. In Aquarius, we are given the opportunity to break free from the prison of illusion and when we achieve this, have the power of clear and rational thought and arguments to help humanity do the same.

Mars in Pisces. Desire submerged in this watery sign can result in lethargy, blunted ambition and feelings of impotency. Men with this placement sometimes feel their "male side" is weak. But emotions bubble away beneath the surface and can manifest as confused resentment and passive-aggression. Some with this combination may resort to victim-like behaviour in an attempt to manipulate people to do what they want.

As the astral field refines, becomes quiet and light-filled, kind action, love and compassion flowing through from Pisces can be radiated to the world. With Mars in this sign, we fight to free ourselves from drowning in the astral currents and when successful, fight to help others to do the same.

6b. Mars in the Houses.

Mars' house represents a life area of major conflict. This is where the desires are very strong and therefore where the ego will fight to get what it wants. This is where we must guard against unthinking emotional impulses and learn to think before we act.

Mars in 1. The ego is courageous, a fighter, and has a tremendous drive to succeed in life. But undisciplined, there is anger and an impulse to attack - oneself or others. This must be curbed and the means to achieve this is through the illumined mind - achieved by life-experience and the desire for continual self-improvement. Then, Mars' fiery force can be harnessed and directed wisely to achieve higher ideals and goals.

Mars in 2. There is a desire to possess everything and everyone, to fight for money and gain. The ego measures its self-worth by its material acquisitions: more money - higher esteem, no money - being worthless. Lower and selfish values and ideals need to be replaced with higher ones. This will bring in abundant energy, prosperity and a desire to fight for the greater prosperity of all.

Mars in 3. Undisciplined fiery passion in the house of communication can result in an angry "motor-mouth" with no filters - firing off attack words without thought of how they hurt or wound. The goal is to think before speaking, especially with siblings, neighbours and relatives. Positively harnessed, there is tremendous energy and enthusiasm to help people in the local environment and to communicate thoughts in a positive way.

Mars in 4. There is war at home. The urge to fight and win arguments with family will create disruption and separations. Some may suffer serious abuse due to evilness being passed down the family line. Either way, the negative patterns must be healed. Fighting for one's right to be free from control and abuse is a good way to use this energy. When successful, there will be a tremendous drive and power to build and maintain a happy family, home, community or spiritual ashram.

Mars in 5. There is trouble with children or lovers when the ego goes on the warpath in this life area. Projecting anger onto children, younger souls or onto lovers will ruin relationships. These impulses must be transmuted and when successful, there will be abundant energy available to bring joy to the lives of loved ones, or to be directed into creative projects, sports, adventures or other pleasurable pastimes.

Mars in 6. Conflict and disruptions at work will erupt when Mars is in the 6th. But projecting one's unhappiness, blame and anger onto co-workers, will bring a backlash. The long-term result could be headaches, inflammations and other disruptions to health. To avoid this, troubled emotions and anger patterns should be healed. When successful, there will be tremendous energy and vitality to benefit health and the career.

Mars in 7.ABfights, urges to control, and blame being projected onto the partner will be the norm until the cause - anger over being hurt in the past; is healed. Wise counselling is required and restraint when the urge to attack starts to rise. The energy should be re-directed into physical activities and adventures that couples can enjoy. Wisely used, Mars' warmth and passion can keep marriages vital and sensual.

Mars in 8. Transformation is required if there are unhealthy sexual predilections or force is being misused in some other way. The desires and emotions need purifying and re-directing into healthier or more positive avenues. The 8th also rules psychology and esoteric sciences and the study of such subjects and self-application of their techniques; these will help to bring about the inner changes. This combination gives great energy and enthusiasm for healthy change. There may be battles over resources and legacies.

Mars in 9. Battles over morals and principles are the rule with Mars in the house of higher learning and wisdom. Some with this combination may become involved with cults and suffer abuse, others may find themselves at war with religious teachings or personnel. Energies should be diverted from fighting teachers or hating those who are different, to expanding one's understanding, knowledge and wisdom. There is a love of travel and a great sense of adventure.

Mars in 10. War with a parent, at work and with authority figures generally, will cause disruptions in the career until anger over being mistreated when in a vulnerable state (often in childhood), is healed. Some with this placement may choose a career that is influenced by Mars, such as becoming a mechanic or user of technology, be involved with automobiles, the military, surgery or hairdressing. Positively, there is tremendous energy and enthusiasm available to create a successful career.

Mars in 11. Fighting with friends or associates in groups and organisations will occur. This is a consequence of anger, the result of unresolved resentments, hurts and grievances from the past being projected onto social associates or organisations. When these are healed, tremendous energy and enthusiasm will be available to pour into favourite causes or group adventures. Some with this combination may become political or revolutionary warriors.

Mars in 12. There is anger in the unconscious, a consequence of past-life abuse. There may be self-harming such as cutting or hitting oneself. These need to be healed to avoid recreating similar events in future lives. If abuse is currently taking place or it occurred in childhood, it is important to bring it into the light so that abusers can be punished and wounds can be healed. On a positive level, there is much energy and enthusiasm available to help people who have been side-lined by life, to pour into private projects that benefit people.

7a. Jupiter in the Signs.

The various ways we expand our consciousness, our wisdom, and the ways brotherliness develops.

Jupiter in Aries. The hot-blooded personality traits of the "ram" expand in ordinary man, but so do courage and leadership. There is tremendous power and enthusiasm to initiate and take the lead in adventures and projects. The higher goal is to develop wise leadership skills. During the period that wisdom begins to affect consciousness, a teacher will come into the life and give advice about what to do next. In this case, "transmute desire into an aspiration for higher things and knowledge into wisdom." When the inner work is done, gradually that which is prophesied will emerge - a wise Aries leader with the skills necessary to direct men and women to their higher good and usefulness.

Jupiter in Taurus. Lust-driven appetites of the "bull" expand in ordinary man with this combination, so that there is a rush to satisfy the lower cravings. There is also an expanded ability to attract abundance and prosperity. But eventually, as the attachments to the material world begin to fade, higher wisdom will be sought. A teacher will appear - in this case, one who is practical and direct in giving the necessary advice - "clean up your life." The goal with this combination is to develop wise-mastery over the material life and not be ruled by a craving for money and things. This means starting a purification program to moderate and balance the lower appetites and re-direct this force into higher creative projects. Mastery over the lower forces results in abundant mental and artistic talent.

Jupiter in Gemini. Uncontrolled fluidity, mental instability and shallowness expand in ordinary man. There are huge dreams, many ideas, a lot of talking, but without practical application. On a search to understand more about life, these people are constantly networking, connecting and exchanging information, they travel far and wide. Then, as the higher way is approached increasing sensitivity to the subtle messages of the soul will be heard. A wise and learned teacher will appear with a message to "Search for wisdom," instigating a search for beauty and truth. The higher goal is to become a master of knowledge and of wisdom and those with this combination have the potential to become this - very wise and loving teachers and communicators.

Jupiter in Cancer. Jupiter is exalted in this sign. Negatively, this can accentuate materialistic tendencies. Unstable emotions will expand and so will hypersensitivity be, resulting in conflicted and unstable relationships. Positively, it gives a loving and supportive family. When the higher way finally calls, a wise and empathetic teacher will appear with a message to, "Balance the emotions and bring them under control." The higher goal is to develop a clear and lighted consciousness, though which wisdom can flow. This will be achieved through spiritual practises and by exerting mental control. Wise people with this combination, radiate wisdom like a lighthouse piercing dark and dangerous waters so that the "lost" are guided home.

Jupiter in Leo. When the ego dominates the nature, the arrogance of the Lion expands. Proud, it is puffed up with its wonderfulness. But generally, so does enthusiasm for life expand, grand displays of fire and emotion, benevolence, generosity and joy. Eventually, when life-reversal occurs, a teacher will appear with the message, "Not thy will, but higher-will should be sought." The higher goal is to become a wise and benevolent leader and this requires decentralisation of the ego and alignment with the soul, the source of wisdom. Self-control and spiritual practises bring this about. Wise leaders with this combination, are charismatic and have the power to warm the hearts of those seeking guidance like the rays of the sun warms the earth.

Jupiter in Virgo. Acquisitiveness, a love of trivia, criticism and judgment expand, obscuring the larger picture. Generally, so too does the ability to work generously and selflessly in the chosen area of service, especially in medicine and health. When the voice of wisdom is finally heard, the impact will cause a reversal of life direction. A prophet will appear with the message - "To become a wise teacher and healer, purify your mind and heart." Right living-habits along with spiritual exercises to bring the mind and heart into balance, are required. Success will enable the foretold wise-teacher to emerge, one whose illuminating discourses and practical instructions will help many to be similarly transformed.

Jupiter in Libra. Negative traits that cause trouble in relationships can be exaggerated, such as indecisiveness and procrastination. But generally, this combination increases wisdom and there is a strong concern for justice. The natural diplomatic skills are enhanced and so is joy to be found in loving relationships. When the voice of wisdom is heard, a teacher will appear with the message, "Find the balanced, central way." The higher goal is to develop a wise and judicious intelligence like that demonstrated by the legendary King Solomon. Expansion of the powers of the finely-honed intellect and bringing it into balance with an open and loving heart, this will bring about the required internal alignment and balance. Consequently, a sage will appear.

Jupiter in Scorpio. Courage and insight are enhanced. But so can lower desire and delusion be, and emotional bias and the distortion of perception. The emotional pain this creates will eventually trigger a search for knowledge and understanding so matters can be improved. A wise teacher will then appear with the message, "Climb out of the swamp of astral control and fight for your spiritual life until you are victorious. Reach for the Light (wisdom)." The higher goal is to balance and master the emotional-desire nature. The battle to do this could extend across lives, but when successful, intelligent-wisdom will be in control of the lower nature. Powerful and transformative teachers and healers could have this combination.

Jupiter in Sagittarius. Appetites are exaggerated and so is the desire to consume something - anything. But generally, the love of travel is enhanced and so is interest in philosophy, study, religion and foreign cultures. These adventures will eventually lead to the higher way and a teacher will appear with the message, "Vision the higher goal, reach it, then pursue another." The higher goal is to develop a Master of the Wisdom. By following and reaching after higher ideals one after another, the pathway to the mountaintop is gradually scaled and the necessary expansions of consciousness are achieved. This combination gives the potential to dispense wisdom like the rays of the sun so that many will be inspired and drawn to listen and follow.

Jupiter in Capricorn. Avarice and material ambitions expand when Jupiter falls in this material sign. But overall it balances conservatism and caution with a more optimistic outlook and boosts the possibility of achieving professional status and career recognition. The higher goal is to develop wisdom in this material world and those with this combination will at some time have a crisis of faith and principle. The message is, "Climb down from the mountain of materiality and scale the mountain of spirituality." If this advice is followed, rapid progress will be made so that consciousness expands. Those who have mastered the material life have the power to construct forms and organisations in the world to better humanity.

Jupiter in Aquarius. Ego-desire for knowledge and control expands with this combination. But so does the search for understanding through scientific experimentation or by seeking wisdom in original ways. These investigations will eventually lead to the higher way. A teacher will appear with the message, "Give all that you have to lift up those in need" - the higher goal with this combination is to become a world server and reformer. If the message is responded to, it will lead to the development of skills and the making of connections with appropriate groups and organizations so a real contribution to world good can be made. It results in a very learned and exceptionally capable humanitarian and teacher, with the power to distribute abundance and prosperity to the masses. Often, this will be through beneficial scientific discoveries.

Jupiter in Pisces. This can accentuate emotions that are already too-fluid and an urge for sensuous satisfactions. It can also enhance idealism, compassion and a spiritual or religious orientation. Development of the intelligence and personality integration will enable the higher way to be found. During this period, a wise teacher will appear with the message, "Follow in the footsteps of a Master and serve humanity." The goal in Pisces is ever world-service. This leads to a search for wisdom and better ways to help the suffering. Eventually, a dedicated server of humanity will emerge, one who gives all to alleviate suffering and to disperse human ignorance. The ultimate task in Pisces is to be a world saviour.

7b. Jupiter in the Houses.

In Jupiter's life area everything is enhanced - including support, fellowship, abundance and good-fortune.

Jupiter in 1. Jupiter brings luck and good fortune, confidence to follow one's dreams and in some, an opportunity to grow in wisdom. The down-side - if discrimination and self-control has not been developed, is a tendency to exaggerate and boast. It is easy to be generous and loving with this combination and it gives those who respond in the higher way, an opportunity to become a very wise teacher.

Jupiter in 2. There is a lucky touch with money and business and if the urge to spend lavishly and hugely is controlled, this can bring financial prosperity. But in return, we are encouraged to pass on the blessings of abundance to others. The golden rule with this combination and what wisdom is trying to teach is that, "To those who give all, then all will be given."

Jupiter in 3. Boastfulness and a lack of proportion can result. But generally, it is easy to be generous with people met during daily life, to have loving communications and kind interactions with neighbours and siblings. In return, blessings will flow back from the environment, from people who will speak kindly of us in return. This combination gives talent with communications and if we go about it in the right way, what we say and write will be distributed widely and have a very positive impact.

Jupiter in 4. Sometimes life may be too busy or noisy, but generally, there is goodwill in the home and ample love and support that will boost the chance for life success. Those with this combination can contribute to the family's well-being and happiness by ensuring that home is a warm and light-filled place and by giving freely of their generosity and wisdom. Blessings will flow back from the family in return.

Jupiter in 5. With the expansive and inclusive Jupiter in the fifth house, the love of pleasure-seeking and irresponsible behaviours could expand. But generally, it enhances personal creativity and talents and boosts loving relationships with children, lovers and younger souls. If these gifts are used to bring joy and love to others and to cultivate their talents; love, joy and luck will flow back with abundance.

Jupiter in 6. Being generous with co-workers as we attend to our daily duties and tasks, this will attract love and support when crises hit the life. A warning though, to avoid being lazy and over-eating and drinking. Moderation is the key to good health. Those who are drawn to helping others have the potential to become very wise and beloved teachers and healers.

Jupiter in 7. No matter what troubles may arise in marriage, with Jupiter located here, they can be fixed. It enhances all manner of one-on-one relationships. It encourages us to use our wisdom to counsel and help others and to be generous and loving with partners. In return, this will attract loving and wise partners - both professional and personal; who will give all that they have to share in return.

Jupiter in 8. Wisdom will develop if we face up to any major life challenge openheartedly and optimistically, and study wise teachings such as psychology or esoteric writings to help navigate our way out of our troubles. As a consequence, we could become a teacher of metaphysics or psychology and use our gifts to help others transform their lives as we changed. Abundance will flow from joint financial endeavours and legacies.

Jupiter in 9. If we are generally responsible in life, then freedom will be given to walk the Spiritual Path of our choosing, to rise in academic fields or to roam the world at will. Life will support our choices and the direction taken. Wise teachers will appear at a crucial times and direct us to the right path to follow. Blessings and rewards will flow to us because of the generous way understanding and wisdom is shared.

Jupiter in 10. There is good-fortune and prosperity in the professional life. If we do the necessary work and are kind and generous with others as high goals are pursued, the potential to achieve real success in life will be given to us. Luck will boost our chances at crucial times, but we must be sure that opportunities are not squandered. Public recognition and acclaim will come if we share our wisdom generously.

Jupiter in 11. All manner of friendships and groups joined for idealistic or social reasons will be enhanced with this combination. We will grow in wisdom and understanding by participating in shared fellowship and in humanitarian causes for the greater good. Spiritual blessings will flow back because of the generosity and joy shared with fellow-searchers.

Jupiter in 12. Freedom will be given to take time out from mainstream life if that is what is desired. This does not mean hiding away from life to avoid dealing with the challenges that mature people normally face. If one is forced to take time out for whatever reason, blessings, understanding and wisdom will be found when least expected. If one's gifts are used selflessly and generously to help others, blessings will flow back from hidden sources.

8a. Saturn in the Signs

Saturn's placement in each sign - as well as the house it is in and its aspects, represents the types of adversities we can face as a consequence of past-life and current karma.

Saturn in Aries. Behaviours that will attract karma are being too stubborn, headstrong and aggressive. In these cases, karma in Aries can come in the form of having hard authority figures ride roughshod over one's feelings, being unfairly blocked from promotion or advancement, or health problems affecting the head or brain. Related fears are - a fear of taking risks, of initiating new projects or fear of failing as a leader. This can lead to resisting any form of confinement or limitation.

The developments required are to discipline the emotions, to think carefully before acting and to be patient. When these have been learnt the power will be given to face adversity courageously and to be a stable and responsible leader and executive. Positive karma will bring respect for demonstrating wise and intelligent leadership, for having a commanding presence that instils confidence and trust, for being a highly respected pioneer in one's field of interest.

Saturn in Taurus. Saturn's goal is to put the brakes on Taurus' natural urge to squander money on life's luxuries. Behaviours that will attract karma are being very stubborn and rigid in thought, unwilling to let go of one's point of view or of possessions and being greedy. In these cases, karma in Taurus can come in the form of being deprived of possessions, bankruptcy and being unfairly disrespected and devalued. Related fears are - a fear of poverty and losing one's material possessions.

Requirements are to develop solid values (non-material) to live by, to be disciplined with money, to live moderately and give generously to others. When these have been learnt, power is given to stand in life like a mountain, able to overcome all adversity in any form. Positive karma can come as steady prosperity, marked success in the chosen profession or work, becoming a highly respected authority or artist.

Saturn in Gemini. Behaviours that will attract karma are harsh and critical words and being judgmental. In these cases, karma in Gemini can come in the form of receiving hard and insensitive communications from authority figures, denied fair right of response, having opinions ignored or disrespected and health problems with the breathing passages or speech. Related fears are - a fear of speaking out or of not being heard.

The development required is to be disciplined with whatever is said and to not harm people in any way through one's communications. When this has been learnt power is given to be an effective and trusted executive, accuracy in thinking and planning and being a straight talker with a strong and solid intelligence. Positive karma will bring respect for being an honest, trustworthy and wise communicator.

Saturn in Cancer. Behaviours that will attract karma are emotional repression and building defensive walls. In these cases, karma in Cancer can come in the form of rejection, ending up isolated and alone, being misunderstood in the family or with people generally or health problems with digestion. The primary fears are being rejected and never finding true love. This can lead to anxiety disorders and depression.

Bringing down the emotional walls is required and learning to trust again so that people can get close enough to have a truly intimate connection. When this has been done it results in emotional stability, inner strength, trust in oneself and the ability to handle all that life brings. Power is given to honour family responsibilities and to be strong and dispassionate if adversity should strike. Positive karma gives the power to build stable and strong emotional unions and healthy family relations.

Saturn in Leo. Behaviours that will attract karma are violations of the Law of Love, abuse of power, or being dogmatic and autocratic. Karma in Leo can come in the form of being subject to harsh and heartless treatment from powerful authority figures or with the law, being publicly humiliated, being denied children or health problems with the heart, blood or circulation. Related fears are - a fear of not being in control, having no personal power, or a fear of being disrespected or humiliated.

The main developments required are selflessness and the wise use of power professionally and personally. When this has been learnt, rulership opportunities will be given. Positive karma can come in the form of being respected for being a wise and intelligent leader, having a regal presence that strengthens and empowers people, being loved and respected or having a strong heart.

Saturn in Virgo. Behaviours that will attract karma are being mean-spirited, being too judgmental and critical or being too materialistic. In these cases, karma can come in the form of being ruled by a mean-spirited perfectionist, being subject to vindictive gossip, loss of possessions, being forced to work in miserly conditions or suffering intestinal disorders. Related fears are - a fear of losing one's possessions or money, a fear that the desired standards of perfection will never be reached.

Never judging or criticising the character of others is required, as is the cultivation of kindness and finding something nice to say about everyone. When these are learnt, power to be an expert or respected elder in one's profession or craft, or being a master healer will be given. Positive karma will come as success in the chosen profession or work, recognition and respect for one's artisanship or technical skills, scientific expertise, or receiving accolades for selfless service.

Saturn in Libra. Saturn is in its exaltation in Libra and those with this combination usually achieve life success because of their diplomatic skills and mature wisdom. Behaviours that attract karma are primarily to do with relationships - dishonesty, deceit and manipulation of significant others. In these cases, karma in Libra can come in the form of difficulties in personal or sexual relations, attracting partners who are venal or cold, being harshly and unfairly judged by partners, going bankrupt, legal troubles or problems with the urinary tract. Related fears are - a fear of intimacy, a fear of making decisions or of being controlled.

The development that is required and the karmic goal are identical - to generally be fair and just so that balanced, stable and grounded relationships are formed. Cultivating a serene and balanced mind and being fair and honest will help to expedite these changes. When these are being demonstrated it means a judicial intelligence and profound insight and wisdom has been developed. Positive karma will bring success and respect in the legal profession and in personal and professional relationships.

Saturn in Scorpio. Behaviours that will attract karma are vengeful retaliation and attacks on people, underhanded manipulations, misuse of the sexual function, forming obsessive and unhealthy attachments and generally succumbing to the darker side of the nature. In these cases, karma in Scorpio can come in the form of impotency, sexual or emotional abuse, being stalked by bad people, unpleasant psychic occurrences, sex-related diseases or psychological disorders. Related fears are - a fear of being annihilated or killed, a fear of retribution, a fear of losing control, a fear of the dark and of the supernatural, or sexual dysfunction. Some with this combination can suppress the emotions with all the dangers to health that can bring.

The developments required are to overcome low desire and delusion by learning to hold the mind steady in the light of wisdom and making decisions based on facts and truth. When successful it means that emotional stability and an acute intelligence that can delve to the root of a problem has been developed. The power to see challenges through until success has been achieved is present and so is the ability to endure adverse hardship and to withstand the darkest evil. Positive karma can come in the form of being a highly respected authority in esotericism, in healing or psychology and general professional, leadership and life success.

Saturn in Sagittarius. The behaviours that primarily attract karma are irresponsibility, greed and wounding people's feelings with thoughtless and harmful words. In these cases, karma in Sagittarius can come in the form of being harshly judged or verbally attacked, being treated shabbily and "ripped off", being the subject of scandal, difficulties with religion or cults or having one's freedom curbed and excesses exposed. Related fears are - a fear of losing one's freedom, one's right to speak out and sometimes a mistrust of foreigners.

The developments required are to demonstrate responsible and ethical behaviours and increased focus and discipline when pursuing ideals and higher goals. This will mean that the life energies are being used more wisely - another goal. Positive karma will bring status, success and respect in higher learning fields such as in academia, philosophy, religion or the Ancient Mysteries.

Saturn in Capricorn. People with Saturn in its own sign, are very comfortable with working hard and carrying responsibilities - especially when this leads to the satisfaction of their worldly ambitions. They make excellent executives and managers and if the law is observed, are destined for professional life success.

Behaviours that will attract karma are any violations of the Law of Love and greedy ambition. In these cases, karma can come in the form of being rejected, being controlled by hard and uncompromising authorities, going bankrupt, having one's dishonest dealings exposed, being humiliated, loss of status and power and being incarcerated. Related fears are - a fear of authority figures, fear of never being successful, or a fear that one is not lovable or likeable.

The developments required are greater sensitivity to the feelings of others and demonstrated integrity and honesty in all business and political dealings. Positive karma will bring success, status and prosperity, becoming a respected elder and leader and taking initiation - which means an expansion of wisdom.

Saturn in Aquarius. The behaviour that attracts karma is being so isolated in a world of one's own thoughts and opinions that one becomes separative and judgmental of people. Selfish individualism is another trait that will attract Saturn's attention. In these cases, karma in Aquarius can come in the form of rejection by friends, being exposed for intellectual errors or theft of intellectual property, harshly judged by rigid-minded authority figures, rejected by friends, being a victim of rebellious action or problems with the ankles, nerves or circulation. Related fears are - a fear of expressing one's true thoughts in case one is wrong or is attacked, a fear of not measuring up intellectually, a fear of having one's freedom or independence taken away.

The main developments that are required are inclusiveness and selflessness. When these are being demonstrated it means the mind is now balanced with wisdom. Positive karma will bring success and respect in the chosen profession or work and for new scientific discoveries or achievements; it will enable solid friendships to be formed and finding one's soul group - like-minded people.

Saturn in Pisces. Saturn in a water sign can lead to trouble with emotional expression, for instance, emotional repression will attract karma. So will an overindulgence in food or drink, addictive behaviours, an extreme love of comfort and a lack compassion and kindness towards others. In these cases, karma can come in the form of being incarcerated and harshly treated, carrying heavy responsibilities without recognition or reward, unfairly forced to sacrifice the life for others, developing a chronic illness or an emotional disorder. Some related fears are - a fear of the unknown, a fear that one will become a victim of others and life, a fear of never finding love or a fear of the religious life.

The developments required are to be more free-flowing with feelings and more responsible in their expression. Positive Saturn in Pisces gives emotional stability, inner strength, self-confidence and ease with carrying heavy responsibilities. Positive karma will bring respect and recognition as a teacher, healer or spiritual leader.

8b. Saturn in the Houses.

This is where karma will be met, where we should work hard and shoulder responsibilities without complaint, where we should be scrupulously honest in our responses; and also, where we can achieve stable success through hard work.

Saturn in 1. There is a reserved approach, sometimes a fear of facing life and of progressing forwards. Karma requires a disciplined and responsible approach to life, but not rigidity or being judgmental. Respect will be gained by being prudent and honest with others.

Saturn in 2. Karma requires that we are conservative with resources and disciplined and responsible with personal money. Related fears are - a fear of being poor or deprived, or a fear of not being respected or valued. Prosperity and respect will be gained by developing self-respect, working hard and being very honest in all financial transactions.

Saturn in 3. Karma requires that we are disciplined and responsible in daily communications and with relatives and neighbours; this is the lesson being taught - to speak the truth, but not harshly. Harmlessness in thought and speech is the goal. This will win respect so that one's opinions will be valued.

Saturn in 4. There is karma in the home, with the parents and family. Something old, rigid or toxic, needs to be healed or cut away. Often this placement forces us to take on family leadership and responsibility - a karmic debt from a past life. Being honest and fair in all familial interactions will build a solid foundation for the life.

Saturn in 5. There are extra responsibilities with children and lovers, which should be embraced to repay karmic debts. A few with this combination may even be denied children. This does not mean being denied love, light-hearted recreation or joy. Those with this combination just have to earn it by being fair and kind with younger, more vulnerable souls.

Saturn in 6. Being responsible and exact in our daily duties and working hard for a living is required. At some time, those with this combination will be asked to provide very solid support for work-mates and should give this support unstintingly and without hesitation. The development of excellent skills will help build a successful professional life. It is important to be flexible in attitude - a rigid mind equals a rigid body and joints.

Saturn in 7. There is an underlying fear of rejection, both generally and in important partnerships and those with this combination should avoid trying to control others to feel secure. If relationships are a test, there is more to discover about oneself and how to interact in a more balanced manner. Enduring love and loyalty will come when the lesson has been learnt.

Saturn in 8. A rigid pattern of behaviour that has been resistant to change requires adjustment. In some, the misuse of sexual force in past lives will bring consequences so that there are periods of forced celibacy, impotency, frigidity or disease. Karma is trying to balance the scales. Being responsible in the use of force, metaphysical knowledge and with other people's money is required. Success will bring respect, as a healer, psychologist or occultist.

Saturn in 9. There is unfinished karmic business concerning morals, religion or with someone or something that has a foreign connection. The urge to big-note oneself as the expert, the one who knows everything, should be avoided. The wise use of knowledge and learning will bring rewards and respect in academic, religious and spiritual circles - or alternatively, involving a foreign country.

Saturn in 10. Karma is in the professional house, which means the pursuit of fame and glory must be based on integrity and honesty. If not, one may rise to a high place, only to be followed by public humiliation and loss. Humility is required and the responsible use of power. When demonstrated, solid success in the career will follow and respect from the public.

Saturn in 11. There is something to be learnt about the type of group associations that are formed and friends chosen to spend time with. Now the task is to choose associates and groups that are respectable and that abide within the law - or suffer the consequences. Positively, Saturn in the 11th gives the ability to form long-term friendships with honourable people who will be supportive when times are difficult. Success that carries responsibilities in politics is also a possibility.

Saturn in 12. Forced retirement out of the main-stream is an option with this combination. The cause may vary, such as ill health, going to prison (this may be psychological), self-isolation to complete projects or a search for self-understanding. This will give time to reflect on life and any decisions made that were not wise or that need reconstructing. Others may choose to serve quietly behind the scenes, helping souls who are lost or are seriously ill and who need rehabilitation. This isolation can be temporary, and lay the foundation for a new cycle of positive involvement with life.

9a. Uranus in the Signs.

Uranus in each sign represents how each generation expresses its independence and changes the world.

Uranus in Aries (2011-2020). The goal for this generation is to bring forwards a new crop of leaders that are original and independent in their approach. "Movers and shakers," they must break free from traditional aspects in society that are seen to be old and limiting to human freedom and lead humanity into a new and ethically higher direction. However, in the masses who are still emotional, this force will increase impulsive, erratic and selfish behaviours that will create conflict and chaos in the world. The individual task is to reorganise the desire nature and develop the scientific mind so that life is viewed more logically. At the higher level, Uranus gives the gifts of intellectual brilliance, intuitive leadership, the will to change things for the better and power to manifest higher goals.

Uranus in Taurus (2019-2027). For this generation, the goal is to bring in new technologies and innovative systems and methods in business and finance, so that the economy and institutions that run it deliver better services for all the people of the world. Banking systems must be reformed and corruption rooted out. However, Uranus falls in this sign. People can be conflict-ridden, erratic and some may have bizarre appetites and desires. Many will succumb to selfish greed and consequently, world finances will worsen for a while and this will create the demand for change. The individual task is to purify the lower appetites and direct desire into higher, creative projects. When this is done, the finer qualities of Taurus can manifest - creative brilliance in business or the arts, power to create harmony and beauty, a steely will and the power of goodness that can destroy darkness and evil.

Uranus in Gemini (2027-2034). The goal for this generation is to bring in new and innovative communications methods so that what people think and have to say can be more rapidly distributed across the world. Generally, this combination gives an original and versatile perception and if circumstances are favourable, mental brilliance. However, in emotional individuals, duality is emphasised instead and the electrification of mind-stuff can cause unreliable and erratic thinking that results in trouble and strife. The task is to resolve duality and this can be done by concentrating on one matter at a time until it has been concluded. Focus and concentration will help to overcome the instability in the lower nature. At the higher level, Uranus gives intellectual and intuitive brilliance and the power to influence people through words. Such people are "Messengers of the Gods." They are able to teach complex esoteric truths in a clear and scientific manner and consequently, can awaken minds to new and higher thoughts.

Uranus in Cancer (2033-2040). This generation's goal is to revolutionise the family unit and what "family" means; to modernise the way families are formed so they better serve modern cultural expectations. However, individually, this combination stirs up the astral nature, which can demonstrate as unpredictable mood swings, explosive emotional eruptions and rebellious outbursts that destabilise and disrupt the family and emotional life. Home life can be transient and chaotic - Uranus is the change planet. The task is to intelligently reorganise the way the emotions are expressed so they are calmer and more balanced. This will enable Uranus to unfold the higher spiritual gifts of Cancer. For example, it gives the will to obliterate ignorance through the application of wisdom in its many forms. People at this level are intuitive Light Bearers who use original methods to transform and improve conditions in mankind.

Uranus in Leo (2039-2046). The goal for this generation is to bring forwards a new crop of leaders and rulership systems and methods, so that the masses are governed in a more dignified and benevolent way. Alternatively, to produce a greater range of original and unique artistic expressions and productions. Individually, there is flair, fire and creative brilliance - as a leader, in the arts or in any field where original ideas and work are admired. The will is strengthened and so is the need to be independent and free of any constraint. However, the unregenerated ego will rebel against authority and demand that all should look to it for leadership and rule. It is an autocratic bully and a troublemaker in groups. The task is to decentralise the ego and render the nature more inclusive. This will align the heart and mind. Then, leadership brilliance will be demonstrated and charismatic magnetism that will attract many followers.

Uranus in Virgo (1961-1969). For this generation, the goal is to revolutionise medicine and healing, to bring in new and innovative methods and health systems so that the people are better served. Individually, rebelliousness is expressed in practical ways. Such as, avoiding the servitude of a boring work-life by acquiring wealth and material possessions; or finding ingenious ways to use modern technology to make a living. But generally, the task is to use the intelligence to serve the higher goal of this combination to improve medicine and health. When wisdom blossoms in the heart and mind, intellectual brilliance and the higher intuition will demonstrate. Those at this level have the will and expertise to raise the health or work conditions and standards in the community and even across the world.

Uranus in Libra (1968-1975). The goal for this generation is to revolutionise relationships generally and marriage specifically. At the broader level, so that modern cultural expectations are better served; at the higher level, so that the union in consciousness between soul-wisdom and the selfish personality is expedited. Individually however, this combination brings wilfulness and strengthens a desire for independence that can cause disruptions and divorce.

There will be many short-lived unions and some may seem bizarre to others or at the least, very unorthodox. The development task is to learn from these experiences and form unions that while honouring traditional commitments, also allow for greater self-expression and freedom. At the higher level, this combination gives a brilliant, judicious intellect that has power to harmonise complex disputes and conflicts.

Uranus in Scorpio (1974-1982). For this generation the goal is to bring to the surface the darkness that lies hidden in human nature - the hate and evil, so they can be destroyed. In some, this force feeds the lower appetites and boosts desire so that the emotions, passions and wilful determinations are enhanced. There may be stealth, stalking, violence and friends becoming predators. Intense sexual urges take some in a dark and illegal direction. Uranus strengthens the intellect and it helps those with this combination to fight their way from the darkness of illusion and lower-desire, to the light of clear-intellect. A scientific program like Raja Yoga (spiritual control through the mind), will be beneficial. Esoterically, Scorpio is considered to be the greater burning ground of trial and testing of the emotional-desire nature. In those who are successful, Uranus (which is exalted in this sign), bestows the intuitive powers of the White Magician - an advanced soul who uses the forces of nature to bring about the greater collective good.

Uranus in Sagittarius (1981-1989). This generation's goal is to revolutionise humanity's beliefs and morals. It does this by bringing to light superstitions, falsehoods or outdated notions that bind the human soul so they can be seen for what they are and radically changed or eliminated. Uranus is comfortable in Sagittarius - the urge to be free is in the sign of freedom, galvanising a love of adventure and travelling. But at the lower level, influenced by the "centaur", the animal appetites are enhanced. Life is adventurous but irresponsible. Friends are sought to carouse with and over-indulge food and drink, to do risky things with and to rebel and cause trouble. The task is to re-direct this force into creative projects, to find and follow a higher way. When the scientific mind develops and esoteric training unfolds the spiritual gifts of Sagittarius, it produces brilliant teachers of the wisdom and true intuitive prophets.

Uranus in Capricorn (1988-1997). The areas in life this generation has to revolutionise are government and the rule of law - rehabilitation must be emphasised rather than punishment. To achieve this, the combination gives business and executive brilliance, heightened ambition and a compelling drive to succeed. The more active, Uranian types in the masses will rebel against authority, conservatism and any restriction of their freedom. Demanding to live by their own laws and dictates, they will try to force these onto others. The development task is to re-direct this power and ambition towards higher, non-material things in life. For instance, in support of ethical and humanitarian organisations that contribute to overall world good. At the higher level, Uranus in Capricorn gives the will, power and ability, to manifest the Plan of God on earth.

Uranus in Aquarius (1996-2004). This generation of independent individuals will refuse to conform to the "ordinary or boring." They are rebellious and unpredictable and will seek out like-minded souls with whom to engineer change more in line with their ideals. Their generational task is to promote human-rights and brotherliness, to transform and revolutionise society on all levels so that its systems and methods benefit the greater, collective good. The individual task is to use the gifts of originality and inventive insight, scientific ability and intellectual brilliance to benefit local projects in the community. At the lower level however, this force will galvanise individuals who have narrow and self-serving goals and who will cause chaos and anarchy when they cannot get their way. The most advanced people who are influenced by this sign are the true World Servers or Water Bearers of humanity. Uranus located here gives the opportunity for those who are born with this combination, to raise humanity up through science or esotericism.

Uranus in Pisces (2004-2012). This generation's goal is to revolutionise non-governmental groups and organisations in the world that care for the suffering in humanity; to modernise them and make them more effective. Individually however, those who are emotional could have their delusions galvanised, causing them to seek out "spiritual" experiences (such as religious cults), which excite and feed the sensual appetites and that bring emotional satisfaction. On another level, fundamentalist religions that rely on superstition and control by fear could feel threatened and retaliate by being aggressive with their particular brand of Old Testament rules. The development task is to use the intelligence to see through delusion and to make wiser decisions based on logic and facts. Pisces produces world saviours who radiate the wisdom and compassion of Deity to comfort and save the suffering. Those with this combination can contribute to this work.

9b. Uranus in the Houses.

The house in which Uranus is located is where we are required to make all things new, where we should take calculated risks and experiment with the new so that we can let go of negative patterns and align more completely with soul-wisdom.

Uranus in 1. Uranus in the house of personal affairs encourages us to be daring, to be different, to develop a new approach to life and create a new image. It urges us to use our initiative, to be original, to always move forwards. Uranus rules science, so this placement also encourages us to make decisions using reason and logic. Like-minded fellows will become friends.

Uranus in 2. A radical change is required in one's attitude towards personal possessions. The goal is to free oneself from the desire for money and wealth, so this does not control the personal values and life direction. New and higher values should be cultivated and resources should be shared with friends and the community. Finances may be chaotic, but generally, original ideas and methods can be used to generate income.

Uranus in 3. Change is required in day to day communications with relatives, neighbours and in the close environment generally. Those with this combination should endeavour to be more independent in thought and speech and more direct in what they say. Shocking people out of their complacency with the unvarnished truth could be part of this experience. Communications can be used to help awaken people's minds.

Uranus in 4. Change is required in the family home and relationships. A more independent approach should be taken to counter-balance old toxic patterns that are corruptive to the family unit. There will be many changes at home so being prepared to adapt or to move will be advantageous. For some there will be opportunities to build a spiritual ashram or to hold occult or scientific discussions with friends at home.

Uranus in 5. Unusual creativity is given with this placement, and/ or the ability to be highly innovative and original in bringing joy to others. There will be unorthodox relationships with children and lovers, who will come into the life in unusual ways. A few with this combination may be denied having their own biological children or have them by resorting to modern science. These creative talents can be used to awaken young minds to higher truths.

Uranus in 6. A more daring and independent approach at work is required and more innovative means to generate a living. Life will support the development of skills in science, with new technology and in alternative areas of health, care and medicine. There could be nervous trouble if things become too chaotic and unmanageable. Treating such disorders and general health problems with alternative medicine will be beneficial. So, will finding original ways to de-stress.

Uranus in 7. Radical change is required in relationships to counter-balance toxic ways of relating that cause divorce. There is a need to be independent in all important partnerships, including not relying on others to supply one's emotional needs. Uranus in this house sometimes indicates divorce. This is not necessarily true, but a difficult relationship would have to dramatically change for the better if it is to survive. Uranus in 7 is helpful if we have to walk away from a bad union and start life over again.

Uranus in 8. Radical transformation is required in the use of sexual force and the handling of joint resources. To facilitate healthy change, sudden and challenging events will force those with this combination to face up to things they have been doing that are detrimental to their spiritual health and general well-being and make the necessary changes. Alternative, psychological or esoteric therapeutical approaches will help.

Uranus in 9. Change and renewal are required in moral and religious beliefs. An exploration of alternative philosophies and teachings should be explored and outdated notions that are limiting personal growth should be eliminated. Travel across the globe will bring diverse experiences and points of view and this will help formulate a new set of moral codes that are more in-line with contemporary spiritual understandings. This placement also gives the talent and ability to present the Ageless Wisdom in new and exciting ways.

Uranus in 10. Exploring more than one career path before settling into a groove is required. Even then, there will be many changes in the career and it is likely to involve science, internet, new technologies or be in a radically new and alternative direction. Either way, the placement gives the opportunity to become renowned for one's unique talents and original ideas. Authority figures will be friends.

Uranus in 11. A renewal of the people and groups chosen to associate with socially and politically, is required. Being daring, radical and experimental when choosing friends will help find people, we are more in tune with. Uranus is the revolutionary planet and we are encouraged to rebel against people and ideas that are unfair and harmful to the greater good. This combination gives an ability to inspire our group-fellows to move in a new and higher direction.

Uranus in 12. The eradication of any patterns of thought or behaviours that are negative and self-defeating is required. This means freeing oneself from subconscious fears and mystical nonsense that controls conscious reality. These negative core beliefs should be brought into light and destroyed with the power of scientific and rational thought. Then, the same can be done to help other people who are similarly affected. Many hidden friends will support attempts to progress forwards in life.

10a. Neptune in the Signs.

In the signs, Neptune represents how each generation expresses its idealism, its glamours and delusions; and individually, what needs to be refined to be more discerning.

Neptune in Aries (1862-1876, 2025-2039). The ideal to be achieved in the first sign Aries, is to produce free-thinking and innovative spiritual leaders and teachers who will guide their followers and faiths into more inclusive ways. However, in the masses, religious fanaticism will flourish along with the emergence of messiahs - true and false. The latter, they will encourage their people to believe that their group or country is the best, the strongest and bravest and to go out militantly to prove it. The Crusades in the Middle-Ages are of this type. On a personal level, the developmental task is to bring about spiritual rebirth or renewal in oneself, to see through illusion and to stand in one's truth.

Neptune in Taurus (1876-1890). In Taurus, the ideal is to dissolve the deep attachment to material life that is embedded in humanity and to refine its values. Artists, musicians and other creative workers all help in the higher task of spiritualising and beautifying humanity. In the process, old selfish attitudes and financial and business structures that do not serve the greater collective good will dissolve and new ones arise. So will new ideas and practical systems that allow for a freer flow of money and resources into areas of need. However, in the masses, values can be confused and greed enhanced so that materialistic people feel entitled to take as much as they can. On a personal level, the task is to resist the sensual lure of the "bull", refine the desire life and spiritualise one's values.

Neptune in Gemini (1889-1902). The ideal to be achieved in Gemini, is to bring forwards new spiritual teachers who will communicate ideas that help humanity become a more inclusive, humanitarian civilisation. However, delusion in Gemini manifests as confusion, misinformation and misunderstandings. Fanatics, who incite hate and evil, coat their words in a glamorous facade so they appeal to man's lower nature - Adolf Hitler is an example. On a personal level, the task is to overcome illusion and hold the mind in the clear light of truth and reality, to enlighten the mind with inspired thought and higher esoteric teachings.

Neptune in Cancer (1916-1928). In Cancer, the ideal is to build the human family into a lighted house. This means refining the way we treat each other so there is greater empathy and compassion. It also means highlighting the vital role that family-life plays in the creation of a healthy and moral society - and giving the family unit and parents greater support. However, as long as selfishness dominates the national psyche, then feelings of entitlement about property and land will rise. World War I erupted in the last cycle as Germany tried to expand its boundaries. The personal task is to clear emotional confusion and transmute selfish desire into a sense of shared inclusiveness.

Neptune in Leo (1915-1928). Neptune's primary task is to bring forwards kind and compassionate leaders who will inspire the masses to follow civilization's highest ideals. However, as long as selfishness and greed dominate, dictators and autocrats will rise who believe they have a divine right to rule and take what they want. This happened in the last cycle and the masses followed in their wake. When Neptune re-enters Leo in 2080, a greater number of evolved souls will seek high-office and use their power to benefit the masses. At the personal level, the task is to be more sensitive to the soul (to love and wisdom) and less responsive to the arrogant ego; to be more inclusive and less autocratic.

Neptune in Virgo (1928-1942). Neptune's passage through Virgo will have a refining effect upon work and health conditions for the masses. For instance, the implementation of more liberal work conditions and subtle improvements in the health system. But Neptune is in detriment in Virgo and under this transit materialism can deepen. For instance, a desire to increase one's material assets and lands, even if it means taking property that belongs to others. World War II started when the Nazis took possession of other countries. On a personal level, Neptune illumines the substance of the lower nature so that the Christ-Spirit (love and wisdom) can express itself through the mind and heart. As this proceeds, the attractions of the material life dissolve and new and higher ideals emerge.

Neptune in Libra (1942-1956). The ideal to be achieved in Libra, is improvement and liberalisation in right human relations and to this end, Neptune's transit refines relationships and sexual habits. It will also liberalise the justice system so that it can better meet the needs of the masses. Old out-dated laws will change and new ideals about marriage and sex will arise and be expressed. In the masses, the last transit gave rise to the liberalisation of sexual expression, which really played out in the 60's. On a personal level, the task is to refine and balance the way relationships are formed and conducted, to be more kind, just and compassionate with partners - intimate and professional. Many idealists who will want to change the laws on marriage and sexual intercourse will be born in this period.

Neptune in Scorpio (1956-1970). In Scorpio, the ideal is to dissolve the darkness that lies within human nature - the hatred and evil; and consequently, to heal people psychologically. Refinement of sexual expression and all matters to do with death are associated with this. Neptune has a distorting effect on those who are susceptible - twisted idealism and unhealthy tastes may rise so that monstrous things are done. Individually, the task is to refine emotional and sexual expression and overcome illusion. Scorpio's Eagle symbol gives the clue on how to do this - take flight like an eagle (rise up into the mind) and soar above the earth (view life from that elevated point of view).

Neptune in Sagittarius (1970-1984). Overall, this transit, has a spiritualising effect upon humanity. The new generation will search for truth, follow their ideals and seek their Holy Grail. In the deluded, Neptune feeds glamours such as religious fanaticism and militancy to achieve one's goals - during the last cycle, terrorism took root. On a personal level, the task is to direct one's life towards the "mountain-top", to always follow the highest ideal and to learn from life so that wisdom develops. In this period, many will find their way to the Spiritual Path and future spiritual teachers will be born - both true teachers and false.

Neptune in Capricorn (1984-1998). Neptune's higher task in this material sign is to dissolve humanity's deep attachment to the material life and to encourage the masses to seek out more subtle treasures and rewards. For instance, serving the greater good through ethical business practices. However, Neptune falls in this sign so its positive effect weakens. In the recent cycle in the USA, materially inspired politicians dissolved regulations that curbed unfair profiteering so that greed flourished. On a personal level, the task is to be ambitious for higher and finer things in life and to manifest these ideals practically.

Neptune in Aquarius (1998-2012). The ideal is to improve human society through science. But as always with a Neptune transit, the ideal is distorted in some. In the recent transit, scientists hired by corporate interests such as the tobacco industry, deliberately confused scientific facts for profit and gain. The same is being done with climate change. Many future scientists will have been born in this recent cycle and in the future, they will lead the way in solving serious problem facing mankind such as the climate problem. On a personal level, the task is to bring the heart and mind into union and to dissolve any impediments that prevent the expression of universal brotherhood. Raja Yoga, a scientific meditation technique would benefit this group.

Neptune in Pisces (2012-2025). Neptune's task in this universal sign, is to subtly redefine the ideals that drive the race forwards - spiritually and materially. As part of this, it will highlight the bad effects of greed so that there will ground-swell in the public to improve things. In the current cycle for instance, attention has been thrown onto corporate greed and the immoral practices of profiteering bankers and other money manipulators. In Pisces, Neptune deepens delusion in those who have not yet developed discrimination. Consequently, such people blindly follow bad leaders as if they were Messiah's. On a personal level, the task is to be more discerning - to overcome delusion and emotionalism and to stand in truth and reality.

10b. Neptune in the Houses.

In Neptune's house we may be looking at life "through rose-coloured glasses." If so, this is where we must deal with the affairs of the house and relate to the people we meet there, practically and discriminatively.

Neptune in 1. Emotional people will look at life through the distorting and glamorous Neptune light, so that things look nicer that they are. This must be overcome. The goal is to avoid being naive about life and to be more discriminating. In spiritually advanced people, there is a clear and transparent approach to life and a compassionate urge to help the suffering.

Neptune in 2. People who have emotional attachments to money, will lack of discernment in how they use it and this could lead to financial losses. It is important to be scrupulously honest with money and possessions and clear about how it is used. But generally, there is a desire to give all to help people. Much good can be done if this is applied intelligently. Neptune in 2, could also cause the leakage of personal vitality.

Neptune in 3. Communications are confused. This is caused either by a tendency to lie by omission, fudging the truth, or naïvely believing everything that is heard. There is a need to train the mind to think clearly, with discernment and to speak the plain truth. Working positively, this placement gives the gift of communicating in a way that inspires and heals people.

Neptune in 4. Something is not right in the home. For example, a parent could be an alcoholic, there could be sexual abuse, or religion is being used to manipulate family members. There is a great need to be very honest in family discussions and to talk about toxic things - not avoid them just to keep the peace or to avoid a scandal. Potentially, love and compassion in the home environment will be nurturing and loving for all.

Neptune in 5. This placement can give inspired creativity and the ability to create beautiful works of art that uplift people. More seriously, it can sometimes indicate something unhealthy going on in relations with children or lovers. If so, everything needs to be brought into the open and dealt with so healing can begin. If this approach is taken, in time there can be compassion and forgiveness.

Neptune in 6. Confusion or unhappiness at work will result in the weakening of vitality and strange illnesses. If this is the case, it is important to be clear and honest about what is going on and to avoid going into denial. Positively, it suggests Neptune-like skills and talents will be of benefit in earning a living in careers such as being a spiritual worker, healer or counsellor, a swim or sailing coach, artist or poet.

Neptune in 7. Intimate relations need refining. It is possible that a lack of trust in oneself to be able to handle rejection is behind the confusion that rises in close unions. This pattern will attract people who are confused, deceitful, weak or addicted. There is a great need to trust, to be transparent and honest - with oneself. This will enable truly beautiful relationships to be formed with people who are both sensitive and ethical.

Neptune in 8. Something unhealthy in the life or psyche needs to be transformed. For instance, an unhealthy emotional attachment to a person or to a cult, or perverse sexual habits or desires. Either way, discrimination is required, sexual cleanness and integrity when handling other people's money. Positively, there is a gift for spiritual healing and for the development of metaphysical gifts. These should be used selflessly.

Neptune in 9. Being hoodwinked by a false teacher is possible. Any message that is insulting to the intelligence or that manipulates through false flattery, should be avoided. If discernment is applied when choosing a path to follow, the right and ethical teacher will appear. The potential exists, if the right teaching or philosophy is followed - and discrimination is applied; to become a spiritual teacher oneself.

Neptune in 10. Best careers are those that involve healing or the spiritual - or for the more creative, in the arts or film. Sometimes it may take some time and many attempts to find a suitable vocation. It is likely that a spiritual experience at work, or an important teacher coming into the life could lead to a positive change in life direction. The potential exists to become someone to whom people look up to, revere and idolise.

Neptune in 11. There is a past-life tendency to be drawn to people who have unhealthy addictions or habits, or who are confused about what they want from life. Consequently, friends and groups need to be reassessed to ensure they are healthy and positive for the current and future life direction. With discernment, the potential exists to find the ideal group in which to thrive and grow spiritually and psychologically.

Neptune in 12. It is possible that past-life religious beliefs that cause fear and guilt are undermining resolve and the ability to move forwards. If so, these need to be pulled up into the light of day so they can be eliminated. Ultra-sensitive to suffering, this placement can lead to the development of compassion and understanding. Giving selflessly to help life's victims will bring many blessings from unseen sources.

11a. Pluto in the Signs.

Pluto transforms each generation it passes through. The negative traits of the sign are highlighted and it is the responsibility of each group to transmute these negatives into their equivalent positives.

Pluto in Aries (1824-1853). This combination gives the power to lead and to initiate; consequently, it brings to the surface a desire for prominence and dominance. In the past, this led to military aggression as groups and countries jostled to further their selfish interests. At the same time, powerful leaders emerge to lead their people's interests on both higher and lower levels. On a personal level, the challenge is to purge emotional impulses that cloud good judgement and to think before acting.

Pluto in Taurus (1853-1883). In this material sign, Pluto's task is to purge the race of greed and avarice, thereby clearing the way for higher values to emerge. As a consequence, materialism is stimulated, the greedy become extreme in their profligacy and disputes over money, property and territory will rise. In response, the suffering masses will demand change and greater accountability and fairness in finance and business, triggering reforms. The personal goal is to develop higher values to live by and to be moderate with spending.

Pluto in Gemini (1883-1914). Pluto's goal in Gemini is to purge the collective mind of ugly and dangerous ideas, thereby clearing the way for higher and more illumined thoughts that will benefit the collective good. Consequently, during this cycle, powerful information blocs and dynamic orators of the lower type emerge and use evil words and ideas to whip up hatred and prejudice. Nazi Adolf Hitler began his rise to power in the previous cycle. Such people are counter-balanced by powerful voices of reason (Roosevelt, Churchill). Purifying the quality of the thought life and learning to speak with goodwill is required at a personal level.

Pluto in Cancer. This cycle (1914-1939), purges aggressive nationalism. Fears about security, family and property arise and some will try to take what belongs to others. This period spanned World War I and the beginning of WWII, which were fights over land and territory. In the aftermath of the wars, the masses, revolted by human-rights abuses demanded greater protection for the rights of all people and the United Nations was born. Pluto in Cancer clears the way for Light Bearers, the wise and intelligent who work to uplift the masses. On a personal level, the challenge is to be balanced in emotional expression and scrupulously honest. This will have an enormous transformative influence for good on the immediate family.

Pluto in Leo (1939-1957). Arrogant war-mongering and aggression is purged in this cycle. In some people, Pluto's transit stimulates a sense of being entitled to take whatever one wants and it brings forwards autocrats who promote this view. It also empowers leaders who will stand in opposition. This happened in World War II, where Roosevelt and Churchill challenged Hitler and Tito. The atrocities committed then, taught society to put in place steps to curb the ambitions of dictators and warmongers. The personal challenge is to develop self-awareness and positive self-rulership, to transform selfish aggression into selfless assertiveness.

Pluto in Virgo (1957-1971). In this earth sign, Pluto purges rank materialism. Consequently, an obsessive need to acquire material possessions and financial gain is stimulated in the masses. The recent transit gave rise to the Consumer Age, the "I want to be a millionaire by age 30" attitude. Greed will gradually be purged as the masses become intelligent and united enough to enforce demands for fairer economic systems. At the higher level, Pluto in Virgo empowers intelligent and hardworking souls who seek no glory, wishing only to serve. Personally, we are required to be less materialistic and more altruistic and giving.

Pluto in Libra (1971-1984). The evil ways that people treat each other are dragged into the light so they can be dealt with. For instance, violence in marriage, sexual exploitation, prostitution, masochism and paedophilia. Once before the public gaze, a mass demand for increased or fairer legal rights and protections for victims will arise. Pluto in Libra empowers legislators, diplomats and moderators who fight for fairness and justice. On a personal level, transforming unhealthy sexual or inter-personal habits is required.

Pluto in Scorpio (1984-1995). This cycle purges dark and evil tendencies in the human psyche, such as paedophilia, prostitution, violence and torture. It brings them up into public awareness so that a cry for change will arise. Pluto in Scorpio empowers healers, psychologists and anyone generally who fights to help or to heal the sick, weak and helpless. The personal challenge is to fight for one's spiritual freedom, to transform the "dark" side of the nature and bring it into the light - then help others to do the same.

Pluto in Sagittarius (1995-2009). The goal is to purge excess generally and corruption in religious institutions. To this end, greed is exposed and evil practices in faith-based organisations. Public revulsion will bring a demand for change and this has happened in this cycle with the exposure of paedophilia in church and government organisations. Inspirational teachers and visionaries will also emerge to direct humanity into the new and higher direction. The transit forces us individually to rid the life of excess and to follow a higher path. Some with this combination may become powerful spiritual teachers.

Pluto in Capricorn (2009-2024). This cycle purges depravity and greed from governments and big business organisations. Profiteering will become so brazen the public will demand that ethical changes are made and put into law to curb such behaviours. Pluto in Capricorn also empowers executives and leaders of both the higher and lower types; it either solidifies greed in the nature or helps to release us from it. On a personal level, those who are ready to take initiation (a marked expansion of consciousness) will be tested to see if they have overcome unhealthy ambition and are free from materialism. If so, rewards will follow.

Pluto in Aquarius (2024-2044). The goal with this combination, is to eliminate separativeness in society and systems of supply that are unfair. First it intensifies selfish individualism and gross inequality in the distribution of goods and services. This will trigger a reaction in the masses and a demand for fairer systems. Pluto in Aquarius empowers groups and scientists who promote radical ideas, whether high or low. On a personal level, the challenge is to make friends with people, to join or support groups or organizations whose endeavours are to reform society for the greater good.

Pluto in Pisces. When Pluto returns here in 2044 to 2068, it will bring another opportunity to purge all that stands between the soul of man and his spiritual freedom. Pluto in Pisces empowers the masses, who without wise leadership, can turn into unruly mobs. Fundamentalist religious leaders who perceive their controls over the masses are slipping, will try to bring back the past in autocratic and cruel ways. The challenge for society is to reform outdated institutions and religions that no longer serve the common good. On a personal level, the goal is to eliminate excess from the life so there is more time and energy available for artistic and creative projects. These kinds of endeavours will have a positive and transformative effect upon the life.

11b. Pluto in the Houses.

Pluto's house is where we must eliminate and transform an old and obsessive habit and make a brand-new beginning.

Pluto in 1. Pluto gives a steely will and people with this combination are often leaders in their field. But in most, the approach to life needs transforming so this power is not misused - there is a need to be less controlling and obsessive, more flexible and detached. On a personal level, when spiritual-will (the command of power for the higher good) has been developed, those with this combination can become leaders with the power to beneficially change the lives of others.

Pluto in 2. Entrenched materialistic attitudes and values must be eliminated, which means speculation can be risky - there could be mega-gains or huge losses. The wisest use of this force is to be minimal when acquiring possessions and to transform one's personal values so there is balance regarding money and possessions. This will bring good karma and prosperity.

Pluto in 3. With this combination, thoughts and words will have a powerful effect for good or ill. Consequently, if a serious matter arises, we must be especially careful that what is said is the truth and that it is being presented in the kindest way possible. Otherwise, there could be serious repercussions. The goal is to be assertive but also harmless in thought and speech. This does not mean being silent if something has to be said. If the local neighbourhood, siblings or other relatives are abusive or dangerous, drastic action should be taken to right things. This may mean cutting that toxicity away and / or moving to a radically new location.

Pluto in 4. Pluto located in the family home needs to be handled with extreme care. Family dynamics could be manipulative and there could be a very toxic family pattern or person that needs to be cut out of the life. Abuse should be reported to authorities and family ties severed if necessary. Sometimes a parent may not be around so those left behind are vulnerable to exploitation or abuse. Positively, those with this combination are given the inner strength to transform their "roots" and to build a new and healthy family environment.

Pluto in 5. The placement is a double-edged sword. On one hand it gives the power to create incredibly gifted children or works of art that can transform people's lives. On the other, it can highlight a tendency to be intensely obsessive with children or lovers, or the reverse situation where we become the target of fixation. If we act circumspectly and set healthy boundaries in these relationships, they can be transformed into something incredible. Sometimes, for karmic reasons, we may be denied having children.

Pluto in 6. There will be disruptions in the working life. This could be because the place of employment goes bankrupt, because we no longer want to put up with a toxic work environment or because of a serious health condition. This will provide the opportunity to assess what we have been doing and go in a radically new direction and find work that we are better suited to. At a higher level, it gives the power to heal and transform and if these skills are developed it can lead to a very rewarding career.

Pluto in 7. This intensifies the desire to have a deep and intense relationship with someone. But care must be taken it does not verge into an obsession or into manipulation and control - either being the controlling one, or being controlled. If so, such a union could become dangerous. Either way, the way we relate in marriage and other formal partnerships will transform because of cathartic experiences that occur. Balance is required. and healthy boundaries should be established in close one-on-one relationships. The power to heal deep psychological wounds that occur as a consequence of rejection is given with this placement.

Pluto in 8. Pluto, the planet of transformation, in the eighth house of transformation, indicates that there are deep emotional issues or sexual habits that need healing or transmuted. We need to be assertive but also discerning in the way vital energies and power are used and act with integrity at all times when handling other people's money - otherwise there could be serious repercussions. Staying away from dangerous people and keeping to the "noble middle path" should be the rule. Positively, there is talent in detection, research, psychology, healing and occult work.

Pluto in 9. Powerful teachers and gurus who radically change the life will be met as we explore the higher teachings for understanding. But it is very important to be discerning and not give one's power to someone who is a crook or charlatan. This is a possibility with this combination. Use the power positively, to transform any obsessive and inflexible beliefs and concepts that limit understanding and wisdom. The potential exists, to be a potent and transformative force for good in the lives of people who are looking for answers to life.

Pluto in 10. Powerful people will be met in the professional life - some good and some who will be abusive; but all will have a transformative effect on the life and on any high goals pursued. Disruptions in the career should be viewed in this light. Change careers if necessary, if a manger or the job itself is dangerous to one's life or reputation, because otherwise the fall-out could be massive. Such experiences can be used to develop confidence, the wise use of power and good managerial skills. The placement potentially indicates a career that transforms the lives of people for the better.

Pluto in 11. Influence from friends and social organisations we belong to, will change the life in profound ways. Because of this, we should ensure that this influence is positive and avoid forming close connections with people who are criminal, dangerous or generally toxic. Such people should be cut out of the life before things go too far. The right friends and groups will have a profound effect for good and by adding our ethical contributions we can help to make the world a better place.

Pluto in 12. If there is abuse going on in private, this must be brought to the attention of authorities or people who can help. Pluto's task is to go deep down and pull poison or evil to the surface, so it can be purged or healed. Even if the fall-out is massive, this must be borne. Healing at a deep root level is required. In turn, one should avoid becoming a secretive manipulator or criminal because the repercussions could result in incarceration. Psychologically, there is a need to transform negative core beliefs buried in the unconscious. Attending to this will release energy for positive use and transform the life in a most incredible way.

12a. Vesta in the Signs.

In each sign, Vesta represents a sacred cause that we should attend to in order to strengthen the inner spiritual flame.

Vesta in Aries. Emotional purification is required and bringing under control the tendency to react too quickly and aggressively. With this combination, we should withdraw periodically to align with the pure flame of spirit and dedicate the life towards becoming a disciplined and thoughtful leader. The freedom to explore and to go boldly forwards into life should be cultivated.

Vesta in Taurus. The desire nature needs purifying and any lustful appetites that keep us in situations or relationships that are unhealthy. Periodic withdrawal into a sacred space, health spa or healing centre to purify the body, mind and spirit will be beneficial. The flame of aspiration for higher and finer things in life should be fanned by visiting holy places, studying wisdom texts or by enjoying and appreciating cultural beauties such as fine art or music.

Vesta in Gemini. The mission is to cultivate the spark of mental-creativity by guarding the visions received in contemplation and original ideas that follow prior to their outer use and expression. Then, when presented to the public, they will be accurate representations of messages received from the sacred source within. Withdrawing periodically to fan the flame of inner creativity is required.

Vesta in Cancer. The mission is to purify the emotional nature so that its storms and tempers no longer dominate the life and relationships. Periodic withdrawal to practice balancing disciplines and meditations to purify and quieten this body, perhaps also to do inner-child healing work will be beneficial. The flame of wisdom that is uncontaminated by glamour should be cultivated and used to guide decision making.

Vesta in Leo. The mission is to nurture the sacred flame of one's true identity by withdrawing periodically (such as in morning meditation), to realign with the soul, and connect with the authentic self by asking and then answering the question, "Who am I?" This will help to lift focus out of the ego and mute its demand to dominate and control. Integrity in leadership should be cultivated and expressed.

Vesta in Virgo. The sacred mission is to nurture the spirit of true love and wisdom that is seeking birth through the conscious self, and to purify the nature and life so it can find expression. Virgo is closely related to the Vestal Virgins, so dedicating oneself fully to this task - in order to better serve others, is required.

Vesta in Libra. The task is to nourish and cultivate the flame of relating with others in a sacred sense, to ensure the energy inter-actions are pure and honest and are uncontaminated by lies or deceit. This will require periodic withdrawals to analyse how we are doing in this regard and making adjustments if necessary. Taking time as a couple to go on retreat, into a private space to renew the passion and fire of the union will be beneficial.

Vesta in Scorpio. Guarding the flame of one's sexuality and preventing contamination through promiscuity, unhealthy thoughts or other misuse is the mission. The same applies to the emotional life. Both need purification and the transformation of any negative patterns or habits. Periods of celibacy or occult practices to bring inner purity and balance will be helpful.

Vesta in Sagittarius. The sacred duty is to guard the flame of aspiration to reach towards the heights and to grow in spirit and understanding. To this end, the lower appetites and pursuit of material pleasures should be curbed and journeys made to sacred places to foster the higher impulse. Protect freedoms, such as the right to explore and practice one's sacred beliefs, morals and philosophies.

Vesta in Capricorn. The mission is to keep aflame moral codes and traditions that are healthy and that contribute positively to personal growth. This is assisted by cutting away unnecessary rules, duties and unhealthy ambitions that bind the soul to the material world. If there is confusion, then periodic withdrawals to assess what to let go of, and which way forwards is the best way to go, will be beneficial. Taking on appropriate responsibilities is part of this experience.

Vesta in Aquarius. The task is to protect the sacred fire that drives humanity forwards into the New Age of universal brotherhood and social equality and to help this progression by contributing original ideas and helpful science. Fighting for the rights of minorities and for right human relations is a sacred duty. Private retreats with like-minded souls to clarify the best way to proceed will strengthen the flame.

Vesta in Pisces. Strengthening the sacred flame of spirit within through silent and reverential contemplation, or through artistic expression is the goal. This will play out naturally in the life as a spontaneous aspiration to serve and to help the needy and suffering. Periodic withdrawals into beautiful spiritual centres or sacred places in forests, will help to strengthen the inner link.

12b. Vesta in the Houses.

Representing as it does the sacred inner-fire of spirit, Vesta's house shows an area in life that needs to be made more sacred or spiritual. This is because something is amiss in that area - spiritual faith or trust has been lost and needs to be recovered.

Vesta in 1. Dedication to a path of self-awareness and to making one's own way through life is required. This is important to help counter-balance a past-life tendency to lose one's identity when in the presence of other people and giving up important personal goals. A clear and positive self-identity will enhance important unions. Periods of self-imposed isolation to help restore faith in oneself should be undertaken.

Vesta in 2. Cultivating the sacred inner flame of spiritual values to live by, of generosity and sharing with those who are in need, is the goal - then expressing these higher principles in the way money is earned and spent. Use periods when resources are scarce, to reinforce the importance of founding one's life upon a bedrock of integrity and honesty. All is given to those who ask nothing for the separated self.

Vesta in 3. The sacred principle to be fostered is that of being harmless in thought and speech, or as our wise grand-mothers used to say - "speak only when you have something kind to say". To this, the life should be dedicated. It is important to get into the habit of keeping silent about contentious issues that are none of one's business and contemplate the wisest thing to say when one is involved.

Vesta in 4. Vesta is very comfortable in the 4th and gives a natural inclination to foster a happy home-hearth, to honour and look after family traditions and parents. This may require sacrificing any career goals. If so and the lesson is learnt, new opportunities will arise - either later in the current life or in the next. Nothing is random in the chart and sometimes we are required to focus on the personal life to round out development.

Vesta in 5. Fostering the flame of personal creativity is required. Time should be dedicated to the development of our God-given talents so they can be used to inspire and uplift - children especially, but also others who come into our care. This will require the sacrificing of normal pleasure-seeking activities that others enjoy. Periodic withdrawal to fan the flame of unconditional love and kindness is a sacred duty.

Vesta in 6. Dedication is required, to develop work skills and talents that will enable a living to be made in a career that is fulfilling and nurturing to the soul. Such a career should benefit the health and wellness of people being treated and also those contacted at work. Personal sacrifices may have to made to achieve this but there will be spiritual rewards. For some, a health crisis will require a reset of the career to one that is more in line with one's heart or soul duty.

Vesta in 7. Creating beautiful relationships that are uncontaminated by lies or deceit is the sacred task. The sacrifice of personal goals so that there is more time to devote to the partner and to the well-being of the union will help keep the flame of joy and love alive. This will also help to balance any karma due to past-life selfishness. Being able to create such unions will come naturally when right-balance has been established with the soul - the source of love and wisdom.

Vesta in 8. The sacred task is to transform any aspects of the emotional life, any unhealthy sexual habits or material attachments because they are hindering spiritual progression. Healing the cause of such trouble is a prerequisite if one is ever to find inner balance and serenity. Periodic withdrawal to study psychology and esoteric subjects is required, so that the knowledges and skills necessary to do such profound work can be learnt and then applied.

Vesta in 9. Spiritual development is the sacred duty. Sacrifices should be made each day so there is time to devote to the study of spirituality, philosophy and esotericism and to pray or practice meditation - steps required to achieve an expansion of consciousness (soul and consciousness are synonyms). Travel to foreign lands and connecting with foreign cultures and religions will also broaden understanding.

Vesta in 10. The sacred task is to be successful in a profession that is aligned with one's highest life or spiritual goal, whatever that is. For some, the duty may be to make things better in the world as a whole, requiring the sacrifice of personal and family life so that more time is available to devote to the responsibilities that come with such a mission. This is a karmic duty, having sacrificed one's professional life for family in a previous life, one can now pursue what was previously denied.

Vesta in 11. The flame of true and unconditional friendship is to be cultivated, the fostering of brotherliness and respect for people we feel allied with because they share higher aspirations - this is the task. On a larger scale, our dedicated efforts could be poured into supporting and working within a group or organization that works to bring about social and humanitarian improvements in the world.

Vesta in 12. Something unresolved in the unconscious, from the past, needs healing and this is the sacred task. The acceptance of life and of whatever has happened is essential for trauma to be healed. A period each day should be dedicated to spiritual discovery, such as - prayer, meditation, the pondering of life's greater mysteries, retreating into nature to wonder at the beauty of creation, or in physical-spiritual practices such as yoga or tai chi.

13a. Juno in the Signs.

Juno represents attitudes we bring to marriage and those we require from the partner and from the union, if we are to be happy.

Juno in Aries. The natural tendency is to be assertive, ardent, fiery and bold in marriage. Liking to be the boss, commitments will be honoured if adequate freedom is given. If not, feeling constricted, trouble could arise leading to a separation. The ideal partner is someone who can match one's fire and move on quickly from problems if they arise. Very jealous and aggressive, there will be a fight if a rival comes on the scene.

Juno in Taurus. Reliability and stability are qualities brought to the marriage. Supplying and attending to the basic necessities of life – a comfortable home, food, sex and money; these are vital for domestic happiness. The ideal partner is someone who has the same values and who will meet these needs. Possessiveness, stubbornness and unwillingness to change one's expectations in marriage are the negatives to avoid.

Juno in Gemini. Clear and excellent communication and willingness to talk through issues is the vital ingredient required for domestic bliss. The ideal marriage partner is someone who is similar - a thinker willing to share ideas, who can discuss many topics, who likes playful words and repartee and likes to travel the world. Trouble will come however, if deceit and lies start to contaminate the union.

Juno in Cancer. Marriage is approached in a nurturing, family-oriented and protective manner. A deep emotional investment is made in marriage and in the partner. So ideally, he or she will be someone who meets one's emotional needs, someone who will be a good parent and provider and who will ensure the home and family is secure. Being too clingy, needy, ultra-sensitive and moody are the negatives to avoid.

Juno in Leo. Taking command of the marriage will come naturally and usually it will be guided with flair and competency. Great demonstrations of love and affection sets the style and energy will be put into keeping romance alive. The ideal partner is someone who will follow and greatly appreciate the fire, warmth and efforts being made - someone to take pride in and who looks good. Arrogant bullying could potentially cause trouble in this union.

Juno in Virgo. Loyal and reliable, committed relationships are projects that need to be worked on and no detail will be overlooked by the owner of this combination, in an effort to do the right thing. From ensuring the needs of the partner are being met, that a healthy lifestyle is maintained and that all material needs are taken care of; all these engross attention. The ideal partner is someone who is similarly practical. Being too critical could cause a divorce.

Juno in Libra. Juno is very comfortable in Libra and its positive qualities are likely to shine through. Wonderfully romantic, flirtatious, social and attractive, these attributes are brought to marriage. The ideal partner is someone who will show due appreciation with lots of attention and gifts and will enjoy creating and living in a harmonious and peaceful environment. Being too superficial, uncommitted and unfaithful are the negatives that could cause a divorce.

Juno in Scorpio. Intensity, passion, sensuousness, healthy sexual appreciation and tremendous loyalty - these are some of the qualities brought to marriage. Once the commitment is made, investment in the partner and union is deep and powerful. The ideal partner will match this intensity of attention and passion and will enjoy spending quiet and private time together to enjoy what each has to offer. Possessiveness, being too controlling, intense jealousy and spiteful retaliation breaks these unions down.

Juno in Sagittarius. People with this combination are freedom loving and adventurous, they love to travel and would like to move the home base around on occasion. Generous and easy going, they are usually easy to live with. Idealistic, they form a picture of the ideal mate and will go on a hunt to find someone who fits the picture. Such a person will be a mate to share the adventure of life with. Irresponsibility, and sometimes problems with gambling or other addictions are negatives that can cause a divorce.

Juno in Capricorn. A serious and conservative approach is taken with marriage, being responsible and working hard to establish financial and material security. The ideal partner is someone who comes with assets, who is similarly responsible and who will be respectful and appreciate the efforts made to look after the family. Ignoring the intimate side of the marriage or the emotional needs of the partner, and sacrificing family time for work - these are negatives that can cause a separation.

Juno in Aquarius. Independent and cerebral, the ideal partner is someone who is first and foremost a friend, someone who is easy to get along with and with whom there is intellectual compatibility. The mate should also have interests outside of the union and be willing to experiment with lifestyle moves or changes. Shared progressive or humanitarian interests will help to cement the union. Being too intellectually remote can cause problems.

Juno in Pisces. With emotions that are inclusive and flowing, romantic, artistic and spiritual, finding a partner who is similar and who appreciates the finer things in life is essential if fulfilment is to be found in marriage. Those with this combination are compassionate and forgiving and will put up with much. However, irresponsibility, infidelity and addictions to drugs or alcohol can sometimes arise - introduced by the person with this combination or the partner.

13b. Juno in the Houses.

Juno in the houses shows areas of life that will be important in marriage.

Juno in 1. Formal partnerships can be enhanced by improving the image or body, developing individual interests outside of marriage, and an independent life approach. The ideal partner will be complementary, will support and encourage this. However, when together as a couple, it will be important to focus with one-pointed attention on the happiness of the partner and the balanced well-being of the union.

Juno in 2. Marriage will be enhanced by contributing financially, by being stable and loyal, and by valuing and appreciating the partner. Shared spiritual values may also be a vital component. Either way, with this combination we should be careful to choose a mate who has the same values or differences could cause a breakdown and divorce.

Juno in 3. The essential glue required to cement unions healthily together is clear and honest communication. This will ensure that there is mutual understanding and that the way to progress forwards as a couple is clear. Shared interests done together on a daily basis will be helpful and the partner may be found close to home or even be associated with the extended family.

Juno in 4. A stable marriage, home and family life; these are essential with this combination. To this end, a partner should be sought who feels the same and who will work to build a secure domestic structure. Mutual nurturing and shared emotional support are vital elements and the mate should be a good parent and provider.

Juno in 5. The ideal partner will be romantic, creative in keeping the spark alive in marriage and is a warm and appreciative lover. Likewise, someone who will enjoy sharing cultural and pleasure activities, and who will be good with children and play with them.

Juno in 6. Formal partnerships will be enhanced by working through crises, accepting one's duty and just generally contributing daily to the responsibilities, duties and tasks that are the nuts and bolts of marriage. The ideal partner should have good hygiene, take an interest in health and work hard so that the union runs smoothly and all material needs are taken care of.

Juno in 7. Important one-on-one unions will be enhanced by developing excellent relationship skills, being fair and cooperative and lavishing love and attention on the partner. These are also the qualities to be looked for in a partner, someone who wants to share his or her life and cohabit in harmony.

Juno in 8. Marriage will be enhanced by contributing to a healthy and passionate sex life and relating to the partner with depth and emotional intensity. The ideal partner will complement this and contribute to joint finances. Such mutual involvement will be transformative and will change the marriage for the better - a requirement of this placement to avoid separation and divorce.

Juno in 9. Travel and adventure are a must in marriage, which will be enhanced by taking long journeys together - whether this journey is intellectual, spiritual or philosophical. For the union to be fulfilling, the partner should have similar morals and beliefs and there needs to a mutual sharing of interests that are higher and more expansive.

Juno in 10. Formal partnerships can be enhanced by gaining professional success, gaining the respect of the partner and by making the success of the partnership an important life goal. It will also be important for the union to be seen to be successful in the eyes of the world, or that the partner is successful. There should be no "washing of dirty linen" in public.

Juno in 11. The glue necessary to cement together a deeply fulfilling union is a solid friendship and a shared vision of how to make the marriage and the world a better place. Mutual social and humanitarian interests being expressed in association with a group or organization will also be beneficial.

Juno in 12. There may be an aversion to marriage because of a lack of interest in traditional unions or because of a sense that it would lead to a loss of freedom even entrapment. Some may find themselves nursing an invalid partner, others may make a commitment to a spiritual marriage. This is not to say one cannot find happiness in marriage with this combination. But if there are psychological or other inhibiting life issues, these need to be worked through.

14a. Ceres in the Signs.

Ceres is the Goddess of the Harvest and from that angle, represents how loving attention and care can bring to fruition, a bounteous crop. The analogy to human relationships is clear. In the chart, Ceres represents the type of nurturing we received when we were children and consequently, the self-esteem we developed and then as adults - the type of nurturing we give to others.

Ceres in Aries. A home-life where we are encouraged to be independent, to explore and be adventurous, will help boost self-esteem. This nurturing style passed on will similarly build confidence in others who come into our care. If, however there was rough treatment or abuse, this development will be stifled, resulting in feelings of shame, intense anger, resentment and explosive outbursts. This should be healed so that the same abuses are not passed on.

Ceres in Taurus. The development of self-worth requires tangible demonstrations of appreciation and affection and for home life to be stable and secure with all the basic necessities being provided. This nurturing style passed on to others will likewise give a sense of security. If, however, there were insufficient resources, money and food, a fear about not having enough, then a compulsion to keep acquiring things as a safety bulwark against the insecurities of life may develop. A greater appreciation of one's own fineness of character and intrinsic worth will be healing.

Ceres in Gemini. Self-esteem will develop if we live in an environment where healthy discussion is encouraged and people listen to - and respect, what we say. Good communication and speaking words of encouragement is essential with this nurturing style. Journeys to places of interest will also be beneficial and will help spark a curiosity about life and interest in others. However, if freedom of speech is met with reprisals and threats, it will result in a fear of speaking up for oneself when it is appropriate to do so.

Ceres in Cancer. Sensitivity, empathy, understanding, having one's emotional needs acknowledged and provided; these are required at home for healthy self-esteem to grow. If, however, there was emotional coldness and rejection, the result will be low self-worth and a deep distrust of intimacy and closeness. Emotional shields will be put up for self-protection. If this has happened, healing should be administered so that similar rejections are not passed on. This nurturing style is empathetic, inclusive and caring.

Ceres in Leo. Good self-worth develops if those we live with are generous with their love, attention and praise and home is filled with fun, creative activities and encouragement to star and shine. This nurturing style passed on to others - especially children, will likewise boost their confidence and ability to go forwards into life. But if there was bullying and humiliation, sensitive feelings will be suppressed for protection and this will have serious implications in relationships and on health. To reverse this, inner healing will have to occur.

Ceres in Virgo. Those with this combination prefer an environment that is well organised, which is clean and hygienic. If there is also praise given for carrying out one's duties meticulously, then self-esteem will flourish. However, unrelenting criticism and judgment in early home life will destroy faith in oneself. This can give rise to an obsession about needing to be perfect, to get everything right - perfectionist tendencies. The goal is to learn to love and appreciate one's goodness and helpfulness, which this combination fosters.

Ceres in Libra. Self-esteem develops in a family atmosphere of peace, beauty and harmony, where we are listened to, are treated fairly and receive love and attention. This nurturing style passed on will foster harmony and balance in all our important relationships. If, however, there was conflict and uncertainty, a fear of intimacy could result and an inability to form harmonious unions. If so, attention should be given to heal this so true happiness with others can be experienced.

Ceres in Scorpio. Self-esteem would develop in a family atmosphere of unwavering emotional support and trust and where parents fought when necessary to protect the family's wellbeing. The same intense attention and unwavering support given to others will be similarly encouraging. However, if home was filled with danger and fear because of abuse, it is vital that any resultant trauma is healed so that the same abuses are not passed on to others.

Ceres in Sagittarius. A home life filled with laughter, adventure and encouragement to go out into the world and explore will result in self-worth and confidence. This nurturing style passed on to others will similarly help to instil an expanded and positive outlook. If, however, there was an abrogation of duties at home because a parent or carer was irresponsible, it could result in a fear of being trapped in a similar domestic situation. Consequently, commitments could be avoided.

Ceres in Capricorn. A family environment where everything is properly structured and organised and everyone has their duties and place will help the development of good self-worth and a responsible attitude to life. The same nurturing style passed on will have a beneficial structuring effect on other people's lives. However, if there was strict discipline without love, so that life was harsh and unforgiving, self-esteem will drop. If so, healing of the inner-child is required so that the same abuses are not passed on.

Ceres in Aquarius. A home life that is friendly, where independence is encouraged and there is lively discussion and sharing of ideas, this will help develop healthy self-worth. If however, one was forced to be independent and self-sufficient because support from others was not forth-coming; low self-esteem could be the result. Additionally, the emotions could be suppressed to avoid being hurt again. In such a case, the inner trauma should be healed so that happy and healthy relationships can be formed in the future.

Ceres in Pisces. Healthy self-worth will flourish if home life is emotionally nurturing and there is compassion and kindness. If, however, in early life there was family irresponsibility with broken promises, lies and addictions those with this combination can grow up confused and have difficulty establishing healthy emotional boundaries. Such traumas must be healed so that similar abuses are not passed on.

14b. Ceres in the Houses.

Ceres in the houses shows where nurturing is needed and from whom.

Ceres in 1. Life will be approached in a nurturing way, with spontaneous caring and sympathy being extended to others and towards life generally. People seeing this would be inclined to be nurturing in return. If, however, there was lack of support in childhood or even in the current life situation, the result could be a deep dislike of one's body image and fear of moving forwards in life. The healing key is to learn to accept oneself, both the good and bad.

Ceres in 2. The nurturing environment required for the development of good self-esteem, is one where we feel valued and appreciated. This is first and foremost. In childhood, living comfortably with the basic essentials provided - such as money, clothing, food and housing; these are also important. If however, there was a lack of appreciation and the essentials to decent living were not provided, an inner void could form that one tries to fill with possessions and money. The healing key is learning to value all that is good and beautiful in oneself.

Ceres in 3. A home environment which has positive communications, where kind words of encouragement are spoken on a daily basis is required for good esteem to flourish. This will help those with this combination to be confident in voicing their opinions. If, however, there was constant judgment and criticism, self-worth will be damaged and result in turn, words being used negatively to wound and hurt people. The remedy is to replace negative self-talk with words of encouragement and love.

Ceres in 4. Emotional comfort and positivity in the home and provision of a domestic environment that is warm and welcoming, these are required if good self-esteem is to flourish. If, however, there was a cold atmosphere where the focus was on the basics in the absence of emotional support and caring, then self-esteem would have suffered. This will result in insecurities about one's value as a homemaker or parent. Nurturing the inner child will help to heal this.

Ceres in 5. A family environment filled with fun, laughter and adventures, where all are encouraged to develop their creative skills and to go out into life with confidence; this will build healthy esteem. But if this is lacking, if self-esteem was squashed because of a lack of love and support, it could result in a restless search for true love through many shallow and unfulfilling romances. The remedy is to learn to love the child within.

Ceres in 6. The environment that will be most nurturing is one which is run efficiently, with great attention to detail and cleanliness, where good hygiene is the rule and attention to health is provided - and praise is lavished when these duties are attended to. These life-skills could provide the basis for a successful career. However, if there was drudgery with no praise or support, low esteem will plummet and depression will impair the health. A lack of confidence in coping with life challenges could arise and hypochondria develop. The inner-child needs healing.

Ceres in 7. Fairness and justice in important relationships - this is essential to the creation of an atmosphere of harmony and balance in the home environment; a vital factor if self-esteem is to flourish. However, if in childhood there was conflict between the parents and an unjust sharing of power - self-worth will fall. This could lead to a codependency situation and the continual demanding of time and attention to try to quieten inner anxiety. The remedy is to learn to have a loving relationship with oneself first.

Ceres in 8. Steady, unwavering emotional support, trust and encouragement is required for self-worth to develop healthily. But if there was abuse, rejection, sexual misconduct or misuse; it will result in a lack of confidence, fears about being able to cope with life and the extinguishment of hope. Consequently, esteem will plummet with resultant depression. The remedy is to go on a search for wisdom and psychological self-understanding. The skills gained to bring about inner-healing can then be used to nurture and heal others.

Ceres in 9. The best environment for self-esteem to flourish is one where freedom is given to explore life and truths in order to form one's own understandings, beliefs and moral standards about life. However, if independent enquiry was squashed by people with fixed minds and ideas, or unscrupulous people used religion or moral platitudes to prey on the innocent; esteem will fall and moral standards suffer. It is vital to escape from this type of corruptive environment and to start a new and independent search for understanding.

Ceres in 10. A life that is prominent in some way, such as - being born in a family with status or achieving public success through one's own hard efforts; this will boost esteem. But the reverse is true if there was notoriety or public shaming from authority figures. Then low self-esteem and negatives such as doubting one's ability to succeed, or shame about appearing in public; could arise. Self-respect will rise if we learn to appreciate the little things achieved every day in life. A career could be based on mentoring people who are seeking to reach their high life goals.

Ceres in 11. Being surrounded by warm and supportive friends who are present in those times when emotional support is needed; is the best environment in which healthy esteem can grow. For others, being in a nurturing society or serving in a humanitarian organisation will provide what is needed. However, if in childhood there was betrayal by friends, rejection and abandonment; low self-esteem and resentment will result in rebellious retaliations. Being one's, own best friend can help such a situation.

Ceres in 12. Some with the placement may feel abandoned psychologically or emotionally and bereft because no comfort is to be found. This placement indicates that self-nurturing should be applied - in private and out of the mainstream of life. For instance, developing a love of nature and of forests, flowers and gardens; this will help to tap into the healing and nurturing currents of nature. Or practicing universal worship of some kind and appreciating the fact that one is "a child of the universe." All these will help.

15a. Pallas Athena in the Signs.

Pallas Athena in the signs represents the different ways we use mental creativity and logic to solve life problems.

Pallas in Aries. Problem-solving is rapid and intuitive. There is a quick grasp of inspired ideas and ability to put them intelligently into action. This and the courage to go where no-one has before gives an original, exciting leadership style. When thwarted, people with this combination can be mentally combative and argumentative.

Pallas in Taurus. A common sense approach is used when problem solving. This practical expertise when married with visionary power and artistic flair, gives the ability to make money in creative ways, to produce products or creations that are both useful and attractive so that people desire them. Negatively expressed, people with this combination can be mentally rigid.

Pallas in Gemini. Problems are solved logically and intelligently. Networking, so everyone is involved in the conversation - brain-storming sessions to look at every aspect of an issue and to study every possible solution until the best way forwards is found. This way, everyone will be happy with the outcome. Hard aspects could manifest as pushing forwards ideas that are not practical or workable.

Pallas in Cancer. The ability to think clearly and dispassionately while in the midst of an emotional upset (one's own or other people's), is the gift of this combination. This, coupled with the natural nurturing characteristics of this sign, leads to wise problem solving that takes into consideration the wants and needs of all involved. Hard aspects show this function is impaired - that emotionalism swamps logical thought.

Pallas in Leo. Charm and charisma are used to get people onside. But there is also an acute and strategic mind that can make very wise decisions under duress, a combination that gives brilliant leadership ability when it is functioning without the usual Leo arrogance. Otherwise, problems are solved by forcing one's ideas onto others and by roaring loudly so that no other voice can be heard.

Pallas in Virgo. The ability to solve life problems is good because of the Virgo ability to scrutinise every detail associated with a problem and to be acutely discriminating when choosing the best way to go. Pallas enhances these natural Virgo abilities and adds leadership style and flair. Negatively aspected, the hyper-critical traits are accentuated and an inability to solve problems because of getting bogged down in details.

Pallas in Libra. Problems are solved through negotiation and consultation - getting everyone involved in the decision making so that a balanced consensus can be reached. Pallas enhances these natural Libra traits and adds an acute ability to quickly find the point of harmony in any dispute and to facilitate a rapid solution to restore peace. Conversely, this process is obstructed through mental agitation.

Pallas in Scorpio. Acute intelligence combines with natural Scorpio courage to find solutions by delving to the roots of an issue no matter how ugly the circumstances may be and by courageously fighting to combat all opposing ideas until victory is secured. Working negatively, the powerful mind is used to destroy people, not ideas.

Pallas in Sagittarius. Problems are solved by looking at the larger picture, drawing from different philosophies and points of view. Then, when all the information is in the open, the acute mind can come in to assess and weigh the relative values so that the best solution is found. Working negatively, thought gets hamstrung between different and opposing moral, religious, philosophical or spiritual points of view.

Pallas in Capricorn. When the ability to vision clearly all best possible outcomes and solutions to a problem, marries with practical Capricorn intelligence; then excellent executives, leaders and managers are produced. It leads to success in the business or professional life. But if this talent is misused so that there is avarice, greed and a disregard for people getting hurt; then karmic retribution will be attracted.

Pallas in Aquarius. With this combination, the clear Aquarian understanding of life's complexities and how to solve them scientifically, marries with the problem-solving excellence of Pallas. This enhances the ability to put lofty ideals into action by harnessing the power of group wisdom and shared efforts to manifest one's goals on the physical plane. Misuse results in a clever but trouble-making rebel.

Pallas in Pisces. Compassionate understanding coupled with clear and intuitive insight about the best way to go, the best thing to do, is used to solve problems. It leads to solutions that - although they may be slower to bring results because of the sensitive appreciation of the human cost; are the most humane. Negatively, in this sign that rules the oceans, powerful emotions could swamp the ability to reason clearly. This needs to be overcome.

15b. Pallas Athena in the Houses.

Pallas Athena in the houses shows where we will focus the creative intelligence to solve problems.

Pallas in 1. The natural problem-solving style is to rely on our own efforts and ingenuity and to act quickly to resolve things. Underlying this is an ability to quickly size up a problem and figure out the best solution. This is especially so if Pallas is conjunct the ascendant. However, unless due consideration is given to the impact made on others, this style can cause trouble in relationships.

Pallas in 2. When faced with a problem, this placement gives the ability to quickly align with one's values, so that there is clarity about the best way to proceed and so the wisest decision can be made. It also gives a clever ability to manifest money creatively and to organise resources and possessions so that life is comfortable and there is enough to share with others.

Pallas in 3. A walking knowledge-bank, day to day problems are solved by communicating with others in the local environment and including them in decision making. This will be appreciated and the creative and visionary solutions proposed will be valued. Others however, may resent what they see as unwanted and advice and busy-body interference.

Pallas in 4. Use of the creative mind to organise family affairs and systems so that everyone is contributing to tasks will ensure home-life runs efficiently and smoothly. This is especially beneficial if mother works. Home decor and layout will also likely be arranged to contribute to efficiency rather than for show. Resentment will arise from anyone who does not like to be organised.

Pallas in 5. One's talents are enhanced with Pallas located in the house of personal creativity. It gives an ability to excel in hobbies such as chess, or sports that require strategic thinking and in gambling. Intelligent children could come into the life and this talent could be used to think up exciting and challenging competitive games for them. Care should be taken not to over-organise or intellectualize affairs of the heart to avoid killing off romance.

Pallas in 6. A career could be based on the ability to problem solve and to organize so that systems and tasks run more efficiently. Skill with new technologies is another avenue that could be pursued and that could bring a living. Balance should accompany zeal to avoid stressing out mentally, causing health problems.

Pallas in 7. If problems should arise in marriage, Pallas' reason and logic can be used positively to ensure that due acknowledgement is given to the needs and wants of the partner while the trouble is being sorted out. Harmony will result if the union meets the needs of both participants and those with this combination have the insight to bring this about. Negatively, some may zealously try to organise the marriage without negotiation, causing resentment.

Pallas in 8. On a professional level, this placement can give expertise in healing, psychology, in esotericism and in organising other people's money or sorting out the sexual or life problems of clients. It also gives the ability to intelligently sort out our one's own problems. Any investigation and practice of occult teachings should be undertaken carefully and with humility to avoid developing mental pride - a danger in metaphysical work that can lead to life and mental-health problems.

Pallas in 9. The placement gives an urge to study and understand higher teachings, different world philosophies, cultures or religions. Alternatively, foreign people, lands and cultures could be the focus. The clarity and insight gained from such investigations could then be used to help others clarify their understandings and to find their own path to wisdom. Moralising and promotion of dogma should be avoided.

Pallas in 10. A natural ability to manage and organise (if developed and intelligently applied), will bring professional success. Alternatively, success could come through the development of one's own creative talent or the devising of a unique service or product and marketing it skilfully so that people clamour for what is being offered. Using one's power or position to force ideas onto others will cause problems.

Pallas in 11. There will be a natural urge to express one's personal creativity through work and interests being done by groups and organisations (humanitarian or political), to solve the problems of society. Programs that are visionary and intelligent in their application will be especially appealing. On a personal level, this energy could be directed into shared endeavours with friends to solve local problems and to create a more ideal outcome for all involved.

Pallas in 12. This combination gives insight into the unconscious so that negative beliefs can be pulled into the light of mind and intelligently dealt with. It also can bring wisdom as a consequence of spending time in isolation because of uncontrollable events or unwise choices. Some may utilise this force by volunteering their time and efforts to help people who are casualties of life get their lives back together again. On a sober note, living too much in the mind and becoming detached from society could cause mental health problems.

16a. Chiron in the Signs.

Chiron's sign indicates childhood experiences that can contribute to emotional wounding and the embedding of associated negative core-beliefs. Using positive affirmations that are the opposite of the negative belief is a way to overwrite the latter. This technique in Raja Yoga is called, "Think an opposite thought". [1]

Chiron in Aries. This combination suggests that family life was filled with bullies who used force and coercion to get their way. If so, negative beliefs such as "I'm bad," or "I'm weak," could form and so could a self-protective instinct such as lightning fast anger and aggression at the first hint of criticism. If these patterns exist, they must be transmuted. The first step is to slow down the process and think before acting. Visualisation exercises can help such as imagining oneself to be a leader and affirming, "I am the master of my life and I create my own destiny!" Chiron's healing style in Aries is dynamic. There is power to expel weakness and to imbue strength to those who need it. Innovative and new approaches will be tried if old methods fail or are no longer appropriate.

Chiron in Taurus. This wound concerns values and resources. It can form if early home life was unstable and insecure because there were insufficient resources and funds to provide essential material necessities. Such experiences can warp values so that the child feels it has no value. Negative beliefs can form such as "I'm worthless" or "Without money I am nothing." To fill the inner void, money and possessions could be hoarded. A remedial exercise is to visualise oneself letting go of possessions, but being rich with love and friendship; then affirming, "I am rich with love and goodness." The Taurus healing style is traditional, practical, is common-sense based and makes use of natural therapies such as herbs and flowers.

---
[1] Light of the soul, Book II, sutra 33.

Chiron in Gemini. This wound involves mis-communication. If the family atmosphere was filled with negative feedback, criticisms, evasions of the truth or outright lies, then negative beliefs such as "I'm stupid", or "It is dangerous to speak," can form. Consequent behaviours are - a lack of confidence in speaking up for oneself, not trusting one's judgment, or fearing honest communication. To help overcome these self-worth issues, endeavour to speak up more often when it is appropriate to do so. A positive affirmation to sound is, "I speak my truth beautifully, sincerely and simply." The Gemini healing style is instructive. It plants positive healing thoughts in the mind to support any external methods and modalities being applied.

Chiron in Cancer. A home-life filled with emotional storms and dramas and that is chaotic and turbulent will disturb the emotional life of the child with this combination. Resultant negative beliefs that could form are, "I'm unprotected", "I'm afraid", or "I'm defenceless." The remedial task is to use the mind to heal and balance the emotional life; to think before acting. A visualisation exercise to use is: see oneself sitting serenely by a very still lake, then affirm, "Peace, be still". The Cancer healing style is intuitive, nurturing and empathetic; it aims to heal the wounded emotions.

Chiron in Leo. Being bullied in childhood would result in the formation of negative beliefs such as "I'm weak", "I'm a coward", or "I can't control anything." Defensive aggression and outrage, and roaring like an injured lion, these are some defensive strategies used by the wounded inner-child to protect itself. An exercise to help repair the inner damage and to learn to stand in one's authentic power, is to visualise God or other power symbol or totem and affirm, "I am That, and That am I." Simultaneously, to search within for courage in challenging times. The Leo healing style radiates power, warmth and energy, seeks to vitalise and to lift up the weak by force of will.

Chiron in Virgo. Unrelenting criticism and judgment in early home life would destroy faith in oneself and give rise to negative core beliefs such as "I'm imperfect", "I'm inadequate", or "I'm a failure." The remedial goal is to learn to love and appreciate oneself – "warts and all". Negative self-talk must be replaced with positive thoughts. An exercise to help is to visualise the love of God flowing through the heart and out into the world to heal. A helpful affirmation is, "I am very thankful for all the love in my life and I find it everywhere." The Virgo healing style is practical. The problem - and the client, are studied meticulously, so that no detail is overlooked and the best healing approach is found and applied.

Chiron in Libra. A home life where the truth was glossed over or hidden in order to keep up appearances, or there was unfair favouritism; this can result in the formation of negative beliefs such as "It isn't fair" or "There must be something wrong with me." A lack of trust in oneself or one's judgment can form and the denial of reality. The remedial goal is to balance the emotions and to be centred in oneself. An exercise is to visualise the Sun setting, perfectly centred and radiant on the horizon of a very still ocean; then affirm, "I am perfectly poised and balanced." Simultaneously, practice being more decisive. In the Libran healing style, an intelligent search is made for the most balanced and unobtrusive healing modality, all options are weighed and counselling is an important part of the remedial approach.

Chiron in Scorpio. Serious abuse in childhood – psychological, emotional and physical; this will result in negative beliefs such as "I'm bad", "I'm dirty", "I'm broken", or "I'm damaged." There will be boiling resentment, anger and a desire to attack to protect oneself. Scorpio gives the power to fight and win and such devastations can be healed with extended therapy. Scorpio exercise is to visualise oneself as a victorious warrior armed with a sword, and affirming, "Warrior am I, and from the battle I emerge triumphant." Simultaneously, the study of occult and psychological science is useful for personal healing and to help heal others. The Scorpio healing style is dynamic. There is power to go to the root of a problem and bring emotional toxicity into the light of awareness so that it can be purged and healed.

Chiron in Sagittarius. Being denied the right to explore life, being sexually abused or subject to nasty religious bias; any of these violations in childhood will result in the formation of negative beliefs. For example, "God hates me" or "I'm evil." A restless rolling-stone attitude may arise and difficulty committing. A remedial goal is to find and pursue an inspiring belief or philosophy and to travel the world, either in mind or body to broaden the horizons. An exercise is to visualise oneself as an archer, firing an arrow that reaches its target; then affirm: "I see the goal. I reach the goal. And then I see another." The Sagittarius healing style is dynamic and directive. There is power to inspire people to be healed through self-belief.

Chiron in Capricorn. A home life that is emotionally cold like a mountain top covered with ice, being judged and treated harshly; this will result in the formation of negative beliefs such as "I'm unlovable", "I'm defective", or "There is something wrong with me." Over-controlling and ultra-disciplined behaviour to reach one's ambitions (and therefore to prove one is okay), is often a consequence. The remedial goal is to heal the inner-child and there are various inner-child healing books available, such as those by John Bradshaw. This applies for all signs. An exercise to help the process is to visualise hugging the inner-child and saying, "I am here. You are safe now." The Capricorn healing style is professional and is common-sense based. All that is best from traditional medicine is applied, all the tried and tested methods.

Chiron in Aquarius. Being isolated emotionally as a child by intelligent carers who were unable to express warmth or empathy, this will result in negative beliefs such as "I'm alone", "I'm invisible", or "I don't matter." The compensatory reaction in this sign often involves withdrawal, becoming extremely detached and mind-focused. An exercise to help is to visualise love radiating from the heart and out into the world for healing; and affirming, "I am filled with the waters of life and love, which I pour out to those in need." The remedial goal is to balance the mind and emotions, to get in touch with the emotions and to express them healthily. To this end, throughout the day, try to engage people at a feeling level. The Aquarius healing style is intellectual and while taking into consideration traditional healing approaches, it will look afield into the untried, the new or into alternative medicine and healing modalities.

Chiron in Pisces. With this combination, if carers had emotional problems and lived in a fantasy world, or the child fell prey to predators because parents were careless, absent or addicts; this will result in negative beliefs forming, such as, "I'm a victim", "I'm helpless", or "I'm bad." In reaction to the emotional wound, as an adult, there could be a sense of wanting to rescue everyone, doing for others what was not done for the child. The remedial goal is to build up good self-esteem and develop healthy emotional boundaries. An exercise to help is to visualise oneself healed, whole and radiating light and love, and affirming, "I am a child of God, perfect and whole." The Pisces healing style is compassionate and empathetic. All aspects of the patient - body, emotions, mind and soul are patiently healed.

16b. Chiron in the Houses.

Chiron's house provides more information about emotional wounds and how to heal them.

Chiron in 1. A healthy sense of self, how we look, and being in control of life; these were impaired in childhood due to the emotions being wounded by parents or carers. Unhealed, they will result in a loss of confidence in oneself and the appearance, when in the company of others. A strong and confident sense of self must be developed. When successful, Chiron in the 1st gives a natural wisdom, the power of self-healing and also the power to heal others through the life-examples that are set.

Chiron in 2. The emotional wound involves a belief that we have no value and are unworthy. It can lead to "poverty consciousness", feeling poor no matter what material assets have been accumulated. Compensatory behaviour can be an exaggerated need for material assets or addictions to food or drink. The remedial goal is to learn to value all the fine, non-material assets we have. For example, appreciating one's inner beauty, goodness or integrity. Chiron in the 2nd gives the power to heal one's self-worth and that of others.

Chiron in 3. This placement indicates a problem with communication - of one's inner feelings and truths and insecurities about being heard or listened to sympathetically. These are consequences of growing up in an environment where there was constant criticism and judgment. The development of public speaking skills will help overcome this. Another task is to learn to communicate truth wisely, in ways that does not injure people. Chiron in the 3rd gives the power to heal by communicating wisdom.

Chiron in 4. This placement indicates trouble in the home during childhood. There was abuse of some form that was damaging to the inner-child, causing emotional wounds that now need healing. It may result in a lack of trust in one's own ability to create a healthy home and family life. Or an unhealthy codependency upon people who are unkind or unworthy, because the inner child is still seeking parental approval. Cutting ties from toxic people and moving away is sometimes necessary. Chiron in the 4th gives the power to heal fears in the unconscious generally and gives innate wisdom on how to form a healthy home base.

Chiron in 5. Unhappy childhood experiences ranging from being denied pleasure outings to sexual abuse; these have caused an emotional wound that will interfere with creative work. It may also induce a sense of guilt about enjoying simple pleasures in life. Until such insecurities are healed, they can affect the ability to form healthy relations with children or impair the ability to have a happy and uncomplicated love-life. Inner-healing will release the creative force of life that flows through the heart. Chiron in the 5th gives the ability to heal others in very creative ways, which includes play, joy and laughter.

Chiron in 6. Crises and hardships early in life and possible serious health problems within the family unit; these have resulted in deep emotional wounds and insecurities. These can take the form of doubting one's ability to cope if a health problem should arise, or anxieties over not being able to make a living. Hypochondria could develop or a work-obsession, so that one becomes driven in one direction or another. Chiron in the 6th indicates the need to heal such anxieties. Success will produce wisdom, because of having healed oneself. It can also produce a very wise and skilled healer.

Chiron in 7. Relationship healing is required. Trouble amongst the parents when growing up, the possibility of a divorce so that the family unit was destroyed; these have resulted in deep emotional wounds that need healing. Anxieties could take the form of lacking confidence in one's ability to form a healthy and enduring partnership, or that unions will eventually end up in open warfare that destroy all who are around. Chiron in the 7th shows the ability to heal such wounds, to develop excellent relationship skills and potentially to become a brilliant counsellor and healer of other people's woes.

Chiron in 8. Emotional trauma needs healing. Contributing causes can be the traumatic loss or death of a parent while a child, or being sexually, emotionally or physically abused. The study of western psychology or/ and Eastern metaphysics, and applying what has been learnt remedially to oneself, this will help bring about the needed inner adjustments. It will also help to restore faith in one's ability to handle major changes or traumas in the future. The insight and skills acquired during the process will give immediate insight into others who have similarly suffered. From such training and healing, one can become a master-healer.

Chiron in 9. Children with this combination, may grow up being indoctrinated by morals and beliefs that are judgmental, narrow and skewed. The consequence of this will be an outlook on life that is similarly twisted and a dislike of any religion or peoples in the world who are different. Such dogmatic ideals should be pulled up into the light of clear analysis so they can be destroyed. This will restore healthy open-mindedness. A questioning and inclusive attitude is vital for both spiritual and physical health. Chiron in the 9th gives the ability to develop a wise outlook and to use what has been learnt to guide and teach others who have similarly had their minds twisted.

Chiron in 10. Indications are that in childhood, shame descended upon the family and its reputation was damaged; alternatively, one's reputation was seriously tarnished in a previous incarnation. Either way, the emotional wound suffered then is still present with consequent low self-esteem. It can initiate behaviours such as constant striving to be better than anyone else, or needing constant reassurances that one is okay. Healing will be achieved when the constant comparing of oneself to others stops and life-contentment is found. Chiron in the 10th gives the potential to make a career out of teaching and healing.

Chiron in 11. Rejection by one's peers, by one's chosen tribe, is perhaps the most powerful and debilitating of all fears. It is primeval. We are gregarious people and need the group we belong to for survival. Chiron in the 11th indicates there has been such a wounding, either in a previous life or early in childhood. Whichever, a negative core belief about rejection needs to be healed. When this has been achieved, it gives an ability to teach friends and groups to similarly heal themselves.

Chiron in 12. A serious emotional wound caused by covert actions, hidden away from the public gaze (this could have occurred in a previous life), has yet to be healed in the unconscious. Until then, the toxicity surrounding such a trauma will have a debilitating effect on the life as well as on physical and psychological health. It can cause a fear of life and people, so that one is vigilantly guarded and unwilling (or unable) to share at a deep intimate level. Such people tend to hide away from life so they will be safe. If there are symptoms like these, therapy assistance is required to resolve the inner damage. If this is done, then Chiron in this house gives the potential to heal the most deeply damaged and wounded of people.

CHAPTER 5. PLANETS IN ASPECT

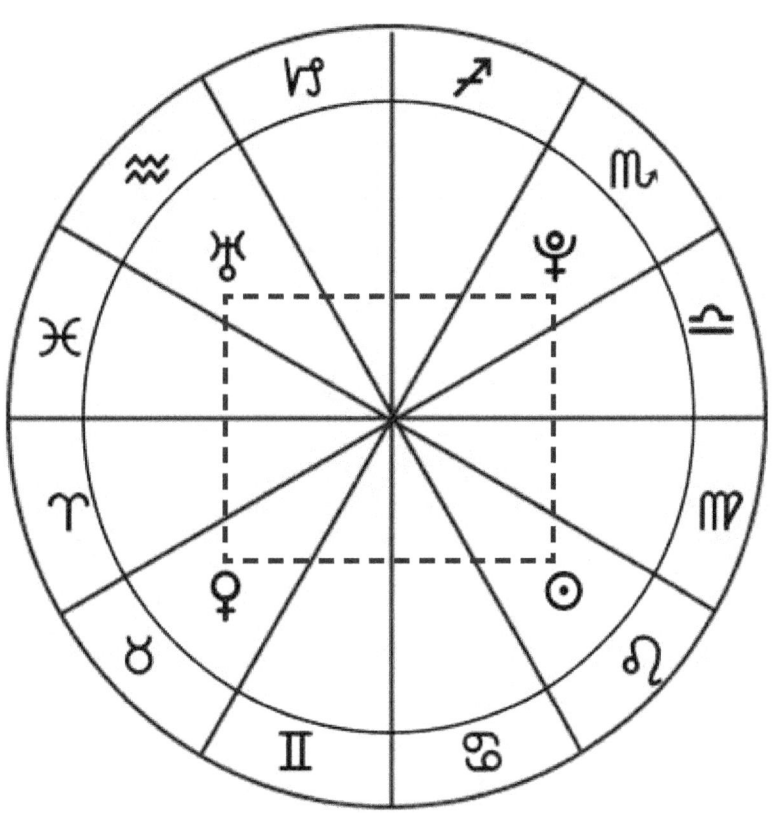

A. ASPECTS OVERVIEW

Planets carry universal energies, but also represent different parts of ourselves. They orbit the Sun at different speeds, travelling 360 degrees to complete one cycle. As they progress, they form angles (aspects) with each other for a while, before they move on. The aspects in the personal chart represent how the different parts of ourselves work together. They indicate whether we will express our energies harmoniously or stressfully.

Major Aspects					
Aspect name	Angle	Orb	Symbol	In the chart	Energy interactions
Conjunction	0	8-10°	☌	Planets together	Easy or hard: intensifies, unites for good or ill.
Square	90	8°	□	3 signs apart	Hard: blocks, challenges, conflict, drive, fights, friction, incentive, tension, represses.
Trine	120	8°	△	4 signs apart	Easy: beneficial, flows with, harmony.
Opposition	180	8°	☍	Opposite sides	Hard: clash or complement, opposes, fights.
Minor aspects					
Sextile	60	4-6°	✶	2 signs apart	Easy: compatible with, constructive growth.
Semi-square	45	5°	∠	1.5 signs apart	Hard: conflict, friction, irritates, hinders.
Inconjunct quincunx	150	5°	⚻	5 signs apart	Hard: cutting away, discord, hidden, imbalance requiring an adjustment, out of sight.
Minor-Minor aspects					
Sesquiquadrate	135	3°	⚼	4 signs + 15°	Hard: conflict, disruption.
Quintile	72	2°	Q	2+ signs apart	Easy: hidden talents, spiritual potential.
Semi-sextile	30	1°	⚻	5 signs apart	Hard: lack of ease, out of sync.

1. Think of Aspects as generally being either "easy" or "hard."

a. Easy aspects indicate easy energy flow, ease within the nature and with others.
   (Trine and sextile)
b. Hard aspects indicate blocked or disrupted energy flow, conflict within and with others.
   (Square, opposition, semi-square, inconjunct or quincunx).
c. Consider conjunctions easy if they consist of the Sun, Moon, Mercury, Venus or Jupiter.
   Consider them hard if Saturn, Uranus, Neptune and Pluto are involved.

2. Finding aspects in the chart.

a. Look for aspects by sign, not by houses.
b. The general rule is: planets around the same degree in complementary signs (fire signs are complimentary with air, and earth signs with water), form easy aspects. Planets opposite each other and in uncomplimentary signs (fire and air signs clash with earth and water signs), form hard aspects. However, if one planet is found at the beginning of a sign, and the other at the end of a sign, this rule does not apply. In this case count the degrees.
c. Use your eye to find aspects. Look at the drawings that follow and memorise the look of the angles for each aspect. You will see that planets opposite each other are in opposition; planets at right angles to each other are square; planets one third of the chart away are triangular.

3. The aspects and their "orbs", or range of influence.

An "orb" is a range of influence; the number of degrees allotted a planet in *aspect* to another planet, in which the aspect is said to be operational. Referring to the chart: as planet B moves away from A, then back towards it on its closing cycle, it forms angles/ aspects. It does not have to make the exact angle, to be in aspect because of the "orb" or extended range of influence on either side of the exact angle.

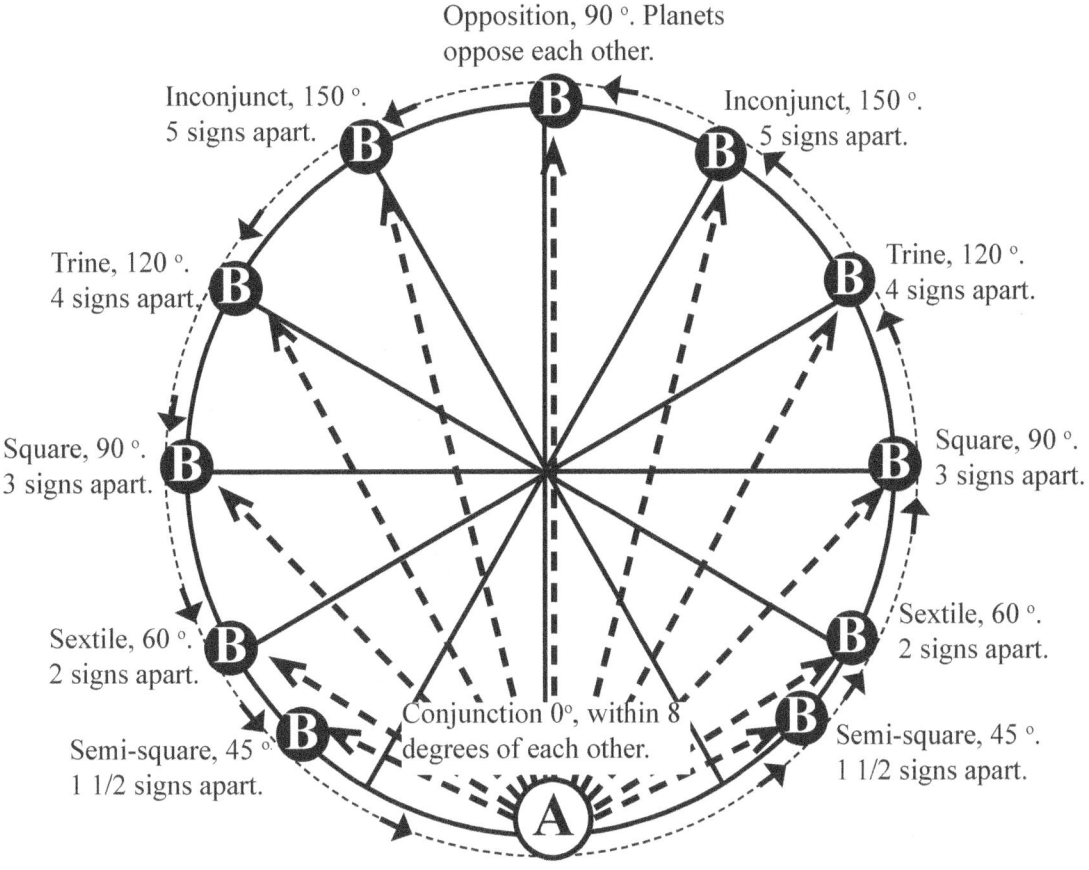

- **Conjunction**: The exact aspect is 0 degrees with an 8-degrees orb. Planet B can be up to 8-degrees either side of planet A.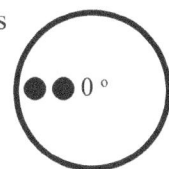

- **Semi-square**: 45° aspect, 4 degrees orb. Planet B can be 41-49 degrees from planet A.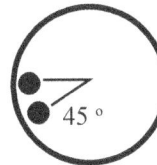

- **Sextile**: 60° aspect, 6 degrees orb. Planet B can be 54-66 degrees from planet A.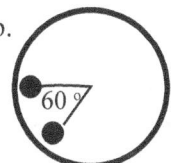

- **Square**: 90° aspect, 8-degrees orb. Planet B can be 82-98 degrees from planet A.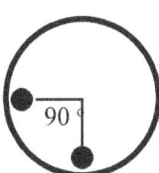

- **Trine**: 120° aspect, 8-degrees orb. Planet B can be 112-128 degrees from planet A.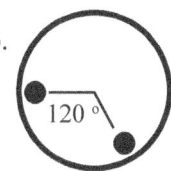

- **Inconjunct, quincunx**: 150° aspect, 3 degrees orb. Planet B can be 147-153 degrees from A.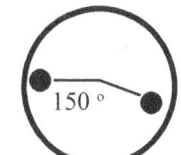

- **Opposition**: 180° aspect, 8-degrees orb. Planet B can be 172-188 degrees from A.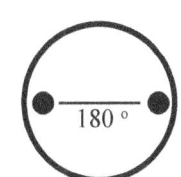

Minor aspects usually are given a 2 to 3 degree orb. The tighter the aspect, the more intense its effect.

A1. The Aspect Grid and Applying and Separating Aspects.

The aspect grid is usually under or beside the natal chart. Prince George's chart is used in the explanation. Each planet has a row and a column.

When two planets are in aspect, the square in the grid where they intersect - by row and column; it shows the aspect. If the square is empty, there is no aspect. But it must be remembered that we key into the computer, our preferences for the aspects - which ones we wish to see and the orb. Four examples are given below.

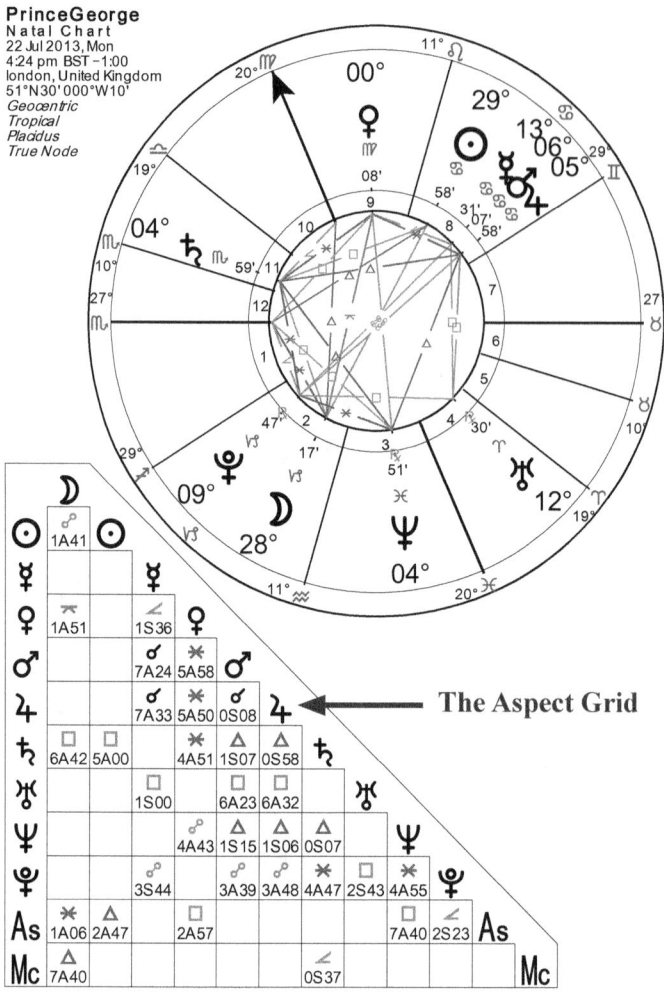

- The aspects of the Moon:
  It is opposition the Sun (☍)
  - is inconjunct Venus (⚻)
  - is square Saturn (□)
  - is sextile the ASC (ascendant) (✶)
  - is trine the MC (Midheaven) (△).

- The aspects of the Sun:
  It is opposition the Moon.
  - is square Saturn (□)
  - is trine the ASC (△).

- The aspects of Uranus: it is square to Mercury, Mars, Jupiter and Pluto.

- The aspects of the Ascendant: it is sextile the Moon, trine the Sun, square Venus and Neptune; and is semi-square Pluto.

Applying and Separating Aspects.

The faster planets move towards the slower planets, make aspects with them, then move away again.

1. When a faster planet moves towards a slower planet to form an aspect (and is in orb of that aspect), this aspect is called "applying"; the exact aspect has not yet been formed. Life events begin with an applying aspect. They keep building and unfolding during this period and the outcome can still be influenced.

2. In Prince George's grid, you will notice that under each aspect symbol, there are figures and an "A" or "S". For example, "1A41" for the Moon-Sun opposition, which means the Moon is applying to the Sun, and is 1 degree 41 minutes from the exact aspect.

3. When the exact aspect is made (both planets are at the same degree), the experience peaks.

4. When a faster moving planet begins to move away from the exact aspect to a slower moving planet - but is still in orb; this is called a "separating" aspect. The energies are dissipating. Now we are dealing with the aftermath of any experiences that began in relation to the aspect. Once the planet has moved beyond the orb of influence, technically, the aspect has finished. However, if serious trauma is involved the aftermath of the event can extend for weeks, months or years.

5. In the chart, there is a separating aspect between Mars and Jupiter ("0S08"), which means Mars is 8 minutes past the exact conjunction with Jupiter.

6. Sometimes the faster planet moves over the slower planet, goes retrograde for a period (reversing backwards over it), then moves forwards again to re-cross the slower planet. This drags out the whole experience, which lasts as long as the whole aspect period lasts.

A2. Major Planet Configurations.

Major planet configurations occur when 3 or more planets are in aspects with each other. They represent types of behaviours we naturally use, how we express our energies in daily life.

1. Stellium: conjunction of 3 or more planets, or 3 planets in a sign.

The energies of the planets and the signs they are in are tremendously intensified. When reading a stellium, start with a personal planet.

Sai Baba had a stellium - four planets connected via conjunctions. His personality was intense (Sun in Scorpio), powerfully influential (Sun conjunct ascendant), and ambitious (conjunct Saturn). He loved (Venus), communicating (Mercury), spiritual matters (Sagittarius). He had power to direct people to the heights (Sagittarius).

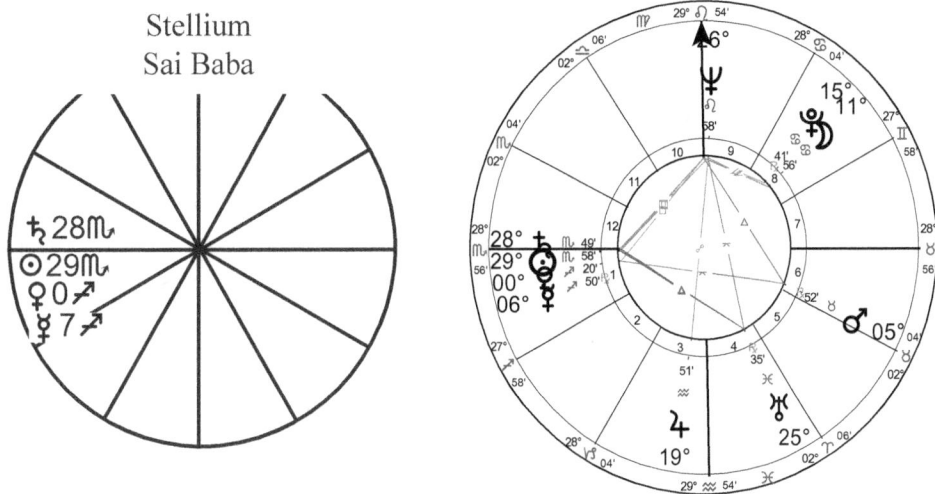

2. Grand Trine: 3 or more planets trine each other.

The trine is considered to be the lucky aspect, so this is triply so. Energy in the pattern flows and this creates harmony. It gives a pleasant disposition, ease and harmony with others and with the environment. Things tend to turn out well for the owner - at least in the areas of life the trine touches. Although the pattern is lucky and things flow, for some this can mean that life is so comfortable they cruise through life, not achieving much.

The Dalai Lama has a Grand Trine. His personality is sensitive and nurturing (Sun in Cancer), and he has the power to influence others with the example he sets in life (Sun conjunct ascendant). There is a tremendous sense of responsibility for the well-being of the suffering masses and to serve them by guiding them spiritually (trine Saturn in Pisces, 9H). This is accompanied with a generous flow of love (trine Jupiter 5H). His luck enabled him to escape from China's malevolence.

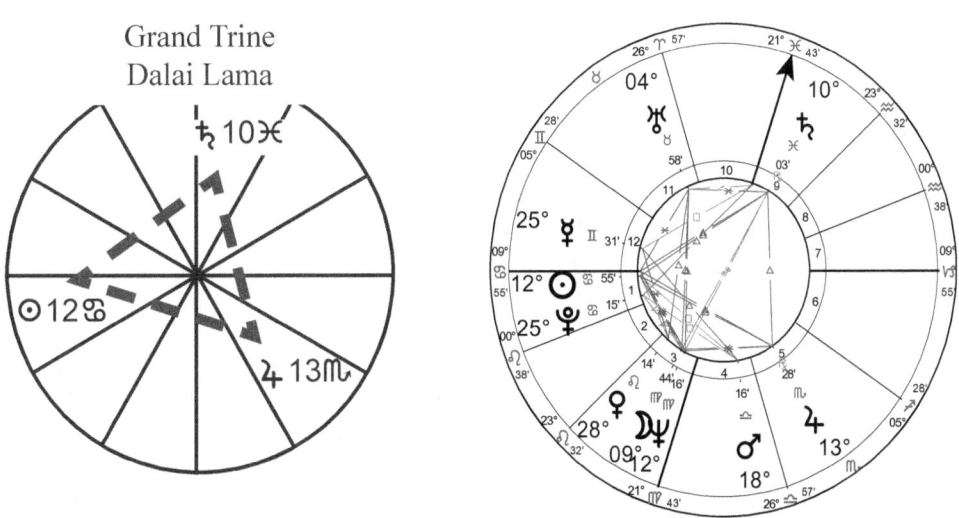

3. T-Square: two planets in opposition, both square the same third planet.

There is inner conflict and dissatisfaction. This drives a person to action to improve things. It is commonly found in the charts of achievers, people who work hard in spite of set-backs, to make something of themselves.

Winston Churchill had three T-Squares. Two of them included Mercury, the planet of oratory. Interpreting Mercury-Uranus-Pluto: Churchill's mind (Mercury) was deep and intense, intellectually brilliant (Uranus), and his tongue had a sting (Mercury in Scorpio). A powerful orator (opposite Pluto), he could destroy people with his words. But he also used its vocal power to lift people up during the dark days of the war.

A powerful variation of this pattern is the Grand Cross (GC), which has a 4th planet that forms a square. In Churchill's chart, if Saturn had been a few degrees later so it formed a square with Pluto; a GC would have been formed. It symbolizes even greater internal conflict than the T-Square. For those who can master this force – such as Churchill, it gives increased energy and drive to succeed. But many find the inner conflict too much to bear.

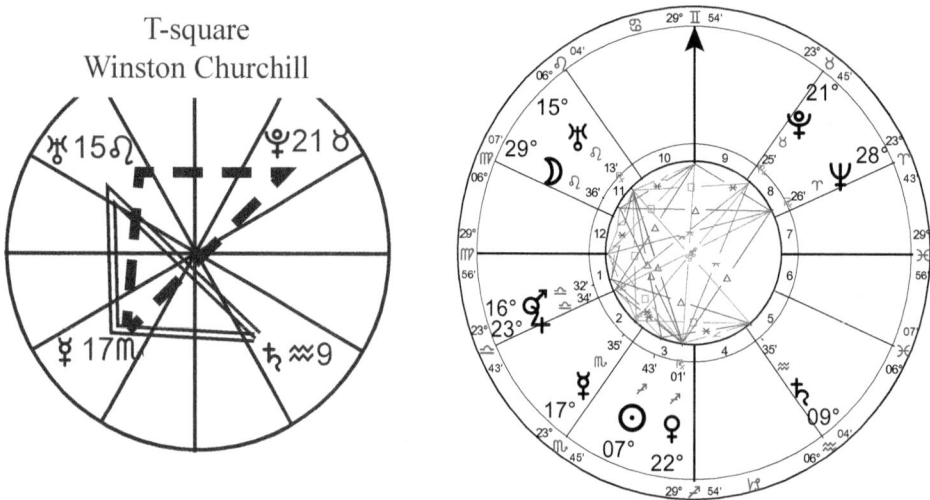

T-square
Winston Churchill

4. Yod, "the Finger of God": two planets sextile each other, both inconjunct the same third planet.

The Yod shows inner conflict that will manifest as external conflict if balance is not found. The goal is to find balance, to reconcile the part of the nature represented by the planet at the apex of the pattern (Jupiter in Diana's chart), with the other two parts represented by the planets that are sextile (Mars and Mercury). These two planets cannot "see" the apex planet. Start by interpreting the two planets that are sextile.

Princess Diana was compassionate in her thoughts (Mercury in Cancer), and passionate about helping and healing people (sextile Mars in Virgo). This part of her nature was out of balance with her huge need for material comfort and for praise (Jupiter, in the 2H of personal money and values). The reading could be flipped so that the sole planet is the positive point. Diana wanted to give all she had to help others (Jupiter), but this conflicted with the duties (Virgo), imposed by her marriage (Mercury 7H). Both are probably true.

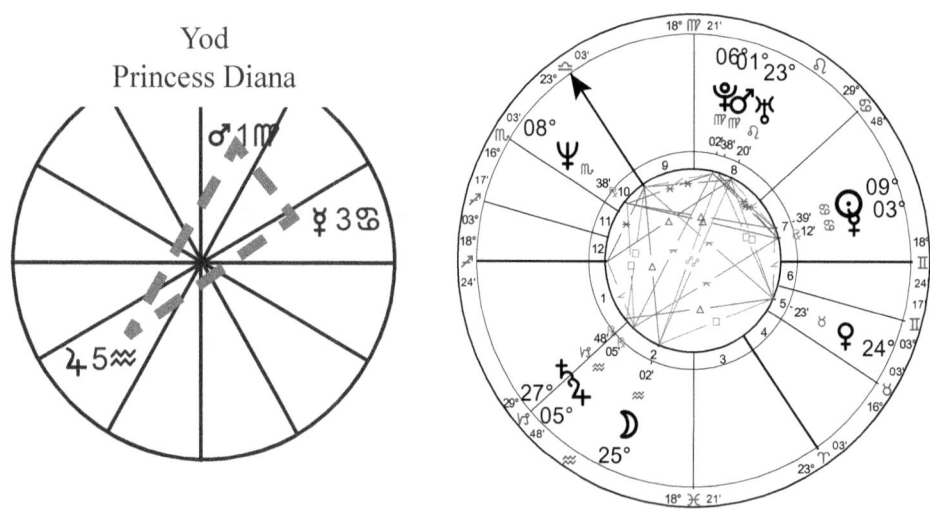

Yod
Princess Diana

A3. Aspects, Planet Patterns, Major Planet Configurations.

To help ground what has been taught so far, Winston Churchill's chart is examined. In the chart, we look firstly at the aspects. Students should verify for themselves which aspects are in play between the various planets and also with the ascendant and MC. Then the arrangements the planets make are examined. We look to see if they conform to any of the recognised Planet Patterns (Bowl, Bucket, etc.). Finally, we look for any Major Planet Configurations that have been formed between the planets. For example, such as a T-square or Grand Trine.

1. Aspects

a. There is one conjunction (☌) between Mars and Jupiter.

b. There are six semi-squares (∠) between Moon-Mars, Sun and Jupiter, Venus-Saturn, the ascendant with Mercury and Uranus, and Uranus with the MC.

c. There are six sextiles (✶) between the Sun and Saturn; Venus with Mars and Jupiter; Mars-Uranus; the MC with the Moon and Neptune.

d. There are five squares (□) Mercury with Saturn and Uranus; Venus with the ascendant; Uranus and Pluto, and the Ascendant and MC.

e. There are seven trines (△) The Moon with Venus and Neptune; Sun and Uranus; Venus with Uranus and Neptune; Mars and Saturn; and Jupiter with the MC.

f. There are three inconjuncts (⚻) between Pluto with Venus and Jupiter; and Neptune and the ascendant.

g. There are four oppositions (☍) between Mercury and Pluto; Venus and the MC; Jupiter and Neptune; and Saturn and Uranus.

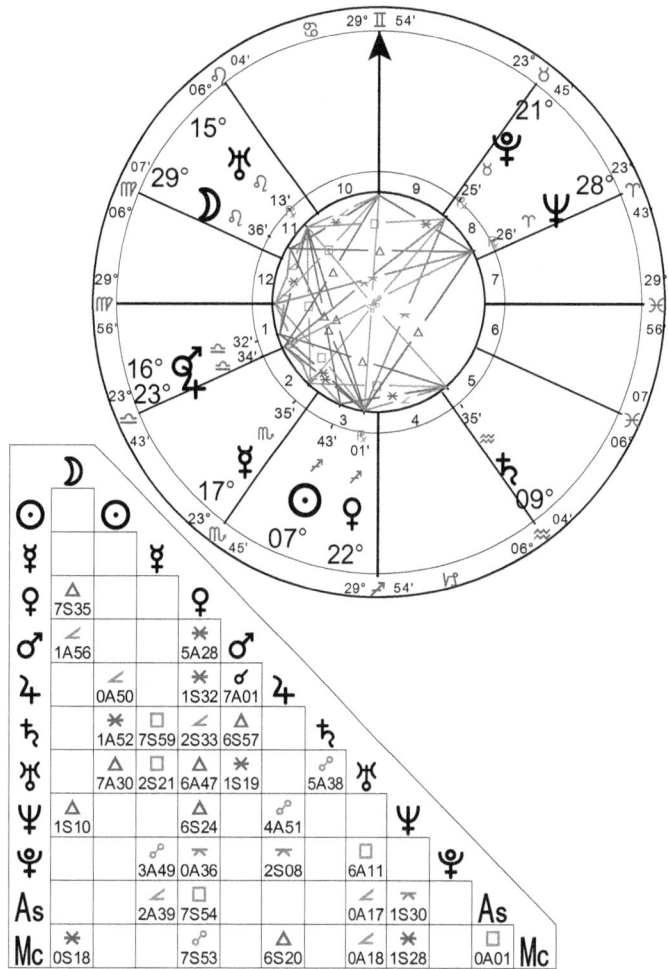

2. Planet Patterns.

Churchill's chart just fits into the "Bucket" pattern. "A single planet (two in this case) opposes all planets on the opposite side. The energy generated by the large group of planets will try to find release through the single planet. It is crucial therefore that the function symbolised by this planet is working well, or congested energy, anger and frustration will result." Pluto and Neptune are the handles of the pattern. They indicate that he was a very idealistic leader (Aries), and powerfully stubborn and driven in pursuing his goals (Taurus).

3. Major Planetary Configurations.

a. There is a T-square between Mercury, Pluto and Uranus; a second one between Uranus, Saturn and Mercury; and a third one between the Ascendant, MC and Venus.

b. There is a Grand Trine between the Moon, Neptune and Venus.

c. There is a Yod between Pluto, Venus and Jupiter.

A4. Reading Aspects

Hard aspects reflect our inner conflicts, which if not healed underlie our life problems. Easy aspects reflect our comfortable expressions. The average person's chart has a mixture of hard and easy aspects.

Sometimes people have more easy aspects than hard - for instance, may have two Grand-Trines and no squares. Life is easier for such people. But sometimes, because life is so easy, they may squander their talents and make nothing of themselves.

It seems that we need a few squares - disappointments with life and ourselves, difficulty in relating with others, rejection and hard-times; to help us make the most of our innate gifts, to strive for goals and to grow psychologically. Two positive keywords for the square, are "incentive" and "drive". Life rejections and disappointments can provide the fuel or incentive that drives us to change - and change is the spiritual goal. We are all evolving in consciousness, are expanding our talents and capabilities. View squares as opportunities for growth. Some charts are so laden with squares, there is a Grand Cross. This indicates a psyche that is constantly at war with itself and with others, so that crisis after crisis seems to dog the person's footsteps.

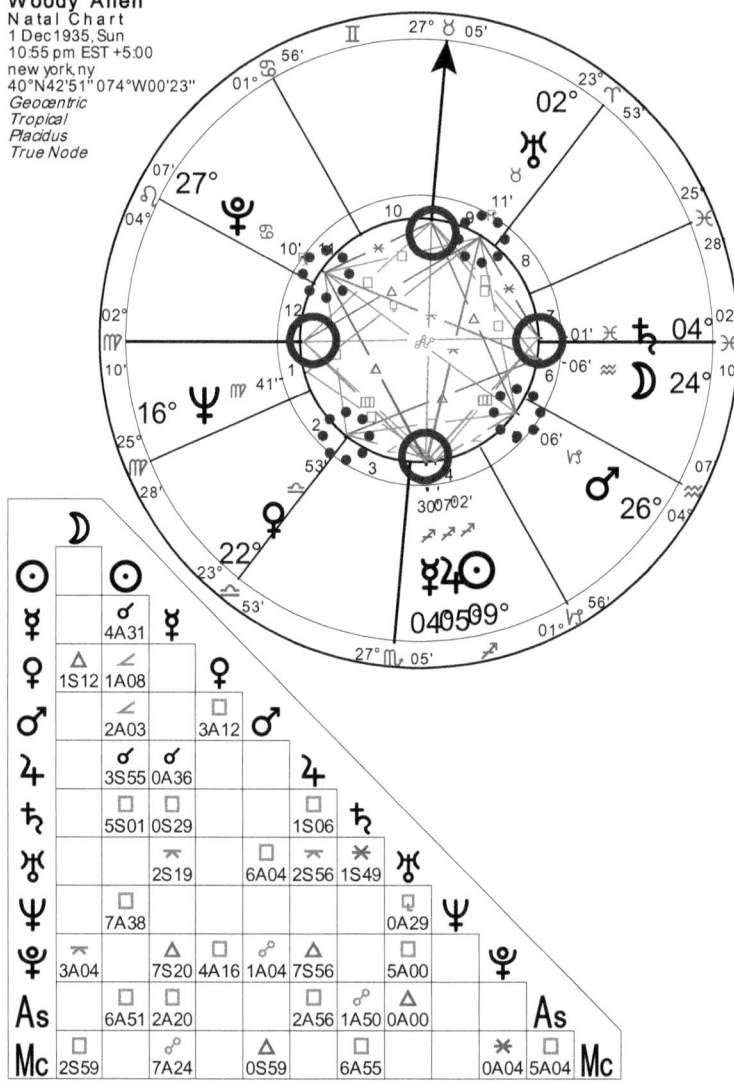

Movie Director Woody Allen has two Grand-Crosses marked out by two different sets of circles (dots and whole circles).

In one cross, one point touches the MC. Through hard work he achieved his movie-directing goals, and his films have been widely acclaimed. But he destroyed his marriage to Mia Farrow and family life when he covertly began an affair with his adopted daughter Soon-Yi Previn. One corner of this cross touches fourth house planets and another touches the cusp of the seventh house of marriage.

The second Grand Cross includes Venus, Mars, Uranus, Pluto, contributing to a nature that has unusual and obsessive desires. Mars (passion) is in the fifth house of children.

Many of us have Grand-Crosses and most of us use the energies in a constructive and healthy way.

When reading aspects.

1. Generally, do conjunctions first, because planets in conjunction work together as a unit.
2. Then you can either read the hard aspects first, and finish with easy aspects, so that the message finishes on a positive note.
3. Or you can read them as they appear on the chart grid, working from the inner planets, outwards. But in this method, still finish each section on a positive note.

B. PLANETS & ASTEROIDS IN ASPECT

Ceaselessly, the planets transit around the Sun, all the while playing upon the planets and points in the chart. What this means of course is that we are being constantly stimulated. The chart maps what happens to us in reality. The vitalisation that we receive is of the nature of the transit planet and the aspect is makes. These are explored in this section.

1. Sun Aspects - Personality Expression.

Sun and Moon. Self-expression and emotions unite. Easy aspects indicate that self-expression and emotions flow together. The basic nature is easy-going and the emotions contribute positively to life generally and in the home and family. Hard aspects are indicative of disharmony between the masculine and feminine natures and with members of the opposite sex. There is a tendency to be continually dragged back into the past, which the Moon is related to. If the sense of self is not strong, then the emotions could dominate healthy self-expression and could undermine the ability to express one's inner power potently. The goal in this case is to strengthen the Sun sign qualities and use them to dominate those of the Moon sign.

Sun-Mercury. Self-expression and communication unite. The only major aspect possible between these two is the conjunction. The desire to express one's truth is compelling and the combination does give the potential to communicate powerfully and effectively. However, unless there is mental strength, it will be hard to be dispassionate. If the mind is dominated by the ego, people will want to talk forcefully about themselves and their own interests. They will be less interested in listening to others or to reason. The signs these two planets are in will either help or be a hindrance to rational thought.

Sun-Venus. Self-expression and love unite. The personality is loving, charming, affectionate, and enjoys the company of other people. There is a love of art and beauty and artistic talent. The semi-square aspect can indicate irritability with partners and relationships that can lead to minor disagreements. At its highest, the combination indicates a personality that is wise and affectionate.

Sun-Mars. Self-expression and passion unite. There is energy and enthusiasm for life, a love of adventure and anything that provides an outlet for the boundless energy that this combination gives. But the conjunction and hard aspects can indicate impetuous foolhardiness, an impulse to take risks that leads to accidents and trouble. A parent figure could have been abusive in childhood and the urge to fight back could arise as angry and heated battles with authority figures. In such a case, a healthy outlet for this force should be found and passion re-directed towards achieving important life goals. Easy aspects imply the personality expresses itself confidently and assertively. The ability to lead will come easily and success will come in life enterprises.

Sun-Jupiter. Self-expression and expansiveness unite. This gives an easy-going, good-humoured and optimistic personality and an enthusiastic approach to life. Expressing itself in larger than life ways, it has a zest for living, for understanding and exploring. Sometimes an out-sized ego arises, an overly optimistic approach to life and a tendency to exaggerate. This is especially true with the conjunction and hard aspects. If so, the challenge is to learn moderation, right proportion and humility. Easy aspects and the conjunction help bring in life abundance and prosperity, a comfortable life, good fortune and success. However, some with this combination can be lazy, self-indulgent and squander life's gifts.

Sun-Saturn. Self-expression and discipline unite, giving a serious, stable, sensible and organised nature. Work and a career will be important and this combination gives ambition and the self-discipline to succeed. In childhood, a father figure may have been strict and imposing and if the repercussions of this are carried into adulthood it can lead to feelings of being restricted and a fear of going beyond safe boundaries. This is especially true of the hard aspects and conjunction. Being kind, generous and gentle with oneself is the remedy. There is a need to create one's own rules and beliefs on which to build the life. Easy aspects lighten the energies. Responsibilities are taken on with a sense of ease. Any of the combinations can lead to professional success. People just have to work harder with the squares.

Sun-Uranus. Self-expression and independence unite. The personality can be impulsive and determined to express its individuality and do things its own way - rebelliousness is embedded in the nature. This combination gives an inventive mind, a pioneering nature, unique talents and the power to be an original and innovative leader. Some take all this too far, are erratic, bizarre in their self-expression. People can view these expressions as arrogant, wilful and disruptive. This is especially true with the conjunction and hard aspects. Overall, this combination gives an interest in unusual, scientific or esoteric subjects. Easy aspects help this electric force to flow well. People will be attracted to the intelligent and friendly persona.

Sun-Neptune. Self-expression and spiritual-sensitivity unite. All aspects of the personality are rendered sensitive and are oriented towards artistry, musicality and idealistic causes. There is a natural urge to pursue the spiritual life. Delusion is always a possibility with all aspects. But there is less chance of succumbing with the easy aspects because it is easier for the personality to retain its sense of self. The conjunction and hard aspects indicate over-sensitivity, viewing life through rose-coloured glasses, being easily overwhelmed by life and becoming addicted to drugs and alcohol in an attempt to escape reality. Such people do not know who they really are or what they want. There is a need to be grounded.

Sun-Pluto. Self-expression and intense will unite, giving a very strong and sometimes an obsessive nature. There is great personal power, and a driving will to express one's deepest self in life, to impose the will generally. The potential exists to become a powerful and effective leader if the right balance of these forces is found. The conjunction and hard aspects give sharp edges. In childhood, some may become a victim of a powerful parent-type figure and the consequent trauma, if unhealed, can lead to explosive rages and potential abuse of oneself or others later. Personal transformation will be an ongoing feature of the life. The challenge for all who have this combination, is to use the power to transform themselves so that this force is expressed positively.

Sun-Vesta. Self-expression and purification unite. Dedication to a self-development program that will help be more authentic and confident is the goal. Any ego excesses that stand in the way of this higher potential must be purified. This is especially so with the conjunction and hard aspects. If extreme egoism is sabotaging the life, time should be taken out of the mainstream to deal with this and to gain clarity regarding life purpose. Those with this combination want to dedicate themselves to a cause of some sort.

Sun-Juno. Self-expression and marriage unite. The personality is drawn to marriage and this combination will help to form strong partnerships. However, the conjunction and hard aspects can indicate selfishness, possessiveness and potential jealousy that can wreck unions. The challenge is to be more aware of the partner's needs and try to find balance with one's own. Easy aspects make this easy. Relationships flow and unions are joyful and mutually beneficial.

Sun-Ceres Self-expression and nurturing unite. If in childhood, attempts at self-expression were rejected by a parent, low self-esteem will result. This is especially so with the conjunction and hard aspects. The goal then is to learn to unconditionally love and accept oneself, to provide the nurturing that was lacking. This will give greater confidence and esteem. The easy aspects indicate that childhood nurturing enabled positive self-esteem to develop. All aspects indicate the potential to help others overcome rejection and low self-esteem.

Sun-Pallas. Self-expression and mental-creativity unite. The personality is creative and intelligent and can see clearly the next step ahead to take. This leads to wise action. Women with this combination can do well in the traditional world of men. Just a note of caution with the conjunction and hard aspects. Ensure the ego does not override the mind. If the will is used to force ideas onto others, this will bring a backlash. The challenge is to learn from life experiences and to apply the wisdom gained. The easy aspects make it easier to succeed professionally, due to being open-minded and easier to get on with.

Sun-Chiron. Self-expression and healing-wisdom unite. If there are unhealed wounds stemming from childhood it can show as a personality that is scared to put itself forwards in life for fear of being hurt. The conjunction and hard aspects can indicate an obsession with caring for a wounded partner or parent and sacrificing the life to this end. If any of these exist, a wise counsellor or teacher should be sought for healing. Self-caring is required to allow one's emotional wounds to heal. The combination potentially gives a compassionate and wise nature and natural healing power. These gifts flow naturally with the easy aspects.

Sun-Nodes. Self-expression and spiritual goals unite. The personality is required to move forwards on the Spiritual Path and to express in life what is learnt. Sun conjunct the north-node helps this to be achieved. The conjunction to the south-node indicates a tendency to get bogged down in the past and this is hindering forwards progression. The challenge is to cut the past away and to be free of it.

Sun-Asc. Self-expression and new beginnings unite. This combination gives a radiant personality and power to shine one's light into life and to influence people. Easy aspects make it easy to do this and power flows naturally. Hard aspects indicate self-expression is difficult, force is not wisely directed and this will cause conflict. The purpose of the soul with this combination, is to learn to express personality power fully and harmoniously into life.

Sun-MC. Self-expression and higher-goals unite. The personality likes to shine in the public eye. It wants status and good standing and therefore has strong ambitions to succeed in the chosen life direction. This will be easier with the conjunction and easy aspects. Hard aspects indicate personality obstacles will stand in the way, but there is a will to succeed that can bring success eventually if illegal methods are avoided. Otherwise, fame could come by being notorious.

2. Moon Aspects - Emotional Expression

Moon-Mercury. Emotions and communications unite, imagination with logic. This manifests as an urge to communicate one's feelings, especially with family. With the hard aspects, because thoughts and speech are strongly affected by the emotions, care should be taken to calm oneself before communicating. Otherwise arguments could erupt and bad decisions could be made. Easy aspects give the ability to communicate thoughts and feelings with ease and clarity. There is an easy and relaxed approach with women and the public. Emotional and family relationships will flow because the right words will be found to ease troubled waters.

Moon-Venus. Emotions and love unite. The goal is to develop loving and nurturing relationships. This will be a challenge for hard aspects. Difficulties in expressing the affections will result in problems in intimate unions - especially within the family; until this is overcome. Easy aspects and the conjunction indicate an easy flow of love and appreciation towards people generally. This will benefit all relationships and help to ease any difficulties that arise. There is charm, love of artistic or creative interests, of beauty and a need for peace and harmony in the home and in family relationships. The public will love any artistic creations.

Moon-Mars. Emotions and passion unite. This gives impulsive and reactive emotions. This tendency is accentuated with the conjunction and hard aspects. The nature is quick-tempered, impatient and irritable; is insensitive to the feelings of others and intolerant. In such a case, anger will cause difficulties in all emotionally based relationships. The goal is to be less reactive and to think before acting. Emotional balance (the easy aspects), results in an assertive, motivated and self-confident nature. There is an ability to recognise opportunities, make the most of them and rise to all challenges. An abundance of positive energy is available to direct into life goals and this will lead to success. Emotional and family relationships will be energetic and potent and relations with the public will be dynamic and positive.

Moon-Jupiter. Emotions and expansiveness unite, giving generosity and warmth. There is optimism about life and a belief that few things will be out of reach. Easy aspects bring luck and success because the benevolent and good-humoured nature has a broad appeal to the public. Consequently, all relationships - but especially those with the family, will be rewarding. Hard aspects indicate imbalance in the emotions, a tendency to excessive, self-indulgent and extravagant behaviours. There may be unrealistic expectations. Moderation is required - this will help ensure family relationships are joy-filled and happy.

Moon-Saturn. Emotions and discipline unite. Positively, this gives a responsible nature, with family and with the public at large. However, the conjunction and hard aspects can indicate deprivation of early nurturing and can manifest as repressed emotions. There can be feelings of insecurity, coldness, ultra-caution, guilt, fear of authority and low self-esteem. The remedy for this is to provide for oneself, the nurturing that was denied by others; to learn to value and accept oneself "warts and all." This will help to build good self-esteem. Easy aspects give an inner self-confidence that helps to build firm foundations in life and stable family relations. Authority figures will be supportive and this will help realise the ambitions.

Moon-Uranus. Emotions and independence unite, there is inventiveness and a love of freedom. Emotionally, the nature likes excitement and has a preference for the unconventional. It does not like to conform, especially in home and family relationships where there will be many changes. The conjunction and hard aspects give an erratic, emotionally unpredictable and stubbornly individualistic nature. In this case, both public and family life will be unstable and unpredictable and remain so until inner harmony is achieved. The easy aspects indicate that the emotions are comfortable with change and enjoy the unexpected, the new and exciting. Freedom will be given to explore life and the family and public will be accepting of any unconventional ideas or creations that are presented.

Moon-Neptune. Feelings and spiritual-sensitivity unite. This gives an ultra-sensitive emotional nature and empathy and compassion for the pain and suffering of others. The family will often have a strong spiritual or artistic component. Contact with sacred places or centres of cultural beauty will help to develop the artistic, spiritual and creative nature. The downside is that it is easy for the feelings to be over-whelmed. This is especially so with the conjunction and hard aspects where the potential exists for reality to be lost in dreams and fantasy. Such people view life through rose-coloured glasses, may try to escape through drugs or religious cults. In such a case, discernment is required and common sense.

Moon-Pluto. Emotions and intense will unite. This gives a deeply passionate nature, prone to explosive outbursts if the emotional nature is not balanced. A love of drama will create problems if it is not well-managed or channelled into a creative outlet. But positively expressed, the will exists to make substantial achievements. There is deep insight into people and an understanding of their motives. The conjunction and hard aspects can indicate abuse - someone with all the power preying on someone weaker. In such a case, professional assistance is required for protection and to help restore emotional health and balance. Intimate and family relationships will be difficult until then. Overall, there will be profound changes in home and family relationships.

Moon-Vesta. Emotions and purification unite. Emotionalism and its power to distort reality and bind us to the past needs to be purified - especially with the hard aspects. Time should be taken out of the mainstream every now and then for regeneration, to dedicate oneself to practises that will clear the emotions and to help gain clarity regarding life purpose. Easy aspects make it easy to do this and also to help other people work through their emotions and find their purpose.

Moon-Juno. Emotions and marriage unite. The ability to commit and give of oneself emotionally in formal relationships is enhanced and this will help to form harmonious and pleasurable unions. This is especially so with the easy aspects, which indicate it will be easy to meet these commitments and to give emotional support to the partner and be supported in return. Hard aspects make this more difficult. There may be a reluctance to commit, or possessiveness and jealousy could tarnish unions. The remedy required is to develop a healthy emotional relationship with oneself first. This will ease all outer emotional relations.

Moon-Ceres. Emotions and nurturing unite. If emotional nurturing was not provided in childhood, if there was rejection by a parent or carer, this will result in low self-esteem. This is more likely to occur with the hard aspects. In such a case, the goal is to nurture and learn to unconditionally love and accept oneself - to provide what was not given by others. Easy aspects indicate that early nurturing and love was provided and this will have resulted a sense of inner well-being and confidence. All aspects give insight into those who suffer from low self-esteem and the power to help them by embracing them with care and understanding.

Moon-Pallas. Emotions and mental-creativity unite. If emotional balance has been established, (more likely with the easy aspects), the intuition will combine well with the mind and executive talents and this will lead to success in the career as well as in life generally. With this combination, women can do well in any traditional male-dominated career. If, however, the emotions are stronger than the intellect and outdated beliefs and notions are pushed onto others (hard aspects); this will bring difficulties and disruptions in family and business relationships. The goal in this case is to be more open-minded.

Moon-Chiron. Emotions and healing-wisdom unite. The aspect indicates that emotional wounding will lead a search for healing and as a consequence, wisdom will be developed. The conjunction and hard aspects indicate the healing process is to occur in this life and until this is achieved, unhappy memories from the past will be projected onto all emotional relations, contaminating them. Partners will be attracted who are similarly cold. A wise counsellor-healer should be consulted to help this process. Easy aspects indicate wisdom was gained in a past-life experience and the gift of healing is available to use in the current life. All aspects indicate that the potential exists to become a sensitive and empathetic healer

Moon-Nodes. Emotions and spiritual-progression unite. Moon conjunct the north-node and easy aspects indicate a desire for progressive growth and to use the home for spiritual or goodwill purposes. The opposite applies for a conjunction to the south-node and hard aspects. There is a tendency to get stuck in negative emotional patterns that bind one to the past. The family could be the problem.

Moon-Asc. Emotions and new beginnings unite. Moon conjunct the ascendant indicates that the mother or women generally, will have a major influence on the life. This will be beneficial with easy aspects and difficult with the hard aspects. The emotions are sensitive, reactive and close to the surface, so are easily seen by onlookers. There may be anxieties about the appearance or dislike of the body image. Easy aspects indicate healthy emotional engagements with women and the public. The purpose of the soul is to purify the emotions and to express them healthily into life.

Moon-MC. Emotions and important-goals unite. The desire to be well regarded by the public and accepted is prominent in the nature. Additionally, emotional security is wanted in the chosen profession and the mother may influence career choices. Easy aspects indicate the family or public will be supportive in the achievement of important life goals. Hard aspects and the conjunction, indicate emotional issues and domestic problems may prevent the desired success.

3. Mercury Aspects - Mental Expression.

Mercury-Venus. Communication and love unite. Communications are intelligent and it is easy to speak affectionately with others, to converse socially with people and get pleasure out of words and thoughts. This combination gives talent with creative writing and art. The semi-square can indicate irritable and scratchy communications with partners and relationships.

Mercury-Mars. Communication and passions unite. This combination speeds up the mind and gives it heat. New ideas are quickly grasped. Speech is forthright, fast. The mind is sharp and has powerful debating skills. Adept at communication, those with this combination defend themselves very well with words. But communications can turn angry and aggressive with hard aspects. Or alternatively, may be repressed so that angry thoughts turn within and affect the nerves. Even so, the mind is sharp and with training, can be used constructively to achieve goals rather than to destroy them through constant verbal combat.

Mercury-Jupiter. Communication and expansiveness unite. There are big ideas and plans and the bigger life-picture is seen. The mind is broad-minded, talkative and has a thirst for knowledge so that travel and education may feature largely in the life. A warm sense of humour and praise for others helps social interactions and this, along with the ability to communicate with people from all walks of life, contributes to life-success. Hard aspects show a mind that exaggerates and that lacks right proportion. In such a case, big ideas and plans can come to naught, promises may not be kept and outright lies told to fool people. Moderation is required.

Mercury-Saturn. Communication and discipline unite. This mind is impressed with seriousness. It is a deep thinker, is logical and practical. With this combination - as children, we may have felt it was unsafe to express an opinion, in case we were rebuked. But as an adult and with the right training, the combination can permit one to become a voice of authority. There is common sense and ability to communicate clearly, without frills and without judgement. This is especially so with easy aspects. Hard aspects and the conjunction give the mind rigidity and difficulty communicating due to an authority figure - probably the father, being critical and repressive in childhood. These inhibitions can be overcome. The remedy is to learn to think kindly of oneself and others.

Mercury-Uranus. Communication and independence unite, giving an independent mind. It is incisive and potentially ingenious and has an interest in progressive topics and original ideas and opinions. There is natural expertise in science and new technologies (such as internet) and esoteric knowledges. Hard aspects can render chaos to the mind - ideas can be bizarre and difficult to understand, thoughts and speech may be erratic, original ideas may be impractical. The wilful defence of one's right to free speech may deny the same right to others with different opinions. The positive use of these energies is more likely with the easy aspects. But hard aspects give an edge to such a mind and it will work well with a little discipline.

Mercury-Neptune. Communication and spiritual-sensitivity unite. This gives an imaginative, artistic mind and the ability to communicate one's talents through oratory, writings or through other creative medias. Such people are inspirational thinkers, orators, preachers, artists, etc. However, the conjunction and hard aspects are more challenging and can indicate a lot of time spent fantasising, vague thoughts that lack accuracy, even a tendency to tell lies. If so, other people will be vague and similarly dishonest.

Mercury-Pluto. Communication and wilfulness unite, giving a keen, probing mind. Social chitchat is avoided in favour of deep and meaningful conversations. Communications are powerful, they carry authority. Words are straight to the point and potent. There is delving and research talent, an interest in the mysterious and meaningful. People with this combination make wonderful research scientists, psychologists and detectives. The conjunction and hard aspects can add a touch of "darkness" to the mind, so there is cruel speech, obsessive thoughts, attempts to destroy people through words or in writing.

Mercury-Vesta. Communication and purification unite. If negative thinking and harmful ways of communicating exist, these need to be purified. It will be useful to take time out of the mainstream for regeneration, to dedicate time to a self-development program that will help expand the way the world is viewed and to practise techniques that will help achieve a clear and peaceful mind and harmlessness in speech. With this combination, the opportunity exists to help others in the same way.

Mercury-Juno. Communication and marriage unite. Thoughts will turn constantly to one's marriage or partner. This accentuates the need for good communication so that the union flows smoothly. Efforts to do this will boost harmonious communications and benefit the commitment. However, hard aspects indicate that relationships could be damaged by the communication of jealous and critical thoughts and words. If so, the challenge is to learn to communicate one's needs to the partner in ways that are positive and kind.

Mercury-Ceres. Communication and nurturing unite. Communications with carers and parents when a child will have a profound impact upon the thought life. If they were negative, if there was criticism, a habit of self-criticising will develop. This is more likely with the hard aspects. If so, the goal is to learn to talk to oneself and to others, in a kind and nurturing way. If early efforts were supported (easy aspects), self-esteem will be good and nurturing and kind speech will flow naturally, boosting the self-esteem of others.

Mercury-Pallas. Communication and mental-creativity unite. Sharp and creative, this mind can vision the future, the best next step forwards to take and what to do to manifest ideas. In a woman, it gives the ability to excel - intellectually and assertively; in traditional male careers. Hard aspects give a sharp edge and determination to force ideas onto others, to judge and criticise. In this case, the challenge is to think kindlier. But generally, this combination gives the potential to succeed in the personal and professional life due to being open-minded, creative and wise.

Mercury-Chiron. Communication and healing-wisdom unite. If early childhood communications were difficult, we can grow up believing something is wrong with us and with what we say. This deepens with the hard aspects - the mind can be rigid and dogmatic and so can thoughts and speech be. If so, courses to develop good communication skills and assertiveness are recommended. But overall, this combination indicates an understanding of people and their issues, the ability to listen sympathetically and give wise counsel. It is a good combination for teaching and healing.

Mercury-Nodes. Mind and spiritual-progression unite. There is a need to develop good communication skills because the destiny is linked to some form of teaching or communication. The conjunction to the north-node and easy aspects will help positive communications to flow. The conjunction to the south-node points to mental attitudes that are retrogressive and that keep one bound to a cycle of negative thinking and ongoing arguments that lead nowhere. The goal is to think more positively about oneself and others.

Mercury-Asc. Communication and new beginnings unite. There is a curiosity about life, a desire to understand what it is all about. There is enjoyment in discovering new ideas and sharing these with others - there will be many journeys of discovery. Communications will play a major role in the life and these will be well received by people who will see one as being an interesting and knowledgeable communicator. This is especially so with the conjunction and easy aspects. Hard aspects indicate some difficulty in getting one's point across clearly and accurately. Confident communication of one's truth, is an important spiritual goal.

Mercury-MC. Communication and higher-goals unite. Good communication will play a key role in achieving important life goals. The profession may involve writing, teaching, publishing, selling or be transport related. Consequently, the development of good communication skills and learning to speak assertively and clearly will help to achieve the desired success. People in authority will be impressed with what one has to say. This is especially so with the conjunction and easy aspects. Hard aspects point to communication conflicts and misunderstandings that can sabotage these goals.

4. Venus Aspects - Expression of Affection.

Venus-Mars. Love and Passion unite. The male and female sides are related to each other and this will help create an attraction to and with the opposite sex. The nature of this attraction and the ease with which it plays out depends upon the signs and aspects. Hard aspects bring challenges - a struggle to balance one's own needs and the needs of the partner. Selfish demands could ruin an otherwise good union. The ideal is to be less demanding, more accepting of oneself and of the other. Easy aspects and the conjunction (well aspected), indicate a talent for relating to the opposite sex, being a loyal and fun-loving partner with an ability to balance intimacy with independence. It will be easy to attract lovers and sex will be satisfying.

Venus-Jupiter. Love and expansiveness unite, giving a fun loving, generous approach in relationships, marriage and towards life generally. Being generous with partners, spoiling and indulging those who are loved - this comes naturally and will bring a blessing to unions. However, with hard aspects there is a need to make sure that one's behaviour does not become extravagant so that financial worries arise causing trouble in the union. Some with this combination can be irresponsible and unwilling to work through problems. There may be a childlike expectancy that someone will always come to the rescue, will always be there to give love and support. But overall, the aspect brings luck in life and love because of the generosity of spirit that this combination represents.

Venus-Saturn. Love and discipline unite. Faithful and loyal, those with this combination are dependable, stable and dutiful partners. It gives an ability to organise social occasions and the ability to form good business, personal and intimate partnerships. Some with this placement become involved romantically with an older person or someone who offers material security. Once formed, important relationships will endure because they are grounded on firm foundations. Easy aspects help such unions flow, helps love to arise and last. Hard aspects and the conjunction however, brings challenges. There may be a fear commitment, an inability to trust and show love. This can play out as trying to control the partner or vice versa, the partner is the controlling one. Such unions can be cold, devoid of love. Learning to love oneself is essential, because then there will be love to give to others.

Venus-Uranus. Love and independence unite. Uranus is called the divorce planet, but this combination can work if there is enough regard for the partner and the relationship. Problems arise (hard aspects and sometimes conjunction), if one insists upon maintaining full individual rights within the relationships and to be free to come and go. Choice of a partner is important, because there is a tendency to get bored and restless in traditional relationships. Spontaneity and intellectual stimulation are needed. Compromise is required to avoid spending the life alone or in short-lived, unstable relationships. However, some bachelor types may prefer this. Easy aspects indicate that freedom, change and excitement can be found in relationships. There is an ability for both partners to express their individual interests, while maintaining a loving union. This combination enables love to be continually refreshed.

Venus-Neptune. Love and spiritual-sensitivity unite. This combination throws a rosy glow over relationships and marriage. Those with this combination may seek a perfect partner who only exists in fairy tales. When a real human being comes along, they are disillusioned. Especially with the conjunction planets and hard aspects. It gives an idealistic but unrealistic way of viewing life. Partners may be attracted who appear wonderful on the surface, but lack substance and stability. The goal is to see oneself and others as they really are, not how we wish they were or could be. In such a case, the emotions should be balanced and one's expectations adjusted. But overall, the urge to find and express beauty is accentuated and there is loving compassion for the less fortunate. A spiritual orientation is present - along with musical and artistic talent. Easy aspects help these to manifest healthily. Hard aspects mean we have to sift through delusion before finding the real thing.

Venus-Pluto. Love and wilfulness unite, bringing drama to personal relationships. In love, there are no half-measures. Pluto adds an intensity and depth of feeling so that one can be consumed with love and passion and expect the partner to feel the same way. This becomes destructive (hard aspects and conjunction), if "love" becomes obsessive and steps are taken to manipulate the partner to keep control. Moderation is required. Easy aspects bring the right balance so although there is the tendency to bond deeply with the loved one, there is also an ability to make the necessary changes demanded to keep the union healthy, balanced and wholesome. But generally, there is a deep well of unending love to give.

Venus-Vesta. Love and purification unite. Any misuse of sexual energy (hard aspects), or ongoing problems in relationships that defy fixing; need attention. The traits causing the problems are also impediments to spiritual progression. If these exist, take time out of life for regeneration, to improve the relationship skills and to find beauty in one's life purpose. Easy aspects indicate that the right balance can be struck, between the personal, intimate life and spiritual endeavours.

Venus-Juno. Love and marriage unite. The ability to commit deeply to a formal relationship is strong. But hard aspects indicate difficulties. There could be a reluctance to marry or to commit fully because flirtatious games are more fun. Alternatively, jealousy and possessiveness could destroy an otherwise healthy union. For harmony's sake, the partner and the relationship need to be more highly valued. Easy aspects indicate that marriage will go well because one is a romantic and will remain so; and a partner will be attracted who be the same. Together, a very beautiful, loving and intimate relationship can be formed.

Venus-Ceres. Love and nurturing unite. Parental nurturing and the love required to develop into a self-confident and loving adult, these come with the easy aspects and the conjunction - so will the ability to nurture people. On the other hand, hard aspects indicate that this kindness was not available resulting in low self-esteem. Without healing, this will impair the ability to nurture children or others. The remedy is to provide the nurturing that was withheld, by being kind to oneself - physically, emotionally, mentally and spiritually.

Venus-Pallas. Love and mental-creativity unite. Wise in the ways of love, mental-creativity and artistic skills can be used to beautify oneself and to enhance all relationships. These skills can also be used to build a successful career that is associated with Venus - such as in art, cosmetics, design or counselling. Hard aspects show that over-thinking, being too analytical and a lack of empathy will harm unions. The challenge is to learn from bad experiences and apply the wisdom gained to build more beautiful relationships in the future.

Venus-Chiron. Love and healing-wisdom unite. Childhood wounds associated with being lovable (or not) will be more serious with hard aspects. Rejections from parents or carers, being deprived of kindness and attention, these will result in difficulties in giving and receiving love. If so, the goal is to learn to unconditionally love and accept oneself. Easy aspects and the conjunction, indicate love and nurturing was provided and this helped to heal emotional wounds from previous lives - or, alternatively, it will be easy to heal hurts suffered in the present life. The gift of this combination (all aspects), is the power to heal through love.

Venus-the Nodes. Love and spiritual-progression unite. The spiritual destiny is linked to the development of harmonious and balanced relationships - with the soul, within oneself and with others. Art or beauty could also be involved. But the end goal is to develop intelligent love and to give this to others. This will be easier with the north-node conjunction and easy aspects. Venus conjunct the south-node and hard aspects indicate that emotional hurts from past relationships have not yet been resolved and are impediments to moving forwards. These must be dealt with to break the binding shackles around the heart.

Venus-Asc. Love and new beginnings unite. There is a nimbus of glowing beauty surrounding those who have the easy aspects and the conjunction to the ascendant. Affectionate and kind (and seen to be so by people looking on); this combination brings popularity and love. Hard aspects indicate clashes between the desire to love and putting it into practice. There is a need to reconcile these conflicts if harmony in intimate and personal relationships is to be found. With all aspects, wisdom is seeking expression into the life.

Venus-MC. Love and higher-goals unite. Those with this combination love to shine in the public eye and the career could reflect Venus' touch, such as those involving art, beauty, colour, harmony and counselling. Relationships and love will always be important. The partner should have a good reputation and relationships should be seen by the public as working well. This is especially so with the conjunction and easy aspects. There should be no "washing of dirty clothes in public." The same ideals remain with hard aspects, but there are impediments. Unwise actions - one's own or the partners, could bring unions into disrepute. Either way, loving relationships and a career that brings pleasure to the life are important life goals.

5. Mars Aspects - Expression of Desire.

Mars-Jupiter. Passion and expansiveness, unite. Energy levels are high, there is abundant courage and a tendency to go where "angels fear to tread." Life is approached with gusto regardless of the consequences. Travel, higher study and religious causes are likely to feature in the life, alternatively - the military, competitive sports or promotional work. For the hard aspects, there is a need to discipline the desire nature and its impulses. Otherwise, anger and rash actions could impede the achievement goals or cause accidents. But overall, enthusiasm and belief in oneself will make it easy to achieve success.

Mars-Saturn. Passion and discipline unite and this is not an easy mix in most cases. This is because Mars wants to leap ahead impulsively and Saturn is discipline personified. This combination often manifests as a feeling that something always blocks the way ahead and this leads to frustration. Hard aspects and the conjunction can manifest as tough discipline in childhood. A father or other authority figure restricting freedom and using the will to force compliance. In such a case, festering anger can smoulder for years and should be dealt with to avoid health problems. In this case, the goal is to find inner peace and direct the pent-up energy into the pursuit of goals. Easy aspects indicate that passion and ambition work harmoniously together and this will lead to life success. The career may involve law and order, the government, the military or administration of authority.

Mars-Uranus. Passion and independence unite. There is a wilful, devil-may-care outlook, a highly independent streak and determination to get one's way. With the conjunction and hard aspects, although there is courage, it is just as likely to be accompanied with foolhardiness. The temper flares easily and is unpredictable. If pornography is studied, the dark side of the nature can rise up and unhealthy sexual tastes. Sexual experimentation is likely, but care needs to be taken if trouble is to be avoided and danger. There is a need to discipline the wild, unruly side of the nature to avoid trouble and accidents. But overall, high energy levels, enthusiasm and innovative talent will bring success in life - especially with the easy aspects.

Mars-Neptune. Passion and spiritual-sensitivity unite - this heightens emotionalism. If the nature is not balanced (conjunction and hard aspects), a yearning for the highs of life and to escape from emotional pain, this can lead to addictive behaviours. Consequently, with this aspect, it is better to avoid alcohol or drugs or to be vigilant that one does not become dependent upon them. Fiery, righteous anger could result in strange viruses and debilitating tiredness. This force can be directed healthily through art, water sports or recreation, in nature studies or going on a spiritual search. With this combination generally, there is an enthusiasm for higher "things."

Mars-Pluto. Passion and wilfulness unite, giving an enormous pool of energy that is very useful in achieving life goals. Highly competitive, those with this combination can do well in activities which require strength, courage and risk-taking. There is self-belief and a passionate drive and will to commit to anything the heart desires (conjunction and easy aspects). But the force can be dangerous if it is not managed carefully. Those who have it like to be in control and to get their way. But if balked - and the emotions are not balanced (conjunction and hard aspects), unreasoning, volcanic outbursts will erupt. The sexual drive will also be strong and should be directed into healthy expression to avoid over-stimulation of the lower appetites. Any excesses need to be moderated.

Mars-Vesta. Passion and purification unite. Emotional and sexual energies need purifying. Dedication to a self-development program that will help balance and refine these forces is important. The work involved will clear perception and give clarity about how to use these energies more wisely in the future. Hard aspects indicate the misuse of emotional and/ or sexual force is sabotaging the life.

In such a case, time should be taken out of mainstream life for a reset and for self-training so these energies can be used more constructively in the future. All aspects indicate the potential to coordinate these forces and direct them towards some dedicated task to help the greater good.

Mars-Juno. Passion and marriage unite. This combination indicates that the physical side of marriage will be important, so a partner should be chosen who also enjoys a passionate sexual life and physical recreational activities. Formal relationships can go well because a lot of energy will be expended into meeting marital commitments. However, the conjunction and hard aspects indicate anger, jealousy, possessiveness and a tendency to project one's stuff onto the partner. These are due to one's own insecurities and should be healed to avoid turning marriage into a battleground. In more serious instances, there could be physical or sexual abuse and in such a case, leaving the union may be for the best.

Mars-Ceres. Passion and nurturing unite. With this combination, physical, hands-on parenting style is welcome. Doing physical recreational things together, going on adventures and being encouraged by a supportive parent all the way, will help build good self-esteem. Being helped to understand sex and its healthy function is another important element. However, the hard aspects and the conjunction indicate physical even sexual abuse. The consequences of this will extend into adulthood if not healed - anger, low self-esteem and potential hurting of others. The goal is to learn to love and accept oneself and respect the sexual function. Positively, the aspect indicates an ability to help build self-esteem in others through physical adventures.

Mars-Pallas. Passion and mental-creativity unite. This combination adds intelligence and creative insight to the brute force of Mars and is a great combination in any avenue of life that requires both - such as in competitive sports where strategy is required. It is also a great asset to have in the corporate world, especially for women, who would do well in the traditional world of men with this force. However, the road to success will not be smooth with the hard aspects and the conjunction. It indicates a tendency to force one's ideas onto others in an aggressive manner, causing conflict and resentment. The challenge is to learn from such experiences and in the future, apply the wisdom gained assertively and not aggressively.

Mars-Chiron. Passion and healing-wisdom unite. Early home life that was too rough, angry or abusive has resulted in emotional wounds that need healing. The problem will not be so severe with easy aspects and in fact, may contribute to self-confidence being developed through physical adventures and play. But hard aspects and the conjunction can indicate serious physical and sexual abuses and if so, cause very deep and debilitating emotional wounds. If these are not healed, they will disrupt the entire life and result in aggressive actions with others. Overall, there is sensitive understanding about these kinds of hurts and a gift for being able to defend and to speak up on behalf of those who have been similarly injured.

Mars-Nodes. Passion and spiritual-progression unite. This combination indicates enthusiasm and passion for self-development and for spiritual growth. These practises will have a physical element, such as with tai chi, yoga or walking meditations. These will come easily with a north-node conjunction and easy aspects. But a conjunction to the south-node and hard aspects, these indicate unhealed emotional hurts from the past are preventing forwards progression. Old battles are still being fought - within oneself and with others. These need to be healed and a deliberate effort made to let go of the past and to move forwards.

Mars-Asc. Passion and new beginnings unite. All aspects indicate high energy and a willingness to take action to assert one's authority and to control the environment. There is a fount of enthusiasm that is very useful when goals are being pursued. There is also an attraction to physical and competitive activities. But with the conjunction and hard aspects, life-approach is aggressive and emotionally reactive and this will cause trouble with others and accidents. People may see those with this combination as being defensive and angry, too blunt and uncompromisingly direct. A wider perspective of life should be developed and tolerance and patience. But positively, there is the will and drive to achieve goals.

Mars-MC. Passion unites with higher goals. There is much energy and enthusiasm available to pour into the profession, to realise one's ambitions and to compete for the higher prize. This is a very useful aspect to have if recognition and professional-life success is desired. However, hard aspects indicate this force is not wisely directed and that anger and rash actions are impediments to higher achievements. In some cases, these could lead to notoriety so that recognition is gained but for all the wrong reasons. When this fiery aspiration is wisely directed, well-earned success will come.

6. Jupiter Aspects - Expansion of Consciousness.

Jupiter-Saturn. Expansiveness and discipline unite. These forces are diametrically opposite - Jupiter expands, Saturn contracts. It can result in feeling torn between a need for freedom and one's duties and responsibilities. Positively applied (the easy aspects), optimism is tempered by common sense, giving the ability to progress forwards nicely within a structured system. This combination is ideal for business and religious explorations. Hard aspects can manifest as a sense of fluctuating between feelings of confidence and failure, of moving forwards only to be blocked. The key is to gain confidence in one's own abilities by trying and testing them in life experience - taking on little projects first and gradually building up to those that are larger. Self-respect will be gained and respect from others.

Jupiter-Uranus. Expansiveness and independence unite. There is enormous energy and enthusiasm for all that is new and wonderful, a desire to explore the unknown and untried and to see what is on the other side of life. This enthusiasm for wider understanding and for independence in expression, extends to higher study, religion, philosophy, esoterica and travel. But the hard aspects give an abrasive touch. An urge to change the world to one's design is not applied wisely and there is impatience and a lack of persistence to see through any changes. For all aspects, there is a restless spirit that wants to travel far. At its highest potentially, it enables us to find true wisdom and knowledge about the mysteries of life.

Jupiter-Neptune. Expansiveness and spiritual-sensitivity unite. This combination expands the urge for exploration and discovery in the spiritual or metaphysical realms. It broadens empathy and compassion and a desire to heal and save the suffering in the world. It also gives talent for music and the arts, the ability to tell stories that can transport listeners to other worlds. Hard aspects and the conjunction however, indicate that emotionalism, delusion and unrealistic expectations will expand. If life is being viewed through "rose-coloured glasses", judgement and the ability to discriminate will be impaired. The antidote is to stop dreaming and be real about life, to keep one's feet on the ground and not get carried away with unrealistic dreams. For all combinations, there will be a call to serve others in one of the caring or spiritual areas.

Jupiter-Pluto. Expansiveness and wilfulness unite, giving an enthusiasm to live life to the fullest. Whatever is done, will be done in a big way. If the ego is kept under control, much can be achieved. There is leadership skill and a style that will be popular because it is characterised by warm enthusiasm and encouragement. This is especially so with the easy aspects. Problems can arise with the conjunction and hard aspects. If the ego expands instead of the heart, grandiose but unrealistic plans can arise. A huge dissatisfaction with society may motivate too radical or destructive actions, bringing a formidable backlash. To get the best out of this combination, to achieve what one's heart is set on - keep a humble spirit.

Jupiter-Vesta. Expansiveness and purification unite. This combination indicates a need to rein in self-indulgent activities which waste time and energy that stand in the way of achieving higher life or spiritual goals. This is especially so with the hard aspects. These emotions and impulses need to be purified. Dedication to a self-development program that will help balance these excesses is required. Easy aspects can give innate wisdom about how to conserve one's enthusiasms sensibly and how to use them to the best advantage in life. Teaching these skills to others is also a possibility.

Jupiter-Juno. Expansiveness and marriage unite. The ability to create a happy marriage or partnership is enhanced, because the nature is easy-going, warm-hearted, generous and there is laughter (which heals). Relationships will be an adventure and partners will be friends as well as lovers. Greater effort will be required however, with the hard aspects. Excesses and selfish indulgences can spoil an otherwise harmonious union. Commitments may be avoided because they interfere with freedom and pleasure-seeking pastimes. For a stable partnership, greater practicality and discipline may be required.

Jupiter-Ceres. Expansiveness and nurturing unite. Generally, early life will have been supportive, with parents being on hand to give encouragement and praise. The household will have rung out with laughter and the hustle and bustle of people going enthusiastically about their business and on adventures and travel. This early start to life will boost self-esteem and self-confidence. Hard aspects can indicate feeling alone or rejected because parents were too preoccupied or attention was spasmodic so that ongoing support could not be relied on. But overall, this is a fortunate combination and indicates trust in the beneficence of the universe to provide.

Jupiter-Pallas. Expansiveness and mental-creativity unite. This combination combines intelligence with wisdom, a most fortunate aspect or ability to have and one that when it is well-directed, will bring success in any area of life. The mind is able to soar into the realms of philosophy, religion etc., to learn from what has been studied and to apply what has been grasped effectively in life. Though this still holds true for the hard aspects, an element of dogma or rigidity in beliefs may exist and a tendency to preach to people will be resented. In this case, the challenge is to expand the mind and be more accepting of other philosophies or beliefs.

Jupiter-Chiron. Expansiveness and healing-wisdom unite. There is a natural generosity of nature and understanding for the less fortunate in life. Another attribute is an ability to encompass other people's personal philosophies without feeling threatened. There is also an attraction to healing, success in such endeavours and an ability to teach the chosen modality. Wisdom will come by learning from life's adversities, by going on a search for inner healing and for answers (especially with the hard aspects). This in turn will provide the necessary training to become a teacher of philosophy, of healing and of life.

Jupiter-Nodes. Expansion and spiritual-progression unite. Jupiter conjunct the north-node and easy aspects indicates that it will be easy to follow a pathway to one's higher aspirations and goals. Life will boost such efforts and bring wise teachers when needed to direct us to the next stage of the journey. In turn, we could inspire others to see the big picture and guide them forwards on their journey. Although this still holds true with a conjunction to the south-node and with hard aspects, indulgences from the past have to be cut away first. Time and energies wasted on excesses and life frivolities bind to the past and these should be freed so they can be redirected towards higher life goals.

Jupiter-Asc. Expansiveness and new beginnings unite. This is a fortunate combination. It gives an expansive and benevolent personality, good humour and generosity of spirit that makes it easy to move forwards into life. Wisdom will be gained through travel, study, teaching, religion or philosophy so that one may become known as a seeker and teacher of knowledge and higher matters. In return, goodwill, benevolence and life abundance will be attracted. The downside with all aspects, is that these gifts and opportunities may be wasted, abandoned in the search for self-indulgent life pleasures. Big ideas and grandiose schemes may come to naught because of an unwillingness to put in the hard work required to ground such endeavours. But generally, there is a blessing over the life and good fortune often flows.

Jupiter-MC. Expansiveness and higher-goals unite. This combination makes it relatively easy to achieve one's higher goals in life, to gain recognition for one's professional or other life achievements. Hard aspects can distort perception so that exaggerations occur, things are seen in a rosier light than they are in actuality, or there is an over-estimation of one's talents. This will delay the desired success. However, Jupiter is always forgiving and with a little reset and adjustment, goals can be achieved.

7. Saturn Aspects - the Disciplining of Consciousness.

Saturn-Uranus. Discipline and independence, unite. These energies are very different and can lead to inner and outer conflict if they fight each other. Uranus needs to be free-ranging while Saturn demands duty and adherence to traditional rules. Trouble will rise with the conjunction and hard aspects if these two extremes fight for control. There could be problems with authority figures, an inability to stick at a job, or a sense of always having one's individual rights trampled upon. The ideal is to balance these two forces, which happens with maturity (facilitated by the easy aspects). Then traditional values can be emphasised when it is appropriate to do so and innovation applied at other times. Learning to compromise and to get one's timing right is essential. But overall, there is a talent for science, technology and computing and the ability to be successful professionally with information technology.

Saturn-Neptune. Discipline and spiritual-sensitivity unite, giving the potential to be both practical and other-worldly. This means that if there is musical or artistic talent or an orientation towards the spiritual life; the ability exists to give these expressions form and to make something practical and long lasting. These forces, when functioning together amicably bring balance between the intuitive and rational sides of the nature. But hard aspects and the conjunction indicate that discipline and spiritual-sensitivity fight. The cautious and conservative side wants to control the artistic-spiritual urges. Sometimes one side will dominate and then the other. Balancing these two will ensure one's forays into the metaphysical world will be sensible. False teachers will be quickly exposed because the cynical side can quickly spot a charlatan. Overall, there is an ability to manifest one's talents and spiritual aspirations practically.

Saturn-Pluto. Discipline and wilfulness unite. This is a very powerful mix of energies and can cause serious trouble if the forces are not handled correctly or are misused. This is more likely with the conjunction and hard aspects. Frustration can give an urge to force one's way through obstacles. If the "obstacles" happen to be people, it can bring a serious or even a dangerous backlash. This combination gives a very wilful nature that does not like to take instructions from anyone - it considers itself to be the law! To get on with people, these traits need to be reined in. Positively expressed, it gives leadership power and organising talent. Qualities that can bring success if due humility is expressed.

Saturn-Vesta. Discipline and purification unite. Easy aspects accentuate positive executive skills, the ability to dedicate oneself to a task and to see it religiously through to completion. Occasional retreats to recuperate one's energies will be beneficial. The conjunction and hard aspects indicate a tendency to overdo things, carrying duties and work too far so that exhaustion sets in and health problems start. Alternatively, low self-esteem and fears about life may require attention. Going into retreat to address and heal emotional problems is required. This will help to clarify one's life purpose, give better structure to the life and greater confidence to move forwards.

Saturn-Juno. Discipline and marriage unite. Those with this combination take their vows seriously. A commitment is a contract to be honoured and endured through, despite what may come. Challenges will arise with the conjunction and hard aspects. The potential exists to be too controlling, possessive and jealous. Or putting one's ambitions ahead of the partnership so that resentment arises. Disappointments may cause one to be "married" to the job to avoid what is going on at home. Balance and giving greater consideration to the partner's needs is required. Easy aspects indicate that the right balance can be struck and that the partner will appreciate having the practical side of the partnership well-managed.

Saturn-Ceres. Discipline and nurturing unite. Early home life was probably well disciplined and organised. Family traditions were observed and duties and responsibilities were allocated and had to be attended to. If this was also accompanied with kindness and concern (the easy aspects), healthy self-esteem would have developed and a mature approach to life. However, if there was meanness, coldness and punishment, if one was rejected and this has not healed; lingering low self-esteem and self-doubt will blight the life. The key here is to provide the nurturing that was missing. Therapy will help.

Saturn-Pallas. Discipline and mental-creativity unite. When this combination works well (easy aspects), it gives the ideal characteristics for professional success - a hard work ethic, intelligence and ability to clearly see the pathway ahead and to make the right decisions at crucial times. There is also a creative and visionary flair. Hard aspects and the conjunction indicate problems at work because of rigidity of ideas and an unwillingness to compromise and negotiate. The challenge is to learn from difficult experiences and apply the wisdom gained to be more accepting of other people and their ideas in the future.

Saturn-Chiron. Discipline and healing-wisdom unite. This is similar to the Saturn-Ceres combination. Early discipline applied with meanness, coldness and punishment (conjunction and hard aspects), rejection by a parent, will cause deep emotional wounds. If these are not healed, it will be difficult to have intimate relations with people in the future. A steely self-defence shield will prevent love and emotions getting through or out. In such a case, therapy should be sought from a wise and patient healer and counsellor. But overall, the potential exists to be a wise authority, counsellor/ healer. For some, this comes naturally. For others with hard aspects, it seems they have to overcome adversity first to gain the necessary insight and wisdom.

Saturn-Nodes. Discipline and spiritual-progression unite. Saturn conjunct north-node and easy aspects. The soul has issued a challenge - to take responsibility for the life and personal growth and to move forward and away from past negative lifestyles and habits. If this does not happen spontaneously (Saturn on the south-node and hard aspects), then adversity in some form or an illness may occur, to force a reassessment of the life and consequent movement in the right and higher direction. Past-life karma to do with the sign and house Saturn is in needs addressing. Overall, Saturn involved with the nodes indicates the importance of attending to one's life duties.

Saturn-Asc. Discipline and new beginnings unite. Saturn represents karma and the connection to the ascendant indicates that because of unwise actions in the past (life), conduct is being monitored to ensure it is upright and proper. Saturn imbues the nature with a sense of duty and responsibility and the way life is approached will be shaped by this. Importance will be placed upon tradition and conservatism. The demeanour will be reserved, serious and dignified. People will see this and give due respect for the hard-work ethic and common-sense values being demonstrated. While this holds true for the conjunction and hard aspects, there will also be rigidity. Feelings of insecurity and rejection will inhibit self-expression, which can be defensive. Such demonstrations will cause the public to lose respect. The remedy is to be kind, generous and gentle with oneself and extend this to others. Positively, this combination offers spiritual growth and influence if the opportunities provided are successfully dealt with and integrity is displayed.

Saturn-MC. Discipline and higher-goals unite. This combination indicates that professional success will be achieved by working hard in the chosen career and attending to all duties and responsibilities. This will gain the respect of those whose influence counts and success will duly follow. However, Saturn puts a caveat on this promise - the conjunction and hard aspects. If the ambitions are accompanied with greed and a desire for power so that the Laws of Love or the morals or laws of man are violated; this will bring retribution and a fall from grace. Being honest and humble is essential. But generally, there will be an attraction to government or conservative professions that carry responsibility - and the ability to succeed in these.

8. Uranus Aspects - the Awakening of Consciousness.

Uranus-Neptune. Independence and spiritual-sensitivity unite. These are generational planets and are only effective on an individual level if aspects are being made to personal planets or to the ascendant or midheaven. This holds true for Pluto as well. However, this combination gives an attraction to all things alternative and unorthodox. Ideals will be ahead of their time and there will be inspired creativity. Science and spirituality unite amicably with the easy aspects, permitting the discovery and understanding of all things metaphysical and esoteric. Hard aspects can result in a dismissive attitude towards all things spiritual or arty - science and the mind rule.

Uranus-Pluto. Independence and wilfulness unite. The combination gives the power or urge to change the status quo and to fight against injustices. It can also give an inflexible will and a desire to try to control and manipulate people (conjunction and hard aspects). In this case, attempts to bring change will be bulldozed through, but will be destructive and counter-productive in the long run. With the easy aspects, the power to bring change will be intelligently applied through negotiation and in consideration of what is best for all. Wise use of this power can bring considerable success.

Uranus-Vesta. Independence and purification unite. This combination gives an amazing ability to dedicate oneself to an intense search and discovery for forward-thinking ideas and inventions. But any selfish or over-the-top behaviours can prevent getting the best from this combination (hard aspects). Talents and energies can be being wasted. In such a case, freedom and quietness should be sought, privacy and space so that concentration can be restored and inspiration gained. In the right environment, brilliant work can be produced.

Uranus-Juno. Independence and marriage unite. Old and outdated attitudes to marriage need to be radically updated. So do unrealistic expectations, jealousies and possessiveness. This combination is teaching us that all things change including people's feelings and what they want. Divorce may be the best option - especially with the hard aspects. Working positively, formal relationships will go well because freshness and excitement is brought into the union. Both parties are comfortable giving the other freedom and space and this will benefit the union.

Uranus-Ceres. Independence and nurturing unite. This combination is teaching us to be more flexible and modern in our nurturing style. Being too hands-on, hovering around anxiously in case a child should stumble in life will not work - greater space should be given to one's charges. Otherwise, children will become dependent upon this attention and lack confidence about moving into life independently. With hard aspects, parents may have absconded from their parental duties so that one had to forage for oneself. If this is the case, then self-nurturing has to be provided and one has to learn to stand independent and alone.

Uranus-Pallas. Independence and mental-creativity unite. Potentially, this can give a brilliant and creative intelligence, one which is ahead of its time. It can give an ability to see clearly the next step ahead to take in any project and talent to manifest one's vision. Women with this combination would do very well in the traditional world of men. While these gifts can come with all aspects, the hard aspects indicate changes are required first. If there is egoism, one's vision will be tied (and distorted) by personal, selfish goals. The challenge is to experiment with the new, learn from experiences and apply wisdom gained to create more skilfully in the future.

Uranus-Chiron. Independence and healing-wisdom unite. At its highest, this combination potentially gives brilliant healing and teaching skills. It gives talent and the ingenuity required to make brilliant scientific discoveries in health and medicine that can bring sudden and spectacular results. With the hard aspects, necessary wisdom will be gained by healing one's emotional wounds first. The studies, explorations and training to achieve this will help to unfold the innate gifts. Overall, there is foresight and innovation and the desire to use one's gifts to help others.

Uranus-Nodes. Independence and spiritual-progression unite. This indicates one's journey will be different, will veer into the new, the alternative and the esoteric. This may require travelling far from one's roots and if so, this will be good for future growth, for self-understanding, to find freedom and achieve one's spiritual goals. A conjunction to the south-node or hard aspects indicates that toxic ties to the past need to be radically cut away. They are binding the soul to matter, to the past and old.

Uranus-Asc. Independence and new beginnings unite. This is the mark of an individualist, someone who needs to "walk to the beat of his or her own drum", and who will rebel if anyone tries to stifle independence. Freeing oneself from unnecessary restrictions that bind the soul is an important evolutionary development. Hard aspects can indicate selfish individualism, a rebellious spirit that has difficulty getting on with people. The requirement to be free is interpreted egotistically, selfishly and wrongly. The spiritual goal is to refresh the approach to life and to be original and innovative, to contribute original and exciting ideas that will help to make society fairer for all.

Uranus-MC. Independence and higher-goals unite. The driving urge behind this combination is freedom to express one's own unique ideas in public life and in the career, which will likely feature science and all manner of new technologies. There may be many changes of professions or goals, until the right fit is found. Hard aspects can make it more difficult to achieve this. There is the tendency to rebel against the status quo, the current authority bodies or authority figures rather than direct this force into inventing and creating something unique.

9. Neptune Aspects - the Refining of Consciousness.

Neptune-Pluto. Spiritual-sensitivity and wilfulness unite. At its highest, this combination indicates power to ground one's highest aspirations and spiritual ideals and also the potential to become a powerful and influential spiritual leader. But generally, this generation will be impelled to transform the nature of spirituality, of religion and its teachings. If these two planets also aspect personal planets, it can indicate deep and beneficial transformations as a consequence of one's spiritual endeavours (easy aspects); or being manipulated by unscrupulous and possibly dangerous people (hard aspects).

Neptune-Vesta. Sensitivity and purification unite. This is a positive mix of spiritually oriented forces. Vesta can ground the otherwise too subtle Neptune influences and solidify the urge to serve the greater good. For instance, by grounding a wish to help people by actually doing something about it. However, hard aspects can indicate the opposite - a tendency to lose touch with reality. The antidote is to do something tangible and practical, such as with volunteer work.

Neptune-Juno. Spiritual-sensitivity and marriage unite. Easy aspects and the conjunction, indicate that formal relationships will go well because partners will likely share the same ideals, creative or spiritual interests and be similarly sensitive and caring. Such a person is a true "soul mate." The conjunction and hard aspects indicate problems. Expectations of the partner and marriage are unrealistic and/ or impractical and require a good dose of common sense. There may be betrayal, lies, problems with addiction. Being clear about what is wanted in marriage and whether it is fair and workable, will help matters.

Neptune-Ceres. Spiritual-sensitivity and nurturing unite. Embracing those in one's care with unconditional love and compassion, cultivating artistic or spiritual interests - this is the parenting style with this combination. Growing up in such an environment will help children to express their artistic and spiritual sides. Hard aspects can indicate something perverse or unhealthy in childhood, parents who may have had strange ways or addictions. Subtle abuse is just as damaging for children as physical abuse. The goal is to unconditionally love and accept oneself and others.

Neptune-Pallas. Spiritual-sensitivity and mental-creativity unite. This combination can help to give shape and form to one's spiritual aspirations. Creative ways can be found to worship or revere God or Life or to express artistic talents. For instance, starting a business that teaches or shares such matters, which is both instructive, inspiring and profitable. The problem with the hard aspects and conjunction, is that material considerations could override moral principles.

Neptune-Chiron. Spiritual-sensitivity and healing-wisdom unite. The healing style is intuitive and the needs of the patient are attended to sensitively and compassionately. Childhood wounds that result from this combination, could come from strange childhood experiences that were confusing, perverse happenings, or betrayals by parents with addictions. This is especially so with the conjunction and hard aspects. The emotional damage could be subtle and only start to cause problems later in life. In such a case, learning to trust in oneself, one's inherent worth and ability to stand strong in life will help. Overall, this combination gives the gift of understanding and compassion for people and spiritual healing talent.

Neptune-Nodes. Spiritual-sensitivity and spiritual-progression unite. Neptune type interests such as meditation, healing, service or art; one or more of these will be very important for one's growth and should be pursued. Neptune on the south-node or hard aspects indicates that spiritual growth is being impaired because of emotionalism, by attempting to escape the harsh realities of life through means such as drugs and alcohol. This all needs to be cleaned up.

Neptune-Asc. Spiritual-sensitivity and new beginnings unite. This combination makes the persona very sensitive. Positively expressed, it gives spiritual discernment and a compassionate urge to help people. At the lower level, it results in emotional hyper-sensitivity and a desire to escape reality through some escapist means. Most of us are somewhere in the middle of these two parameters. Hard aspects can manifest as being so naive about life, one becomes a victim of con-artists or of delusion. The spiritual goal is to refine emotional expression so that wisdom and understanding can shine through. Unencumbered by disturbed emotions, it will be easier to see the way forwards in life.

Neptune-MC. Spiritual-sensitivity and higher-goals unite. The higher destiny or career is linked to the expression of one's artistic and creative talents or through avenues that provide expression for the healing or spiritual aspirations. However, hard aspects and the conjunction can confuse or hide high life goals. We can be unclear about what it is we really want to do. A journey of discovery is required to find out what resides in the heart and what it wants to do. In such a case, it is the journey that is important and not the goal.

10. Pluto Aspects - the Transformation of Consciousness.

Pluto-Vesta. Wilfulness and purification unite. Working positively, this combination gives an ability to focus powerfully on one's spiritual life or on other very important life missions. This concentration of force will bear results for good or ill, depending upon the motivation. Working negatively (conjunction and hard aspects), this force may be used to control or manipulate people. If so, the emotional pain and serious consequences that Pluto brings will provide an incentive to change. Quiet and private spiritual practices to renew one's connection with the soul is recommended. Working positively, much good can be done to help people.

Pluto-Juno. Wilfulness and marriage unite. The ultimate goal of this combination is to transform any negative attitudes involving marriage. For instance, becoming obsessed with a partner and trying to control and manipulate him or her to get one's way. The underlying problem is that one does not have a mature and balanced relationship with oneself - hence the skills are not in place to relate well with others. These must be developed. Overall, the potential exists to create a relationship that is deeply fulfilling and satisfying. Easy aspects help such a union to manifest.

Pluto-Ceres. Wilfulness and nurturing unite. This combination indicates that the parenting style could involve a "tough-love" approach, commando-style parenting. It is usually applied to children who are wilfully out of control. But skill is required to get the right mix, to ensure abuse does not arise. It would be useful in managing young offenders who break the law. Negatively (conjunction and hard aspects), early life can be tough, even abusive so that self-esteem plummets and emotional disorders arise. But there is much healing potential and an effort should be made to regain confidence.

Pluto-Pallas. Wilfulness and mental-creativity unite. Working well, this combination indicates an intelligent and creative use of inner power to create the type of life or career that is wanted. There is insight and an ability to read people's motives. These are excellent attributes to have generally and especially in the business world. Women in particular will benefit, enabling them to do well in the traditional world of men. Misused (conjunction and hard aspects), there is a compelling urge to force one's will onto others, to manipulate in clever but underhanded ways. But overall, there is intelligent leadership talent, which will bring success if it is used correctly.

Pluto-Chiron. Wilfulness and healing-wisdom unite. This combination indicates traumatic events in early life, serious losses or even abuse, which leave their mark in the form of emotional wounds and negative core beliefs about the self. This is especially so with the conjunction and hard aspects. If this is the case, it is important to seek inner-child or emotional healing for the problem, otherwise the trauma will plague the life. Working positively (all aspects potentially), the darker side of life is understood. If it has been experienced but in time wounds have healed, people with this combination can help others who have been similarly traumatised. There is powerful healing potential.

Pluto-Nodes. Wilfulness and spiritual-progression unite. This combination indicates that the life will be positively transformed and so will the personality. Pluto located on the south-node or square it, this indicates that powerful people or circumstances from the past are preventing this regeneration. It is vital these be cut away. Traits of the south node sign need to be eliminated - they are binding the soul to matter. Simultaneously, the positive qualities of the north-node sign need to be cultivated. Power is available to transform others.

Pluto-Asc. Wilfulness and new beginnings unite. The perspective of life will continually transform due to enormous challenges faced in life. But strength is given. Such people walk through life with courage. Power surrounds the persona and others sit up and take notice because of the intensity of will being radiated. Such people are often catalysts for change because of this impact. The conjunction and hard aspects indicate this force may be misused to control and manipulate people. If so, this must be resisted. The soul's purpose is to use this power wisely for self-healing and to help transform the lives of people for the better.

Pluto-MC. Wilfulness and higher-goals unite. People with this combination have what it takes to do well in management. The career may involve delving to the bottom of things and uncovering the truth by bringing hidden things into the light so they can be examined - such as in detective work, applied psychology or occult investigations. However, care needs to be taken with the conjunction and hard aspects to avoid becoming obsessed about getting power and being manipulative or destructive in doing so. This will bring a powerful backlash from people in authority. But generally, the aspect shows that insightfulness and once the will to achieve is applied (if the energy is managed well), success will follow.

11. Vesta Aspects - Purification.

Vesta-Juno. Purification and relationship commitment. A serious effort will be made to develop a good marriage and to ensure home is a happy place. But hard aspects indicate that possessiveness and jealousy may ruin relationships. If so, dedicating oneself to a program to develop good relationship skills and to understand that one is worthy of love, is required. A career could be made in marriage and relationship counselling.

Vesta-Ceres. Purification and self-acceptance unite. A concerted effort will be made to nurture and care for those we are responsible for. But hard aspects indicate that self-esteem was harmed while growing up. Perhaps home life was very efficient, spartan, there were rules to follow and high expectations, a lack of emotional support and nurturing. A program dedicated to the development of self-love and acceptance is required. Once healed, these skills can be used to help others similarly affected.

Vesta-Pallas. Purification and mental-creativity unite. This combination gives the ability to dedicate oneself with one-pointed focus to a cause, a career or to anything else in life that needs an intelligent, concentrated approach. It will help women excel in male-dominated areas. The downside is a too narrow approach based upon rigid beliefs, or being unable to put the brakes on from a hectic life so that burn-out occurs. In such cases, time should be taken out of the mainstream to reconnect with nature and the Divine, for healing and regeneration.

Vesta-Chiron. Purification and healing-wisdom unite. If emotional wounds were suffered during childhood due to neglect because parents were too busy with their own concerns, or they had ideas and beliefs that were rigid and damaging to self-esteem; these need healing. A dedicated therapy program designed to get rid of negative beliefs such as "I'm a failure" or "I'm not good enough," should be undertaken. This will help expand understanding and give clarity about one's life purpose. This combination gives the potential to be a healer with a mission to help and save.

Vesta-Nodes. Purification and spiritual-progression unite. This combination indicates that dedication to a higher calling or important spiritual goal is required. So is applying any and all necessary disciplines in order to be successful in these endeavours. But hard aspects and Vesta conjunct the south-node, these indicate that something negative in the character or from the past is binding the soul. Purification of the emotions is required and discipline to cut away any unhealthy life-links.

Vesta-ASC. Purification and new beginnings unite. The soul's plan is to live a pure and simple life and to be dedicated to a higher, worthy mission. This approach is necessary if important life and spiritual goals are to be reached. Hard aspects indicate a lack of balance, perhaps being unnecessarily austere in one's approach to life, or pursuing other missions that are at odds with one's true heart desire. If so, a readjustment is required.

Vesta-MC. Purification and higher-goals unite. This statement is similar to the previous one involving the ascendant, because both suggest dedication and discipline should be applied to achieve important life goals. The difference between the two goals, is that the ascendant goals are linked to self-development, while the MC goals are linked to career achievements. However, the latter could also be part of the soul's plan. Hard aspects indicate other interests could sabotage the desired achievement.

12. Juno Aspects - Marriage Committment.

Juno-Ceres. Marriage and nurturing unite. With the conjunction and easy aspects, the ability to commit in formal relationships and build harmonious relationships is good. Caring and nurturing the partner and family comes naturally and consequently; formal relationships will be pleasurable and harmonious. This remains a potential with hard aspects. But until feelings of unworthiness and low self-esteem are healed, until those with this combination learn to unconditionally love and accept themselves as they are; intimate relationships could be ruined with jealousy, suspicion and resentment. Being more sensitive and attentive to other people's needs and learning to value the benefits of a good union; these will help to form healthier bonds.

Juno-Pallas. Marriage and mental-creativity unite. The conjunction and easy aspects indicate an innate ability to intelligently understand what needs to be done to create harmony in marriage and to resolve disputes. Consequently, there is an opportunity to build a career out of marriage and couple counselling. Hard aspects indicate that jealousies, possessiveness, rigid views and beliefs may sabotage unions. If formal partnerships are difficult, owning up to one's contribution to the trouble is required and taking steps to change the pattern. The remedy is to become more accepting and forgiving, lower any unrealistic expectations and to look for the good in others rather than focusing on any negatives.

Juno-Chiron. Marriage and healing-wisdom unite. All combinations indicate that deep emotional wounds have occurred in marriage - either in this, or a past life. The troubled union may have been that of the parents, and hurt from that dysfunction affected the entire family. The goal now, is to heal these wounds if they still exist (conjunction and hard aspects). Easy aspects indicate wisdom in such matters, the result of emerging from trauma with a healthy outlook and knowledge of how to make relationship adjustments that benefit all unions. Consequently, this combination gives the opportunity to succeed in marriage and to make a career out of relationship counselling.

Juno-Nodes. Marriage and spiritual-progression unite. This combination indicates much is to be learnt about intimate unions. Learning how to harmonise conflicting forces that arise when in close association with another - this will contribute to better relations generally with others and benefit the future direction. This applies to all aspects. However, the conjunction to the south-node and hard aspects indicate a repetitive pattern of jealousy and possessiveness, which hinders forwards progression and binds the soul to the past. It is important to heal this, to be free from the old and move into the new.

Juno-Asc. Marriage and new beginnings unite. All aspects indicate that the development of healthy intimate relationship with the marriage partner is part of the soul's purpose in this life. But the right balance should be struck. Hard aspects indicate that in the past, spiritual growth was sacrificed because of a jealous partner or too much time was diverted into a demanding marriage. That should not be allowed to happen again. Straightening this out now will help to ensure that in future incarnations, partners will be supportive.

Juno-MC. Marriage and higher-goals unite. Marriage is linked with the career or with status. For some, it may mean that marriage should be successful and happy and shown with pride to the world. There is nothing wrong with this, unless it is being done to try to compensate for fears about being unworthy in one's own right, or having no value if the union is seen to be less than perfect. The hard aspects indicate something needs addressing along these lines. In some cases, the spouse may achieve recognition and fame or one's career could be associated with the marriage industry. In other cases, habitual bachelors may be married to the job.

13. Ceres Aspects - Self-Acceptance.

Ceres-Pallas. Self-acceptance and mental-creativity unite. Positively applied, there is an ability to intelligently understand how to nurture people so that healthy self-esteem and confidence develops. In most cases, parents would have been encouraging and supportive and this gift was fostered then. In contrast, hard aspects show an unhappy childhood with critical and demanding parents. The consequence of this is a tendency to attack oneself with negative thoughts for not being good enough. If so, the ability to heal oneself through the use of creative visualisation and positive affirmations is associated with this combination.

Ceres-Chiron Nurturing and healing-wisdom unite. Emotional wounds, the consequent of rejection by a parent or carer is associated with this combination - especially with the hard aspects. In such a case, emotional hurts, low self-esteem and a subsequent inability to trust others needs healing. A deep understanding about human nature and how to nurture people so they feel good about themselves will arise as this is done. Easy aspects indicate this wisdom is present and is a natural gift that can be used to heal people who have suffered parental rejection.

Ceres-Nodes. Nurturing and spiritual-progression unite. All aspects indicate that an important goal in life is to learn to love and accept oneself - this is especially true with the conjunction to the south-node and hard aspects. The tendency to get stuck in feelings of low self-esteem, coupled with a powerful fear of rejection; this is preventing healthy life interaction and forwards progression. Developing an inner sense of security, which is based on healthy esteem is the goal. This can then be used to assist others to unconditionally love and accept themselves. The conjunction to the north-node and easy aspects helps the expression of this.

Ceres-Asc. Self-acceptance and new beginnings unite. An important spiritual goal with this combination, is to develop a strong and healthy sense of self and to nurture others as the road of life is travelled. These qualities may be present at birth with the conjunction and easy aspects; and if so, people will see these characteristics and be supportive and nurturing in return. "What goes around, comes around." There is work to be done with the hard aspects, a need to heal an acute sense of grief and abandonment. Learning to love and accept oneself is the key. This then can be extended to others.

Ceres-MC. Self-acceptance and higher-goals unite. If low-esteem is present (more likely with the hard aspects), an important life goal is to heal this and to learn to love and accept oneself. Not only is this vital for inner-development, but so that career goals will not be adversely affected. This negativity and self-doubt will be seen by those in power and will likely inhibit opportunities. The conjunction and easy aspects indicate that self-confidence will help the career blossom and that nurturing others in some way could form the basis of a successful career.

14. Pallas Aspects - Mental Creativity.

Pallas-Chiron. Mental-creativity and healing-wisdom unite. With all aspects, the potential exists to be an intelligent and effective healer who can combine science and natural healing methods successfully. However, with the conjunction and hard aspects potential creativity may not be flowing due to emotional wounds from childhood. To restore the inner spiritual flow, the challenge is to broaden one's understanding about life, gain knowledge about emotional traumas and how to heal them; then use this wisdom to heal oneself.

Pallas Athene-Nodes. Mental-creativity and spiritual-progression unite. This combination indicates there is a need to learn how to use one's mental-creativity constructively and develop any innate talents because higher life goals are linked to helping others in one way or another. But with Pallas conjunct the south-node or with hard aspects this will not be easy. There is work to be done first. Trying to force rigid or narrow attitudes onto others will cause trouble and bind one to the past. The goal is to intelligently heal any emotional traumas underlying this behaviour, to cut away the past and start to move forwards again towards a new and better life.

Pallas Athene-Asc. Mental-creativity and new beginnings unite. All aspects indicate that an important spiritual goal is to approach life intelligently and to use one's mental-creativity wisely, to help others as life's road is travelled. This will be a challenge for those with the hard aspects, who will try to force rigid or narrow ideas and beliefs onto others. It is an important part of the soul's plan for life, that such attitudes are healed. Success will bring greater life opportunities and an easier pathway to walk.

Pallas Athene-MC. Mental-creativity and higher-goals unite. There is an ability to use one's mental-creativity and talent to succeed in the career and to achieve higher goals. For women, this combination gives the ability to do well in traditional male fields. Challenges that come from hard aspects and that could stand in the way of success, are rigid attitudes and narrow mindedness. In such a case, the intelligent creative talents should be used to heal these patterns and to figure out what needs to be done to succeed.

15. Chiron Aspects - Inner Healing.

Chiron-Nodes. Healing-wisdom and spiritual-progression unite. Chiron in any aspect to the nodes indicates that in order to progress forwards in life, emotional wounds must be healed. This is especially true with a conjunction to the south-node and hard aspects. Any ties to the past that are toxic and unproductive should be cut away. Another possibility is that a physical illness may alter the course of the life in an important and positive way. There is the potential to be a skilled healer and teacher.

Chiron-Asc. Healing-wisdom and new beginnings unite. Natural and wise healing ability will be present from birth (especially with the easy aspects and conjunction) and development and utilisation of this talent to do good in the world is part of the soul's plan. This development may be the consequence of having to heal oneself first, of emotional wounds that cause a fear about approaching life. An incentive to help and heal could also result from observing the suffering in the world and the good that healers do to alleviate it.

Chiron-MC. Healing-wisdom and higher-goals unite. This combination links healing to the professional life and the ability to have a successful career in one or other of the many modalities connected with health. This is especially true with the conjunction and easy aspects. Hard aspects may delay this. Emotional wounds suffered as a consequence of being treated harshly by authority figures in childhood must be dealt with or negative behaviours could disrupt an otherwise promising vocation.

16. North and South Nodes Aspects

Nodes-Asc. If the north-node conjuncts the ascendant, or makes easy aspects; it emphasises the qualities of the ascendant sign, and the need for their development to achieve spiritual purpose. If however, the south-node is conjunct or makes hard aspects to the ascendant; the negatives of the rising sign are impeding spiritual progression and must be replaced with the positive traits.

Nodes-MC. A north-node conjunction to the MC or easy aspects, emphasises the important of the career and that it should be in alignment with one's spiritual goals. The same applies with the hard aspects, but impediments have to be worked through first. However, home and family must come before a career, when the south-node conjuncts the MC and the north-node is on the 4th house cusp,

CHAPTER 6. EXERCISES TO INTERPRET A NATAL CHART

ARIES

"I Am First"

Fiery - Fast

Selfish, Aggressive, Emotional, Initiating, Intelligent Leaders.

Expertise in interpreting a natal chart evolves over time. The immediate goal is to train the mind to make rapid associations between the astrology symbol and what it means. This requires learning what symbols mean then practicing reading them together in a chart. The more this is done, the greater will one's skill-set as an astrologer become. Here are some tips.

A spiritual-philosophical way to approach a chart reading is to understand that everyone is a soul (in consciousness), on a journey to enlightenment that spans lives. We begin as imperfect beings and end up as illumined and wise. We achieve this elevated state through life experience, by learning from our mistakes and by making changes. What we are doing metaphysically, is removing psychological traits in our nature that are obstacles between ourselves and the soul (spiritual love and wisdom). Hard aspects in the chart should be interpreted from this angle - a character issue that needs to be straightened out.

We should also remember we are reading for a sensitive soul who has all the hopes, dreams and wishes for a successful and happy life that we all share.

> "The psycho-spiritual goal of astrology readings is to help clients gain deeper insight into their characters by better understanding the energy inter-actions of the natal chart. This involves highlighting the positive elements in the chart and potentials for life-success. It also involves pointing out inner adjustments that are required within the nature to straighten out any energy-kinks (hard aspects) that are contributing to life or health problems. Overall, this will help those we counsel live a more fulfilling and happier life."

The reading should chart a course that is accurate in interpretation - the tough aspects are not dodged but are delivered in a sensitive way that does not reinforce fears and sends the person away with a sense of foreboding. It helps to have counselling training.

1. When reading planets well placed by sign and easy aspects, generally use positive keywords.
2. When reading planets not well placed by sign with hard aspects, start with negative keywords for the hard aspect to describe the negative pattern being played out. Then end with positive keywords - how the energy should be used and the benefits that will flow when the change is made. Apply therapy, how the pattern can be changed. Use common sense advice. Include any easy aspects the planet makes to other planets or points in the chart. Finally, address how making changes will benefit the life.

To demonstrate this, imagine that a male client says he is unlucky in love and he has been accused of being stingy with money. You see in the chart there is a Venus-Saturn square. Here is how it could be addressed.

(1) "Your relationship difficulties are shown in the chart. You have a fear of intimacy and of being rejected. Most people have the latter, but it is accentuated in you, the result of being rejected in the past. You are ultra-cautious and this affects other parts of your life, such as with money. Do you identify with this?" [Discussion follows, giving the client the opportunity to talk about his experiences]. (2) Apply therapy. Then (3) "Your chart also shows that you have the ability to build an enduring relationship. If you make the recommended changes, if you learn to be kinder to yourself and more generous, a stable and long-lasting love will come to you in the future." Always hold out hope.

> In the following exercises, work with your own or someone else's chart. Each planet, sign, house and aspect are given keywords. These are connected with conjunctions - "connecting words," which link these various factors together. This technique will help you to get started interpreting. Initially, some of the phrases may not make sense. But jiggle the words around and add a few of your own until you come out with something meaningful. Use the "Keywords" page to help you do these exercises. This is the "nuts and bolts" section of your training. Put in as much time as possible to get a flow going. If it seems hard, remember that you are developing your brain power, accelerating your understanding and developing skills that can help people. Use the astrology play - cards given in a later section to help this process.

Exercise 1: Read planets in signs.

Start by reading your own chart.

Column 1: contains symbols of the planets

Column 2: contains keywords for the planet.

Column 3. contains the connecting conjunctions.

Column 4: contains the symbol for the sign the planet is in.

Column 5: contains keywords for the signs.

1	2	3	4	5
Planet	*Keywords for the Planet*	*Conjunctions or connecting words*	*Sign*	*Keywords for the Sign*
☉	My personality	is	♋	defensive, sensitive
☽	My emotions	are	♓	fluid, emotional
Asc	My approach to life	is	♉	practical, grounded
☿	My mind	is	♋	emotional, defensive
♀	My affections	are	♊	adaptable
♂	My desires	are	♌	grand and royal
♃	The urge to grow	is expressed	♓	inclusively
♄	One's ambitions	is expressed	♋	defensively, sensitively
♅	Urge for independence	is expressed	♎	intelligently
♆	Urge for spiritual union	is expressed	♐	expansively
♇	Urge to control	is expressed	♎	diplomatically

To get the most out of these exercises, draw up your own table and practice with many charts. Once the data is entered, the next step is to convert each statement into something understandable and readable. Here are some suggestions. Keep things simple in the early stages. Change keywords if you can think of a better one while interpreting.

1. Sun in Cancer: my personality is defensive and sensitive.

2. Moon in Pisces: my emotions are fluid and emotional.

3. Ascendant in Taurus: I approach life practically, am grounded.

4. Mercury in Cancer: my mind is affected by the emotions.

5. Venus in Gemini: my affections are adaptable, can be superficial.

6. Mars in Leo: my desires are expressed in a grand and royal way.

7. Jupiter in Pisces: my urge to grow, to understand is expressed fluidly, with feeling.

8. Saturn in Cancer: I express my ambitions sensitively, defensively.

9. Uranus in Libra: independence is expressed intelligently, to maintain harmony.

10. Neptune in Sagittarius: The urge for spiritual understanding is expressed expansively, enthusiastically.

11. Pluto in Libra: my urge to control and to survive is expressed diplomatically.

Exercise 2: Read planets in aspect to other planets.

In this exercise, only the personal planets and the ascendant are used. They form the core of the nature - the personality, the mind and the emotions. The other planets, when they aspect the personal planets; impress their nature upon that part of the personality. In (1) are the symbols for the first planet and its sign and keywords for both. In (2), are the aspects and keywords for the aspect, or in other cases, connecting words. In (3), are the symbols and keywords for the second planet and its sign.

	1		2		3	
	Planet 1 & Sign Keywords		*Aspects and Keywords*		*Planet 2 & Sign Keywords*	
1	☉ ♋	The personality is defensive, emotional.	□	in contrast	♃ ♈	expansive, bold
2	☽ ♌	The emotions are dramatic.	△	and	♅ ♐	independent, free.
3	As ♑	Life is approached - with discipline, reserve.	☍	conflicting	☉ ♋	personality. sensitivity
4	☿ ♒	The mind is intellectual	☌	and	♆ ♒	intuitive *(no need to repeat a keyword for the sign).*
			□	also	♇ ♉	intense, stubborn.
5	♀ ♍	The affections are discriminating.	∠	incompatible with	☽ ♌	dramatic emotions
			△	flow with	♄ ♉	caution & common-sense
6	♂ ♏	The desires are intense, deep.	✶	and	As ♑	stable

1. Sun in Cancer square Jupiter in Aries. The personality is defensive and emotional, in contrast with another side of the nature that is bold and wants to grow and expand. These sides fight each other.

2. Moon in Leo trine Uranus in Sagittarius. The emotions are dramatic, there is an emotional need to be independent and free.

3. Ascendant in Capricorn opposing the Sun in Cancer. Life is approached with discipline and reserve and this conflicts with the sensitive personality.

4. Mercury in Aquarius conjunct Neptune in Aquarius. The person is a thinker, an intellectual and is also intuitive. Mercury square Pluto in Taurus. But there is also intense stubbornness, rigidity.

5. Venus in Virgo trine Saturn in Taurus. In romantic matters, there is an element of caution and a tendency to over-analyse. Venus semi-square Moon in Leo. This is incompatible with the dramatic and warm emotions. This contrasting mix of feelings indicates there will be conflict in relationships.

   (Note how in this statement, an opinion has been made "there will be conflict in relationships." It is well understood in psychology, that inner conflict translates into outer conflict. Adding extra information like this is part of the psychological astrology craft).

6. Mars in Scorpio sextile ascendant in Capricorn. However, the desires are intense and compatible with a stable and cautious approach to life.

Notice how the keywords are joined together with conjunctions to make the various statements understandable and so that they flow. Adverb conjunctions like "however", "yet" or but" are very useful when knitting together the hard aspects or contrasting parts of the personality.

Exercise 3: Read planets, in signs, in houses.

Reading planets in signs is extended to the houses.

Column 1: contains the planet-sign symbols and keywords.

Column 2: contains connecting words.

Column 3: contains the houses keywords.

	1		2	3	
	Keywords: planets in signs.		*Connecting words*	*Keywords: houses*	
1	☉ ♋	The personality is defensive, sensitive	and is also	5	creative
2	☽ ♓	The emotions are fluid, emotional	and	1	personal
3	☿ ♋	The mind is affected by the emotions	and	5	children
4	♀ ♊	The affections are adaptable	with	4	family
5	♂ ♌	The desires are grand and royal	at	6	work
6	♃ ♓	The urge to grow	is	1	personal
7	♄ ♋	Repressed emotions	focus on	5	children
8	♅ ♎	Individualism is moderated	in the	10	career
9	♆ ♐	Spiritual ideals	are kept	12	private
10	♇ ♎	Power is expressed diplomatically	in the	10	career

The next step as always, is to convert the data into something readable. Play around with the connecting words to get the best fit. Try to add additional sentences to the base data.

1. The personality is sensitive and defensive. Focus is on recreational activities, children and lovers. These interests are soothing for the emotions.
2. The emotions are fluid, emotional and very expressive. He/ she wants to save people. Onlookers can see this side of the character.
3. The ability to think clearly is affected by the emotions. Creative work and hobbies, spending time with children; these interests are soothing to the mind.
4. The affections are adaptable, are communicative. Loving dialogue with the family, in the home is important.
5. The desires are expressed in a grand and royal way, especially at work. Physical and mechanical work-skills may be developed. There could be conflict at work.
6. The urge to grow and understand is expressed fluidly, with feeling. Personal growth is an important personal goal.
7. There is a tendency to repress the emotions. Especially in regard to children of lovers. This will cause difficulties in these relationships.
8. The need to be independent is expressed diplomatically, in the career.
9. Spiritual ideals and beliefs are wide-ranging. But this side of the nature is kept private and may not be expressed in the outer life.
10. The need to be in control is expressed diplomatically, in the career. (This statement can be extended to include the type of people one will meet in the vocation - Pluto in the 10th). This will be necessary to keep on the good side of powerful authority figures encountered at work.

Exercise 4: Read the houses - Prince Charles' chart.

Signs on each house cusp symbolise our attitudes to the different life areas. In this exercise we will use Prince Charles' chart. In column 1 are the numbers of the houses and keywords. In column 2 are the signs on each house cusp and keywords. Note that houses 5 and 11 have intercepted signs - these are signs that are not on a cusp. This happens in some systems such as Placidus (which is the system used for Charles' chart), where houses can be wider than 30 degrees.

1		2	
House Number and Keywords		*Sign on Cusp and Keywords*	
1 & As	His approach to life	♌	royal and grand
2	Charles attitude to money	♌	royal and grand
3	Method of communication	♍	discrimination
4	Attitude to family	♎	balanced, he tries to be fair
5	Attitude to children is	♏ ♐	intense and also philosophical
6	Attitude to work	♑	ambitious
7	Attitude to marriage	♒	intellectual, detached
8	Ability to transform	♒	intellectual, detached
9	Moral expression	♓	adaptable, compassionate
10	Attitude to career	♈	leadership
11	Attitude to friends	♉ ♊	stable and communicative
12	Self-undoing	♋	hiding his emotions

Interpretations for some of the houses.

House 1-2. Charles approaches life grandly and has luxurious tastes with money.

House 3. Charles chooses his words carefully when he communicates.

House 4. He likes a balanced and harmonious home life. He tries to be fair.

House 5. With his children, he can be intense and hands-on. But over time, will become more philosophical.

House 6. Charles' attitude to work is ambitious and conservative.

House 7. Towards marriage, Charles' can be quite detached. He would prefer a partner who was his equal intellectually.

House 10. Charles was born to be a leader. He is competitive and assertive.

House 12. Charles' major negative is that he tends to keep his emotions private, to himself.

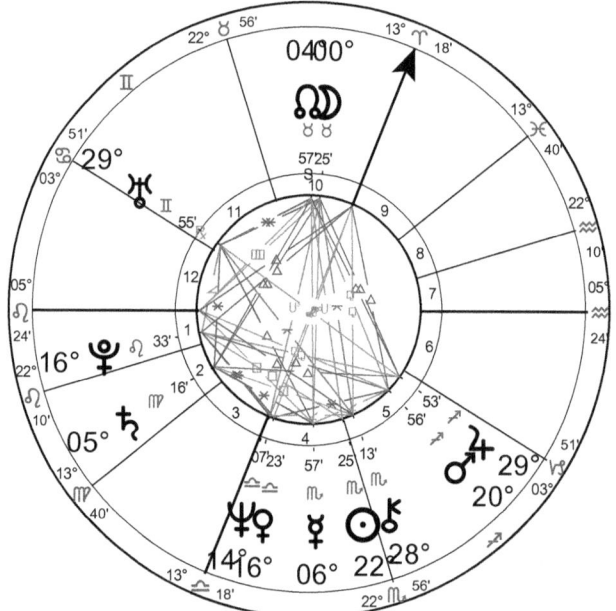

Exercise 5: Read houses, signs on cusps and planets in the houses - Princess Diana.

This is an extension of Exercise 4, where attitudes to houses were interpreted. This is repeated with Diana's chart, but adds planets in the houses. In column 1 are the house numbers and the signs on the house cusp. In column 2 are the planets in the house and the signs they are in.

1		2	
House Number and Keywords		*Planets and Signs*	
2♑︎♒︎	Attitude to money	♃♒︎	expansion of humanities
		☽♒︎	emotionally detached
		⚷♓︎	emotional childhood wounds
5♉︎	Attitude to children, lovers	♀♉︎	practical, hands-on and sensuous (lovers)
7♊︎	Attitude to marriage	☉♋︎	emotional, defensive
		☿♋︎	communicates emotions/ emotionally
8♋︎♌︎	Ability to deal with trauma, major losses	♅♌︎	changes quickly, with dignity
		☊♌︎	.. to progress forwards
		♂♍︎	passive aggressive
		♇♍︎	destructively critical
10♎︎	Attitude to career, status, high goals	♆♏︎	idealistic, intense focus

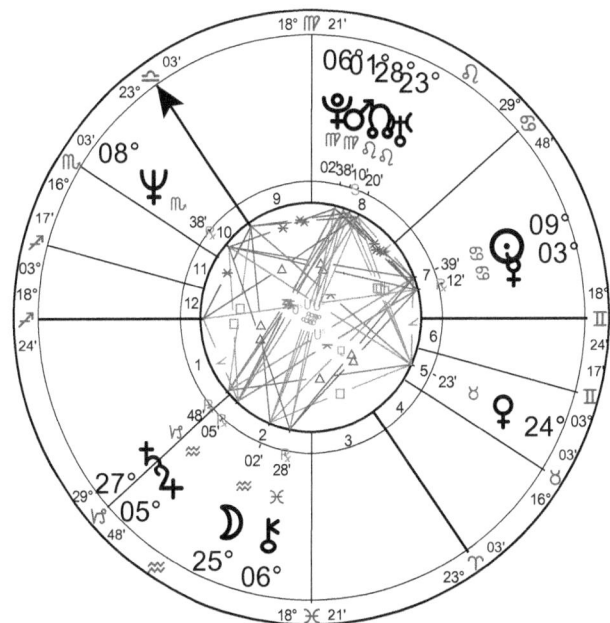

House 2. Diana's values were practical (Capricorn), but also humane (Aquarius) - she liked to share. She was very generous (Jupiter) with people, with humanity (Aquarius). She wanted to heal the hurts of the world (Chiron) and giving of her time and money was a way to do this.

House 5. She was practical and hands-on with her children and sensuous as a lover.

House 7. Diana's initial attitude to marriage was to communicate freely and lightly (Gemini on the seventh house cusp). But once her emotions were engaged (Sun in Cancer), she could be sensitive, protective and defensive. When unhappy, she would communicate emotionally, withdraw into her shell, be moody and sulk (Mercury in Cancer retrograde).

House 8. Emotional hurts (Cancer) would compel Diana to transform herself and her life so she could be in control (Leo). Meditation and other New Age practises (Uranus), helped her to move forwards (node). However, at a deeper level (planets in a third sign in the house - Virgo), anger and resentment, attack thoughts about others and herself (Mars, Virgo) festered. This would be self-destructive (Pluto) if not healed.

House 10. A very important goal of Diana's (MC) was to be fair with everyone and considerate. She was idealistic (Neptune) and intense and would fight (Scorpio) for her causes.

Exercise 6: Reading the rulers of houses.

This is an extension of Exercise 5 and Princess Diana's chart will be used again. The ruler of a house, is the planet that rules the sign on the house cusp. Its location in the chart, symbolises where we go to: (1) Resolve the matters of the original house, or (2) to get that houses needs met, (3) to express the energy of the original house.

Note that in Diana's chart, Saturn rules the second house because Capricorn on the cusp. Saturn is at the end of the first house and is conjunct the second house cusp. There is a rule - when a planet is at the end of a house and within 5 degrees conjunct of the next house's cusp, the planet is influential in the next house. This is important with planets in the twelfth house that are conjunct the ascendant. That planet's influence will not be hidden, but will be obvious.

House 2. The first ruler of the second house is Saturn. Diana's values were practical (Capricorn), and she was very careful to conserve her resources and personal money (Saturn conjunct the second house cusp). The second ruler of house 2 is Uranus (Aquarius intercepted). But her humanitarian side wanted to share (Aquarius), and she would use her influence to gather resources and money (Uranus in the eighth house of other people's money), for her causes.

House 5. The ruler of the fifth house is Venus, with Taurus on the cusp. Diana was very practical and hands-on with her children. She would put her whole attention onto this task (Venus is in the 5th).

House 7. The ruler of the seventh house is Mercury and it is in the 7th, in Cancer. With Gemini, Diana very much wanted to communicate with her husband. But when emotionally hurt, she could sulk and vent her hurt feelings (Mercury retrograde in Cancer). This cause a breakdown of communication with her older and more mature husband.

House 8. The first ruler of the eighth house is the Moon, with Cancer on the cusp. The way she handled her emotions (detaching emotionally and going into old stuff - Moon in Aquarius conjunct the south-node), needed to be transformed. The second ruler is the Sun, with Leo intercepted in the 8th. She needed to learn to stand up for herself in marriage (Sun in seventh house).

House 10. The ruler of the tenth house is Venus, with Libra on the MC. In her profession, Diana would be fair and considerate. She could be very creative in her work, charm people and bring them pleasure (Venus).

Exercise 7: Reading the rulers of houses that have no planets in them.

Houses with no planets in them are just as important as houses that have planets. The planet ruler of the house, its sign, house and aspects represent that house's affairs. If the ruler of a house is afflicted, there will be conflict in that house. If it is well aspected with many easy aspects, things will run relatively smoothly. Diana's fourth house has no planets and ruler Mars is primarily afflicted in the eighth house

1		2		3	
House & Sign		*Ruler, its Sign & House*		*Planets and Signs*	
4♈	Home life was fiery	♂♍8	There was conflict and criticism. This caused trauma. Mother "died" (left the home.	☍ ☽ ♒2	To cope, she detached emotionally
				⚻ ♄ ♑1	She felt she had no control, was afraid.
				✶ ☿ ♋7	It helped to talk to her therapist.
				☌ ♆ ♌	With effort and drawing on her courage, she could work through her traumas, heal, make the necessary transformations and move forwards.

Home life was fiery, challenging. Mother leaving was traumatic, emotionally very painful. She was shocked (Uranus) devastated (Pluto), afraid (Saturn). Therapy helped her to cope. Her courage would help her heal and move forwards.

Exercise 8: Read planets, in signs, in houses - in aspect to - other planets, in signs, in houses.

In column 1, are the first planets to be analysed, in their signs and houses. Column 2 has the aspects. Column 3 has the aspected planets, in their signs and houses. Just one keyword for each component will do.

	1		2	3	
	Planet 1 in Signs, Houses		*Aspect*	*Planet 2 in Signs, Houses*	
1	☽ ♓ 1	Very sensitive emotions, close to the surface, easily seen by people.	△	☉ ♋ 5	Sensitive and nurturing personality that enjoys children.
			△	☿ ♋ 5	Pleasure in communicating.
2	♀ ♊ 3	Affections communicative, with siblings, neighbours.	☍	♅ ♐ 9	Wants freedom, travel, prefers alternative philosophies.
3	♂ ♌ 6	Likes to be the boss at work and assert control.	□	♄ ♉ 3	Stubborn and fixed attitudes in communications.

1. Our subject is very sensitive emotionally and people can see this. She derives much enjoyment being with children, nurturing them, playing games they enjoy and talking with them.
2. She enjoys socialising and conversing with siblings and neighbours, but may put some people off with her New Age, perhaps bizarre beliefs. However, she has the charm to bring people around.
3. At work, she likes to be the boss and to be in control of what she is doing. This, and being too conservative and a disciplinarian, will cause problems with her co-workers. She should get her own business, be self-employed.

Exercise 9: use cards to help you develop your interpretive skill.

On the following pages are cards with the astrology symbols drawn upon them. Photocopy the cards onto light card. On the back of the sign cards, write SIGNS. On the back of the planet cards, write PLANETS. On the back of the house cards write HOUSES. On the back of the aspect cards write ASPECTS.

Use the cards to help become fluid in your readings.

As you do the previous exercises, extend your practice by using the cards. For instance:

When doing Exercise 1, "Read Planets in Signs", select randomly one planet card and one sign card and read them. Do this repeatedly until you become fluent with putting the symbols together.

As you do Exercise 2, "Read Planets in Signs in aspect to other Planets in Signs," select a planet card, a sign card and an aspect card, and then another planet, sign and aspect card. Then read them.

When doing Exercise 3, "Read Planets, in Signs, in houses," select one planet card, one sign card and one house card; then another planet, sign and house card. Then read them. Do this for all the exercises.

All these exercises and use of cards are designed to help students develop their astrological interpretive skills. At the end of it all, what makes the difference between being a good astrologer and a great one, is ongoing practice - reading charts! The more fluidly we can connect the symbols to the qualities they represent, the easier and faster it becomes to read a chart.

ARIES "I Am First" Fiery - Fast The Ram  Selfish, Aggressive, Emotional. Initiating, Intelligent Leaders.	**TAURUS** "I Desire" Earth - Fixed The Bull  Desirous, Stubborn. Stable, Persevering, Loyal, Artistic.	**GEMINI** "I Think" Air - Adaptable The Twins  Superficial, Dual. Changeable. Clever, Intelligent, Versatile.
CANCER "I Feel" Water - Fast The Crab  Defensive, Moody, Emotional. Sensitive, Nurturing, Protective.	**LEO** "I Rule" Fiery - Fixed The Lion  Arrogant, Controlling. Regal, Self-aware, Dignified Leadership.	**VIRGO** "I Analyse" Earth - Adaptable The Virgin  Critical, Perfectionist. Discriminating, Kind, Intelligent, Healing.
LIBRA "I Weigh" Air - Fast The Scales  Indecisive, Imbalance. Poised, Balanced, Fair, Just, Intelligent.	**SCORPIO** "I Fight" Water - Fixed The Scorpion  Aggressive, Vengeful. Deep Passions, Warrior, Courage.	**SAGITTARIUS** "I Vision" Fiery - Adaptable The Centaur  Extravagant, Boasting. Visionary, Idealistic, Prophetic, Spiritual.

CAPRICORN "I Work" Earth - Fast The Goat  Ruthless Ambition. Responsible, Sage, Disciplined, Stoic.	**AQUARIUS** "I Know" Air- Fixed The Water-Bearer  Fixed-minded, Detached. Friendly, Intelligent, Serving.	**PISCES** "I Serve" Water - Adaptable The Fishes  Too Fluid, Delusional. Compassionate, Kind, Arty, Self-Sacrificing.
SUN  The SELF, the Personality. the Ego, the Identity. Personal Power & Authority".	**MOON**  The EMOTIONS, emotional habits & patterns. 'Prison of the Soul pattern" - negative core beliefs.	**MERCURY**  The MIND, Communication, Thoughts.
VENUS  The AFFECTIONS, Love, Relationships, Partnerships, potential Intelligent Love.	**MARS**  The DESIRES, Sex, Passion, Emotions. Anger, Cruelty, Courage, Warriorship, Spiritual Aspiration.	**JUPITER** ♃ *EXPANDS*, Wasteful, Boastful. Teaches, Widens, Good Fortune, Wisdom, Visionary, Prophetic.

SATURN  *CONTRACTS* Hardens, Blocks. Disciplines, Responsibilities, an Opportunity to overcome Karma.	**URANUS** 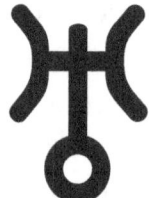 *AWAKENS* to "the New", Shatters the old, Sudden, Unusual, Different, Friends, Selfish Individualism.	**NEPTUNE**  *DISSOLVES* the old. Illusion, Rose-coloured glasses. Compassion, Sensitivity, Idealism, Spiritual.
PLUTO  *TRANSFORMS, DESTROYS* the old & crystallised so the new life can be birthed. Power & Control.	**ASCENDANT**  *IMAGE,* how people see us; our *APPROACH* to *LIFE,* how we View life. The head and physical body.	**CONJUNCTION**  UNITES, MERGES with, for "good or ill".
OPPOSITION  OPPOSES, FIGHTS, DEBATES, ARGUES, IMBALANCE. DEBATES with, RECONCILES, COMPLEMENTS.	**TRINE**  EASY, FLOWING, HARMONY. GOOD FORTUNE, SUCCESS, COMPLEMENTARY, COMPATIBLE.	**SQUARE**  BLOCKS, DENIES, REPRESSES, HATES. SUCCESS, GROWTH through STRUGGLE & EFFORT.

Chapter 6: Exercises to Interpret a Natal Chart - 149

SEXTILE	SEMI-SQUARE	INCONJUNCT
	∠	
POSITIVE ENERGY, CONSTRUCTIVE GROWTH, COMPATIBLE.	MINOR CONFLICTS, & OBSTACLES. IRRITATION, DISAGREEABLE, DISLIKES.	IN CONFLICT, IMBALANCE, EITHER OR, CUT AWAY, BRING INTO BALANCE.
HOUSE 1 "I AM!" ME, MINE. (Related to Aries) **Personal Interests, the Body, the Appearance.**	**HOUSE 2** "I HAVE" (Related to Taurus) **PERSONAL VALUES, RESOURCES, MONEY, POSSESSIONS.**	**HOUSE 3** "I THINK" (Related to Gemini) **COMMUNICATION. SIBLINGS, NEIGHBOURS.**
HOUSE 4 "MY HOME & FAMILY.' (Related to Cancer) **MOTHER.**	**HOUSE 5** "I CREATE" (Related to Leo) **PLEASURE, HOBBIES, LOVERS, ROMANCE, CHILDREN**	**HOUSE 6** "I SERVE" (Related to Virgo) **WORK, HEALTH.**

HOUSE 7 **"MY PARTNER"** (Related to Libra) **MARRIAGE, FORMAL PARTNERS**	**HOUSE 8** **"DEATH, TRANSFORMATION"** (Related to Scorpio) **Other People's Money, Emotional Trauma. Inheritances, the Occult**	**HOUSE 9** **"MY BELIEFS & MORALS"** (Related to Sag.) **RELIGION, HIGHER LEARNING, the SPIRITUAL PATH.**
HOUSE 10 **"MY PROFESSION, CAREER."** (Related to Capricorn). **STATUS, FAME, RECOGNITION. FATHER.**	**HOUSE 11** **"MY GROUPS & FRIENDS".** (Related to Aquarius.) **Hopes & Wishes, Group Creativity. Politics.**	**HOUSE 12** **"MY PRIVATE MATTERS. SELF-UNDOING".** (Related to Pisces.) **Hidden things, the Unconscious. Large institutions.**

CHAPTER 7. LOVE, CAREER, HEALTH, CHILDREN & DEATH

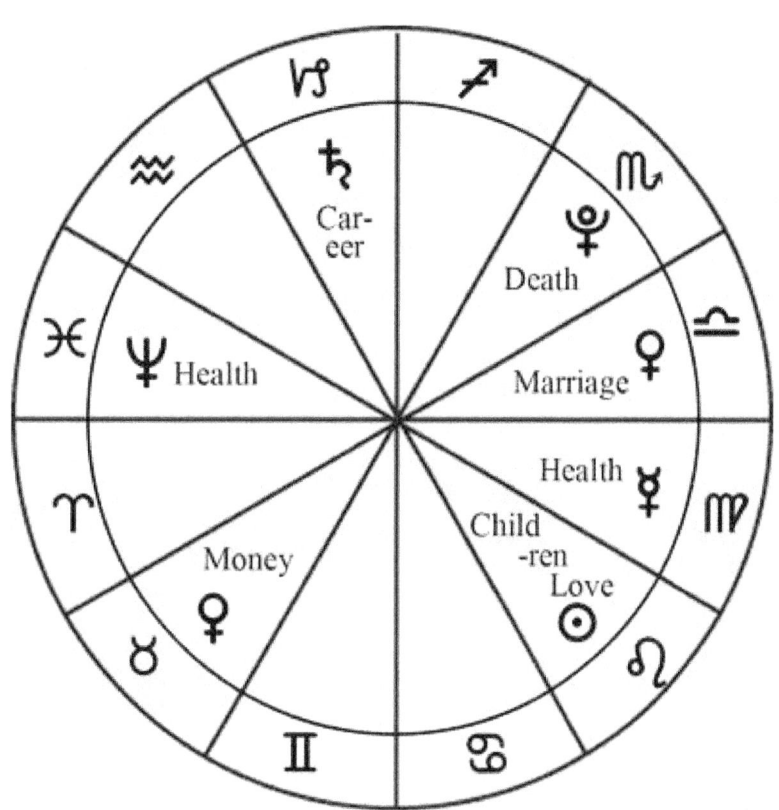

1. Love and Relationships

A person's ability to give and receive love is represented primarily by Venus, its sign, house and aspects. If a relationship between two people is being analysed, then:

- Study Venus in both charts.
- Use the Synastry or chart comparison technique.
- Use the combined or composite-midpoint chart of the two people involved. The composite Sun is placed midpoint between each person's Sun, the composite Moon is placed at the midway point and so on. This is the chart of the relationship. Astrology software will create this chart.

The marriage of Joanne Woodward and Paul Newman will be used as an example. Woodward was born at 4:00 am on 27 February 1930, Thomasville, Georgia. Newman was born 6:30 am, 26 January 1925, Cleveland Heights Ohio. They married in 1958 and had two children. Their marriage was one of the most long lasting in Hollywood. When asked the secret of their contentment, Joanne replied, "Who's contented? We may divorce next year. But we like each other a lot and have great respect for each other. We feel very comfortable together. We don't believe in being together all the time. We spend about half the year together, and have nothing in common." She cared nothing for his race cars or politics and he had no interest in her interests in opera and dance. But the relationship worked. Astrology shows why.

a. The ability to give and receive love.

Examine the personal planets.

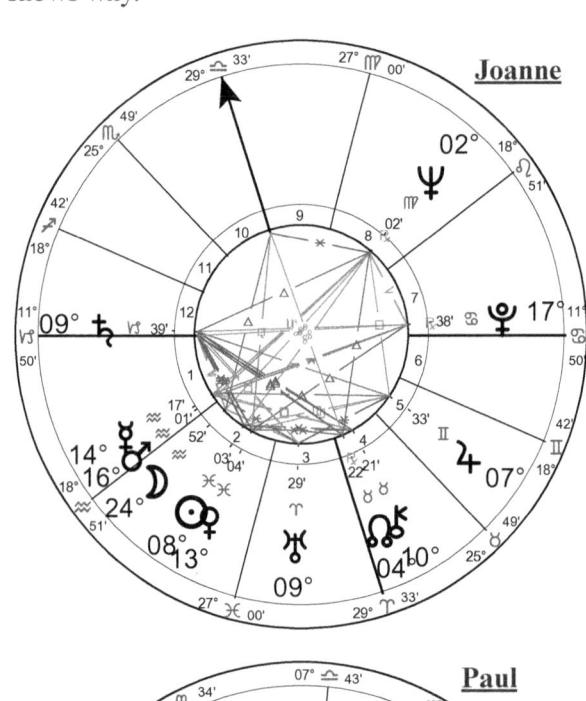

1. Venus. It will be relatively easy to give and receive love and to establish a fulfilling relationship if Venus is well placed - in Taurus, Libra, Pisces, in an angular house and it has easy aspects. Hard aspects indicate that relationships will be difficult until skills have been developed. In a man's chart, Venus represents the type of women he will admire and be attracted to. In a woman's chart, Mars represents the type of man admired and found attractive.

Joanne has Venus exalted in Pisces with great aspects. Venus was in Paul's first house with a mixture of aspects.

2. The Moon. The Moon is very important in intimate relationships because it represents our emotional needs and how we get on with others daily. No matter how powerful a sexual attraction may be, if we cannot live with the person the relationship will break down. Afflictions to the Moon indicate difficulties expressing the emotions and forming intimate relationships. A well aspected Moon gives emotional health and ease in a domestic situation.

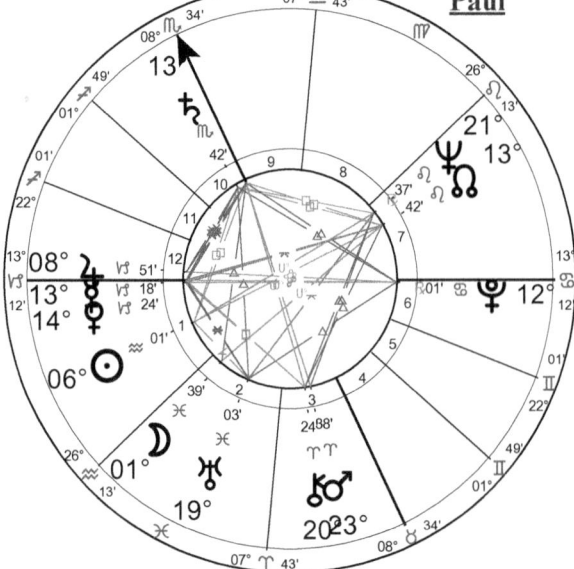

Both Joanne and Paul's Moons were not well aspected. Joanne's had difficulties and Paul's was unaspected. They spent a lot of time apart.

3. Mercury. A well aspected Mercury indicating good communication skills is a plus. In contrast, people with hard aspects to Mercury should be encouraged to develop effective communication skills.

Both had Mercury-Jupiter aspects indicating a great sense of humour and the ability to laugh together.

4. Uranian or Saturnian? If Saturn dominates the character, the person is basically cautious, reserved, responsible, is able to make a commitment and will want a more conventional type of relationship. Uranus dominated individuals are highly individualistic and independent. They need a lot of freedom and are comfortable with unconventional arrangements. To identify if a person is more Uranian or Saturnian in expression, look for major aspects from the personal planets or the ascendant to them; or look to see if one of these planets is on the ascendant, in the first house or on the MC. It will not be a good fit if these two types get together. If a person has a mixture of Uranus and Saturn aspects, there is greater flexibility.

Joanne and Paul, they were a mixture of both, so were compatible in this regard.

b. The Synastry Chart.

There are three steps in setting up a synastry chart:

- Person B's planets are placed in A's houses, and examined for the impact they make in the houses.
- This is repeated with A's planets in B's houses.
- The aspects between A's planets and B's planets are examined for compatibility.

1. Planets in houses.

In love relationships, it is favourable for the partners personal planets to be in the 5th of love affairs, and in the 11th of friendships - it is good to have a lover as a friend.

Joanne's Jupiter falls in Paul's 5th.

For marriage, planets in the 7th of marriage and the 4th of home and family are fortunate. Unfavourable houses, especially if the planets are afflicted, are 6 (love becomes a duty or hard work), 8 (the relationship can be too intense which may lead to divorce), and 12 (hidden agendas spoil things). If planets in these houses are well aspected, it helps matters.

Paul's Juno is in Joanne's eleventh house. Joanne's Juno was on Paul's ascendant. These add to marriage compatibility.

Houses 2, 6 and 10 are good for professional relationships. Well aspected planets in the 3rd giving good communication and in the 9th - giving a shared search for understanding are good for any relationship.

Paul's Sun, Mercury, Venus fall in Joanne's first house, indicating he will support her personal interests and goals. Joanne's Sun, Moon and Venus fall in Paul's second house - she will support his values. Paul's Jupiter also falls on Joanne's ascendant - he will be generous with her, support her, laugh with her and encourage her to grow.

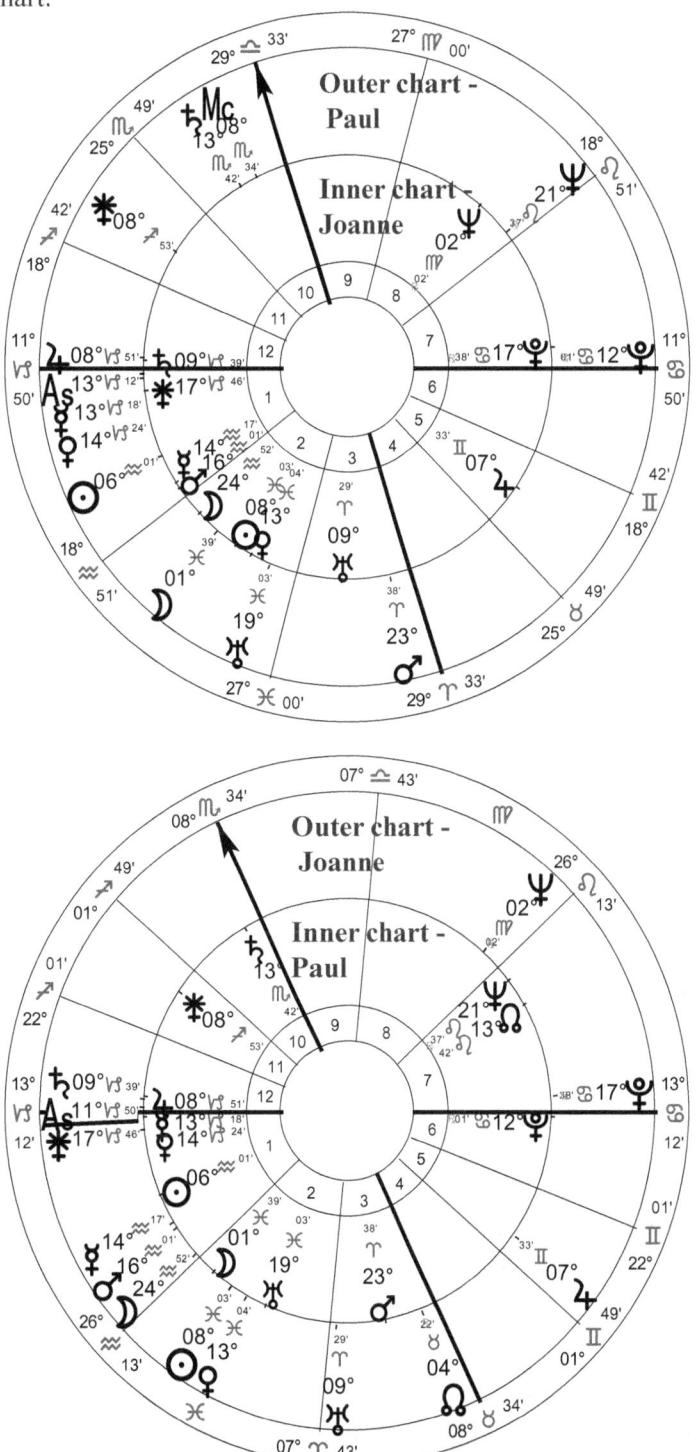

2. Examine aspects between planets.

Check Sun to Sun (ego compatibility), Moon to Moon (emotional compatibility), Juno to Juno (marriage commitment compatibility), Mercury to Mercury (communication compatibility), Venus to Venus (love) and Mars to Mars (sex and passion).

Hard aspects, or planets in signs that are incompatible, indicate energy difficulties that must be balanced if there is to be relationship harmony. Fire and air signs are compatible, so are earth and water signs. If there are hard aspects, see if there are compensating easy aspects to other planets. For example, if the two Suns clash, but they have easy aspects to Jupiter; the clash of egos can be eased through laughter. Or if the Moons are trine, tension can be eased through emotional compatibility. If there is no aspect between two planets, check to see if the signs they are in are compatible.

In love relationships, look for favourable aspects between the Sun (male force) and Moon (female energy) and between Mars (male sexual energy) and Venus (feminine energy). Oppositions - usually considered to be difficult aspects, are viewed differently in intimate relationships. An opposition between one person's Sun and the others Moon, or between Venus and Mars these are favourable because they indicate a magnetic attraction between the two. Good Jupiter aspects bring friendship to any relationship.

Both Joanne and Paul were cerebral and although they had different interests, they communicated well (Paul Sun in Aquarius conjunct Joanne's Mercury in Aquarius). They loved a lot and laughed a lot together (Paul's Sun trine Joanne's Jupiter, fifth house).

Paul's Moon is conjunct Joanne's Sun. These symbols of husband and wife or man and woman, when they come together like this, it is a very beneficial aspect for marriage. Further, Paul's Moon is conjunct Joanne's, giving emotional empathy. Their Venus' are sextile and their Mars are compatible (Joanne's Mars in Aquarius sextile Paul's Mars in Aries. This latter explains Paul's life-long passion for car racing).

They both had the same signs on the ascendant and seventh house, indicating similar attitudes towards life and marriage - both disciplined and professional personally, but emotional and nurturing in marriage - and both very intensely involved with each other (their Pluto's are conjunct).

Paul's Juno is in freedom-loving Sagittarius in the eleventh house. He loved racing cars (Mars in Aries) and being with his friends, different to Joanne's more traditional and conservative approach to marriage (Juno in Capricorn). But the marriage worked because she let him have his freedom (Paul's Juno trine Joanne's Uranus in Aries)

Regarding being Uranian or Saturnian. They were a mixture. Paul has Saturn on the MC trine Uranus, and his Sun in Aquarius. Joanne had Saturn on the ascendant and three personal planets in Aquarius. This means they would honour family and relationship traditions, while also being explorative and giving each other space.

c. The Composite Chart.

The composite-midpoint chart is the energy chart of the relationship and is read like a natal chart. For example, Mercury in the chart - its sign and aspects, indicates how the two people communicate, the seventh house represents the marriage, etc. Usually there are a combination of easy and hard aspects. If the hard aspects outweight the easy ones, it is often very hard to maintain a long-term intimate relationship. Many hard aspects indicate many conflicts - more than the good times; so, the union may be too hard to maintain. However, if there are strong Saturn or Virgo links, people may feel they are duty bound to stay together. Many easy aspects indicate greater harmony.

1. The Sun.

A strongly aspected Sun gives heart and vitality to the relationship. Hard aspects give strong energies between the two, but the relationship could destruct through ego conflicts.

2. The Moon.

In any type of relationship which requires two people to live or relate together closely, it is important the Moon is well placed or aspected. Otherwise cohabiting will be difficult. Easy Sun/ Moon aspects are very good omens for a successful union.

3. Venus.

Favourable aspects, a conjunction and even an opposition aspect, between Venus and the Sun or Venus and the Moon; this is very good for love relationships. Favourable aspects between Venus and Mars emphasise intense romantic, passionate and sexual attraction. Venus/ Pluto aspects give a very deep, intense relationship, and both people are transformed by the connection. It can become obsessive or destructive under hard aspects.

The Sun is conjunct the Moon and Venus on the second house of values - love and the relationships are vitalised, they shared common values and domestic habits. Opposite Neptune, eighth house - they were very idealistic about the things that were important to them and had to make adjustments over their differences. Consequently, they both transformed because of their willingness to do this for the well-being of the union. Sex (8th) was most likely very healing for their marriage when they had serious differences. It would likely help Joanne overcome any rigid beliefs she held (Moon in Aquarius), about how a marriage should be.

4. Juno. Marriage compatibility.

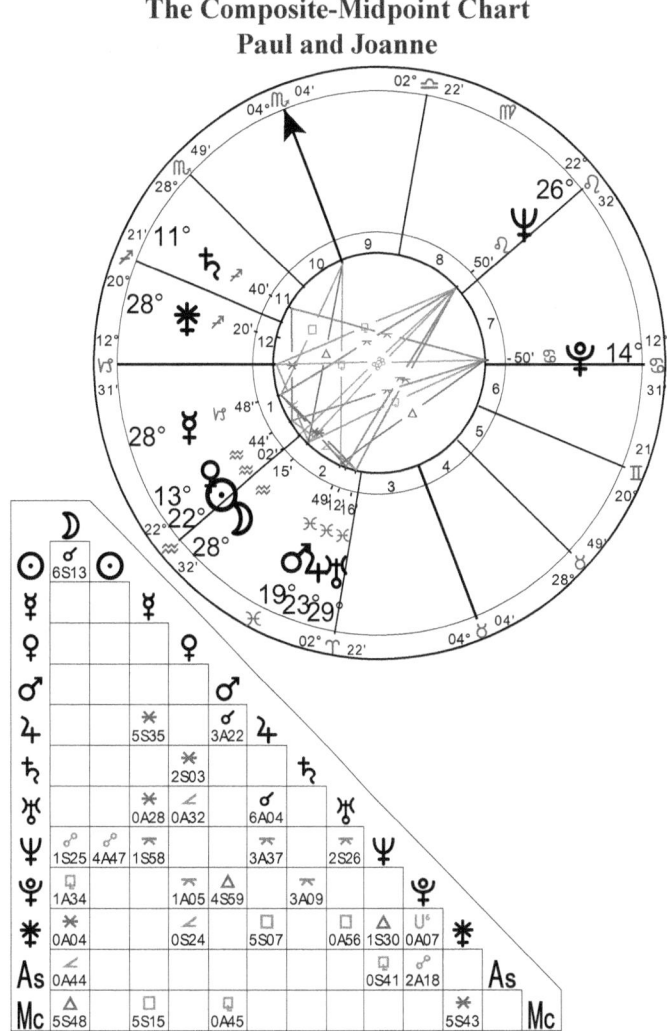

**The Composite-Midpoint Chart
Paul and Joanne**

Within the marriage, they were freedom loving and adventurous (Juno in Sagittarius). Because Paul's Juno was in Sagittarius and Joanne's in Capricorn, it shows she made an adjustment to fit in with his need for independence and freedom. Generous and easy going with each other, compassionate and forgiving (Juno trine Neptune), they kept their marriage troubles private (Juno in 12, square Uranus-Jupiter). They had blazing rows, perhaps even resorted to physical altercations over jealousy issues (Juno square Jupiter-Uranus conjunct Mars). But passionate sex and emotional sharing helped them overcome their issues (Mars-Jupiter-Uranus in Pisces, Neptune the ruler).

Pluto, the planet of radical change and transformation is in Cancer on the seventh house cusp - in their individual charts and in the synastry and composite charts. This indicates the marriage would transform them both individually.

5. Mercury. Easy aspects indicate compatibility in communication.

Although they disagreed about their ideals (Mercury inconjunct Neptune), they would have down-to-earth conversations about their personal issues (Mercury in Capricorn) and could laugh their way out of conflict (sextile Jupiter). They did not dwell on issues for too long (sextile Uranus), but would move on quickly.

6. Other planets.

They blended their physical energies well (Mars conjunct Jupiter and Uranus). Jupiter brings friendship and good fortune - it was comfortable in its own sign Pisces and located in the second house of money, they created wealth together.

2. Work and Career

The first jobs most people get are more Saturnian because there is a need to get established and make money. Later, people may try to find a career which satisfies an inner need for fulfilment and expression. This often occurs after the mid-life period 42 - 45 years, and the Chiron Return at 50 years.

1. Examine the 2nd house of money.

The second house of money indicates prosperity. Check to see if there is a planet link with the 10th. Harmonious aspects between the rulers of these two houses or to planets in either house indicate career success and prosperity. Hard aspects do not rule our prosperity. It may be a little harder to manifest what is desired.

2. Examine the 10th house of career and recognition.

The sign on the 10th, any planets in the 10th or the ruler of the 10th - its sign and house; all these can indicate a compatible career. The primary indicators of career success are well aspected planets in the tenth house and on the MC. Hard aspects to the 10th or MC could also indicate success, but challenges need to be overcome first. It is better to have challenging aspects to the 10th than no aspects at all. A "T-Square" planetary configuration which gives a driving urge to succeed is helpful, especially if it involves the 10th.

3. Examine the 6th house of work skills and conditions.

The sixth house is the primary representative of work and work skills. This house, the sign on the cusp, the ruler and its sign and house, and any planets in the 6th; these represent potential skills that with development, could benefit the working life. Finding links between the 6th and 2nd planets can likewise indicate potential prosperity that can come from such skills. A Grand Trine that links these three houses is good to have.

4. Careers associated with the signs and planets.

Aries and Mars. Careers which allow the expression of initiative, exploration, ideas, drive and physical energy. Managers, leaders, supervisors. Selling, marketing, travelling and entrepreneurs. Sports, athletes and competition; surgery and hairdressing. *Mars:* tradesmen and blue-collar workers generally. Careers involving carpentering, cars, engineering, iron-work, machinery, metal-work, tools, utensils. War and the military.

Taurus and Venus. Careers which require reliability, practical application and commitment. Finance, banking, the handling of money, valuables, luxury items and business generally. Working the land, farming, real estate. Handling food, chef, restaurant owner. The arts, decorating, interior design, designing, fashion, modelling, beauty industries, social events and singing - many Taureans have beautiful voices.

Gemini and Mercury. Any of the communication, information, travelling, marketing, teaching technologies, industries and trades. Academic careers, administration, book-keeping, entrepreneurship, interpreting, journalism, learning and teaching, lecturing, linguists, merchandising, office work, public relations, publishing, reporting, selling, speaking, teaching, tour guide, translator, travelling, writing. All transport industries.

Cancer and the Moon. Industries and vocations connected with women, domesticity, the home or family, nurturing and with the public generally. Mediums and metaphysical workers. Healing, service, hospitality, nursing, food. Careers connected with childbirth, pregnancy, babies, child care. Careers involving white liquids or fluids and water. Organising, administration and real estate.

Leo and the Sun. Managers, dignitaries, leaders, presidents, authoritarians, statesmen, kings, rulers, magistrates, supervisors and self-employment. Sports, working with children and all creative areas - art, theatre, acting, performance, dance and social activities. *The Sun:* heart specialist, goldsmiths.

Virgo and Mercury. Any career which requires attention to detail, such as that done by accountants, administrators, analysts, librarians, lab technician and research scientists. Also, communications, customer service, clerical work and veterinarian. Importantly, all health modalities and associated technologies, hygiene, nutrition and diet.

Libra and Venus. The arts, beauty, fashion, decorating, graphic artist, interior design and social activities. Careers where personal presentation, charm and good looks count. Balancing of relationships - customer service, diplomacy, counselling, ombudsman, psychology, conflict resolution and mediating. The legal system - lawyers, barristers, judges and courtroom aides.

Scorpio, Mars and Pluto. War, death, handling other people's money: assisted dying, blood banks, butchers, hospices, inheritances, insurance, investments, legacies, the military, soldiers, stock-market, tax department, undertakers, weaponry and wills. Industries involved with reproduction and sex. Research, detectives, exorcist, metaphysician, the esoteric or occult. Psychology, healing and surgery. The underworld - sanitation, criminals, refuse, subversive activities, spying. *Pluto:* atomic weapons and nuclear missiles.

Sagittarius and Jupiter. Institutions of higher education, libraries and philosophy. Religious work, morality and philanthropy. Far distance travelling, foreign countries, people and cultures, import-exporting, international finance, tourist and adventure-park guide. All careers that involve gambling and growth: advertising, marketing, promotion, publishing, risk-taking and selling. Sports: archery, coaching, horses, jockeys and vets. *Jupiter:* spreading optimism and humour.

Capricorn and Saturn. Large institutions (conservative and traditional), bodies of power and authority: law enforcement and government. Bankers, executives, leaders, managers, stockbrokers, supervisors and trustees. *Saturn:* industries connected with the earth, land and property - architect, construction trades, farming, mining, minerals, pottery and real estate. Work with the elderly, death and time.

Aquarius and Uranus. Humanitarian groups, social work, politics, revolutions, new reforms and all pioneering initiatives. Anything modern, alternative, esoteric, new technology, internet, computing. Science, electricity, invention, aviation, television. Astrology, cosmology, genetics, human sciences and metaphysics.

Pisces and Neptune. Healing, nurturing, caring, serving industries and vocations. Counselling, psychiatry, hospice or mental health worker, nursing. Religious and mystical or psychic workers. The arts: dance, film, music, photography, poetry, storytelling and theatre. Fantasy and illusion. Trades connected with the ocean - boat-building, sailing, sailors, shipping. *Neptune:* anaesthetics, drugs and alcohol.

5. Careers associated with the Houses.

1. Careers where appearance and presentation are important - the goal is to be appealing or attractive to the public, to sell oneself. Self-employment also is related to this house.
2. Handling money, banking, dealing with valuables, possessions, trade, investments. Psychologist - dealing with values, self-esteem. Art and beauty products and services. Being in business generally.
3. Communications, education, publishing, speaking, teaching. All careers and trades involved in the writing, production and marketing of ideas, books, including delivering, transport and travelling.
4. Family businesses, domestic industries, building trades, real estate. All trades and services connected with family life and the houses we live in. Working from home is another possibility.
5. Creative vocations, theatre, social organiser, match-making bureau, pleasure and amusement activities, gambling, speculation, sports. Working with children.
6. Health work, nutritionist, dietary planning. Development of work skills associated with the sign on the cusp or planets in the house. Workplace organiser, vet, working with small animals.
7. Counselling, negotiation, marriage-divorce industries, lawyer, legal work and industries.
8. Careers dealing with other people's money and property - debt, bankruptcy, joint finances, investments, taxes, wills and legacies. Industries involved with death and sex. Psychology and esotericism.
9. Careers involving overseas countries and people, travel, import-export, emigration. Those connected with places of higher learning, religion and philosophy.
10. Careers where one gains recognition and status. Government, managers, administrators, organisers, employers, authority figures, judges, chief executives. Self-employment.
11. Politics, humanitarian organisations, group endeavours, club activities, social work, friendship bureaus, selling hopes and dreams.
12. Universal service work. Careers in large institutions such as prisons, hospitals and working with the disadvantaged. "Retreat" spiritual, health and well-being centres. Working with large animals.

3. Health

The signs and planets rule different parts of our body and our psychology. Stress and life-style issues can affect health and these are shown in the chart as the hard aspects between planets. Medical astrology is a specialist science but some suggestions are made here.

1. Examine the Sun Sign.

The Sun is the source of pranic vitality and good vitalisation of the body cells and organs equals good health. Its energy is prophylactic - it kills all germs and frees from disease. This activity is reflected in the body by the immune system, which the Sun governs. It is a subset of the cardiovascular system and uses blood vessels to send out its army of white defender cells to fight infection. The Sun governs the cardiovascular system, which includes the heart organ, arteries, capillaries, veins, blood and bloodstream. The heart plays a similar role in our physical system as the sun does in the solar system. It distributes life, vitality and nourishment to every cell in the body through blood circulation.

A well placed and well aspected Sun in the natal chart promotes a positive psychological outlook on life and is the most positive indicator of good health. It indicates a heart that has an excellent ability to absorb prana, thus vitalising cell life and boosting the power of the immune system. Easy aspects to the Sun from Mars and Jupiter boost vitality. This is because the brute animal strength of Mars and the expansive power of Jupiter, support, promote and strengthen the Sun's power. Even hard aspects (square, semi-square, opposition, conjunction) are better than none. In this case, energy is available, though if misused can lead to burn-out.

Afflictions to the Sun indicate heart and circulation problems, depletion of vitality and lowered resistance to disease. The Sun sign often points to a part of the body that will suffer if vitality or immunity should falter. Sometimes solar function is potentially impaired if the Sun is in Virgo, Pisces, or the sixth and twelfth houses, which govern illness and hospitalisation. This does not mean that illness naturally follows such placements; there may be other compensating factors in the chart. What it does mean is that attention should be given to diet, exercise and living a moderate lifestyle to help strengthen vitality and health.

Interestingly, germs are living organisms that find their way into the human mechanism through the medium of the life force, which in its turn, uses the heart and the bloodstream as its agents of distribution.

2. Examine the Moon.

In Alice Bailey's book Esoteric Healing, we are informed that most individual diseases are caused by our own psychology - primarily disturbed emotions (90% cause of disease). So, examination of the Moon - and also of Mars and Neptune (which are given as the rulers of the emotional solar plexus chakra), their signs and aspects; will give insight into emotional expression. Any hard aspects to these planets could indicate potential health problems as a consequence of the misuse of the emotions. Disruptive emotions can cause congestion in energy flows in the body. This means that organs are not being adequately vitalised and this is a precursor to the onset of disease.

3. Examine the 6th and 12th house.

These are the health houses. The 6th rules acute health conditions. The 12th rules chronic health conditions that require hospitalisation or other specialist ongoing attention. The sign on the sixth house cusp, the ruler and planets in the 6th; these can indicate a part of the body that could be more easily affected if ill-health should strike and the type of illnesses that could arise. For example, Gemini - mental and breathing disorders.; Saturn in the 6th or the ruler of the 6th - illnesses associated with cold and chills. Hard aspects from malefics to the 6th or to its ruler, or located in the 6th or 12th can increase the likelihood of illness. They represent stress that is not being alleviated.

4. Illnesses by hard aspects.

Hard aspects and planet patterns such as the T-Square, these show tension in the personality. In such cases, people may suppress their emotions or have volcanic rages. Either way, there is a disruption to energy flow. The planets involved in such a pattern can show the type of diseases, the organs and systems that can be affected if the stress being generated is not alleviated.

5. Signs and planet rulership's of the body and associated illnesses.

Aries and Mars: rule the head, brain, face and nose. Aries governs the pineal gland. Injuries to the head or brain, headaches, teeth, migraine, stroke, head fevers, eye problems, brain congestion. *Mars*: inflammation, infections, acute disease, fevers, blood problems, bruises, wounds, acidosis, burns, irritation, ulcers, surgery, sharp pain, muscular disorders, haemorrhages, accidents, fractures, infectious diseases.

Taurus and Venus: rule the limbic system, the throat, thyroid gland, the mouth and beginning of the alimentary canal. Earache, sore throats, swollen throat glands, mumps, abscesses, thyroid problems, laryngitis, gum disease, obesity through overeating.

Gemini and Mercury: rule the central nervous system, neurons, nerve fluid, the airways, lungs, breathing organs, respiration, speech organs, ears, hearing, eyes, thymus gland, shoulders, arms, hands and upper body-movement. Allergies, asthma, lung disorders, bronchitis, pneumonia, pleurisy, nervous disorders, neuralgia, mental stress, respiration problems, emphysema, speech defects, breathing disorders - asthma, problems with the hands, locomotive disorders.

Cancer and the Moon: rule the breasts, abdomen, stomach, the pancreas gland, female reproductive organs and processes such as menstruation, pregnancy and child-raising. White body fluids (including co-rulership of the lymphatic system), the watery sacs in body, tears, white blood cells, brain and bone matter and stem-cells. Water retention leading to obesity, flatulence, breast cancer, allergies, diseases caused by wrong diet. Moodiness, emotional-based problems.

Leo and the Sun: rule the cardiovascular system especially the heart, lower lungs, the immune system, co-rules the thymus, sternum, the spine and vertebrae. *The Sun:* rules vision via the eyes and cell-life. Autoimmune diseases, heart disease, problems with the blood, fevers, high temperatures, high blood pressure, sunstroke, sunburn, spinal meningitis, back pains, angina, anaemia, inflammation, low vitality.

Virgo and Mercury: rule intestinal digestion, the small and large intestines, the bowels, the colon, the pylorus, the duodenum, the appendix and co-rules the anus (with Scorpio), which is the end point of digestion. Malnutrition, appendicitis, colic, digestive and bowel problems, food allergies, parasites and wind.

Libra and Venus: rule the pancreas, kidneys, bladder, ureters, co-rule the adrenals with Scorpio, and rule the belt-area of the body including vertebrae in that region. Lumbago, urinary tract problems, kidney diseases of all types. Blood sugar imbalance, kidneys and pancreas disorders. *Venus*: female reproductive processes, genitals and the pancreas. Over-relaxes (prolapses), problems with periods, diabetes through overindulgence with sugar, addictions to sweet foods and laziness.

Scorpio, Mars and Pluto: rule the reproductive organs generally - primarily in men, the elimination organs, the adrenals and fight and flight impulse. Hernia, piles, venereal diseases, menstrual irregularities, prostrate trouble, kidney infections and adrenal troubles. *Pluto*: rules the will to survive. Malformation, massive infections, malignancies, obsessive anxiety disorders.

Sagittarius and Jupiter: rule the hips, thighs, mobility and problems such as sciatica and movement problems. *Jupiter:* rules the liver, the arteries and growth generally. Liver problems such as jaundice, hepatitis and cirrhosis of liver. Diseases caused through excess - obesity, gout, enlarged organs and cell overgrowth such as in cancer.

Capricorn and Saturn: rule the skeleton, skin, teeth, spine, knees and all joints. Rheumatism, bone dislocation, colds and chills, arthritis, knee problems, deafness, dental problems, stiffness. *Saturn*: chronic diseases, problems with the skeleton - rigidity, calcification, crystallisation. Obstructions, malnutrition, skin diseases, hair loss, under-activity, weaknesses generally and depression.

Aquarius and Uranus: rule DNA, the ankles, blood circulation and corule the nervous system. Genetic diseases, gene mutations, leg cramps, ankle problems, varicose veins, anaemia and other problems with blood quality. *Uranus*: neurons and synapses. Spasms, epilepsy, sudden illnesses, cramps, convulsions, ruptures, seizures, twitching, restlessness. Stress-related illnesses, sudden accidents especially from electricity.

Pisces and Neptune: rule the feet and lymphatic system. Cystic fibrosis, bunions, viruses, allergies, mucus, devitalisation, general weakness, gout. Alcoholism, psychosomatic illnesses, delusions, drug and alcohol addictions. *Neptune*: the blood stream, hidden or obscure illnesses.

4. Children, Childbirth, Fertility

A question sometimes asked is, "Can I have children?" Here is where to look in the chart.

1. The 5th house

- If children are desired, it helps to have the fertile signs - Cancer, Scorpio and Pisces, on the fifth house of Children cusp. Taurus is also helpful, since the Moon is exalted in that sign. Consequently, it is not helpful to have barren signs on the 5th - Gemini, Leo, Virgo.
- It is helpful to have the ruler of the 5th in one of the fertile signs and well aspected.
- It helps to have the benefics Venus and Jupiter, or the Moon (these three are "the givers" of children), in the 5th and well aspected, or any planet in the 5th be well aspected, especially by the Moon or Jupiter. Consequently, it is not helpful to have malefics in the 5th. Pluto (loss, death, denial). Saturn and Mars deny children. Uranus can indicate difficulty conceiving or carrying full term. It can also indicate children coming by unorthodox means, such as by adoption. Neptune, loss through unknown causes.
- Several planets in the 5th indicate being surrounded by children. These may be children of one's own body, or children that come by other means, such as by adoption, by marrying someone with children or working with them such as in school teaching or sports coaching. Sometimes planets here represent characteristics of the different offspring, the first planet representing the first child, the second planet the second child, etc.

2. The Moon and Cancer

- The sign Cancer and its ruling planet Moon rule childbirth and child-raising. They should be examined in both male and female charts as indicators of potential parenthood. They are the primary rulers of the female reproductive system and female fertility.
- When children are wanted, the best signs for the Moon to be in are Cancer (in dignity) and Taurus (exalted). It also helps if the Moon is well aspected - especially by Venus or Jupiter or located in the 5th.
- Consequently, the Moon poorly placed in Capricorn or Scorpio is not helpful. Neither is it in cadent houses, or if it has hard aspect from malefics. Hard lunar afflictions in female charts indicate conception, pregnancy and child-raising problems.

Weigh the odds. Often, indications regarding children are mixed which means that there may be some initial problems or delays with conception or birth which can be overcome with care. If there have been difficulties ask for the medical report. Weigh the positive indications against the negative, before making a final decision to the question "Can I have children?" But even if matters look bleak, never say "no". Try to leave hope intact.

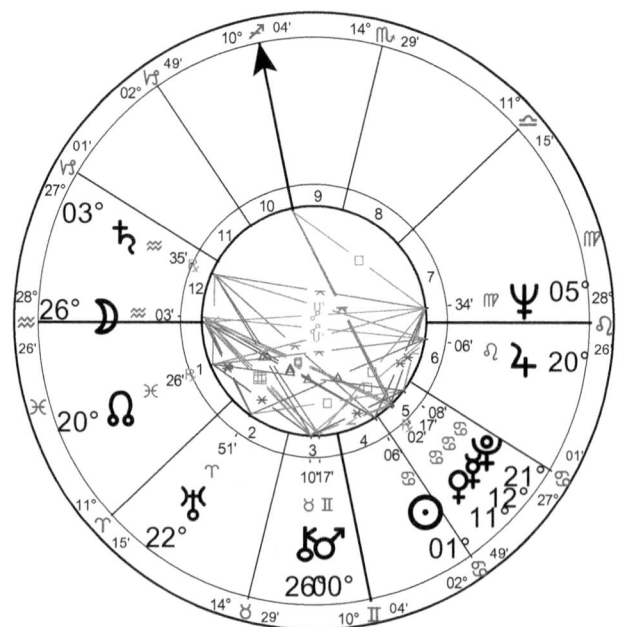

Princess Soraya, born 22 June 1932, 10:30 pm, Isfahan Iran.

Soraya was the queen consort of the Shah of Iran who she married in 1951. When doctors told her and the shah, that she was infertile and would never have children, they divorced in 1958.

She had Cancer on the fifth house and Venus within it - these are fortunate. But unfortunately, Pluto - the "drastic" planet, was also in the 5th. It squares Uranus, which suggests a genetic difficulty.

The Moon is opposed by Jupiter, which is in Leo, a barren sign; and it is deposed by Uranus, reinforcing the genetic difficulty.

5. Death and Life Endings

The eighth house which rules death - the sign on the cusp, the location and status of the ruler and planets in the 8th; these represent the nature of the death and circumstances surrounding it.

The fourth house is the other area to be examined because it rules "life-endings." The sign on the cusp, the ruler, and planets in the 4H indicate the circumstances that surround us at the end of the life.

President John Fitzgerald Kennedy

The chart of JFK is an interesting example to study because we all know the circumstances surrounding his death.

- He was assassinated - shot in the head.
- He was surrounded by thousands of people at the time.
- There was confusion about the identity of the assailant.
- People mourned his passing.

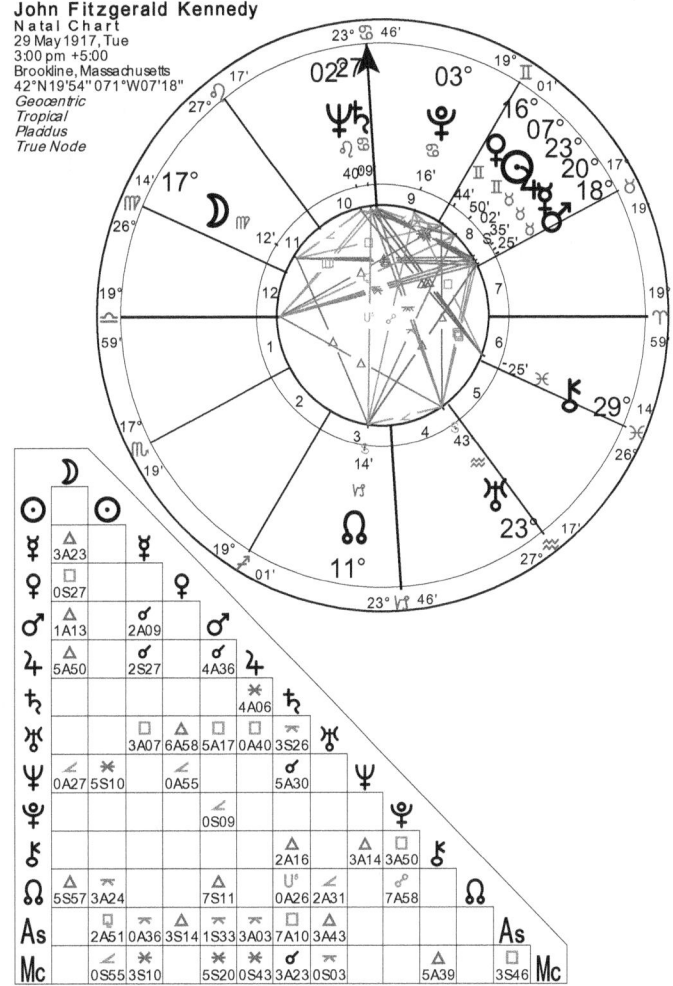

The eighth house has five planets (Mars, Mercury, Jupiter, Sun and Venus, in that order).

- Many planets in the 8th - many people witnessed JFK's passing. Many planets can also indicate many factors involved in a death.
- It would be a very public death - Venus (the ruler the 8th, with Taurus on the cusp) squares the Moon, which rules the public. The Moon also rules the Midheaven - a death in the open.
- Mars is the first planet in the 8th, inconjunct the ascendant - the first house is related to the head. He died - shot in the head, while travelling in a car, elements ruled by Mars.
- Mars square Uranus in the 4th. He was assassinated by a partisan countryman. It was politically motivated. This is shown a second time by Venus square the Moon (someone from "home"), in the eleventh house of politics.
- There has been conjecture that the Mafia were behind the killing. The eighth house and Pluto rule "the underworld", so this is a possibility.
- Confusion surrounded the circumstances of his death (Venus semi-square Neptune). In any event, his death was going to be controversial and argued about (Mars-Mercury square Uranus). It would be big news and would shock both his countrymen and the world (Mercury conjunct Jupiter, Venus in Gemini square the Moon).
- Sun sextile Neptune - there would be grief.
- Uranus rules politics and its placement in the 4th indicates political activity until the end of his days. Saturn rules the fourth house of life-endings and is conjunct the MC in Cancer - he was in office at the end of his life, and held in high esteem. He had a very public funeral.

When JFK died on November 22 1963, Mars by solar-arc was moving over Pluto, the planet of death.

READING CHARTS

Beginner students often feel over-whelmed when looking at a chart for the first time. The planets and patterns look alien and the mind gets confused and over-whelmed. This can be overcome if readings are approached with a clear method in mind - such as is given here. The chart of Sean Connery is used to demonstrate a simple method.

In later sections of this chapter, five specialist areas have been covered - relationships, career, health, children and death. Once the basic character reading has been completed, if there are no special requests from the client then do a quick overview of relationships, career and health. But usually, clients book a reading with an astrologer because there is an issue involved - most often, relationships. Each topic has been comprehensively covered to help students build up expertise when reading these areas.

A Simple Natal Chart Format

1. Briefly, look at the Planetary Pattern and the Mode and Elements.

Just do this briefly. Identifying the pattern and dominant mode and element (if there is one) is a way to get the mind working and a "feeling" for the person's character.

2. Then focus the reading around the Sun, the personal planets and ascendant.

a   Start with the Sun - the personality. Read it in its sign, house and aspects (do this for all planets). It is the heart of the personality and all the other planets should be related back to it. Using the analogy of a car, the Sun in Aries could be likened to a Ferrari - a personality that wants to race. All the other planets are like parts of the engine and interior of the car that affect the speed and handling of this race car.

b.   Read the emotions, the Moon.

c.   Read the ascendant, the appearance, image and how life is approached.

d.   Read Mercury - how the mind thinks.

e.   Read the affections - Venus; how easy it will be to give and receive love.

f.   Read the passions, the desires - Mars.

g.   Then read any of the other planets that are making important statements if they have not already been included in the reading of the personal planets.

Example: Natal Chart Reading - Sean Connery

Scottish actor Sean Connery was born on the 25th of August, 1930, in Fountainbridge, Edinburgh, Scotland, at 18:05 pm.

1. The Planetary Pattern.

The pattern is a Bucket. Here is the definition: *"A single planet opposes all planets on the opposite side. The energy generated by the large group of planets will try to find release through the single planet. It is crucial therefore that the function symbolised by this planet is working well, or congested energy, anger and frustration will result."* Saturn is the handle of the bucket in Sean's chart and sits on the Capricorn ascendant. What this tells us about him, is that he is very disciplined in the way he approaches life and what people think about him. No matter what is going on in the rest of his life, he is very careful about his image and what the public sees.

2. Note the breakdown of elements.

Sean is outstandingly an earth element person. Three of his personal planets are in an earth sign (the Sun, Mercury, Venus in Virgo). As previously mentioned, his ascendant and the handle of the bucket are in Capricorn, a cardinal-earth sign. This gives him a cautious, practical and pragmatic nature. These down-to-earth traits are foundational in his nature.

3. Read Connery's personality - the Sun.

- Sun in Virgo in the seventh house. Sean's personality is intelligent, discerning and analytical. Marriage and close one-on-one partnerships are important to him.
- Sun conjunct Neptune. This aspect softens his analytical side; he is sensitive, artistic and compassionate.
- Sun semi-square Venus in Libra, eighth house. Sometimes he can be a little selfish with his affections and if so, this will cause issues with partners.
- Sun sextile Mars in Gemini, sixth house. He is passionate about his work, where he is versatile and a good communicator. He likes physical work.
- Sun trine Saturn in Capricorn, conjunct ascendant. Sean is responsible, hard-working and ambitious. This is the way he approaches life, how people see him and what they like about him.
- Sun sesquiquadrate Uranus in Aries, second house. He can be selfish with money.
- Sun trine north-node in the third house. He likes to have a plan, how he can progress forwards into life. If he takes the initiative (node in Aries), things should flow.

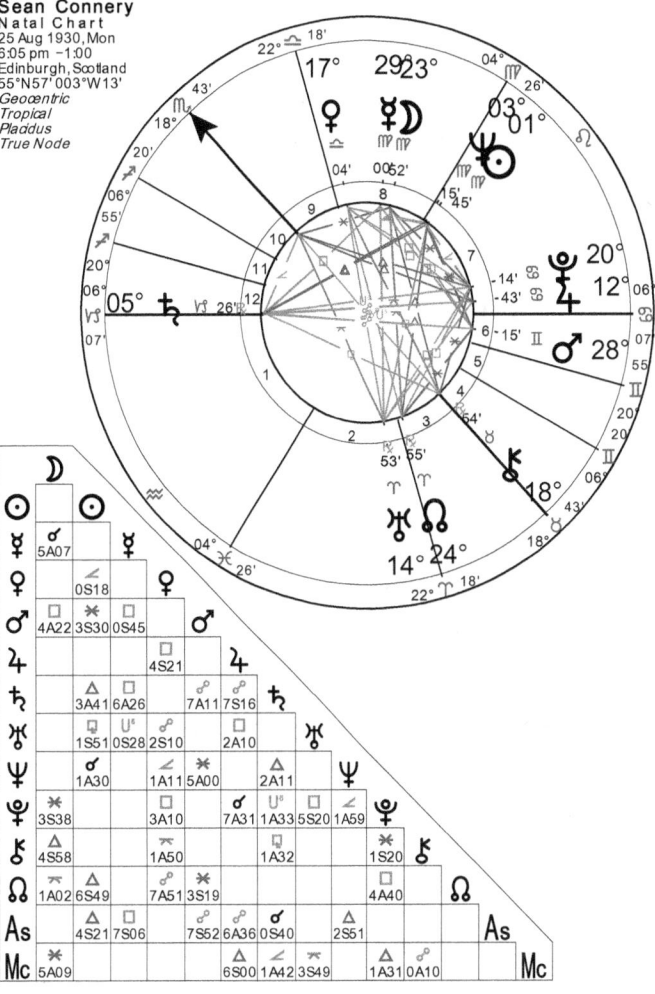

Summary. Sean is intelligent, analytical and also sensitive and artistic. Marriage is very important to him but he needs to be more considerate at times. He is passionate about his work, is a good communicator and hard working. People respect him. He likes to have a plan about how to progress forwards in life.

> Remember, the chart represents character at birth. If you are reading for a mature person, it is possible that hard aspects in the nature have been straightened. So, while Sean may have been "selfish with money" when young, it is just as possible he adjusted this as he matured.

4. Read the emotions, the Moon.

- Moon in Virgo in the eighth house. Sean can be irritable if things do not go his way - especially in business and in the handling of shared resources and money.
- Moon conjunct Mercury in Virgo, eighth house. He likes deep and intelligent conversations.
- Moon square Mars in Gemini, sixth house. He can be angry and sarcastic if things go wrong at work. He is a perfectionist
- Moon sextile MC. His imagination will help him achieve success in his career.
- Moon inconjunct north-node in Aries, third house. He needs to adjust his tendency to criticise, be more straight-forwards with what he says.
- Moon trine Chiron. Wounds from childhood compelled him to seek emotional healing.

Summary. Sean can be irritable if things do not go his way. He will criticise people he is unhappy with - especially in business and when handling money. In his work he tries very hard to get everything perfect and this has helped him achieve success in his career. He must heal any heal childhood wounds that remain unresolved and learn to speak kindlier when he is irritated.

5. Read the ascendant, the appearance and how life is approached.

Ascendant trine the Sun has already been done with the Sun, so there is no need to repeat it.

- Ascendant in Capricorn. Sean approaches life in a cautious and responsible way.
- Ascendant conjunct Saturn. He can be conservative and serious.
- Ascendant square Mercury in Virgo, eighth house. He will criticise people who disagree with how he wants to do things. Especially in business.
- Ascendant opposite Mars in Gemini, sixth house. He can be argumentative.
- Ascendant opposed by Jupiter in Cancer, seventh house. He can exaggerate issues.
- Ascendant trine Neptune in Virgo seventh house. He is a kind and compassion person and the understanding he receives from partners will help him overcome his niggardly side.

Summary. Sean approaches life in a cautious and responsible way and this is how people see him. He will criticise people who disagree with how he wants to do things and argue - especially when money or inheritances are involved. He can exaggerate issues to try to get his way. But essentially, he is a kind and compassion person and the understanding he receives from partners will help him overcome this side of his nature.

6. Read Mercury - how the mind thinks.

Mercury has already been done extensively with the Sun, Moon and ascendant, so there is no need to repeat it. This often happens because Mercury orbits very close to the Sun.

7. Read the affections - Venus; how easy it will be to give and receive love.

Note that Connery only has hard aspects to Venus. This indicates he had/ has issues expressing his affections, which he needed to sort out.

- Venus in Libra in the 8th. Sean is a romantic. He adores beautiful women and making love to them.
- Venus opposing Uranus in Aries, second house. His independent side does not like restrictions that a committed relationship places upon him.
- Venus square Jupiter and Pluto in Cancer, seventh house. He can become obsessed with a partner when he is in love. Major problems will arise in relationships if he tries to control his partner by using force.
- Venus conjunct the south-node. The previous statement "He can become obsessed with a partner," this is an old pattern. Giving the partner greater freedoms and independence would help him overcome it. This is important, because the compulsion is interfering with his spiritual growth.
- Venus semi-square Neptune in Virgo, seventh house. Sometimes he has unrealistic expectations.

Summary. Sean is a romantic. He adores beautiful women and making love to them. Sometimes he has unrealistic expectations and can become obsessed with a partner and create problems by trying to control her. Giving the partner greater freedoms and independence would help him overcome this and is a positive move forwards for Connery. It will help him overcome his possessiveness. When he gets the balance right, his intimate relationships will be more harmonious.

8. Read the passions, the desires - Mars.

- Mars in Gemini in the sixth house. Sean is passionate about his work and will debate and argue to try to get things right.
- Mars opposing Saturn on the ascendant. When obstacles arise, frustration can compel him to argue and to fight.
- Mars sextile Neptune in Virgo, 7th and eighth houses. It will help to direct his frustrations and energies into his artistic interests.
- Mars sextile the north-node. It also helps to direct his energies into new projects that he initiates. This will help his spiritual progression in life.

Summary. Sean is passionate about his work and is an assertive communicator and debater. He can get frustrated with delays and be argumentative. It helps to direct his energies into his artistic interests and new projects that he initiates. This will help him progress forwards in life.

> By focusing the reading upon the personal planets and ascendant, all the planets were involved. So, there is no need to redo the outer planets. Once the basic character reading has been completed, other specialist areas such as career and health can be done.

9. Career opportunities for Sean Connery.

When considering a career, look to see if there is a link between the second house of money and the 10th of profession, or to the 6th of work. For Connery, Neptune, ruler of the 2nd, sextiles Mars in the sixth house. In turn, Mars is a ruler of the 10th with Scorpio ruling that house. This generally indicates that if the right choices are made, he should have a successful career and make money from it. We know that he did.

a. *The 2nd house - making money.* Connery's house of money is ruled by Neptune, with Pisces on the cusp. Neptune is in analytical Virgo, trine Saturn on the ascendant and sextile Mars in Gemini in the sixth house. This indicates that if he presents the right mature, tough-guy image and works intelligently to develop his craft (Saturn on the ascendant, Mars in Gemini 6), he can make a career and money out of selling illusion (Neptune).

b. *The 6th house of work skills.* With Gemini on the sixth house cusp, the development of good communication skills would enhance his career opportunities. Mars is in the 6th in Gemini and Connery started his career doing manual labour. In his movie career, he became famous playing the fictional spy 007, James Bond; a tough, masculine man's man (Mars sextile Neptune). He communicated this excellently, and the money started rolling in.

c. *The 10th house of profession and fame.* Scorpio is on the 10th and it rules amongst other things, death, weaponry, sex and spying. All the attributes of James Bond that made Connery famous. If Connery had chosen not to go into acting, it is likely he would have been successful in other ways.

10. Soul purpose and spiritual direction.

a. *The Ascendant Sign - soul purpose.* The first place to look in the chart is at the ascendant sign, which represents the purpose of the soul - the qualities to develop and things to do so that greater love and wisdom is developed and expressed in the life. With the Capricorn ascendant, this is to be "ambitious for the greater good, to use one's powers, resources and influence to benefit humanitarian causes." This purpose is ruled by Saturn, since it is the esoteric ruler of Capricorn - as well as the exoteric. The chart listing the esoteric planet rulers is in the "Planets" Chapter, Ascendant section. With Saturn on the ascendant, Connery's appearance and actions would be scrutinised and judged. He was required to act with integrity and to be authentic in his life demonstration. Otherwise, people would see his fakeness and judge him.

b. *The Sun Sign.* The Sun represents the personality, the lower self. The spiritual goal is always to develop the positive traits of the Sun Sign.

c. *The Moon Sign (in Virgo), the prison of the soul pattern.* An emotional need to criticise people, is the problem pattern. This infects the mind, so it becomes hypercritical and demands perfection in this imperfect world. This must be purified. Vulcan, the purifier, is the esoteric ruler of Virgo. The need to transform these negative traits are emphasised with the Moon in the eighth house.

d. *The Moon's north and south nodes.* With the north-node in Aries (third house), positive traits such as using the initiative, courage and assertiveness must be expressed, to counterbalance Libra south-node negatives such as indecision and procrastination. Communicating what he thinks to those around him is another important goal for Connery. He has definitely achieved this through his movie career.

> This is a simple interpretation and a guideline to help students get started. Once a basic technique has been mastered and there is greater familiarity in navigating a chart, then experiment with different models or let the reading unfold in a manner that seems to suit the chart or the client. As previously stated, the key to becoming a proficient and excellent astrologer, is to keep reading charts on an ongoing basis.

CHAPTER 8. MANUAL CALCULATIONS - NATAL and PROGRESSIONS.

Time Zone Map

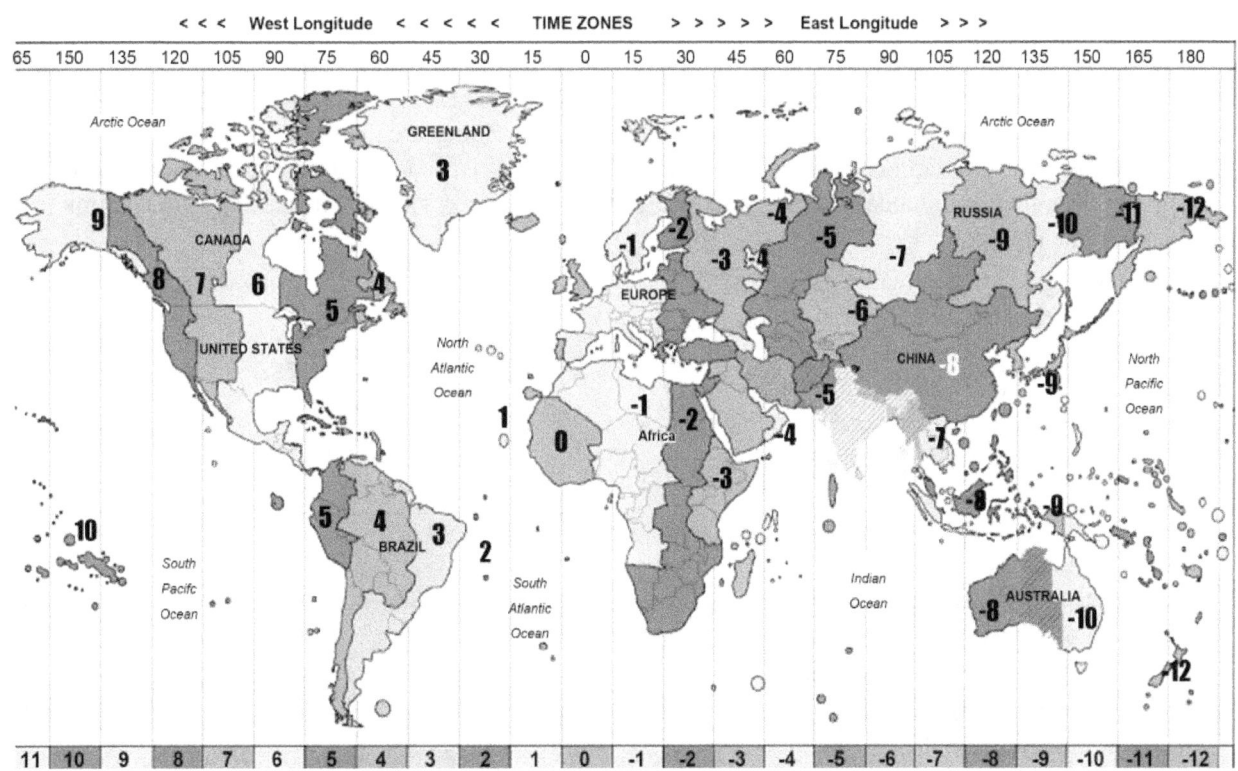

Basic tools required to calculate a Natal Chart

1. An Ephemeris. It contains the daily position of each planet at midnight (if a Midnight Ephemeris is used), or at noon (Noon Ephemeris). The American Ephemeris for the 20th and 21st Centuries (Midnight) by Neil F. Michelsen is recommended. It is calculated for Greenwich, England, which is located at 0 degrees longitude.
2. Book of Tables. This is needed to help find the House Cusps of the chart. The Michelsen Book of Tables is recommended and it is used in the following examples. It includes both Placidus and Koch House Systems.
3. An Atlas. The International Atlas by Thomas Shanks is recommended. It lists all the countries in the world (except USA) which is in a separate atlas - The American Atlas. Both contain Time Zones and time changes (Daylight, Wartime). This information is also obtained via a Google search online. The atlas gives three important pieces of information that are required to calculate the House Cusps.
    - The longitude and latitude of any given birthplace.
    - The Time Zone.
    - When Daylight Saving (added hours for summer time) and wartime apply.
4. A calculator. To work out the maths.

A. GUIDE TO NATAL CHART ERECTION

In this section, a guide is given for the manual erection of a natal chart - to find House Cusps and planets for a local birth time. Examples for Southern and Northern latitudes are given.

The first step is to convert the local time of birth to Local Sidereal Time. This is because the Ephemeris tables are set at Greenwich Mean Time (GMT), which means the local birth time has to be converted to GMT in order to use them. GMT is time at the Greenwich prime meridian line or zero-degree longitude point, which runs through Greenwich, England. It is also called Universal Time (UT), because it is the standard time for astronomers, astrologers, etc. From this meridian, all other Time Zones are measured.

Geographically, the Earth is divided by two imaginary sets of latitude and longitude circles. Every spot on earth has its own latitude and longitude. When the houses are being calculated, this information is factored into the equation.

Longitude begins at Greenwich and radiates out East and West. Longitude East of Greenwich is appended with "E" for East (for example 60E20). Longitude West of Greenwich is appended with a "W" (60W20). The highest degrees of longitude are 179E59 or 179W59. The point where 180E00 and 180W00 meet is called the International Date Line, which mostly runs through water to avoid half a country being one day behind the other.

"Meridian" is a synonym for latitude. The first meridian of 0 degrees is located at Greenwich, UK. Latitude or the first meridian starts at 0 ° at the equator. Latitudes north of the equator are appended with "N". Latitudes south of the equator are appended with "S". Latitude is at its maximum at 90 degrees, north or south.

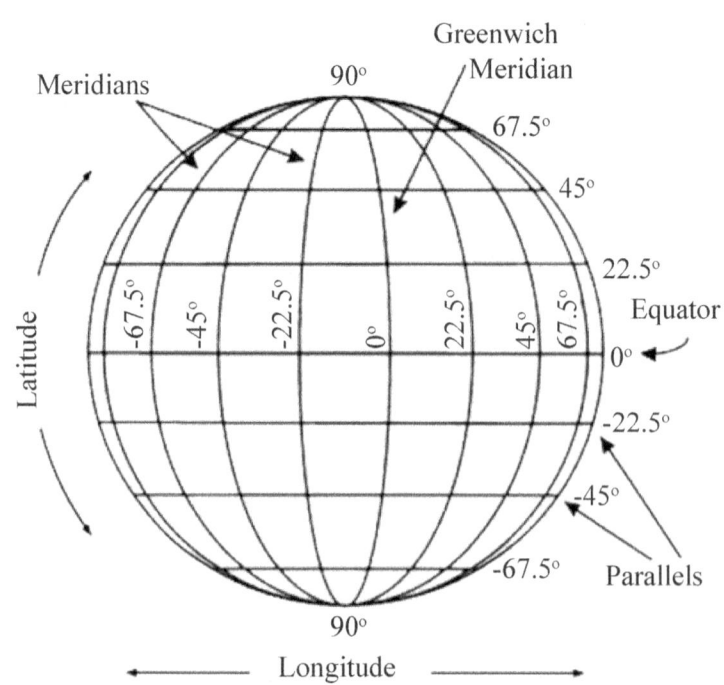

Worksheet 1:
Calculate Natal House Cusps (Placidus) - Southern Latitude

Use Michelsen's Midnight Ephemeris and Tables of Houses for Placidus.

The first example chart is for Helen Maxine Reddy. She was an Australian-American singer. During the 1970's, she enjoyed international success, especially in the United States where she placed 15 singles in the Top 40 of the Billboard Hot 100. Her signature hit was "I Am Woman".

Step 1. Convert the local time of birth to Local Sidereal Time (LST - Lines 1 to 16)

Overview of steps involved.
  a. The Sidereal Time at midnight on the GMT birthdate is found.
  b. To this is added the GMT of Birth.
  c. To this is added the solar-Sidereal Time correction made to the GMT of Birth.
       = This gives the Sidereal Time of Birth at Greenwich.
  d. A time correction is made for longitude (added for East, subtracted for West)
       = This gives the Local Sidereal Time for Northern Latitudes
  e. For Southern Latitudes, add 12-hours.

Example: Helen Reddy, 25 October 1941, GMT 07:50, ST 10:03:14.

a.	ST at Greenwich on 25/10 1941		10:03:14	Sid Time on 25 October
b.	GMT of Birth	+	07:50:00	
c.	Sidereal Correction on GMT	+	00:01:17	
	= ST of birth at Greenwich	=	10:03:14	
d.	Correction on Longitude	+	09:39:52	
e.	Add 12-hours (Melbourne 37S47).			
	= LST Southern Latitudes	=	31:43:06	
	Subtract 24-hours	=	07:43:06	(to bring time under 24hrs).

1. Write the local time of birth into Line 1. Use the 24-hour clock.

Line 1 - Reddy was born at 17:50:00.

2. Identify if Daylight Savings Time (DST) was in effect.

The practice of adding an hour to time in summer is widespread. This is called Daylight Saving Time (DST). Additionally, during the World Wars many countries adopted War Time and a few had Double Summer Time (advanced the clock by 2 hours). Daylight Saving Time is always subtracted.

Line 2 - For Reddy there was no DST so the line is left empty.

3. Calculate the Standard Time of Birth.

Line 3 - Reddy's Standard Time of Birth was 17:50:00.

4 and 5. Calculate the Greenwich Mean Time of birth (convert standard time to GMT).

(4). Identify the Time Zone of the Birth Place.

Time Zone is added to local time of birth if the birth was West of Greenwich; subtracted if East.

Line 4 - Reddy's Time Zone was East (AEST -10). So, this is subtracted.

(5). Calculate the GMT of Birth (from Lines 1, 2, 3, 4), and also record the result on Line 8.

Line 5 - Reddy's GMT of Birth was 07:50:00.

6. Clarify GMT Date of Birth. It is important when finding the GMT of Birth, to note which actual *date* it falls on. This is because, when local time is converted to GMT, the birthdate can move backwards into the previous day (for eastern Time Zones), or forwards into the following day (for western Time Zones).

Line 6 - Identify the GMT Date of Birth and write it on this line. Reddy's GMT Date was 25 October 1941, the same date as at her local place of birth.

Worksheet 1: Calculate Natal House Cusps (Placidus) - Southern Latitude

Name: Helen Reddy
Place of Birth: Melbourne Australia
Birth: 25th October 1941
Time: 5.50 pm
Time Zone: AEST - 10 hrs
Latitude: 37S47
Longitude: 144E58

Step 1. Convert local time of birth to Local Sidereal Time				
		Hours	Minutes	Seconds
1. Local time of birth - use 24 hour clock.		17	50	00
2. Subtract Daylight Saving if in effect. *(Always subtract DST)*.	-			
3. Equals Standard time of birth.	=	17	50	00
4. From Time Zones, find Standard Time Zone difference to GMT. *(Add 24 hours if needed to subtract)*. **West ADD /East MINUS.**	-	10	00	00
5. Equals **GMT of birth.** *(Record on Line 8)*.	=	07	50	00
6. Clarify **GMT Date of birth** *(Same day? Day before? Day after?)*.	**GMT date Birth = 25/10/1941**			
7. From Ephemeris GMT date, find Sidereal Time of Birth.		02	11	57
8. *Record GMT of birth from Line 5.*	+	7	50	0
9. From Table II, find Sidereal Correction value *(Less than 4 mins)*.	+		1	17
10. Calculate **Sidereal Time of Birth at Greenwich.**	=	10	03	14
11. From Table III, find Longitudinal Correction. *(Reddy's is 144E58). (You cam also divide longitude by 15)*. **West MINUS / East ADD.**	+	09	39	52
12. Calculate **North Latitude Local Sidereal Time** *(Lines 10 and 11)*.	=			
13. For Southern Latitudes, always add 12 hours.	+	12	00	00
14. Calculate **Southern Local Sidereal Time** *(Lines 10, 11 and 13.)*	=	31	43	06
15. *If result is over 24 hrs minus 24 hrs; over 48 hrs minus 48 hrs.*	-	24	00	00
16. Final result is the **Southern Latitude LST.**	=	**07**	**43**	**06**
Step 2. Calculate the House Cusps - use the Table of Houses (TOH)				
17. From TOH, find LST just under than the client's (07:43:06).	-	07	40	00
18. Subtract from client's LST *(Line 16. It is always less than 4 minutes)*.	=		03	06
19. Convert result to seconds.	=			186"
20. Divide result by 240 (seconds) = Constant decimal (CD).	**Result CD = 0.775 = 0.8**			

Latitude 37S47, round to 38S		MC	11th	12th	ASC	2nd	3rd
21. TOH, larger LST (07:44:00, Lat 38)		24♋06	27♌07	26♍27	21♎07	18♏58	20♐22
22. TOH smaller LST (07:40:00, Lat 38).	-	23♋10	26♌10	25♍33	20♎18	18♏07	19♐28
23. Calculate difference over 4 minutes.	=	00 56	00 57	00 54	00 49	00 51	00 54
24. Convert result to minutes.	=	56	57	54	49	51	54
25. Multiply result by CD. *(Round out figs)*.	x	45	45	43	39	41	43
26. **Calculate cusps** - add line 25 to line 22.	=	23♋55	26♌55	26♍16	20♎57	18♏48	20♐11
27. **Reverse Sign** for Southern Latitudes	=	23♑55	26♒55	26♓16	20♈57	18♉48	20♊11
Computer generated figures		23♑53	26♒52	26♓14	20♈58	18♉50	20♊12

Here are some examples to find the GMT time and date of birth.

a. Born in New York, USA, at 8 pm, 30 January 1985.

Born at time	20:00:00	NY, 30 January 1985.
Time zone EST	+ 05:00:00	Eastern Standard Time Zone.
GMT	25:00:00	subtract 24-hours
GMT date 31 Jan	01:00:00	1 am, the day *after* the local birthdate.

In this example, there was no Daylight Saving, so the standard time zone applied - Eastern Standard Time, EST +5. Because the birth was West of Greenwich, the Time Zone was *added* to local time. This moved the GMT Date of Birth forwards into the next day, 31 January (1am). The 31st was the GMT work-date in the Ephemeris.

b. Born in New York, USA, 3 am, 30 June 1985.

Born at time	03:00:00	NY, 30 June 1985.
Time zone EDT	+ 04:00:00	Eastern Daylight Saving Time Zone.
GMT date 30 June	07:00:00	7 am, the *same* day as the local birthdate.

This birth was also in New York, but six months later than that the first example. Daylight Saving Time was in effect, consequently the Time Zone was EDT +4. Adding the time zone did not push the date forwards into the following day. The GMT Date of Birth remained the same as the local birthdate - 30th June. The 30th was the GMT work-date in the Ephemeris.

c. Born in Auckland NZ, 6am, 30 June 1985.

Born at time	06:00:00	Auckland NZ, 30 June 1985.
Time zone NZT	- 12:00:00	NZ Standard Time.
GMT date 29 June	18:00:00	6pm, the day *before* the local birthdate.

This birth was also on the 30th June, but in Southern Latitudes. There was no Daylight Saving, so the time zone was NZT -12. Because the birth was East of Greenwich, the Time Zone was *subtracted*. This moved the GMT Date of Birth backwards into the previous day. The 29th of June was the GMT work-date in the Ephemeris.

7-16. Calculate the Local Sidereal Time (ST) of Birth.

The Sidereal Time taken from the Ephemeris is used to calculate House Cusps. Sidereal Time is star time, so called because a sidereal day is the time it takes for the Earth to complete one rotation about its axis with respect to the fixed stars. The sidereal day is 3 minutes 56 seconds shorter than the solar day. The Ephemeris uses Sidereal Time because it is more accurate than solar time.

> *Exercise:* Look up your day of birth in a Midnight Ephemeris, then look at the 2nd Column. It is headed "Sid. Time." This is the Sidereal Time at midnight for that day. Notice how Sidereal Time increases each day by 3 minutes 56 seconds. The sidereal year begins around 22 September, 0 hours, as the Sun moves into Libra.

(7) *Using the GMT date, from the Ephemeris, find the ST of Birth for that date.*

Line 7 - Reddy's GMT ST on 25 October 1941, was 02:11:57.

(8) *The GMT of Birth (from Line 5) was previously recorded on this line.*

Line 8 - The GMT of Birth is always added. Reddy's GMT was 7:50:00.

(9) *Using Table II "Solar-Sidereal Time Correction Table", make a correction for the GMT of Birth - (Line 8 - 7:50:00).* This correction converts solar time to sidereal. It is always less than 4 minutes.

> *Exercise.* Go to Table II in Michelsen's. Note that the "hours" go across the top, and "minutes" go down each side. Each column is divided into minutes and seconds. For 7 hours and 50 minutes, find the column headed "7h", go down the column until you reach the row intersecting with "50" minutes. The correction is 1 minute 17 seconds. This correction is always less than 4 minutes and is always added.

Line 9 - The correction is 1 minute 17 seconds.

(10) Calculate Sidereal Time of Birth at Greenwich (Lines 7, 8 and 9).

Line 10 - Reddy's, was 10:03:14.

(11) Using "Table III, Time Correction for Longitude," make a time correction for the birthplace longitude. If longitude is East the correction is added, for West it is subtracted.

Exercise: Using Table III, note that the table is divided into Degrees and Minutes at the top. Longitude for Reddy's birthplace - Melbourne, Australia, is 144E58. In the "Degrees" columns, find 144 - the correction is 9 hours 36 minutes. In the "Minutes" column, find "58" - the correction is 3 minutes 52 seconds. Added together, the total correction is 9 hours 39 minutes 52 seconds. Write this figure on Line 11.

Line 11 - Longitude correction for Reddy is 9:39:52. It is added because longitude is East.

(12) Because Reddy was a South Latitude birth, the line (for North Latitudes) is left empty.

(13) For South Latitude births:

Line 13 - Add twelve hours.

(14) Calculate the Local Sidereal Time - from Lines 10, 11, and 13.

Line 14 - Reddy's Local Sidereal Time was 31:43:06.

(15) On this line, time is brought back to under 24 hours - subtract either 24 or 48 hours to do this.

(16) The result is the final Local Sidereal Time of Birth.

Line 16 - Reddy's Local Sidereal Time was 07:43:06.

Step 2. Calculate the House Cusps (Lines 17 to 27).

17-18. From Table of Houses (TOH), find the difference between the LST Table figures and Reddy's.

Go to the Placidus Tables and find the LST figures. They are in the top left-hand corner of each table. Note that the LST in each table increases by 4 minutes. Now find the LST that is just under Reddy's. Enter this LST figure onto Line 17.

Line 17 - Since Reddy's LST is 07:43:06, the lower LST figure of 07:40:00 is selected.

(18) Calculate the difference between Reddy's LST and lower Tables figure (subtract Line 17 from 16).

Line 18 - LST difference for Reddy was 00:03:06.

19-20. Find the Constant Decimal (CD).

The CD is used in house cusp calculations. Save it in the calculator's memory.

(19) Convert the Local Sidereal Time difference to seconds.

Line 19 - Reddy's LST difference in seconds is 186 seconds.

(20) Divide Line 19 total by 240 (the number of seconds in 4 minutes).

Line 20 - Reddy's CD is 0.8 (rounded from 0.775).

21-27. Find the House Cusps

(21-23) Find Reddy's House Cusps in the TOH - choose the cusps for Latitude 38 (37S47).

Go to the Placidus TOH and find the LST's that are just larger and lower than Reddy's (07:43:06).

Line 21 - TOH figures just larger are 07:44:00 - write the House Cusps (Lat. 38) on this line.

Line 22 - TOH figures just under Reddy's are 07:40:00 - write the lower House Cusps (Latitude 38) on this line.

Line 23 - Calculate the difference (subtract 22 from 21).

(24-25) Find the distance each House Cusp moved for Reddy - apply the CD.

    Line 24 - Convert any degrees to minutes.

    Line 25 - For each House Cusp, multiply the result by the CD and round out decimals.

(26-27) Calculate Reddy's House Cusps

    Line 26 - Calculate cusps. Add Line 25 to Line 22 (the lower house cusp figures).
             If this was a North Latitude birth, these figures would be the final House Cusps.

    Line 27 - For a Southern Latitude birth, reverse the signs.

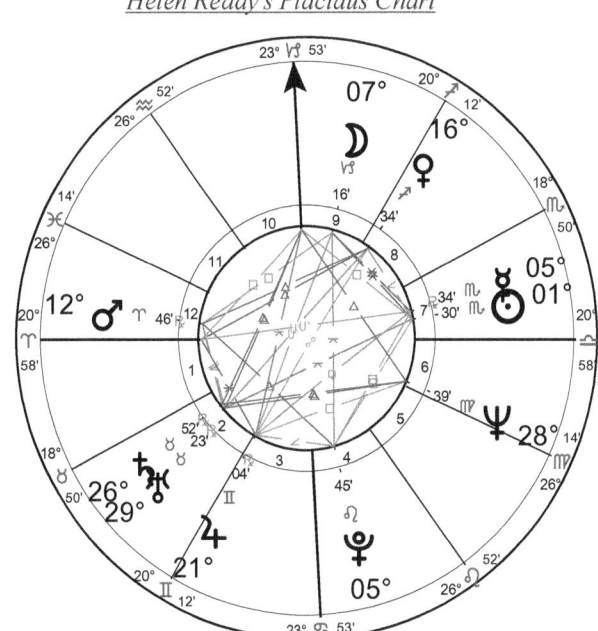

Helen Reddy's Placidus Chart

Compare computer generated House Cusp figures to those manually prepared

When calculations for House Cusps are done manually and compared to a computer-generated chart, there are usually differences. This is caused by rounding decimal figures out - a factor that is also built into the tables.

As long as this difference is within one degree, that is acceptable.

When Helen Reddy's computer-generated house cusp figures are compared to those produced by this exercise, the greatest variation is three minutes.

Erecting Birth Charts when the time is unknown.

If a birth date is available, but no birth time, a chart can still be set up - by using an Equal House system where all houses are 30 degrees wide. This system is called "0 Aries" - the cusp of the 1st house is set at 0 Aries, the cusp of the 2nd house is set at 0 Taurus, etc. This utilises the fact that each sign is related to the house of the same number. So, any planets in Aries will be in the 1st house, planets in Taurus will be in the 2nd, etc. There is no ascendant or midheaven. It works well. All inter-planet aspects will be accurate excepting for the Moon, which can move up to 13 degrees a day. Setting the chart for 12pm will minimise the give or take error.

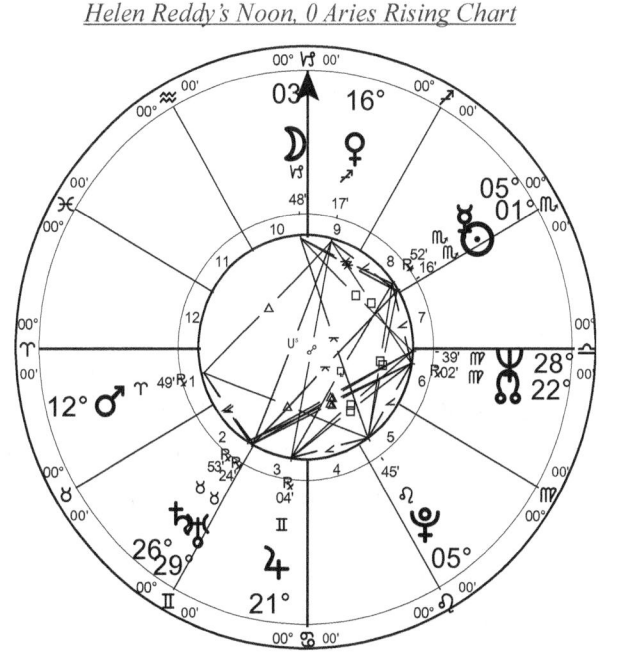

Helen Reddy's Noon, 0 Aries Rising Chart

Reddy's 0-Aries Rising chart is shown here. Since she had Aries rising anyway, there is not such a great variation. Interestingly, it places the Moon in Capricorn on the pseudo MC, which indicates a profession that has strong links to women. Her hit song, "I am woman" and public Women's Lib activism, these had a galvanising effect on women.

Guide for Worksheet 2: Calculate Planet Positions

Use Michelsen's Midnight Ephemeris and Book of Tables for Placidus.

Working with Reddy's GMT and Date of Birth (07:50:00, 25 October), 3 steps are required.

- Step 1: Find out how far planets travel in a day (or half a day for the Moon).
- Step 2: Find out how far Reddy's planets moved on that day.
- Step 3: Calculate Reddy's planet positions.

Step 1: Find out how far planets travel in a day (or half a day for the Moon).

1-2. In the Ephemeris, find the 2 dates you will be working with and record the planet positions.

The first date is the GMT Date AFTER birth. This is recorded on Line 1. The second date is the GMT Date of Birth (which is midnight before birth). This is recorded on Line 2.

    Line 1 - Write in Reddy's planet positions for the day AFTER birth - the 26th October.

    Line 2 - Write in the planetary positions on the day of birth (Midnight Tables) - the 25th.

Because the Moon moves so quickly, there are midnight (0 hr) and noon (Noon) figures given for it.

- If the GMT of Birth was before noon, then the "0 hr" figures will be the "before" figures; and the "Noon" figures will be the after figures - on the GMT date. Reddy's GMT was before noon.
- If however, the GMT of Birth was after noon, then the "Noon" figures will be the "before" figures; and the "0 hr" figures on the following day, will be the "after" figures.

    Line 1 - Moon. Record the "Noon" ("after") figures on the 25th October - 09:44:50.

    Line 2 - Moon. Record the midnight ("before") figures on the 25th October - 02:36:21.

3. Calculate planet travel over 24 hrs - or over 12 hours for the Moon.

Pay special attention to any planets that are retrograde. If so, a reversal in calculation is required. Instead of Line 2 being subtracted from 1, Line 1 is subtracted from 2. Similarly, Line 4c (or 4) is subtracted from Line 2. To check your work, ensure your answers lie between Lines 1 and 2 figures. In Reddy's chart, Mercury, Jupiter, Saturn and Uranus are retrograde.

    Line 3 - Calculate all planet travels, subtracting Line 2 from 1. (1 from 2 for retrogrades).

Step 2: Find out how far Reddy's planets moved that day.

4. Use three tables from Michelsen's "Book of Tables" to work out the travel.

- Table V, the Diurnal (Daily) Motion of the SUN. *(How far the Sun travels in a day)*
- Table VI, the Semi-diurnal Motion of the MOON. *(How far the Moon travels in half a day)*
- Table VII, the Diurnal Motion of the PLANETS. *(How far the planets travel in a day)*

    <u>For example, finding the distance travelled by Helen Reddy's Sun.</u>

    i. Table V. Note that the top header row lists the range of distances travelled by the Sun - from 57' 12" to 61' 10". Each column increases by 2 seconds.

    ii. Note that the "hours" figures are at the bottom of the table and "minutes" at the top.

    iii. The distance travelled by Reddy's Sun in 24hrs was 59' 51".

    iv. In the Tables, top row, 59' 51" falls between 59' 50" and 59' 52". <u>Either can be chosen</u>.

    v. 59' 52" was selected. Distance travelled from GMT: 7 hours = 17' 28", and 50-minutes - 2' 05".

    Line 4a - From the Tables, write in distance travelled for GMT hours (Reddy's is 7 hours). Do the same for Line 4, for the outer planets.

    Line 4b - Write in the distance travelled for GMT minutes (Reddy's is 50 minutes)

    Line 4c - Add Lines 4a and 4b for total distance Reddy's planets travelled.

Step 3: Calculate Reddy's planet positions.

5. Calculate the planet positions.

Add Line 4c (total distance), to Line 2 (planet positions at midnight). Round out figures.

    Line 5   Calculate Reddy's planet positions.

    Line 6   Round out figures and include sign glyphs.

Worksheet 2: Find Planet Positions
Using Midnight Ephemeris and Michelsen's Table of Houses V, VI, VII

Name: Helen Reddy   GMT Birth Date: 25 October 1951   GMT of Birth: 07:50

Planet and sign	☉ ♏			☽ ♑			☿ ♏ ℞			⚷ ♐			♂ ♈ ℞		
	d	m	s	d	m	s	d	m	s	d	m	s	d	m	s
1. Planets <u>after</u> birth (26th)	02	11	00	09	44	50	04	44	00	17	20	00	12	38	00
2. Planets, <u>before</u> birth (25th)	01	11	09	02	36	21	05	58	00	16	12	00	12	51	00
3. Calculate travel in 24/12hrs. Subtract line 2 from 1 *		59	51	07	08	29	01	14	00	01	08	00		13	00
4a. Tables V, VI or VII. Distance travelled for GMT hours (07)		17	28	04	10	15		21	53		19	50		03	48
4b. Tables V, VI or VII, distance travelled for GMT minutes (50)		02	05		29	48		02	36		02	22			27
4c. Add lines 4a, 4b. Total distance travelled	+	19	33	04	40	03	−	24	29	+	22	12	−	04	15
5. Calculate positions. Add line 4c to line 2. Minus for retrograde.	01	30	42	07	16	24	05	33	31	16	34	12	12	46	45
6. Round out figures.	1♏31			7♑16			5♏34 ℞			16♐34			12♈46 ℞		
Computer figures	1♏30			7♑16			5♏34 ℞			16♐34			12♈46 ℞		

Planet and sign	♃ ♊ ℞			♄ ♉ ℞			♅ ♉ ℞			♆ ♍			♇ ♌		
	d	m	s	d	m	s	d	m	s	d	m	s	d	m	s
1. Planets <u>after</u> birth (26th)	21	02	00	26	50	00	29	22	00	28	41	00	05	45	00
2. Planets, <u>before</u> birth (25th)	21	05	00	26	54	00	29	24	00	28	39	00	05	45	00
3. Travel in 24/ 12 hrs.		03	00		04	00		02	00		03	00		00	00
4. Travel for GMT (hrs + mins)	−		59	−	01	18	−		39	+		59	+		
5. Calculate positions. Add line 4 to line 2; minus for retrograde	21	04	01	26	52	42	29	23	21	28	39	59	5	45	
6. Round out figures.	21♊04 ℞			26♉53 ℞			29♉23 ℞			28♍40			5♌45		
Computer figures	21♊04 ℞			26♉52 ℞			29♉23 ℞			28♍39			5♌45		

* For retrograde planets, subtract lines 1 from line 2, or line 5 from 2.

This completes the exercise for Helen Reddy, born in Australia - Southern Latitudes.

The second example that follows is for Princess Diana, the first wife of Prince Charles of Wales and mother of Prince William and Prince Harry. Diana's charisma, friendliness, glamour and good works made her an international icon and earned her an enduring popularity. This was exacerbated by her tumultuous private life and the acrimonious collapse of her marriage. Media attention and public mourning were extensive after her death in a car crash in a Paris tunnel in 1997 and subsequent televised funeral. Her legacy had a deep impact on the royal family and British society.

Worksheet 1: Calculate Natal House Cusps (Placidus) - Northern Latitude

Name: Princess Diana
Place of Birth: Sandringham England
Birth: 1st July 1961
Time: 19:45 pm
Time Zone: BST - 1 hrs
Latitude: 52N50
Longitude: 000E30

Step 1. Convert local time of birth to Local Sidereal Time					
			h	m	s
1. Local time of birth - use 24 hour clock.			19	45	00
2. Subtract daylight saving if in effect. *(Always subtract DST)*.		-	01	00	00
3. Equals Standard time of birth.		=	18	45	00
4. From Time Zones, find Standard Time Zone difference to GMT. *(Add 24 hours if needed to subtract)*. **West ADD /East MINUS.**			00	00	00
5. Equals **GMT of birth.** *(Record on Line 8)*.		=	18	45	00
6. Clarify **GMT Date of birth** *(Same day? Day before? Day after?)*.		**GMT date of Birth = 1/7/1961**			
7. From Ephemeris GMT date, find Sidereal Time of birth.			18	35	14
8. *Record GMT of birth from Line 5.*		+	18	45	0
9. From Table II, find Sidereal Correction value *(Less than 4 mins)*.		+		3	05
10. Calculate **Sidereal Time of birth at Greenwich.**		=	37	23	19
11. From Table III, find Longitudinal Correction. *(Diana's is 000E30)*. *(You cam also divide longitude by 15)*. **West MINUS / East ADD.**		+	0	02	00
12. Calculate **North Latitude Local Sidereal Time** *(Lines 10 and 11)*.		=	37	25	19
13. For Southern Latitudes, always add 12 hours.		+			
14. Calculate **Southern Local Sidereal Time** *(Lines 10, 11 and 13.)*		=			
15. *If result is over 24 hrs minus 24 hrs; over 48 hrs minus 48 hrs.*		-	24	00	00
16. Final result is the **Southern Latitude LST.**		=	**13**	**25**	**19**
Step 2. Calculate the House Cusps - use the Table of Houses (TOH)					
17. From TOH, find the LST just under the client's (13:25:19)		-	13	24	00
18. Subtract from client's LST *(line 16. It is always less than 4 minutes)*		=		01	19
19. Convert result to seconds		=			79"
20. Divide result by 240 (seconds) = Constant decimal (CD)			**Result CD = 0.33**		
Latitude 52N50, round to 53N	MC	11th	12th	ASC	2nd	3rd
21. TOH, larger LST (13:28:00, Lat 53).	23♎46	16♏36	03♐43	18♐45	00♒29	19♓14
22. TOH smaller LST (13:24:00, Lat 53). -	22♎42	15♏43	02♐56	17♐57	29♑14	17♓54
23. Calculate difference over 4 minutes. =	01 04	00 53	00 47	00 48	01 15	01 20
24. Convert result to minutes. =	64	53	47	48	75	80
25. Multiply result by CD. *(Round out figs)*. x	19	21	16	16	25	26
26. **Calculate cusps** - add line 25 to line 22. =	23♎01	16♏04	03♐12	18♐13	29♑39	18♓20
27. **Reverse Sign** for Southern Latitudes =						
Computer generated figures	23♎03	16♏03	03♐17	18♐24	29♑48	18♓21

Worksheet 2: Find Planet Positions
Using Midnight Ephemeris and Michelsen's Table of Houses V, VI, VII

Name: Princess Diana   GMT Birth Date: 1 July 1961   GMT of Birth: 18:45

Planet and sign	☉ ♋			☽ ♒			☿ ♋ ℞			♀ ♉			♂ ♍		
	d	m	s	d	m	s	d	m	s	d	m	s	d	m	s
1. Planet positions, after birth	09	52	17	28	14	52	03	06	00	24	37		01	47	
2. Planet positions, before birth	08	55	06	20	53	40	03	36	00	23	36		01	11	
3. Calculate travel in 24hr, 12hr for Moon. Subtract line 2 from 1 *	00	57	11	07	21	12	00	30	00	01	01	00		36	00
4a. Tables V, VI or VII. Distance travelled for GMT hours (18)	00	42	54	03	41	00		22	30		45	45		27	00
4b. Tables V, VI or VII, distance travelled for GMT minutes (45)		01	47		27	38		00	56		01	54		01	08
4c. Add lines 4a, 4b. Total distance travelled	+	44	41	04	08	38	−	23	26	+	47	39	+	28	08
5. Calculate positions. Add line 4c to line 2. Minus for retrograde.	09	39	47	25	02	18	03	12	34	24	23	39	01	39	08
6. Round out figures.	9♋40			25♒02			3♋13			24♉24			1♍39		
Computer figures	9♋39			25♒02			3♋12 ℞			24♉23			1♍38		

Planet and sign	♃ ♒ ℞			♄ ♑ ℞			♅ ♌			♆ ♏ ℞			♇ ♍		
	d	m	s	d	m	s	d	m	s	d	m	s	d	m	s
1. Planet positions, after birth	05	04	00	27	48	00	23	21	00	08	38	00	06	03	00
2. Planet positions, before birth	05	11	00	27	52	00	23	18	00	08	39	00	06	02	00
3. Calculate travel in 24/ 12 hrs. *		07			04			03			01			01	
4. Travel for GMT (hrs, mns, scs)	−	05	28	−	03	08	+	03	08	−		47	+		47
5. Calculate positions. Add line 4 to line 2; minus for retrograde	05	05	32	27	48	52	23	21	08	08	38	13	06	02	47
6. Round out figures.	5♒06 ℞			27♑49 ℞			23♌21			8♏38 ℞			6♍02		
Computer figures	5♒05 ℞			27♑48 ℞			23♌20			8♏38 ℞			6♍02		

* For retrograde planets, subtract lines 1 and 5 from line 2.

Here is Princess Diana's chart.

If the calculated figures for the House Cusps are examined you will see that they all lie within a degree of being exact from the computer calculated chart. The widest variation is the ascendant - descendant axis, 11 minutes from exact; then the 2nd - 8th houses that are 9 minutes from exact. The MC - IC are 2 minutes out and the remaining houses have a 1-minute difference.

When the planet figures are examined. The Moon, Neptune and Pluto figures are exact. All the other planets are 1 minute from being exact.

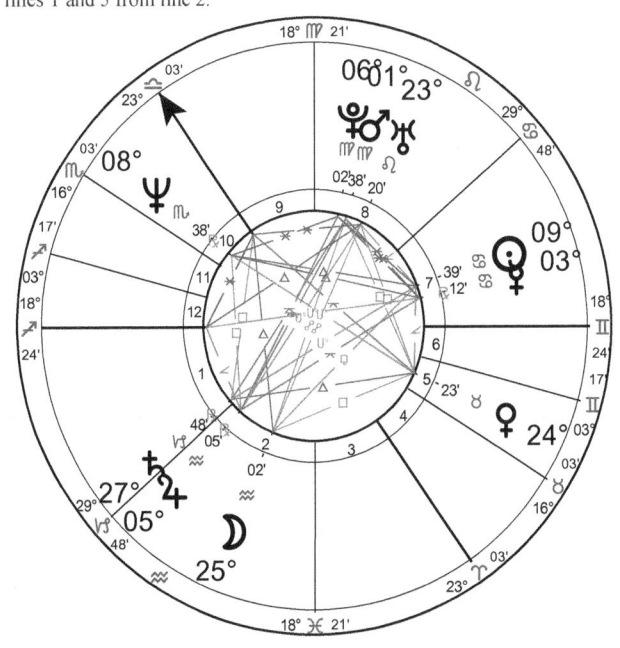

B. CALCULATING THE ACD AND MANUAL PROGRESSIONS.

This section is for those who wish to learn how to manually calculate Secondary Progressions. The philosophy underlying progressions, is each day after birth represents a year in the life.

Guide for Worksheet 3: Find the Adjusted Calculation Date (ACD).

The ACD is used with secondary progressions and the Ephemeris (Midnight or Noon tables). It is the date each year, when the progressed planet positions in the Ephemeris are exact. Once the ACD has been found, it means you can look at any line in the Ephemeris after birth, and know that the planet progressions on that line, for that progressed year, are exact for the ACD date.

A Midnight Ephemeris is used in these examples, but the same method applies for a noon Ephemeris. In the latter, the ACD will be different by six months, to account for the 12-hour difference in planet positions between the Midnight and Noon Ephemerides. The method used here is simple.

- The GMT of Birth and date of birth are identified.
- GMT is subtracted from 24 hours.
- The result is added to the Sidereal Time of the GMT date.
- The result is the interim ACD Sidereal Time.
- Search backwards in the Ephemeris from the GMT date, to find the Sidereal Time that is closest.
- The date of this Sidereal Time is the ACD. Here is an example.

When searching backwards in the Ephemeris for the ACD, it is vital to note whether you go into the year previous to birth (as for Jane's, whose ACD is in 1949), or if you stay in the same year (Jane's GMT date was 1950). This is vital, because the ACD you finally come up with is the start date for counting years into the future. Write the ACD you come up with (day-month-year), into the Ephemeris, beside the GMT date.

Worksheet 3: find the Adjusted Calculated Date (24 hours minus the GMT)
Working with a midnight Ephemeris

	Example: Jane, born 17 July 1950; GMT 13.43. The GMT date of birth is also 17 July.				
1	24 hours		24	00	00
2	Subtract the GMT of birth	-	13	43	00
3	Result		10	17	00
4	Add result to the ST for the GMT Date of birth - 17 July 1950	ST +	19	37	00
5	Result		29	54	00
6	Subtract from 24 hours if result is greater than 24.		5	54	00
7	From birthdate, search backwards for closest ST - closest is:-	Sid Time	**5**	**52**	**59**
8	Closest ST of 5:52:59, falls on 20 December <u>1949.</u>		**ACD: 20 December 1949**		
9	Jane's ACD went back into the previous year before birth - 1949. Consequently ...				
10	**In the Ephemeris, besides Jane's birthdate (17 July 1950), write 20 Dec 1949.** - Then, on 18 July, write 20 Dec 1950. - On 19 July, write 20 Dec 1951, etc.				

For Jane, this means:
- The Ephemeris planets on 17-Jul-1950, are the ACD progressions for 20-Dec-1949. (This was pre-birth).
- The Ephemeris planets on 18-Jul-1950, are the ACD progressions for 20-Dec-1950. (She was 5 months).
- The Ephemeris planets on 19-Jul-1950, are the ACD progressions for 20-Dec-1951. (She was 17 months).
- And so on.

Two further ACD examples are given here.

The first is for Princess Diana - her ACD was in the year previous to her GMT Date of Birth (DOB). The second is for Barbara, specially chosen because her ACD was in the same year as her GMT Date of Birth.

Worksheet 3: find the Adjusted Calculated Date (24 hours minus the GMT)
Working with a midnight Ephemeris

	Example: Princess Diana, born 1 July 1961; GMT 18.45. GMT DOB same day.				
1	24 hours		24	00	00
2	Subtract the GMT of birth	-	18	45	00
3	Result		05	15	00
4	Add result to the Sidereal Time for the GMT Date of birth	*ST +*	18	35	14
5	Result		23	50	14
6	Subtract from 24 hours if result is greater than 24.				
7	From birthdate, search backwards for closest ST - closest is:-	*Sid Time*	23	51	56
8	Closest ST of 23:51:56, falls on 19 September 1960.		**ACD: 19 September 1960**		
9	Diana's ACD went back into the previous year - 1960. Consequently ...				
10	**In the Ephemeris, besides Diana's birthdate 1 July 1961, write 19 Sep 1960 (pre-birth).** On 2 July 1961, write 19 Sep 1961. (Diana was 2 and a half months old). On 3 July 1961, write 19 Sep 1962, etc. (Diana was 14 and a half months old). On 7 August 1961, write 19 Sep 1997. (Diana was just over 36 years).				
11	Diana was 36 when she died on 31 August 1997. 36 days after birth equals Ephemeris date 7-Aug-1961 ~ the ACD year was 1997 (1961+36=1997; 19-Sept). The Sun was at 14♌15 on 7-Aug-1961. In the computer-progressed chart to 19 September 1997, the progressed Sun was at 14♌14. *Any difference under 1 degree is OK.*		14	♌	15

In the next example, the ACD remains in the same year as the birth year.

	Example: Barbara, born 30 June 1944; GMT 02:04. GMT DOB are on the same day.				
1	24 hours		24	00	00
2	Subtract the GMT of birth	-	02	04	00
3	Result		21	56	00
4	Add result to the Sidereal Time for the GMT Date of birth	*ST +*	18	31	44
5	Result		40	27	44
6	Subtract from 24 hours if result is greater than 24.		16	27	44
7	From birthdate, search backwards for closest ST - closest is:-	*Sid Time*	16	29	31
8	Closest ST of 16:29:31, falls on 30 May 1944.		**ACD: 30 May 1944**		
9	Barbara's ACD was the same as the birth year - 1944. Consequently				
10	**In the Ephemeris, besides Barbara's birthdate (30 June 1944), write 30 May 1944 (pre-birth).** Then, on 1 July, write 30 May 1945. (Barbara was 11 months). On 2 July 1944, write 30 May 1946, etc. (Barbara was 23 months). On 23 July 1944, write 30 May 1967. (Barbara was almost 23).				
11	In the Ephemeris, on 23 July 1944, 23 days after birth, the Sun moved into Leo (0♌0). The ACD for that date was 30 May 1967 (1944+23=1967). In the computer-progressed chart to 30 May 1967, the progressed Sun was at 0♌0.		00	♌	00

Guide for Worksheet 4: Calculate Progressed Planets

Princess Diana died on 31 August 1997, just before her 1997 ACD return in September. The task in this exercise is to progress her planets to the day she died. Choose the two ACD's to work with - the ACD dates before and after the incident. **

L1   ACD after incident, 19-Sep-97 (planet positions on 7-Aug-1961). Also record these on L7.

L2   ACD before 19-Sep-96 (6-Aug-1961).

L3   Find distance personal planets travel over the *year*. Subtract L2 from L1 (reverse for retrogrades). The planets from Jupiter outwards travel so slowly, their positions can be quickly adjusted if necessary.

L4   Convert the travel to minutes.

L5   Work out *daily* travel - divide L4 by 365.

L6   Work out the number of days between the event and the ACD - Diana died 19 days before the 1997 ACD.

L7   *(Recorded from L1)*

L8   Calculate travel in 19 days (L5 x L6).

L9-L10. Work out progressions on 31 August (L8 subtracted from L7) and round out figures.

In the year, Jupiter moved 7', Saturn 4', Uranus 4', Neptune 1' and Pluto 0.1'; so their positions (for 19 days) did not change. If the travel was say for 6 months, you would halve the yearly travel and take off 3.5' for Jupiter, 2' for Saturn and Uranus and .5' for Neptune.

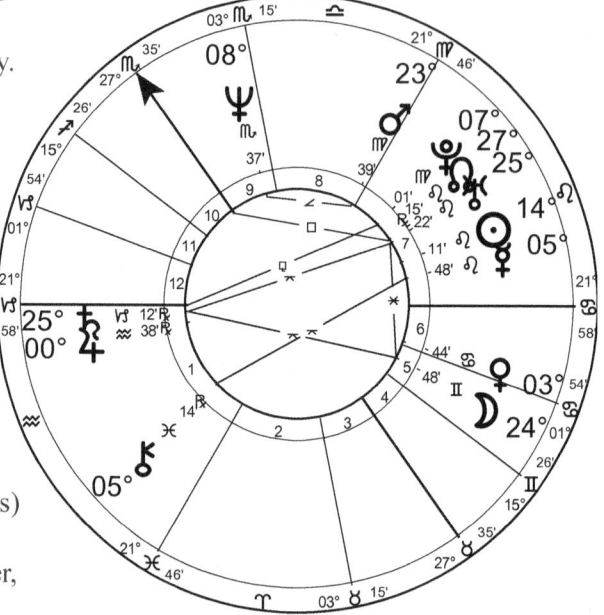

Diana. Secondary Progressions for DEATH, 31 August 1997.

Worksheet 4: Method to find the Progressed Planets using the Adjusted Calculation Date
Round out figures

Diana's death 31-Aug-1997, fell between ACD dates of 7th & 6th August 1961.	☽ ♊			☉ ♌			☿ ♌		♀ ♋		♂ ♍	
	d	m	s	d	m	s	d	m	d	m	d	m
1. Planets on 7-Aug-1961 = ACD 19-Sep-97 *(record L7)*	25	27	11	14	14	56	05	56	03	48	23	41
2. Planets on 6-Aug-1961 = ACD 19-Sep-96.	13	00	03	13	17	25	03	54	02	40	23	04
3. Travel over year *(L2 minus L1, reversed if retrograde)*	12	21	08	00	57	31	02	2	01	8		38
4. Convert travel to minutes		741			88			122		68		38
5. Work out daily travel *(L4 / 365)*		2.03			0.2			0.3		0.2		0.1
6. Work out the number of days the planets travel for incident.	There is **19 days travel** from 31-Aug-1997 to ACD 19-Sep-1997.											
7. Planets on 7-Aug-1961 = ACD 19-Sep-97.	25	27	11	14	14	56	05	56	03	48	23	41
8. Work out distance planets travel in 19 days *(L5 x L6)*.		38	34		05	00		06		04		02
9. Planet progressions for 31-Aug-1997 *(subtract L8 from L7)*	24	48	37	14	09	56	05	50	03	44	23	39
10. Rounded out	24 ♊ 49			14 ♌ 10			5 ♌ 50		3 ♋ 44		23 ♍ 39	

** As previously mentioned, when progressing planets to a target-day, you choose the two ACD years - before and after the incident. Once you have worked out how far the planets progress during the year, you have to decide which ACD year to use, to make the necessary adjustments. Generally, choose the ACD date closest to the incident, as explained below.

- In Diana's case, because she died 19 days before her 1997 ACD, the 1997 planet positions were used and 19 days of travel was subtracted.
- But let us say for example, she died 19 days after her 1996 ACD (6-Aug-1961), then the 1961 planet positions would have been selected to work with, and 19 days of travel would have been added.

Day Calculator

	Jan	Feb	Mar	Apr	May	Jun	Jul	Aug	Sep	Oct	Nov	Dec
1	1	32	60	91	121	152	182	213	244	274	305	335
2	2	33	61	92	122	153	183	214	245	275	306	336
3	3	34	62	93	123	154	184	215	246	276	307	337
4	4	35	63	94	124	155	185	216	247	277	308	338
5	5	36	64	95	125	156	186	217	248	278	309	339
6	6	37	65	96	126	157	187	218	249	279	310	340
7	7	38	66	97	127	158	188	219	250	280	311	341
8	8	39	67	98	128	159	189	220	251	281	312	342
9	9	40	68	99	129	160	190	221	252	282	313	343
10	10	41	69	100	130	161	191	222	253	283	314	344
11	11	42	70	101	131	162	192	223	254	284	315	345
12	12	43	71	102	132	163	193	224	255	285	316	346
13	13	44	72	103	133	164	194	225	256	286	317	347
14	14	45	73	104	134	165	195	226	257	287	318	348
15	15	46	74	105	135	166	196	227	258	288	319	349
16	16	47	75	106	136	167	197	228	259	289	320	350
17	17	48	76	107	137	168	198	229	260	290	321	351
18	18	49	77	108	138	169	199	230	261	291	322	352
19	19	50	78	109	139	170	200	231	262	292	323	353
20	20	51	79	110	140	171	201	232	263	293	324	354
21	21	52	80	111	141	172	202	233	264	294	325	355
22	22	53	81	112	142	173	203	234	265	295	326	356
23	23	54	82	113	143	174	204	235	266	296	327	357
24	24	55	83	114	144	175	205	236	267	297	328	358
25	25	56	84	115	145	176	206	237	268	298	329	359
26	26	57	85	116	146	177	207	238	269	299	330	360
27	27	58	86	117	147	178	208	239	270	300	331	361
28	28	59	87	118	148	179	209	240	271	301	332	362
29	29	**	88	119	149	180	210	241	272	302	333	363
30	30		89	120	150	181	211	242	273	303	334	364
31	31		90		151		212	243		304		365

The Day Calculator is very useful for helping to work out how many days a planet travels between an ACD date and a date of interest.

CHAPTER 9. LOOKING TO THE FUTURE

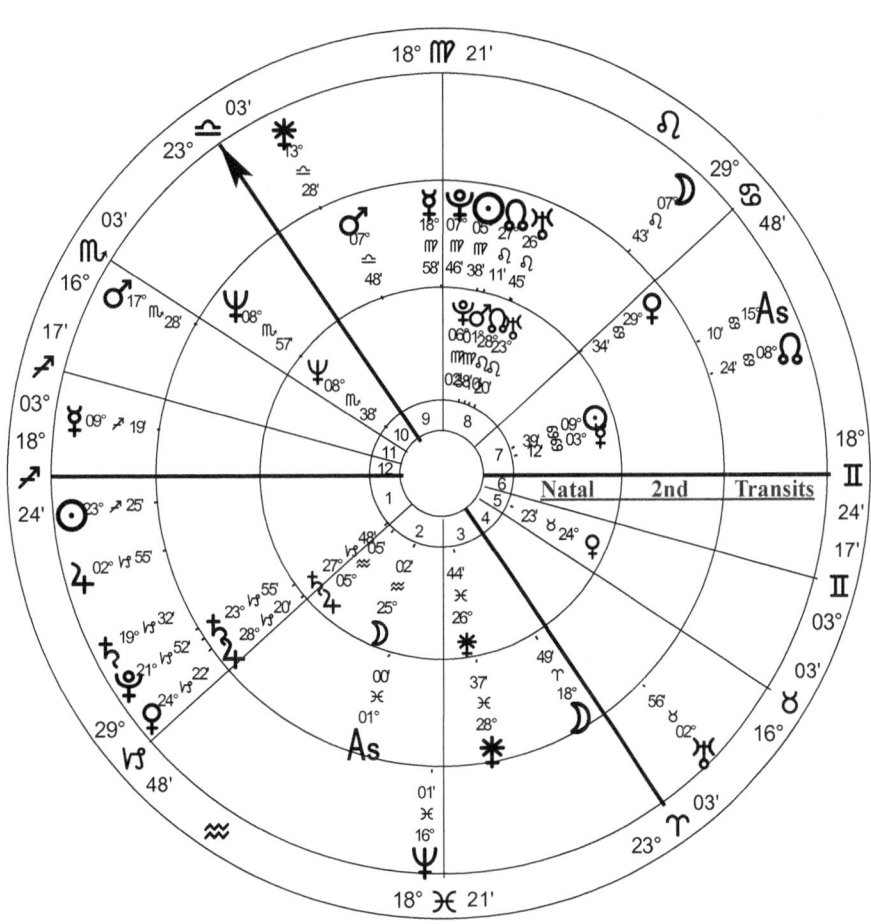

Five methods are examined - secondary progressions, solar-arc directions, transits, eclipses and solar returns. These are the most popular methods used by astrologers to look into the future or into the past. They indicate prevailing energy influences and trends affecting a person at any time in the life. Astrology software will produce a chart for each of these four methods. They can also be manually calculated by using the Ephemeris.

1. Secondary Progressions

1. Definition and purpose.

"Secondary Progressions" refers to an astrology method of determining the internal developments of the birth pattern - the evolution of consciousness, for any given age in the life.

2. How progressions work.

a. The system is based on the notion that "one day equals a year," - each day after birth, symbolises a year in time. For example:

- The planet positions the day after birth symbolise the influences in the 2nd year of life.
- The planet positions the 10th day after birth symbolise the influences in the 10th year of life.
- The planet positions the 50th day after birth symbolise the influences in the 50th year of life.

b. The progressed chart - the migration of the planets, ascendant and MC into new signs and houses; these indicate the nature of the internal changes that are being experienced.

c. The timing of a progression depends upon the speed of the planet. It starts when the moving planet's approach is approximately one degree away from the exact aspect to the natal planet. Its influence peaks in intensity when exact; then fades gradually and ends when approximately 30 minutes past the aspect. The goal is to identify exactly when a progression starts, peaks then ends. This invaluable knowledge enables us to gain greater control over events happening in the life.

3. How progressions are used.

Progressions are commonly used in two ways. First, the progressed chart is set up for the date of a significant life-event, so the influences that were active can be studied. Secondly, the astrologer sets the chart up for a period of interest. For instance, a client asks for the astrology influences in the coming year to be read.

a. The tri-wheel arrangement is the most common model as this example shows.
   - Natal chart is in the centre.
   - Secondary-progressions is in the middle.
   - The outermost wheel has the planet transits.

   Progressions are always studied in relation to the natal chart. The natal chart is what we start with. The progressed chart is who we are becoming.

b. Only work with the personal planet progressions - and the ascendant, MC and Jupiter. Saturn, Uranus, Neptune and Pluto progress so slowly, they make no new aspects, staying close to their natal position.

c. As a personal planet progresses - as it goes into new signs and houses and aspects natal (and also progressed) planets and points; that part of the nature the progressed personal planet represents is stimulated.

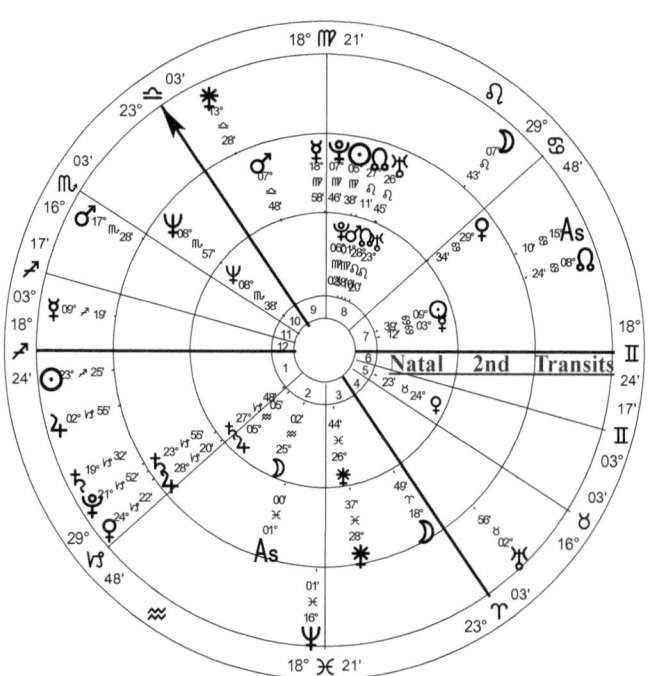

d. The sign a planet is progressing through, it colours, affects and changes that part of the character represented by the planet.

e. The house a planet is progressing through brings people and experiences into the life to represent its interests. For example, the seventh house brings in potential partners, the tenth house brings career opportunities, the third house brings new communications.

f. The natal planet or point being aspected by the progressed planet, is the part of the old life, the old nature, which is being affected and forced to change. The house or houses which that affected planet rules, these affairs are also being energised and changed.

4. Each progressed planet affects us according to its nature.

- **Sun**. The sign and house the Sun is moving through, they show the energies and life experiences that are promoting the expression of personal will and authority. When the progressed Sun makes an aspect to the natal chart, it means the personality is being offered an opportunity be wiser and more mature in the way it handles the affairs of the natal planet. This opportunity will either be challenging (hard aspects and conjunctions to malefics), or generally pleasurable (easy aspects and conjunctions to benign planets). The Sun progresses approximately one degree a year (59').

    Example 1: progressed planets changing signs. A part of the character begins to change when a progressed planet moves into a new sign. For example, Princess Diana married Charles in 1981 when her progressed Sun was still in shy and sensitive Cancer. But it moved into Leo in 1983, two years later. Her shy, sensitive side took on new regal qualities and she became more independent and demanding of her rights. If she had lived, 30 years later (approximately), the Sun would have progressed into Virgo and she would have gradually assumed the discriminating qualities of that sign.

    Example 2: progressed planets changing houses. It is also very significant when a planet progresses into a new house. When Diana married Charles, her progressed Sun was on the cusp of, and moving into, her eighth house of death and transformation. Was this prophetic? She began a cycle which totally transformed her life, brought on severe emotional trauma and led to an untimely death.

- **Ascendant**. It represents new beginnings and interests. It also represents growth experiences that are part of the plan of the soul.

- **Midheaven**. It brings changes to the career and higher goals. It progresses the same rate as the Sun.

- **Moon**. It triggers major emotional events. The house it is moving through shows where the emotions and everyday concerns are focused. The sign it is moving through colours emotional expression. The aspects it makes activates different parts of the life. The Moon progresses approximately 1 degree a month. It completes one cycle of the chart, returning to its natal position in 28-30 years. This completes a major emotional cycle and the beginning of a new one.

- **Mercury**. Its house, sign and aspects, show how and where mental attention is currently being focused and the nature of communications that are occurring. It also represents travel. It progresses approximately 1 degree, 40 minutes a year.

- **Venus**. Its house, sign and aspects show how and where love and affection are currently being expressed. It also relates to artistic and financial matters. Venus also progresses approximately 1 degree 40 minutes a year; but fractionally slower than Mercury.

- **Mars**. Its house, sign and aspects show how and where the passions are currently being expressed. It brings energy, physical contact, new projects and in the case of hard aspects including conjunctions - conflict and accidents. Mars progresses approximately 35 minutes a year.

- **Jupiter**. Its house, sign and aspects show how and where life is expanding with wisdom and understanding. It brings rewards, benefits, expansion and travel. Jupiter progresses approximately 11-13 minutes a year.

2. Primary or Solar-Arc Directions

1. Definition and purpose.

The purpose of this system is identical to Secondary Progressions. "Solar-arc directions" refers to an astrology method of determining the internal developments of the birth pattern for any given age in the life.

2. How solar-arc directions work.

The entire chart rotates as a unit, moves forwards through the signs and houses *at the same rate as the Sun*. The Sun progresses one degree - or more accurately, 59 minutes, each year. This means the entire chart just progresses forwards, one degree (almost) a year. This makes the system easy to use. The positions of the solar-arc planets can be figured out quickly, without needing to make a calculation.

3. How solar-arc directions are used.

The greatest usefulness of directions (along with the simplicity of timing), is that the outer planets come into play. They bring their influences to bear on the natal chart, which is not done with secondary progressions. This is especially useful for instance with health. Aspects being made from directed malefics are often involved when a serious health crisis hits.

3. Transits

1. Definition and purpose.

Transits are the movements of the planets over a planet or sensitive point in the natal chart (over our energy system), at any given time. Transits indicate an external development or influence that is activating a personality function shown in the natal chart. Consequently, the transit is unfolding a natal potential through the experiences that it introduces into the life.

2. How transits are used.

Work primarily with the outer planet transits. They have greater impact and their influence is longer lasting. The inner planets from the Sun to Venus, their transit periods last from a couple of hours (the Moon) to one to three days for the Sun, Mercury and Venus. This means they do not bring profound changes into the life, though sometimes they trigger them as they aspect the outer planets. Mars is different. It takes almost 2 years to orbit the Sun and its aspects can trigger conflicts and accidents.

Here is a list of planets and the time they take to orbit the Sun.

- Sun. Its cycle is one year. It moves approximately 1 degree a day, therefore its influence on a natal planet or point lasts 1-2 days. Its movement through a sign lasts approximately a month. Because it moves 1 degree a day, its movement through a house lasts for as long as the number of degrees which that house contains.
- Moon. Its orbit around the Earth takes 27 days. Its influence on a natal planet lasts for 2-3 hours. It moves approximately 11 to 13 degrees a day and takes two and a half days to move through a sign.
- Mercury. Its orbit is 88 days. It moves approximately 1.5 degrees a day. But it always stays close to the Sun, and due to its retrograde action, completes one circulation of the chart in just over a year.
- Venus. Its orbit is 224 days. It moves about 1.3 degrees a day. But it also travels with the Sun (as viewed from earth), and due to retrograde action completes one circulation of the chart just before or after the Sun.
- Mars. Its orbit takes 687 days. It spends approximately two months in each sign.
- Jupiter. Its orbit takes 12 years, and it spends approximately one year in each sign.
- Saturn. Its orbit takes 28-29 years and it takes 2.5 years to move through each sign.
- Uranus. Its orbit takes 84 years approximately and it spends approximately 7 years in each sign.
- Neptune. Its orbit takes 165 years and it spends approximately 14 years in each sign.
- Pluto. Its orbit is 249 years. Because its orbit is oval-shaped, when it is closer to the Sun it moves faster through a sign (10-11 years), and slower when further away (up to 25 years).

The effects of Mars and Uranus transits are felt immediately their aspects begin, and peak when they are exact. Pluto could fit into this group. The effects of Saturn and Neptune are often experienced after first contact or when the aspects are waning. Saturn's effect can drag on long after it has moved on.

3. The timing of transits.

The period of influence of a transit depends upon the speed of the planet. The retrograde action of transits means that sometimes they pass over the same point three times - even five times for Neptune and Pluto. First contact is when the transit moves over the natal planet, second contact when it retrogrades over it and the final contact as it moves over it again.

The goal is to identify exactly the period of influence of the transit. When the transit planet makes an applying aspect to the natal planet the experience is forming. When the aspect is exact, the event births. When the transit planet goes retrograde the event is drawn out, there is a pause as proceedings sort themselves out. Then as the transit planet starts moving forwards again (for the second time) to the exact aspect, a new level of the experience unfolds. Perhaps more information comes to light. The major impact of the experience lasts from the first to the last contact.

Consider the nature of the transit planet involved. It represents the type of changes occurring and the type of people coming into the life. It can be compared to a visitor coming to one's house. If entry is denied to a Pluto visitor, he may break the door down and destroy the house for good measure. A Neptune visitor may look wonderful and promise much, but may leave at night with the family silver. A Jupiter trine visitor could be the smiling person advising one of a million-dollar lottery win.

- **Sun**. It energises and throws light. As it transits through each sign, the energies and qualities of that sign are distributed to us.
- **Moon**. It influences the emotional nature and the house it is in indicates focal topics.
- **Mercury**. It brings communications, short journeys, study and teaching, trading and merchandising.
- **Venus**. It brings affection, social occasions, artistic pursuits and it can influence financial matters. The house it is currently moving through indicates where love may be found.
- **Mars**. It shows where physical and passionate energy is being focused - negatively, it brings battles, conflict, disruption and accidents.
- **Jupiter**. It brings expansion, rewards, prosperity, adventure or just good fun. Some of its effects are long distance travel, academic or philosophical studies, teachers and teaching and religious matters. Expansive periods occur when it comes back to its natal position, conjuncts, sextiles or trines itself or the Sun.
- **Saturn**. Transiting Saturn provides opportunities to restructure the life and get it onto a solid footing. To this end, it tests us with adversity. If crystallised attitudes and self-defeating habits are operating, it slows the rhythm of life so everything which is not working is magnified. A bad relationship or situation can then be seen for exactly what it is. This enables us to make changes so the life we live is authentic and real.

  The most important Saturn transits occur at approximately ages 28-29 and 58-60. These are called "Saturn Returns," periods when Saturn comes back to its natal position. Also important is the age period 42-45 when Saturn opposes its natal position. Those are very testing "sort out your life" periods.
- **Uranus**. Through sudden, exciting or shattering experiences, Uranus changes the life completely. It cuts away limiting ties, encourages us to experiment, to throw off the past and to be free. Uranus brings excitement into the life, but it may not last for long. Uranus relationships are often transient.
- **Neptune**. It subtly and slowly dissolves old patterns and boundaries, encouraging us to escape from restrictions. It tunes us into subtler realms and encourages us to follow our higher ideals. It brings spirituality, art and music. If we are not grounded - if emotionalism dominates, it brings fantasy, illusion and a desire to escape life's hard knocks.
- **Pluto**. It represents where and how major and often painful changes are taking place and it brings us into contact with people or situations which drive this change. It eliminates and transforms our old patterns. It cuts away the past making room for the new. It makes experiences deeply meaningful.

4. Eclipses

A solar eclipse occurs when the moon gets between earth and the Sun, and the Moon casts a shadow over earth. A solar eclipse occurs when the moon passes directly between the Sun and earth and its shadows fall upon earth's surface.

- When an eclipse makes an impact on the natal or progressed chart, it represents an unforeseen event is coming into the life that can set us on a totally new path.
- Lunar eclipses herald emotionally-charged changes. Solar eclipses, vitalisation of the physical body and affairs in the outer life.
- The sign and house the eclipse occurs in, directly influence the nature of the event.
- The method involved to bring about this change can be easy or hard. This depends upon the type of aspect the eclipse point makes. As usual, hard aspects (and conjunctions) hard experiences, etc. However, the eclipse effect can be moderated. For example, an eclipse on the Sun can represent lowered vitality. But if the Sun has many easy natal or transit aspects; these aspects are vitalised as well, bringing more fortunate results.
- Events can manifest just before or after an eclipse occurs, or unfold within a year after the eclipse.
- The key to making the most of an eclipse is to remember that something old has to go (the obscuring aspect), so that something new can come in.

5. Example: transits, progressions, directions: Princess Diana

1. The progressed Sun.
- The progressed Sun entered Leo approximately 14 years before she died. As the personality was imbued with Leo leadership qualities, Diana became more assertive and self-confident.
- The Sun entered the eighth house of death, rebirth and transformation just before it went into Leo - 15 years previously. Her personality changed profoundly - a consequence of becoming very famous in the world and of the emotional trauma she suffered in her unhappy marriage. If she had lived, the eighth house experience would have lasted 48 years. There are 48-degrees from the cusp of the eighth house to that of the 9th.

2. Love and Marriage.
- When Diana married Charles on 29 July 1981, transit Neptune was on her ascendant. From there it squared her natal Juno during that period and for a couple of years after. She was blinded by adoration for Charles. But the marriage was for show and as she realised this and discovered Charles' betrayal with Camilla, she was emotionally wounded and grieved deeply.
- Uranus is often referred to as the divorce planet. When Diana and Charles divorced on 28 August 1996, solar-arc Uranus was at 26 Virgo, opposite natal Juno.
- Just before her death, the progressed Moon entered the seventh house of marriage. By then she had met Dodi El Fayed and appeared to be in love with him. If she lived and it all worked out, she could have married him.
- Progressed Mars was at 23 Virgo 39 in the ninth house. It was making a trine to natal Venus at 24 Taurus in the fifth house of love affairs. This aspect indicates a passionate love affair with a foreigner, which would receive world-wide public attention (Venus rules the MC, with Libra on that point).
- The progressed Moon would have crossed the natal Sun 15 months after she died (it moves 1 degree a month) - a propitious time for marriage. It would have remained in the seventh house for another 36 months approximately, before crossing into the eighth house.

Chapter 9: Looking to the Future - 189

3. Death.

The death of an individual does not always show in the chart, especially if it is unexpected. But it does register in the charts of loved ones who are left behind. Often, death can be a welcome release from physical impairment or disease. Another point is that the type of aspects under which death can happen - hard aspects involving the eighth house of death and malefics such as Saturn and Pluto. These occur regularly throughout the life and are usually indicative of psychological or emotional death-rebirth experiences (changes in character). Often, beneficial Jupiter is involved during the death process.

Diana has several indicators of death.

- Before her death, in March 1997, there was an eclipse at 3 Libra. It squared natal Mercury (3 degrees of Cancer), ruler of the 8th and of transport. This seems to have triggered events.
- With Cancer on the eighth house cusp, the Moon rules death. Solar-arc Moon was in the final degree of the zodiac - 29 Pisces. This indicates a major cycle is ending (this incarnation) and a new one is beginning.
- Mercury rules transport. Transit Mercury was retrograde in the 8th, conjunct natal Pluto, the planet that rules death. As we know, Diana died in a car accident.
- Additionally, transit Pluto was inconjunct natal Mercury - death involving a short car-journey.
- The second ruler of the 8th is the Sun, with Leo intercepted in that house. Transit Sun was in the 8th conjunct Pluto and opposite solar-arc Jupiter. The progressed Sun was also in the 8th, opposite transit Jupiter. It is unlikely Diana suffered for any length of time with beneficial Jupiter involved. Jupiter also rules the ascendant - Diana's body.

Chart erected for 31 August 1997; the day Diana died.

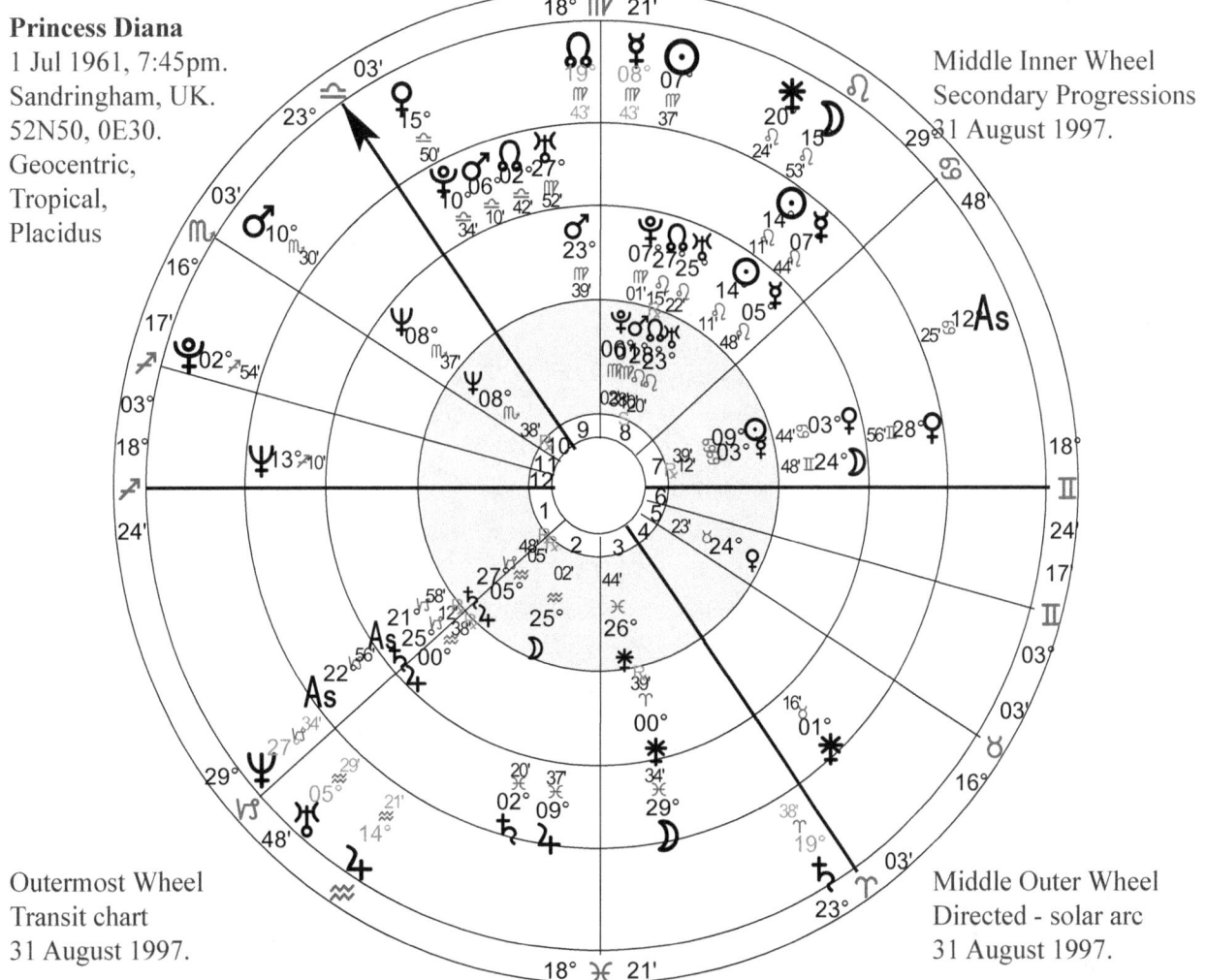

Princess Diana
1 Jul 1961, 7:45pm.
Sandringham, UK.
52N50, 0E30.
Geocentric,
Tropical,
Placidus

Middle Inner Wheel
Secondary Progressions
31 August 1997.

Outermost Wheel
Transit chart
31 August 1997.

Middle Outer Wheel
Directed - solar arc
31 August 1997.

190 - Learn Astrology

6. Solar Return Charts

1. Definition and purpose.

The Solar Return chart indicates influences of the coming year in an individual's life.

2. How solar returns work.

The Solar Return Chart is erected for the moment the Sun returns to its exact position at the time of birth - at the location one happens to be at, when the return occurs. Diana's location on 1 July 1997 was reported to be in London and the Return Chart was set up at that location.

3. How solar returns are used.

It is read like a natal chart - but just for the year ahead.

a. The ascendant sign:
   - Cardinal: a year of action, new projects.
   - Fixed Signs: a year to consolidate things.
   - Mutable Signs: changes, flux, mental focus or preparation for the near future.
   - The planet ruler of the ascendant will give more information about important indications in the year.

b. Planets on angles (8-degree orb): will have the major impact in the year. Of secondary importance are planets on other cusps.

c. Planets: interpret as for a natal chart. If most planets are in angular houses, it is a year of new activity; in succedent houses a year of consolidation; in cadent houses a quiet or introspective year.
   - Sun: The most important life area, where the primary focus is. Its aspects are important.
   - Moon: where primary emotional needs are focused and general changes occur.
   - Asc: how the year is approached, and where (location of planet ruling Asc.)

Diana's 1997 Solar Return Chart

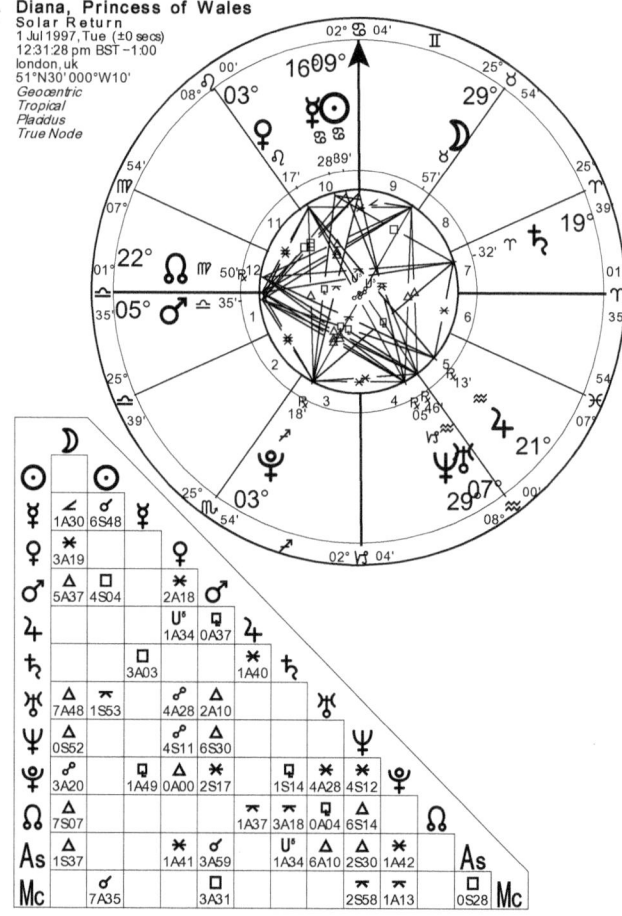

1. On the angles are cardinal signs. This was a year of action and change for Diana.

2. In March 1997, there was an eclipse at 3 Libra, on the Return chart ascendant, which rules the physical body; and on Mars, which was located there. Mars rules cars, accidents, drunken men, and in the Return chart it rules the eighth house of death. A serious warning was given about the consequences of rash and hasty decisions.

   Driver Henri Paul was drunk at the time. He had been on leave but was called back to drive Diana.

3. Pluto, the natural ruler of the eighth house of death is in Sagittarius (pleasure seeking involved), and is in the third house of short distance travel and transport. Her death would be traumatic for the public (Pluto opposite the Moon).

5. The Sun and Mercury were in the tenth house. Diana's accident and death (Sun square Mars), would be in the news, would make headlines. If she had not died, she would be in the news for her humanitarian work (the Sun rules her eleventh house), or some other reason.

Final Page

Finally, we come to the end of this book, a step by step guide for new students to astrology, to help them construct and read a natal chart and future trends in life.

Astrology is a science of self-understanding.

Those who persevere in their efforts to master the science are developing skills that will enable them to gain mastery over themselves and their life.

Astrology is a key to Self-Mastery.

This is the deeper and true purpose of the craft - mastery over the processes of living on this planet. Astrology gives us self-understanding about who we are, what we are meant to do in this life and how to get there. This is the key to Self-mastery.

"Know thyself," is the ancient Greek injunction.

Astrology gives us the means to scientifically study ourselves as energy beings, and the transformations we need to make in consciousness, in order to gain Self-mastery and bring ourselves into harmony with universal flow. To this end, the Eastern Master Djwhal Khul said:

> "If each one of us would scientifically regard ourselves as centres of force, holding the matter of our bodies within our radius of control, and thus working through and in them, we should have a hypothesis whereby the entire cosmic scheme could be interpreted."

Astrology is a cosmic science, which trains us to do what the Great ones do - to be masters of the energies of life and to control and intelligently work with the energies of the signs and planets. This is our task! To all who study the science -

"Welcome to the Guild of Astrologers!"

Appendix

Worksheet 1: Calculate Natal House Cusps (Placidus)

Name: Birth: Latitude:
Place of Birth: Time: Longitude:
  Time Zone:

Step 1. Convert local time of birth to Local Sidereal Time				
		Hours	Minutes	Seconds
1. Local time of birth - use 24 hour clock.				
2. Subtract daylight saving if in effect. *(Always subtract DST)*.	-			
3. Equals Standard time of birth.	=			
4. From Time Zones, find Standard Time Zone difference to GMT. *(Add 24 hours if needed to subtract).* **West ADD /East MINUS.**	+/-			
5. Equals **GMT of birth.** *(Record on Line 8).*	=			
6. Identify **GMT Date of birth** *(Same day? Day before? Day after?).*	**GMT date Birth =**			
7. From Ephemeris GMT date, find Sidereal Time of birth.				
8. *Record GMT of birth from Line 5.*	+			
9. From Table II, find Sidereal Correction value *(Less than 4 mins).*	+			
10. Calculate **Sidereal Time of birth at Greenwich.**	=			
11. From Table III, find Longitudinal Correction. *(You cam also divide longitude by 15).* **West MINUS / East ADD.**	+/-			
12. Calculate **North Latitude Local Sidereal Time** *(Lines 10 and 11).*	=			
13. For Southern Latitudes, always add 12 hours.	+			
14. Calculate **Southern Local Sidereal Time** *(Lines 10, 11 and 13.)*	=			
15. *If result is over 24 hrs* **minus** *24 hrs; over 48 hrs* **minus** *48 hrs.*	-			
16. Final result is the **Southern Latitude LST.**	=			
Step 2. Calculate the House Cusps - use the Table of Houses (TOH)				
17. From BOT, find LST just under than the client's	-			
18. Subtract from client's LST *(Line 16. It is always less than 4 minutes)*	=			
19. Convert result to seconds	=			
20. Divide result by 240 (seconds) = Constant decimal (CD)	**Result CD =**			

		MC	11th	12th	ASC	2nd	3rd
21. TOH, figures for larger LST							
22. Minus smaller LST figures	-						
23. Calculate difference over 4 minutes.	=						
24. Convert result to minutes.	=						
25. Multiply result by CD. *(Round out figs).*	x						
26. **Calculate cusps** - *add line 25 to line 22.*	=						
27. **Reverse Sign** for Southern Latitudes	=						

Worksheet 2: Find Planet Positions
Using Midnight Ephemeris and Michelsen's Table of Houses V, VI, VII

Name: GMT Birth Date: GMT time of birth:

Planet and sign	☉			☽			☿			♀			♂		
	d	m	s	d	m	s	d	m	s	d	m	s	d	m	s
1. Planet positions, *after* birth															
2. Planet positions, *before* birth															
3. Calculate travel: in 24hr, 12hr for Moon															
4a. Tables V, VI or VII. Distance travelled for GMT hours (18)															
4b. Tables V, VI or VII, distance travelled for GMT minutes (45)															
4c. Add lines 4a, 4b. Total distance travelled															
5. Calculate positions. Add line 4c to line 2. Minus for retrograde.															
6. Round out figures.															

Planet and sign	♃			♄			♅			♆			♇		
	d	m	s	d	m	s	d	m	s	d	m	s	d	m	s
1. Planets AFTER birth															
2. Planets BEFORE birth															
3. Travel in 24hrs.															
4. Travel for GMT (hrs + mins)															
5. Calculate positions. Add line 4 to line 2; minus for retrograde															
6. Round out figures.															

Worksheet 3: find the Adjusted Calculated Date (24 hours minus the GMT)
Working with a midnight Ephemeris

	Name:	GMT of Birth:	GMT Birthdate:	
1	24 hours			
2	Subtract the GMT of birth		-	
3	Result			
4	Add result to the ST for the GMT Date of birth		ST +	
5	Result			
6	Subtract from 24 hours if result is greater than 24.			
7	From birthdate, search backwards for ST closest		Sid Time	
8	Closest ST and date it falls on		**ACD:**	
9	Did the ACD go back into the previous year or remain in the same year?			
10	In Ephemeris, on GMT birthdate (write in the ACD - day, month, year 0). 1 day after (write in the ACD - day, month, year 1) 2 days after (write in the ACD - day, month, year 2) and so on.			

Worksheet 4: Method to find the Progressed Planets using the Adjusted Calculation Date
Round out figures

	☽			☉			☿		♀		♂	
	d	m	s	d	m	s	d	m	d	m	d	m
1. Planets later ACD *(record on L7)*												
2. Planets earlier ACD												
3. Travel over year *(L2 minus L1, reversed if retrograde)*												
4. Convert travel to minutes												
5. Work out daily travel *(L4 / 365)*												
6. Work out the number of days the planets travel for incident.												
7. Planets later ACD *(from L1)*												
8. Work out distance planets travel *(L5 x L6)*.												
9. Progressions *(subtract L8 from L7)*												
10. Rounded out												

Outer planets, assess positions

	Later ACD	Earlier ACD	Diff	Progressions
Jupiter				
Saturn				
Uranus				
Neptune				
Pluto				

Glossary

Afflicted planet. A planet that is in a sign where it falls or is in detriment, it is unaspected or has multiple hard aspects to other planets, or it is retrograde. The planet's expression is distorted. The function it represents in the personality needs rehabilitating.

Angular houses. These houses represent the physical plane cornerstones of life - the 1st house (self), 4th (home), 7th (marriage) and 10th (career).

Applying aspect. When a faster planet moves towards a slower planet to form an aspect (and is in orb of that aspect), this aspect is called "applying"; the exact aspect has not yet been formed. Life events begin with an applying aspect.

Ascendant (ASC). The degree of the zodiac rising over the Eastern horizon at the moment of birth. It represents the body, physical characteristics, the image etc.

Aspects. These are specifically defined geometric angles between planets. When two planets form one of these angles (for example, are 90 degrees apart, the square aspect), they are said to be in aspect with each other.

Asteroids. The asteroid belt lies between the orbits of Mars and Jupiter.

Astrology branches or methods

- Electional astrology: attempts to choose the best time for any event.
- Esoteric astrology: The astrology of the purpose of the soul. Each sign is read at three levels to cater for the three levels of consciousness we evolve through - spirit, soul and average man.
- Horary astrology: attempts to answer questions by casting a chart.
- Mundane Astrology: The influence of the planets on countries, cities or the masses.
- Medical astrology: using the chart to analyse health.
- Natal astrology: interpretation of the potential in a natal chart.
- Sidereal astrology: places the planets in the constellations, rather than in the signs of the zodiac, which is tropical astrology. Tropical and sidereal used to coincide in the ancient past (for example the Sun entered 1 degree Aries at the same time), but because of the precession of the equinoxes, no longer do so. The tropical zodiac is no longer is based on astronomical reality but is an imaginary circle of signs around the Earth.
- Solar Return astrology. A chart erected for the moment when the Sun each year returns to its exact position at the time of birth. It is said to indicate the influences in the coming year.
- Synastry: compares planets and points between two people's charts to determine compatibility.

Barren signs. Gemini, Leo, Virgo.

Benefics. Fortunate and helpful planets. Jupiter is the greater benefic and Venus the lesser.

Birthchart - see natal chart.

Book of Tables. Tables that list the degrees of the signs on the different House Cusps for the different latitudes, changing every 4 minutes of Sidereal Time. From these tables, the House Cusps, MC and ascendant of an individual natal chart is determined. Calculations in this book uses Michelsen's Book of Tables.

Bowl planet pattern. The planets are in six consecutive signs or houses. Individuals with this pattern are self-contained and have high ideals or goals which they strive to realise.

Bucket planet pattern. A single planet opposes all planets on the opposite side. The energy generated by the large group of planets will try to find release through the single planet. It is crucial therefore that the function symbolised by this planet is working well. The handle can have a maximum of 2 planets.

Bundle planet pattern. The planets are contained within a trine, four signs or four houses. This cocktail of forces gives a very intense personality type. Bundle people are single-minded, self-mobilised trail blazers.

Cadent houses. The 3rd, 6th, 9th and 12th houses. "Cadent" is defined as being "rhythmic" in vibration, or harmonious - adjectives applied to mutable signs. These houses are related to the Mental Plane, are more particularly concerned with the mind and with learning.

Career houses. The tenth house is the true career house, but the sixth house of work can also indicate a person's employment or circumstances to do with the career.

Celestial Equator. The projection of Earth's equator into space.

Conjunction aspect. Two planets or points in the chart are at the same degree of the zodiac - within 8-degrees of each other. The aspect can be harmonious if the two are compatible, or challenging if they are not.

Composite chart. It is determined by finding the midpoint between two people's planets and points. It is said to be the chart of the relationship and shows compatibility.

Consciousness. Self-awareness. On the Path to Enlightenment, consciousness evolves three times - from ignorance or body-animal awareness, to soul consciousness to spiritual awareness.

Daylight Saving Time (DST) is the practice of setting the clocks forward one hour from standard time during the summer months, and back again in the fall or autumn, in order to make better use of natural daylight.

Decanate. One third of a sign or 10 degrees. There are three decanates in every sign.

Detriment planet. The planet is located in the sign opposite the one it rules, for instance, Saturn is in detriment in Cancer.

Dignity, planet. This occurs when a planet is located in the sign it rules, such as Saturn in Capricorn. The planet's positive qualities are strengthened.

Dispositor. "Disposits" is an astrology term that can be defined as one planet having power over another. A planet disposits any planet which is in the sign it rules. This dispositing planet modifies the disposited planet. For example, if Mars the God of War is disposited in Libra, then Venus' energy will tone down or modify its aggression. The unruly traits will be socialised to a certain extent.

Ecliptic. The apparent path of the Sun through the heavens.

Eclipse, Lunar. The earth passes between the Moon and Sun and throws a shadow on the Moon.

Eclipse, Solar. The Moon passes between the earth and Sun and throws a shadow on the Sun.

Elements of the signs. The signs all represent one of the four elements - fire, earth, air and water.

Elevated planet (most). This is the planet closest to the MC of the chart. What the planet symbolises - and the sign it is in, will have an important influence on the life for good or ill.

Enlightenment. Spiritual Awareness, consciousness infused with the love and wisdom of the soul. On the Path to Enlightenment, consciousness evolves three times - from ignorance or body-animal awareness, to soul consciousness to spiritual awareness.

Ephemeris. The astrologer's calendar. An astronomical table listing the daily position of the planets.

Esoteric: The words "esoteric" and "occult" signify "that which is hidden from normal view." They are concerned with the subtler world of energies and forces, which all outer forms veil and hide. Man's primary esoteric force is the soul.

Esoteric Astrology is the astrology of the soul, the science of the energies and forces of the soul that are hidden behind the outer physical form.

Exalted planet. This occurs when a planet is in the sign which gives the most positive expression of its power. The qualities the planet represents are strengthened and enhanced.

Falls, planet. The planet is located in the sign that because of this sign's nature, gives the most negative expression of its force. The sign a planet falls in, is opposite to the sign in which it is exalted. For instance, Saturn falls in Aries, and is exalted in Libra.

Fixed stars. All stars are called "fixed" because they appear not to move when compared to the planets of our solar system.

Fruitful signs. These are the water signs - Cancer, Scorpio, Pisces.

Glyphs. A glyph is a hieroglyphic character or symbol. There are glyphs for each sign and planet. Planet glyphs are usually (but not always) broken down into three common elements: A circle denoting spirit, a crescent denoting the soul and a cross denoting physical matter or life. Sign glyphs are more obtuse. Some seem to represent the animal traits but generally, all try to convey the spirit aspect of the sign.

GMT date. Conversion of local time to GMT when calculating House Cusps, means that sometimes the GMT Date of Birth falls after the local birthday (West of Greenwich), or before (longitudes East).

Grand Trine. A major planet configuration where 3 planets trine each other. The trine is considered to be the lucky aspect, so this is triply so. Energy in the pattern flows and this creates harmony.

Greenwich Mean Time or GMT. It is time at the Greenwich prime meridian line or zero-degree longitude point, which runs through Greenwich, England. It is also called Universal Time (UT), because it is the standard time for astronomers, astrologers and navigators, etc. From this meridian, all other Time Zones are measured. Most Table of Houses are configured from Greenwich.

Health houses. These are the 6th (acute illnesses) and the 12th (chronic diseases).

Horoscope - see natal chart.

Houses. They represent different life areas.

House Systems. There are various house systems, Placidus and Equal House are two favourite methods.
- Equal House: divides the birthchart into 12 equal parts, beginning with the degree of the Ascendant. Employed by ancient astrologers before the meridian was used. When a birth time is unknown, some astrologers use the Equal House system, placing zero degrees Aries on the ascendant.
- Placidus: cusps are determined by the time it takes for the Sun to move from one point to another.

IC, Imum Coeli, nadir. Imum Coeli is literally "the undersky", the lowest point of the chart, opposite the midheaven. Also called the nadir. In Placidus, it is the same as the fourth house cusp.

Imum Coeli - see IC.

Inconjunct or quincunx aspect. Two planets or points in the chart within 150 degrees of each other (with a 3 degree orb). It is a hard aspect that requires an adjustment.

Initiation, spiritual. A marked expansion of wisdom, the result of study and effort to be more inclusive, loving and wise in one's interactions with others.

Intercepted signs. A sign which is not on the cusp of any house in the chart. This occurs when a house has more than 30 degrees. The qualities of the sign are considered to be hidden.

Latitude. The angular distance of a place north or south of the earth's equator, or of the equator of a celestial object, usually expressed in degrees and minutes.

Local Sidereal Time (LST). This is star time at the local place of birth.

Locomotive planet pattern. Planets fill two thirds of the chart. These personality types have a driving urge to action. They are idealists who are often involved with solving the community's problems.

Longitude. The distance of any place, East or West of Greenwich, England, which is the zero longitude point.

Malefics. Traditionally, planets which exert negative of unfortunate influences. Saturn was the greater malefic and Mars the lesser. Today, Pluto, Neptune and Uranus are included in this list. In modern psychological astrology, they are no longer considered malefic, but rather are opportunities to change and grow, which is what evolution requires of us.

MC - see Midheaven

Medium Coeli - see Midheaven.

Midheaven (MC), zenith. The noon position of the Sun, and highest point of the chart. It is the cusp of the tenth house and represents the highest goals in life.

Midpoints. The point midway between two planets or points. This is a dynamic energy point of the nature of the two planets combined, which is activated if a third natal planet is at that point or transits it. If the two planets have hostile energies, it will be an explosive point.

Mode. The signs vibrate to three modes - cardinal (fast), fixed (slow) and mutable (flexible).

Moon's Nodes. These are the two points at which the orbit of the Moon intersects the ecliptic. They are related to the future and the past. The North Node or Dragon's Head indicates the future, a progressive move forward. The other polarity is called the South Node or Dragon's Tail. It indicates negative attitudes that bind us to the past.

Mutual reception. Two planets that are located in each other's signs, are said to be in mutual reception. This brings a harmonising effect between the two planets.

Nadir - see IC.

Natal astrology. Reading the potential in the chart - one's strengths, weaknesses and adjustments that need to be made to bring about an increased awareness of self.

Natal chart (synonymous with birthchart or horoscope). A chart erected for the moment of birth, showing a map of the planets, in signs and houses.

Nodes - see Moon's Nodes.

Opposition aspect. Two planets or points in the chart within 180 degrees of each other (8-degree orb). The opposition is found by dividing the circle by 2. It is a hard, challenging aspect.

Orb. An "orb" is a range of influence; the number of degrees allotted a planet in *aspect* to another planet.

Personal planets. Sun, Moon, Mercury, Venus and Mars. They are called personal planets because they represent aspects of the personal self - the personality (Sun), emotions (Moon), mind (Mercury), affections (Venus) and passions (Mars).

Planet Patterns. There are six recognised patterns, each one representing a recognised personality type - Bowl, Bundle, Bucket, Locomotive, Seesaw, Splash; and a seventh non-conformist pattern - the Splay.

Precession of Equinoxes. The phenomenon of the vernal equinox point moving backward along the ecliptic (from Aries, to Pisces, into Aquarius), is due to the wobbling of the Earth as it rotates on its axis. It moves at the rate of 30 degrees every 2,150 years. This movement is the reason why the sidereal and tropical zodiacs no longer coincide.

Primary or solar-arc directions. The entire chart progresses forward through the signs at the same rate of the Sun, 59 minutes per year. It is based on the notion that "one day equals a year," - each day after birth, symbolises a year in time.

Progressed chart - see Secondary Progression chart.

Quincunx or inconjunct aspect. Two planets or points in the chart within 150 degrees of each other (with a 3 degree orb). It is a hard aspect that requires an adjustment.

Quintile aspect. A minor aspect of 72 degrees, which is found by dividing the circle by 5. A latent or spiritual talent.

Rectification. A method of determining the ascendant and House Cusps when the precise moment of birth is not known. This is due to the timing of important events and conditions in the life.

Retrograde planets. The Sun and Moon are never retrograde. The retrograde effect occurs when a planet appears to be moving backwards as a faster planet passes it. This phenomenon is interpreted by astrologers as being karmic. Because of misuse in a previous life, the individual is being re-educated in the right use of the principles symbolised by the planet.

Rising sign. The Ascendant. It is the sign on the eastern horizon at the time of birth.

Sabian symbols. Clairvoyant images for each degree of the zodiac.

Secondary Progression chart. From a natal chart, the progressed chart is calculated forwards or backwards in time, to a specific date, using the "one day equals a year" calculation method.

Secondary Progressions. It is based on the notion that "one day equals a year." The planet positions on each day after birth, symbolise events occurring in the life year by year.

Seesaw planet pattern. The planets oppose each other across the chart. These personality types thrive on conflict and excitement. Their natural inclination is to swing to extremes and back and forth.

Semi-square aspect. Two planets or points in the chart within 45 degrees of each other (4-degree orb). The semi-square is found by dividing the circle by 8. It is a hard, militant type aspect.

Separating aspect. When a faster moving planet begins to move away from the exact aspect to a slower moving planet - but is still in orb; this is called a "separating" aspect. The energies are dissipating.

Sesquiquadrate aspect. A minor aspect of 135 degrees. Disruption needing resolution.

Sextile aspect. Two planets or points in the chart within 60 degrees of each other (with a 4 to 6 degree orb). The sextile is found by dividing the circle by 6. It is a constructive, beneficial aspect.

Sidereal Time is star time, so called because a sidereal day is the time it takes for the Earth to complete one rotation about its axis with respect to the fixed stars. The sidereal day is 3 minutes 56 seconds shorter than the solar day.

Sign symbols. Most are animal and represent the "animal" traits of the sign. Three signs have human symbols (Gemini, Virgo and Aquarius). People born in these signs are said to be more human (intelligent) than those born in the animal signs. Libra is alone is having an inorganic symbol - the Scales. Perhaps there is nothing naturally occurring in nature that more correctly represents the balancing attributes of this sign.

Signs. The zodiac signs, 30 degree segments of the ecliptic, the apparent path of the Sun around the Earth. They express the energies of the constellations of the same name, although they no longer coincide.

Solar-arc or primary directions. The entire chart progresses forward through the signs at the same rate of the Sun, 59 minutes per year. It is based on the notion that "one day equals a year," - each day after birth, symbolises a year in time.

Solar-arc chart. From a natal chart, the solar-arc chart is calculated forwards or backwards in time, at the same rate of the Sun, 59 minutes per year.

Solar Return charts. They are erected for the moment the Sun returns to its exact position at the time of birth, using the longitude and latitude of the current location.

Soul. The higher spiritual aspect of our nature, spiritual love and wisdom.

Soul Purpose. It is connected to the ascendant sign. At a higher level, the ascendant represents the purpose of the soul that seeks to increase its light and influence in our consciousness.

Splash planet pattern. Not more than one planetary conjunction or 4 houses empty. This personality type can be more impersonal than the others - they tend to take a broad view of life. They are very versatile and can do several things at once. This could lead to a "jack of all trades, master of none" approach to life.

Splay planet pattern. There are three irregular planet groups in the pattern - but any other non-conforming planet arrangement fits into this category. These are the nonconformists of the zodiac.

Square aspect. Two planets or points in the chart within 90 to 98-degrees of each other. The square is found by dividing the circle by 4. It is a hard, challenging aspect.

Stationary. A planet appears to stand still when its motion is changing from direct to retrograde, or vice versa. It applies to all planets but the Sun and Moon. This period intensifies the power of the planet's expression.

Stellium. A major planet configuration of 3 or more planets all conjunct. The two outermost planets in a stellium (A and C) do not have to be conjunct, as long as the intermediate planet (B) is conjunct them both. A stellium is also formed with 3 or more planets in one sign. The energies of the planets and the signs they are in are tremendously intensified. When reading a stellium, start with a personal planet.

Succedent houses. "Succedent" is defined as "coming next", they follow the angular houses. They are the 2nd, 5th, 8th and 11th houses. They are related to the Emotional Plane and determine how we feel about money (2), love (5), sex (8) and friends (11). Planets located here are instrumental in determining whether emotional experiences in the various houses/ life areas, will be easy or difficult.

Symbols, sign and planet. The symbols that represent each sign are supposed to convey the essential nature of that sign.

T-Square. A major planet configuration where two planets in opposition, both square the same third planet. There is inner conflict and dissatisfaction. This drives a person to action to improve things.

Time Zones. Geographic regions within which the same standard time is used

Transforming planets. These are the five non-personal planets (Jupiter, Saturn, Uranus, Neptune and Pluto). These transformative forces are the agents of evolution and their interactions with the personality (planets) bring experiences that force or encourage us to change, to let go of the past and move into the future.

Transits. The movement of a planet over a planet or sensitive point in the natal chart at any given time.

Trine aspect. Two planets or points in the chart within 120 degrees of each other (with an 8-degree orb). The trine is found by dividing the circle by 3. It is an easy, beneficial aspect.

Tropical zodiac. The zodiac of the signs. It is an imaginary circle of signs along the ecliptic.

Unaspected planet. There are no major aspects to other planets. This is very important if the planet affected is one of the personal planets - the Sun, Moon, Mercury, Venus and Mars. It symbolises an undeveloped and alienated part of the psyche which needs to be integrated back into the personality. The dispositor planet holds the key to integration.

Universal Time (UT). Greenwich mean time, zero degrees longitude. All the other standard Time Zones are determined by using UT as the start point.

Void of course. Applies to a planet, especially the Moon, which has completed all aspects to other planets before leaving the sign it is in. When the Moon is void-of-course it is said to represent a period which lacks creative force, and no new tasks should be started.

Vulcan. An undiscovered planet that orbits between the Sun and Mercury. It is used in esoteric astrology, ruling Taurus and Virgo on higher levels. Its orbit is between the Sun and Mercury. In the chart, it is found between the Sun and Mercury, within 8-degrees of the Sun.

Yod or the "Finger of God". A major planet configuration where two planets sextile each other and both quincunx the same third planet. The Yod shows inner conflict that will manifest as external conflict if balance is not found.

Zodiac. Literally, a circle of small animals. A ring or bond around the heavens that is divided into 12 signs of 30 degrees (longitude each). The planets move through the zodiac.

Index

Symbols

1 Chart: 0 Aries ascendant chart 173
1 Chart: Allen, Woody 116
1 Chart: Charles, Prince 142
1 Chart: Churchill, Winston 114–115
1 Chart: Connery, Sean 163
1 Chart: Day Calculator 180
1 Chart: Diana, Princess 114, 143, 177
  progressed 180, 189
  solar return 190
1 Chart: Kennedy, President 161
1 Chart: Prince George 112
1 Chart: Reddy, Helen 173
1 Chart: Soraya, Princess 160
1 Charts: Woodward and Newman 117–118, 155
1 Chart X 49
1 Drawing: Aspects 111
1 Drawing: Houses 5, 47–51
1 Drawing: the Zodiac 3
1 Map: Time Zones 167
1 Table: Astrology Signs and Planet Rulers 33
1 Table: Major Aspects 110
1 Table: Planet Strengths by Sign 30
1 Table: Signs - Elements - Modes - Symbols 3
1 Table: Signs: Elements, Modes, Symbols 3
1 Table: Signs & Ruling Planets 4

A

Accidents 38, 117, 125–126, 159, 185–187, 190
Adjusted Calculation Date 178–181
Afflicted planets 30, 195
Air element 8
Aldebaran 12
Allen, Woody 116
Angles 50
Angular houses 51, 195
Antahkarana 54
Antares 13
Applying aspects 112
Aquarius 3–4, 6, 8–9, 11, 13, 24, 30, 33–34, 36, 41, 52, 58, 61, 63, 65, 68, 70, 74, 80, 84, 87, 90, 93, 95, 98, 100, 103, 106, 140, 143–144, 150, 154–155, 157, 159, 198–199
  Hercules Labour 24
  Main Section 24
  water-bearer, the 11
Archer, Sagittarius 13, 22, 105
Aries 3–4, 6, 8–10, 12–13, 29–30, 33–34, 37–38, 40, 43, 45, 50, 52–53, 60–61, 64, 67, 69, 72, 76, 79, 82, 85, 89, 92, 95, 97, 99, 102, 104, 115, 140, 149, 154, 156, 159, 162–165, 173, 195–197
  Hercules Labour 14
  Main Section 14
  ram, the 10
Aristotle 2
Arrow, Sagittarius 11, 13, 22, 105
Artemis 17
Ascendant 10, 33–34, 39–43, 48, 50, 53, 60–61, 71, 103, 112–113, 121, 124, 130, 134, 140, 144, 153–154, 161, 162–165, 173, 184, 188–189, 190, 197
  defined 195
  Main Section 33
  purpose of the soul 33, 53, 60–61, 71, 119, 121, 165, 199
  signs 60–61
  spiritual goal 33
  zero degrees Aries 197
ASC - see Ascendant 195
Aspect grid 50, 112
ASPECTS 109–137
  applying and separating 112, 187, 195
  conjunction 112, 115
    defined 110–111, 195
  defined 5, 195
  easy or hard aspects defined 110, 116
  finding 110, 115
  grid 112
  hard aspects defined 30, 110, 154
    health 158
  inconjunct 112, 114–115
    defined 110–111, 198
  opposition 112, 114–115
    defined 110–111, 197
  orbs 111
  overview 5, 110
  quincuncx - see inconjunct 198
  quintile
    defined 110, 198
  reading aspects 116
  semi-sextile
    defined 110
  semi-square 112, 115
    defined 110–111, 198
  separating aspects 198
  sesquiquadrate
    defined 110, 198
  sextile 112, 114–115, 198
    defined 110–111
  square 112, 114–115
    defined 110–111
  trine 112–113, 115
    defined 110–111
Asteroids 4, 6, 44–46, 195
  in signs and houses 95–107
Astral (emotional) 8, 19, 35, 65, 77, 80, 86
Astrology
  branches or methods 195
  chart components 49
  defined 2–3
  ethics 7
  houses 63–71
  natal 197
  psychological or spiritual tool 7
  purpose of the soul 195
  to learn 7
Atlas 168

B

Baba, Sai 113
Benefics 195
Bowl planet pattern 31, 115, 195, 198
Bucket planet pattern 31, 115–116, 162, 195, 198
Bull, Taurus 10, 12, 15
Bundle planet pattern 31, 195, 198

C

CALCULATION, NATAL 167–178
  constant decimal 172
  planets 177–178
Cancer 3–4, 4, 6, 8–11, 12, 17, 29–30, 33, 35, 38–40, 42, 50, 52, 54, 60, 62, 65, 68–69, 72, 74, 76, 79, 82, 86, 89, 92, 95, 97, 100, 102, 105, 113–114, 139–140, 143–144, 149, 155–156, 159–161, 164, 185, 189, 196
  children 160
  crab, the 10
  Hercules Labour 17
  Main Section 17

Index - 201

Capricorn 3–4, 6, 8–9, 11, 13, 23, 29–30, 30, 33, 35, 38–40, 42–43, 50, 52, 56–57, 61, 63–65, 68, 70, 74, 77, 80, 83, 87, 90, 93, 95, 98, 100, 103, 106, 140, 143–144, 150–154, 154–155, 157, 159–160, 196
   goat, the 11
   Hercules Labour 23
   Main Section 23
Cardinal mode 9
Career 6, 14, 30, 50, 50–51, 51, 53, 66, 68, 71, 78, 80, 85, 88, 94, 96, 101–103, 107, 117, 120–121, 124–125, 130–136, 141–143, 156, 162–163, 165, 185, 195
   Main Section 156–157
Celestial Equator 3, 195
Celestial sphere 3
Centaur, Chiron 46
Centaur, Sagittarius 4, 11, 22, 61–62, 87
Ceres 4, 6, 44–45, 118, 120, 122, 124, 126–127, 129–130, 132–136
   aspects (main) 135
   in houses 101–102
   in signs 99–100
   Main Section 45
Charles, Prince 142, 175, 185, 188
Charts
   composite chart defined 196
   erecting for unknown time 173
   natal chart defined 197
   secondary progression chart defined 198
   solar-arc chart defined 198
   solar return chart defined 198
Children 6, 16, 18, 35–36, 46, 51–52, 55, 63, 66–69, 71, 75, 78, 81, 82, 85, 88, 91, 94, 96, 99–100, 103, 107, 116, 121, 124, 130, 132–133, 141–145, 152, 156–157, 160, 162
   childbirth 156, 160
Chiron 4, 6, 44, 46, 118, 120, 122, 124, 126, 128–129, 131–136, 143, 156, 163
   aspects (main) 136
   in houses 106–107
   in signs 104–106
   Main Section 46
Churchill, Winston 114–115
Composite Chart 154–155
   defined 196

Conjunction aspect defined 5, 110–111, 195
Connery, Sean 162–165
Consciousness 2
   defined 2, 196
   group 24
Constant Decimal 172–173
Crab, Cancer 10, 12, 17, 60, 62

D

Day Calculator 180
Daylight Saving Time 169, 196
Death 6, 25, 43, 52, 56, 161, 189
Decanates, decans 9, 196
Descendant 50
Desire 15
Detriment planets 30, 196
Diana, Princess 143–144, 175, 177, 179–180, 185, 188–190
Dignity, planets 30
Dispositor, disposits 29–30, 196

E

Eagle, Scorpio 11, 21, 90
Earth element 8
Easy aspects 34–44, 46, 110, 116–121, 123–125, 127, 129, 131–132, 134–135, 155, 158
Eclipses 188
   lunar and solar 196
Ecliptic 3, 196
Eighth house, (8th) 5–6, 21, 43, 49–52, 71, 94, 144, 155, 161, 163–165, 185, 188–189, 190
   Main Section 56
Electional astrology 195
Elements of the signs 8, 196
Elevated planet 30, 196
Eleventh house, (11th) 5–6, 24, 41, 49–52, 153–154, 161, 190
   Main Section 58
Emotional, emotions 4, 6, 8, 10–11, 12, 17, 21, 25, 29, 33, 35, 38, 42, 51, 52, 56–58, 60–63, 65–67, 70, 72–76, 79–82, 86–87, 91, 95, 98, 100–101, 103–107, 117, 119–121, 124–125, 127, 129, 132, 134–136, 139–146, 150–152, 152, 158, 185, 198–199
   isolation 65
   refine 17
Enlightenment 2, 13, 77

defined 138, 196
Ephemeris 168–169, 171, 174, 178, 184, 196
Equal House system 5, 197
Equator 168
Erecting Birth Charts when the time is unknown 173
Esoteric
   astrology 29, 33, 195, 196
   group 69
   healing 158
   ruler 33, 53, 165
Ethics of astrology work 7
Exalted, planets 30, 196
EXERCISES 137–150
   1: Read planets in signs 139
   2: Read planets in aspect to other planets 140
   3: Read planets, in signs, in houses 141
   4: Read the houses 142
   5: Read houses, signs on cusps and planets in the houses 143
   6: Reading the rulers of houses 144
   8: Read planets, in signs, in houses 145
   9: Using cards 145–150

F

Falls, falling - planets
   defined 30, 196
Father 6, 32, 57
Fertility 160
Fifth house, (5th) 5–6, 18, 34, 49–52, 55, 81, 116, 144, 154, 160, 188
   Main Section 55
Finger of God 199
Fire element 8
First house, (1st) 5–6, 14, 33, 48–53, 57, 144, 152–153, 161
   Main Section 53
Fishes, Pisces 11, 13, 25
Fixed mode 9
Fixed stars 171, 196, 198
Fourth house, (4th) 5–6, 17, 33, 35, 44, 49–52, 116, 144, 161, 197
   Main Section 54
Fruitful signs 196

G

Gemini 3–4, 6, 8–10, 12, 16, 30, 33,

36, 39, 51–52, 54, 60, 62, 64, 67, 69, 72, 76, 79, 82, 86, 89, 92, 95, 97, 100, 102, 105, 139, 143–144, 149, 156–161, 163–165, 195, 198
   Hercules Labour 16
   Main Section 16
   twins, the 10
George, Prince 112
Glyphs 12, 29, 196
GMT Date of birth 169, 196
Goat, Capricorn 11, 13, 23, 61, 63
Grand Cross planet pattern 114, 116
Grand Trine planet pattern 113, 115, 156, 196
Greenwich Mean Time (GMT) 168–176, 196
   examples 171
Greenwich Meridian 168

H

Hard aspects 34–42, 44–46, 102, 110, 116–117, 119–125, 127–132, 134–136, 138, 152, 154, 156, 158
Harding, Karl Ludwig 44
Health 5–7, 17, 19, 25, 38, 46, 55, 58, 63, 66, 69, 71–72, 75–76, 78, 80–83, 85–86, 88, 90, 94–96, 99–101, 103–104, 107, 120, 125, 129, 131, 136, 138, 156–158, 158–159, 162, 165–166, 186, 195
Hercules Labours 14–25
Hitler, Adolf 89, 92
Home & Family 4–6, 10–11, 17, 44, 50, 52, 54, 63, 65–66, 68–69, 71–72, 75–76, 78–79, 81–82, 84, 88–89, 91–92, 94, 96–98, 100–107, 116–117, 119–121, 134, 141–142, 144, 153–154, 156–157
HOUSES 47, 197
   1st, first 14, 33, 48–50, 52–53, 68, 144, 152–153, 161, 195
      Main Section 53
   2nd, second 15, 49, 50, 52–53, 144, 153, 155–156, 163–165
      Main Section 53
   3rd, third 16, 49, 52, 54, 74, 163, 165, 185, 190
      Main Section 54
   4th, fourth 17, 33, 35, 44, 49–50, 52, 54, 116, 136, 144, 153, 161, 197
      Main Section 54
   5th, fifth 18, 34, 49, 52, 55, 81, 116, 144, 153, 154, 160, 188
      Main Section 55
   6th, sixth 19, 36, 49, 52, 55, 78, 153, 156, 158, 163–165, 195
      health 158
      Main Section 55
   7th, seventh 20, 33, 44–45, 49–50, 52, 53, 55, 56, 116, 143–144, 153, 154, 154–155, 163–164, 188
      Main Section 56
   8th, eighth 21, 43, 49, 52, 56, 71, 94, 144, 153, 155, 161, 163–165, 185, 188–189, 190
      Main Section 56
   9th, ninth 22, 49, 52, 54, 57, 188
      Main Section 57
   10th, tenth 23, 30, 33, 49–51, 52, 54, 57–58, 144, 153, 156, 185, 190, 195, 197
      Main Section 57
   11th, eleventh 24, 41, 49, 52, 58, 153–154, 161, 190, 199
      Main Section 58
   12th, twelfth 25, 42, 49, 51–52, 58, 153, 158, 195
      health 158
      Main Section 58
   activation of 5
   and the seasons 51
   angular houses 51, 195
   cadent houses 51, 195
   governed by signs 52
   how they are formed 48
   overview 5
   succeedent houses 51, 199
House Systems 197

I

IC, Imum Coeli, nadir 197
Illness, ill-health 44, 58, 71, 76, 84, 129, 136, 158
Imum Coeli - see IC 50
Inconjunct aspect defined 5, 110–111, 197
Infertile 160
Initiation, spiritual 13, 18, 21, 22–24, 52, 57, 84, 93, 197
   1st 18
   2nd 21
   3rd 24
Intercepted Signs 142, 144, 189, 197
International Date Line 168

J

Jung, Carl G. 2
Juno 4, 6, 44–45, 118, 120, 122, 124, 126–127, 129–135, 153, 153–155, 188
   aspects (main) 134–135
   in houses 98–99
   in signs 97–98
   Juno to Juno aspect 154
   Main Section 44–45
   marriage 6, 44–45, 97–99
Jupiter 4, 6, 9, 17, 19, 29–30, 32, 35, 39, 44, 49, 53, 79–82, 110, 112–115, 117, 119, 121, 123, 125, 127–128, 139–141, 143, 152–155, 157–161, 164, 174, 184–186, 189, 195, 199
   aspects (main) 127–128
   detriment 19, 30
   dignified 30
   exalted 17, 30, 79
   expansion 4, 39, 80, 127–128, 185, 187
   falls 30, 80, 153
   in houses 81–82
   in signs 79–80
   King of the Gods 32
   Main Section 39

K

Kennedy, John President 161
Keywords Summary Page 6
Kowal, Charles T. 46

L

Lama, Dalai 113
Latitude 168, 197–198
Leo 3–4, 6, 8–10, 12, 18, 30, 33–34, 36, 41, 50, 52, 55, 60, 62, 65, 68, 70, 73, 76, 79, 82, 86, 89–90, 92, 95, 97, 100, 102, 105, 139–140, 143–144, 149, 156, 159–160, 185, 188–189, 195
   Hercules Labour 18
   lion, the 10
   Main Section 18
Libra 3–4, 6, 8–9, 11–13, 20, 29–30, 33–34, 37–38, 40, 43, 45, 50, 52, 56, 61–62, 65, 67, 70, 73, 77, 80, 83, 86, 90, 92, 95, 98, 100, 102, 105, 139, 144, 150, 156, 159, 163–166, 171, 188–189, 190, 196, 198
   Hercules Labour 20
   Main Section 20

scales, the 11
Life Endings 161
Lion, Leo 10, 12, 60, 62, 79
Local Sidereal Time (LST) 171, 171–174, 197
Locomotive planet pattern 31, 197
Longitude 168–171, 196–199
LOOKING to the FUTURE 183–191
Love 6, 11–12, 15–22, 25, 29, 33, 35, 37, 39, 42, 45, 51, 55, 57, 60–61, 63–65, 68, 70–78, 80–82, 84–85, 87, 89–91, 95–102, 104–107, 113, 117–121, 123–126, 129, 132–135, 138, 162–169, 185, 187–188, 199
Lovers 6, 16–17, 29, 37, 55, 63, 66, 69, 74, 78, 81, 85, 88, 91, 94, 123, 127, 141, 143
LST 197
Lunar eclipse 188

M

Major Planet Configurations 113
Malefic Planets 55, 158, 160, 185–186, 189
    defined 29, 197
Mansions of the Moon 48
Marriage 4, 20, 37, 44–45, 50–52, 56, 81, 86, 90, 92, 94, 97–99, 104, 114, 116, 118, 120, 122–124, 126–127, 129–135, 142–144, 152–155, 157, 175, 188, 195
Mars 4, 6, 9, 15, 17, 19–20, 23, 29–30, 32–33, 33, 35, 38, 49, 53, 60, 76–79, 112, 114–117, 119, 121, 123, 125–126, 139–140, 143–144, 154–161, 162–165, 185–188, 190, 195–197, 199
    aspects (main) 125–126
    detriment 15, 20, 30, 38, 77
    dignified 30
    exalted 23, 30, 77
    falls, falling 38
    God of War 23, 29, 32, 196
    in houses 78–79
    in signs 76–77
    Main Section 38
    Mars to Mars aspect 154
    passion, desire, sex 4, 6, 19, 29, 38, 76–78, 116–117, 119, 123, 125–126, 154–155, 157
    unaspected 38
MC - see midheaven 197

Medical Astrology 158, 195
Medium Coeli - see midheaven 197
Mercury 4, 6, 16, 19, 22, 25, 29–30, 32, 33, 36, 49, 69–72, 110, 112–117, 121–123, 139–140, 143–144, 152–156, 159, 161, 162–164, 174, 185–187, 189, 190, 197, 199
    aspects (main) 121–123
    composite chart 155
    detriment 22, 30, 36
    dignified, dignity 19, 30
    exalted 30, 70
    falls, falling 25, 30, 36
    in houses 71–72
    in relationships 152
    in signs 19, 22, 25, 69–70
    Main Section 36
    Mercury to Mercury aspect 154
    Messenger of the Gods 32
    unaspected 30, 36
Meridians 168
Michelsen Book of Tables 168, 195
Michelsen Ephemeris 168–171
Midheaven, MC, Medium Coeli
    defined 50, 197
Midpoints 152, 154, 196, 197
Mind
    abstract 36, 41, 70
    air-mind 69–70
    collective 6, 57, 75, 92
    concrete 36, 54
    earth-mind 69–70
    fire-mind 69–70
    illumined 12, 18, 36, 69–70, 77–78
    lower 19, 36, 69–70, 74
    purifying 62
    scientific 21, 24, 41, 85, 87
    subconscious 35
    water-mind 69
Modes of the signs 9, 197
Money 5–6, 15, 37, 51–53, 56, 63, 66, 69, 71–72, 74–75, 77–79, 81–85, 88–94, 96–97, 99, 101–104, 114, 138, 142–144, 150, 155–157, 157, 163–165, 199
Moon 4, 6, 15, 17, 21, 23, 29–32, 32, 35, 44–45, 48–49, 60, 64–67, 110, 112, 115, 117, 119–121, 139–140, 144, 147, 162, 163–165, 196–199
    aspects (main) 119–121
    children 160

composite chart 154
detriment 23, 30, 65
dignified 17, 30
emotions 6, 35, 119–121, 152, 162–163, 185
exalted 15, 30, 160
falls 21, 30
health 158
in houses 66–67
in relationships 152
in signs 15, 21, 64–65
Main Section 35
Moon to Moon aspect 154
Mother-Matter 32
unaspected 35, 152
Moon's Nodes 35–36, 67–69, 119, 121–122, 124, 126, 128–129, 131–136, 197
    in houses 68–69
    in signs 67–68
    Main Section 35
Morrison, Al 46
Most elevated planet 30
Mother 6, 17, 45, 54, 67, 103, 121, 175
Mundane Astrology 195
Mutable mode 9
Mutual Reception 29, 197

N

Nadir - see IC 197
Natal Astrology
    defined 2, 195, 197
    to learn 7
Natal Chart 4–5, 7, 46, 48, 50, 112, 138, 154, 158, 168, 184–186, 190, 195, 199
    defined 197
    how it is formed 48
Neptune 4, 6, 17, 19, 29–30, 32, 42, 49, 52, 89–92, 91, 110, 112, 115, 118, 120, 122–123, 125, 127, 130, 131–132, 139–140, 143, 155, 157, 161–165, 163–165, 184, 186–188, 197, 199
    aspects (main) 131–132
    delusion 42, 89–90, 118, 124, 127, 132
    detriment 19, 30, 90
    dignified 30
    exalted 17, 30
    falls 30, 90
    idealism, ideals 4, 6, 32, 42, 89–90, 131, 155, 187

in houses 91–92
in signs 17, 19, 89–90
King of the Oceans 32
Main Section 42
refines, refined, refinement 4, 6, 42, 89–90
rose-coloured glasses 42, 91, 118, 120, 127
Newman, Paul 152–155
Ninth house, (9th) 5–6, 22, 49, 52, 54, 188
Main Section 57
Nodes - see Moon's Nodes 197

O

Occult 196
Olbers, Heinrich Wilhelm 44
Opposition aspect defined 5, 110–111, 197
Orb, aspect 111, 197

P

Pallas Athena 4, 6, 25, 44–46, 118, 120, 122, 124, 126, 128–129, 131–136
aspects (main) 136
in houses 103–104
in signs 102–103
Main Section 45–46
Path, Evolution 41
Path, Noble Middle 61–62, 94
Path, Spiritual 8, 12, 19, 22, 43, 54, 57, 70, 81, 90, 119
enlightenment 196
Personality (the) 4–6, 13–16, 18–20, 24, 29–33, 36, 39, 41, 43, 53–55, 57, 60–64, 72–74, 76–77, 79–80, 86, 113, 117–119, 128, 133, 139–141, 145, 158, 162–163, 165, 185–187, 195, 197, 198–200
Personal planets 6, 30, 39–43, 130–131, 140, 152–154, 162, 199
defined 4, 29, 33, 197
Phoenix, Scorpio 11, 21
Piazzi, Giuseppe 44
Pisces 3–4, 6, 8–9, 11, 13, 25, 30, 33, 36–37, 39, 42, 51–52, 58, 61, 63, 65, 68, 70, 74, 77, 80, 84, 87, 90, 93, 96, 98, 100, 103, 106, 113, 139, 150, 155, 157–160, 165–166, 189, 196–197
fishes, the 11
Hercules Labour 25
Main Section 25

Placidus House System 33, 49, 142, 169–170, 174–175, 197
defined 5, 197
Planet calculations 174–175
PLANETS 27–45
are agents 3
careers 156
configurations 113
dispositors 29
evolutionary forces 4
glyphs 29
health 159
in society 29
malefics 197
most elevated 30
outer, growth Planets 4
overview of planets 4
patterns
defined 31, 158, 198
find 115
personalities 29
personal planets 4, 33
retrograde 29, 198
strengths
afflicted - defined 30, 144, 195
detriment - defined 30, 34, 196
dignity - defined 30, 196
elevated - defined 196
exalted - defined 30, 196
falls, falling - defined 30, 195–196
unaspected - defined 30, 195, 199
transforming planets 39
PLANETS in ASPECT 117–136
PLANETS in SIGNS, HOUSES 59–107
Plato 2
Pluto 4, 6, 21, 29–30, 32, 35, 38, 43, 49, 92–94, 110, 112, 114–116, 118, 120, 122, 124–125, 127, 129–133, 139–141, 143–144, 154–155, 157, 159–161, 164, 184, 186–189, 190, 197, 199
aspects (main) 132
destroys, destruction 4, 6, 43, 132
detriment 30
dignified 30
exalted 30
falls 30
God of the Underworld 32
in houses 93–94
in signs 92–93
Main Section 43
transforms, transformation 4, 6, 43, 92, 94–95, 118, 155, 187
Pollux and Castor. 12
Precession of Equinoxes 195, 198
Prison of the soul 12, 35, 64, 165
Purpose of the soul 2, 53, 60–61, 71, 119, 121, 165, 195, 199

Q

Quincunx aspect defined 110–111, 197
Quintile aspect defined 5, 110, 198

R

Ram, Aries 10, 12, 14, 60–61
Reddy, Helen 169–175
Regulus 12
Relationship/s 6, 16–17, 19–20, 23, 30, 37, 44–45, 48, 56, 64, 66, 68, 72–74, 88, 94, 99, 101, 107, 118, 120, 123–125, 127, 132–135, 138, 147, 152–155, 164, 187, 196
Religion 5–6, 22, 25, 39, 42, 57, 64, 67, 71, 75, 80, 83, 85, 91, 101, 107, 127–128, 131, 157
Retrograde planets 30, 34, 112, 143, 144, 186–187, 189, 195, 199
defined 29, 198
Rising sign - see Ascendant 53
Rose-coloured glasses 42

S

Sabian symbols defined 198
Sagittarius 3–4, 6, 8–9, 9, 11, 13, 22, 30, 33, 36, 39, 43, 49, 51–52, 57, 61–63, 65, 67, 70, 73, 77, 80, 83, 87, 90, 93, 95, 98, 100, 103, 105, 113, 139–140, 154–155, 157, 159, 190
centaur, the 22
Hercules Labour 22
Main Section 22
Saturn 4, 6, 14, 17–18, 20, 23, 29–30, 32, 35, 38, 40, 49, 56, 61, 82–85, 84, 110, 112–115, 117, 119, 121, 123, 125, 127, 128–130, 138–140, 144, 153–154, 157–161, 162–165, 165, 174, 184, 186–188, 196–197, 199
aspects (main) 128–130
detriment 17, 18, 30, 196
dignified 23, 30
discipline 4, 40, 82–83, 117, 119, 121–123, 125, 127–130

exalted 20, 30, 196
falls 30
in houses 84–85
in signs 17, 18, 23, 82–84
karma 4, 18, 20, 40, 61, 82–85, 129–130
Lord of Karma 40
Main Section 40
the Reaper of Souls 32
Scales, Libra 11, 13, 20, 62, 198
Scorpio 3–4, 6, 8–9, 11, 13, 15, 21, 30, 33, 35, 37–38, 41, 43, 45, 52, 56, 61–62, 65, 67, 70, 73, 77, 80, 83, 87, 90, 93, 95, 98, 100, 103, 105, 113–114, 140, 143, 150, 157, 159–160, 165, 196
    Hercules Labour 21
    Main Section 21
    scorpion, the 11
Scorpion 11, 21, 62
Secondary Progressions 186, 189
    defined 184, 198
    secondary progression chart defined 198
Second house, (2nd) 5–6, 49–53, 156, 165, 199
    Main Section 53
Seesaw planet pattern 31, 198–199
Self-undoing 5, 52, 58
Semi-sextile aspect defined 110
Semi-square aspect defined 5, 110–111, 198
Separating aspects 112, 198
Sesquiquadrate aspect defined 5, 110, 198
Seventh house, (7th) 5–6, 20, 33, 44–45, 49–52, 55–56, 116, 143–144, 154–155, 163–164, 185, 188
    Main Section 56
Sex 5–6, 15, 21–22, 32, 37–38, 43, 51, 55–56, 65, 69, 71–75, 83, 90, 97, 99, 117, 123, 126, 147, 154–155, 157, 165, 199
Sextile aspect defined 5, 110–111, 198
Sidereal astrology 195
Sidereal time 171–172, 198
Signs 7, 198
    are agents 3
    barren 160, 195
    careers 156
    elements 3, 8, 196
    fertile 160
    fruitful 196

gifts of the gods 32
glyphs 12
health 159
intercepted 197
modes 3, 9
symbols 3, 10, 198
zodiac 3, 8, 198
Sixth house, (6th) 5–6, 19, 49–52, 156, 158, 163–165, 195
    Main Section 55
Socrates 2
Solar-Arc Directions 184
    defined 186, 198
    solar-arc chart defined 198
Solar eclipse 188
Solar Return astrology - defined 195
Solar Return Charts 190
    defined 198
    Princess Diana 190
Soraya, Princess 160
Soul 4, 11, 12–17, 20–24, 24, 29, 33–39, 41–42, 53–58, 60–62, 69–74, 76–77, 79, 86–89, 93, 95–97, 106, 124, 132, 138
    advanced 13, 87
    and consciousness are synonyms 97
    awareness 2
    binding 131, 133–135
    blinded 13
    challenge 129
    control 16, 18
    defined 2, 65, 89, 138, 199
    development 33
    group 56, 58, 84
    inspired vocation 57
    mate, mates 56, 131
    message of 33
    messages 69, 79
    of man 22
    plan 71, 134, 136
    represented by Venus 37
    seeking release 13
    synonym 2, 97
    uses ill health 55
    younger 13
Soul-illumined mind 12
Soul Purpose 2, 33, 53, 60–61, 119, 121, 133, 135, 165, 199
Spica 12
Spiritual
    awareness 2, 196
    defined 2
    direction 165

goal of the signs 12, 14–25
path, see Path, Spiritual 54–55
Splash, planet pattern 31, 198–199
Splay, planet pattern 31, 198, 199
Square aspect defined 5, 110–111, 199
Stellium planet pattern 113, 199
Succeedent houses 51, 199
Sun 3, 3–6, 9, 14, 17–18, 20, 24, 29–30, 32, 33–45, 48–50, 53, 61–64, 67, 76, 105, 110, 112–113, 115, 117–119, 139–140, 143–144, 158–159, 161, 162–170, 171, 174, 185–189, 190, 195–199
    aspects (main) 117–119
    composite chart 154
    detriment 24, 30
    dignified 18, 30
    exalted 14, 30, 53
    falls 20, 30
    Father-God 32
    health 158
    in houses 63–64
    in signs 61–62
    Main Section 34
    personality 4, 6, 24, 33–34, 61–64, 113, 117–119, 139–141, 162–163, 165, 185, 188
    physical sun 24
    progressed 188
    Ra, eye of 32
    Sun to Sun aspect 154
    unaspected 34
    veiling and unveiling
        Vulcan 60
Symbols, sign and planet 199
Synastry
    chart 153–154
    defined 195

T

Table of Houses 168, 195
Taurus 3–4, 6, 8–10, 30, 32–35, 33, 35, 37–38, 41, 43, 49, 52–53, 60, 62, 64, 67, 69, 72, 76, 79, 82, 86, 89, 92, 95, 97, 99, 102, 104, 115, 139–140, 144, 149, 152, 156, 159–161, 173, 188, 199
    bull, the 10
    Hercules Labour 15
    Main Section 15
Tenth house, (10th) 5–6, 23, 30, 33, 49–52, 156, 165, 185, 190, 195, 197

Main Section 57
Third house, (3rd) 5–6, 16, 49–52, 54, 106, 163, 165, 185, 190
  Main Section 54
Time Zones 167–169, 199
Transforming planets 6
  defined 39, 199
Transits 186, 186–187, 199
Trine aspect defined 5, 110–111, 199
Tropical
  Astrology 3
  Zodiac 3, 199
T-Square planet pattern 114–115, 156, 158, 199
Twelfth house, (12th) 5–6, 25, 42, 49–52, 144, 158
  Main Section 58
Twins, Gemini 10, 12, 16, 62

U

Unaspected planet 30, 199
Universal Time (UT) 168, 196, 199
Uranian or Saturnian relationships 153
Uranus 4, 6, 15, 18, 21, 29–31, 32, 35, 41, 49, 56, 85–89, 110, 112, 114–116, 118, 120–121, 123, 125, 127–128, 130–131, 139–141, 143–144, 153–157, 159–161, 163–164, 174, 184, 186–188, 197, 199
  abstract mind 41
  aspects (main) 130–131
  awakens 4, 6, 15, 41, 130
  detriment 18, 30
  dignified 30
  exalted 21, 30, 87
  falls 15, 30, 86
  in houses 88–89
  in signs 85–87
  Main Section 41
  scientific mind 41
  Sky-God 32

V

Values 5–6, 16, 37, 52–53, 63, 68, 71, 73–74, 78, 82, 88–89, 92–93, 96–98, 98, 103–104, 114, 128, 130, 143–144, 153, 155, 157
Venus 4, 6, 14–15, 17, 19, 21, 25, 29–30, 32, 33, 37, 49, 72–75, 110, 112–113, 115–117, 119, 121, 123–125, 138–140, 144–145, 152–156, 159–160, 161, 162–164, 185–188, 195–197, 199
  aspects (main) 123
  composite chart 155
  detriment 14, 21, 30, 37, 72, 73
  dignified 30
  exalted 25, 30, 74, 152
  falls, falling 19, 30, 37, 73
  Goddess of Beauty 32
  in houses 74–75
  in relationships 152
  in signs 14, 17, 19, 25, 72–74
  love and affection 6, 15, 25, 29, 33, 37, 72–75, 117, 119, 121, 123–125, 152, 154–155, 162, 164, 185, 187
  Main Section 37
  mind 74
  relationships 6, 29, 32, 37, 72–75, 117, 119, 121, 123–125, 140, 152, 154–156, 164
  soul-love 21
  unaspected 37
  Venus to Venus aspect 154
Vesta 4, 6, 44, 95–97, 118, 120, 122, 124–125, 127, 129–134
  aspects (main) 133–134
  in houses 96–97
  in signs 95–96
  Main Section 44
Virgin, Vesta 44
Virgin, Virgo 10, 12, 19
Virgo 3–4, 6, 8–10, 12, 19, 30, 33, 36–37, 39, 42, 45, 50–52, 55, 60–62, 65, 68, 70, 73, 76, 80–81, 83, 86, 90, 92, 95, 97, 100, 102, 105, 114, 140, 143, 149, 154, 156, 158–160, 162–165, 185, 188, 195, 198, 199
  Hercules Labour 19
  Main Section 19
  virgin, the 10
Void of course 30, 199
Vulcan
  defined 165, 199
  overview 33

W

Water-Bearer, Aquarius 11, 24, 61
Water element 8
Woodward, Joanne 152–155
Work 5–6, 23, 71, 117, 147, 156–157, 186
Worksheet 1: House Cusps 169–171, 176, 192
Worksheet 2: Planets 174–175, 178–179, 180–181
Worksheet 3: Find ACD 193
Worksheet 4: Progressed Planets 194

Y

Yod planet pattern 114–115, 199

Z

Zach, Baron Franz Xaver von 44
Zenith 50
Zodiac 199
  chart/ horoscope 48
  family 11, 17
  messengers 32
  nonconformists 31
  people 15
  signs 8–9, 32, 189
  warriors 21
Zubeneschamali 13